Dark Matter

Dark Matter

A Guide to Alexander Kluge and Oskar Negt

Richard Langston

VERSO

London • New York

First published by Verso 2020
© Richard Langston 2020

1 3 5 7 9 10 8 6 4 2

Verso
UK: 6 Meard Street, London W1F 0EG
US: 20 Jay Street, Suite 1010, Brooklyn, NY 11201
versobooks.com

Verso is the imprint of New Left Books

ISBN-13: 978-1-78873-517-9
ISBN-13: 978-1-78873-516-2 (HBK)
ISBN-13: 978-1-78873-518-6 (UK EBK)
ISBN-13: 978-1-78873-519-3 (US EBK)

British Library Cataloguing in Publication Data
A catalogue record for this book is available from the British Library

Library of Congress Cataloging-in-Publication Data
A catalog record for this book is available from the Library of Congress

Typeset in Minion Pro by MJ&N Gavan, Truro, Cornwall
Printed and bound by CPI Group (UK) Ltd, Croydon CR0 4YY

For REL Jr. (1939–2016)

Contents

Introduction to Gravitational Thinking

Cornerstones of Collaborative Philosophy

Aesthetic Praxis: Video, Television, Film, Literature

Epilogue

List of Illustrations

Introduction

Chapter 1

can thus assume the route represented by, but can also take countless other routes."

Figure 1.4. Three degrees of abstract social experience and three subjective responses: these "six dimensions … contain within themselves the additional dimensions of the political, the historical, the realization of labor power, feelings, consciousness, revolutionary transformation, as well as the horizontal and the vertical (the dimensions best known to sensuous perception), which, for their part, include place, time, punctuality, space, movement, non-movement, relationalities and differentiations."

Figure 1.5. Human evolution versus cyborg intervention: *Left*, "Mutational change of the human hand (natural)"; *right*, "The labor economy's valorization of a mutated hand in terms of the human hand's augmentation into an effective tool of labor. Sketch by Prof. Meixner."

Chapter 2

Figures 2.1–2.4. The epochs of the hand's decline: manipulative action, the hand as motor, machine operators, the computer programmer. From top to bottom: *Yesterday Girl* (1966); *The Patriot* (1979); *Part-Time Work of a Domestic Slave* (1973); and *The Assault of the Present on the Rest of Time* (1985).

Figure 2.5. "'And windows are to a house what the five senses are to the head.' Here: eyes without eyelids."

Figure 2.6. "'This is an important moment. For this reason the eyes are shut.'"

Figure 2.7. "Whoever laughs at fairy tales was never in distress."

Figures 2.8–2.13. From top to bottom: the mugged Yugoslavian diamond smuggler in prostitute Bette's apartment; Betty's pimp, Kurt Schleich, uses a candle to determine the victim's vital signs; Betty prepares a remedy between an incandescent light bulb hanging before a window and three lit candles; Betty and Kurt read to their patient; Betty's crushed lipstick as inconclusive evidence; the final kiss under a crescent moon.

Chapter 7

Chapter 8

Chapter 9

Acknowledgments

Dark Matter began with the author's recognition that it would be a long time in the making. Part of its gestation included the author's involvement with the translation of *History and Obstinacy*, participation in the founding of the *Alexander Kluge-Jahrbuch*, and the publication of the anthology *Difference and Orientation*, containing new translations of Alexander Kluge's essays on aesthetics and poetics, all of which have allowed for sustained reflection on and deep immersion into the complexities of and interconnections between Alexander Kluge's and Oskar Negt's works.

Without the support from an array of organizations this book would have never seen the light of day. The research for and writing of the following essays were graciously underwritten, above all, by a stipend from the Alexander von Humboldt Foundation during the 2011–12 academic years. The College of Arts and Sciences, the Center for European Studies, UNC Global, and the University Research Council, all based at the University of North Carolina at Chapel Hill, also made vital resources available for its completion. The Franklin Humanities Institute at Duke University provided opportunities for dialogue and research necessary for the book's early gestation. The publication of *Dark Matter* was made possible by generous support from the following institutions at the University of North Carolina at Chapel Hill: the Department of Germanic and Slavic Languages and Literatures, the Institute for the Arts and

Humanities (Schwab Academic Excellence Award), and the Office of the Vice Chancellor for Research.

Above all, Alexander Kluge's and Oskar Negt's personal involvement and support at various stages in the research and writing of this book have been sources of indispensable guidance and inspiration for which the author is endlessly grateful.

Special thanks goes to senior editor Sebastian Budgen of Verso Books, who has been an invaluable advocate and supporter of *Dark Matter*. Copyeditor Brian Baughan also deserves recognition for his meticulous review of the manuscript. The author is endlessly grateful to Anselm Kiefer, whose kind generosity and helpful staff (Eva König) made possible the book's cover illustration.

As with any massive undertaking, a huge cast of tremendously smart people helped make this book reality. Leslie Adelson, Nora Alter, Barbara Barnak, Claudia Benthien, Frauke Berndt, Rory Bradley, Thomas Combrink, John Davidson, Gülsen Döhr, Eric Downing, Devin Fore, Zita Gottschling, Randall Halle, Marita Hüttepohl, Christian Jäger, Stephan Jansen, Lutz Koepnick, Karin Krauthausen, Jakob Krebs, Alice Kuzniar, Richard Lambert, Peter McIsaac, Matthew Miller, Johannes von Moltke, Christopher Pavsek, Inga Pollmann, Tobias Rüther, Klaus Sachs-Hombach, Christian Schulte, Cyrus Shahan, Winfried Siebers, Rainer Stollmann, Gabriel Trop, Joseph Vogl, Robert Watson, Beata Wiggen, Emma Woelk, and Guido Zurstiege have made vital contributions both big and small all along the way, for which the author is endlessly grateful.

The seed for this book dates back to an accidental phone call made in the summer of 1999. It was Alexander Kluge who answered. The actual project finally set sail in earnest in 2008. Since then the ideas and arguments within this book incubated at handfuls of conferences held by the German Studies Association, the Society for Cinema and Media Studies, and the Modern Language Association. Lectures held at the Johann Wolfgang Goethe-Universität Frankfurt am Main, King's College of London, the Université de Liège, the Humboldt-Universität zu Berlin, the University of Waterloo, Bowdoin College, Duke University, Princeton University, Universtität Tübingen, Universität Zürich, and the University of North Carolina at Chapel Hill were also valuable opportunities for testing and shaping this book's readings and arguments. Earlier bilingual drafts of portions from two chapters of this book have been previously published: a truncated version of chapter 4 was published as "Permanent

Catastrophe and Everyday Life: Remediation of the Political in Kluge's *Vermischte Nachrichten* and Chernobyl Broadcasts" in the inaugural issue of the *Alexander Kluge Jahrbuch* (1 [2014]: 101–23) and an initial draft of chapter 8 appeared in *Ästhetik und Allgemeine Kunstwissenschaft* (Sonderheft 7: *Ambiguity in Contemporary German Art and Literature* [2018]: 135–50) as "Specters of Ambivalence: Notes on Alexander Kluge's Ambiguous Forms." The author thanks the *Germanic Review* for permission to reproduce "Toward an Ethics of Fantasy: The Kantian Dialogues of Oskar Negt and Alexander Kluge" (85.4 [2010]: 271–93) as chapter 6.

Note on Citations and Translations

Of the three principal collaborations by Oskar Negt and Alexander Kluge discussed in the following pages, only two have been translated into English: *Public Sphere and Experience* and *History and Obstinacy*. Because the second of these two titles is a significantly truncated edition of the German original prepared in large part by just Kluge, both the original *Geschichte und Eigensinn* and its English translation are regularly cited throughout *Dark Matter*. Although *History and Obstinacy* is attributed first to Kluge and then to Negt in order to reflect the former's lead role, *Dark Matter* uses both this new and the old attributions depending on whether the German original or the English translation is under discussion. When neither the original nor the translation are in play, *Dark Matter* defaults to the author's customary attribution, namely Negt and Kluge. When discussed in the context of their publication histories, both the German and English titles are given where appropriate. Citations identify the respective edition addressed but refrain from supplying cross-references to the original or the translation. Not every instance of the English translation can be found in the German, and much of the German is not included in the translation.

Arguably, one of the most important methodological features of the Frankfurt School that Negt and Kluge retain is the primacy of the particular (*das Besondere*) over the universal (*das Allgemeine*) and, to this end, *Dark Matter* has incorporated the particularities of Kluge's aesthetic praxis prominently into each of its chapters. This is why the book's title lists Kluge first. In almost every case, the considerable pool of available English translations of Kluge's work have been used. Conversely, very little of Negt's twenty-two-volume collected works is available in English. Translations of German originals were used only in those cases where existing translations fell short or simply did not exist. All in all, *Dark Matter* has strived to engage both commercially available texts and those available in the public domain that English-language readers can engage themselves without necessarily knowing German.

Unless otherwise noted, all English translations throughout *Dark Matter* from the German are those of the author.

Two things fill the mind with ever new and increasing admiration and reverence, the more often and more steadily one reflects on them: *the starry heavens above me and the moral law within me.*

—Immanuel Kant, *Critique of Practical Reason* (1788)

You are false images,
Faces of radiant flame;
Heart's warmth and tenderness
And soul you cannot claim.

—Karl Marx, "Song to the Stars" (1836)

Kant's starry firmament now shines only in the dark night of pure cognition, it no longer lights any solitary wanderer's path (for to be a man in the new world is to be solitary.) And the inner light affords evidence of security, or its illusion, only to the wanderer's next step.

—Georg Lukács, *The Theory of the Novel* (1916)

Just as the harmony of the spheres depends on the orbits of stars which do not come in contact with each other, so the existence of the *mundus intelligibilis* depends on the unbridgeable distance between pure essences. Every idea is a sun and is related to other ideas just as suns are related to each other.

—Walter Benjamin, *The Origin of German Tragic Drama* (1928)

The constellation of the existing and the nonexisting is the utopic figure of art.

—Theodor W. Adorno, *Aesthetic Theory* (1970)

Self-preservation, as the rational principle with which the creation is endowed, requires a space between the systems that exhausts gravitation.

—Hans Blumenberg, *The Genesis of the Copernican World* (1975)

Introduction to
Gravitational Thinking

Figure 0.1. Alexander Kluge, "*The Death of Marat* and Other Images from the Time after 1789, Explained by Oskar Negt," *10 till 11*, RTL, October 9, 1989. © Alexander Kluge.

Figure 0.2. Alexander Kluge, "Heraclitus, the Obscure: Oskar Negt on Heidegger and Heraclitus," *10 till 11*, RTL, April 1, 1996. © Alexander Kluge.

Figure 0.3. Alexander Kluge, "Man Is Only Fully Human When He Plays," *Primetime/Spätausgabe*, RTL, November 13, 2005. © Alexander Kluge.

Figures 0.1–0.3: Thinking together. Three face-to-face conversations between Oskar Negt and Alexander Kluge, 1989–2005.

Dark Matter: In Defiance of Catastrophic Modernity

From Constellations to Force Fields

What if thinking were like the cosmos?

This question was certainly on Walter Benjamin's mind when he composed the "epistemo-critical prologue" to his landmark habilitation on tragic drama published in 1928. The "basic task of philosophy," he proffered therein, is to redeem all the many bits of profane knowledge about sundry phenomena inundating modern human experience by arranging them into constellations such that unified ideas emerge. "Ideas are to objects," he summarized with the aid of analogy, "as constellations are to stars."[1] In his quest to move philosophical thinking beyond the reign of institutionalized philosophy's doctrinal systems along with its codified forms, Benjamin sought inspiration in the luminous matter visible throughout the heavens at the same time when astronomers began amassing evidence that the cosmos was largely composed of a mysterious substance invisible to the human eye, more dense than any matter known to science, and vastly more formidable than any of the familiar celestial bodies gravitationally bound to our solar system.[2] A radical proposition

---

1 Walter Benjamin, *The Origin of German Tragic Drama*, trans. John Osborne (London: Verso, 1998) 34.

2 Benjamin 27. Benjamin began his habilitation in earnest in 1923 and submitted it in 1925 to no avail. One year after its publication in 1928, American astronomer Edwin

for solving a massive discrepancy between the measurable mass of gigantic galaxy clusters and the unanticipated high velocities observed among
their individual parts, the hypothesis called "dark matter," first advanced
in the year 1933, posited that some other imperceptible matter exert-
ing tremendous gravitational pull had to be responsible for astonishing
galactic speeds of up to 2 million miles per hour.[3] Roughly five decades
later, physical cosmologists and particle physicists began to accept that
daring thesis from 1933 that only a tiny fraction of all matter in the
universe is as we experience it in our everyday lives.[4] The rest, nearly
85 percent of the universe's total mass, contains none of the atomic
particles found in ordinary matter, and refrains from emitting and inter-
acting with electromagnetic radiation, thus making its presence known
only indirectly by virtue of its tremendous gravitational pull capable of
warping the curvature of space-time and with it the passage of light. So,
right when Benjamin sought inspiration for his metaphysical realism in
cosmic forms, astronomers not only garnered evidence of an expanding universe but also proposed a theory upending the solid ground on
which modern terrestrials once firmly stood. Now a mere speck in a possibly infinite sea of dark matter, astronomers suddenly found themselves,
albeit briefly, in the shoes of ancients like Anaxagoras, the pre-Socratic
philosopher who saw in the cosmos's unattainable infiniteness "the true
reference point of contemplation."[5]

Hubble published evidence suggesting that the universe was expanding in spite of Albert
Einstein's initial grasp of a static universe in his general theory of relativity from 1915.
Building on research that dated back to 1925, the Swiss-American astronomer Fritz
Zwicky coined "dark matter" in 1933 even though colleagues Jan Oort in Leiden and
Knut Lundmark in Lund had each observed missing matter in the universe years earlier.
See: Lisa Randall, *Dark Matter and the Dinosaurs: The Astounding Interconnectedness of
the Universe* (New York: Ecco, 2015) 12–14.

3 F. Zwicky, "Rotverschiebung von extragalaktischen Nebeln," *Helvetica Physica
Acta* 6 (1933): 125. Evalyn Gate, *Einstein's Telescope: The Hunt for Dark Matter and Dark
Energy in the Universe* (New York: W.W. Norton, 2009) 21–22. See also: J. Richard Gott,
The Cosmic Web: Mysterious Architecture of the Universe (Princeton: Princeton Univer-
sity Press, 2016) 28–40.

4 Sidney van den Bergh, "The Early History of Dark Matter," *Publications of the
Astronomical Society of the Pacific* 111.760 (June 1999): 659.

5 Hans Blumenberg, *The Genesis of the Copernican World*, trans. Robert M. Wallace
(Cambridge, MA: MIT Press, 1987) 11, 10, 9. Paul Feyerabend similarly notes "a new
period in the history of science commences with a *backward movement* that returns us to
an earlier stage where theories were more vague and had smaller empirical content." See:
Against Method, 3rd ed. (London: Verso, 1993) 114.

Unaware of dark matter, the importance of gravitation for thinking did not pass Benjamin up. Not long after the publication of his habilitation, Benjamin mused further on the value of the constellation, declaring it akin to that increasingly fragile, seemingly extinct human capacity to perceive similarities between macrocosm and microcosm.[6] "Millennia ago," he recalled in an unpublished fragment from 1933, "the arrangement of stars wove itself into a human's existence at the moment of their birth according to the principle of similarity whereby the spirits and forces of life congealed in accordance to a model that was already mapped out in the cosmos."[7] Even though modernity's scientific method, with its "reduction of physical questions to questions of pure analysis," eventually destroyed what another kindred philosopher called analogy's "realism," Benjamin's investment in the fate of the mimetic faculty— along with auratic experience—was not necessarily adverse to the language of science.[8] In fact, the very clue to dark matter's likelihood, a non-geocentric understanding of gravity—nothing less than the hallmark of the Copernican Revolution—served as the basis for another emergent analogy that recurs intermittently throughout Benjamin's writings. Consider, for example, his early account of Fyodor Dostoevsky's *The Idiot* that sees "every event" and "all things and people" "gravitat[ing]" toward and "orbit[ing]" around the novel's center, namely its protagonist Prince Myshkin.[9] In the first draft of his artwork essay from 1935, he suggests that cinema exerts a tremendous "gravitational pull" on spectators thanks to its imagined ability to reproduce life.[10] Reading a poem like Charles Baudelaire's "L'âme du vin" or Else Lasker-Schüler's "Mein blaues Klavier" as a philologist would an ancient text—such that it "casts

6 Walter Benjamin, "Doctrine of the Similar," trans. Michael W. Jennings, in *Selected Works*, vol. 2: *1927–1934*, eds. Michael W. Jennings et al. (Cambridge, MA: Belknap Press, 1999) 694–98.

7 Walter Benjamin, "The Lamp," in *Selected Works*, vol. 2, 692. Translation modified. See also: Walter Benjamin, "On Astrology," trans. Rodney Livingstone, *Selected Works*, vol. 2, 684–85.

8 Hans Blumenberg, *Shipwreck with Spectator: Paradigm of a Metaphor for Existence*, trans. Steven Randall (Cambridge, MA: MIT Press, 1997) 95.

9 Walter Benjamin, "Dostoevsky's *The Idiot*," trans. Rodney Livingstone et al., in *Selected Works*, vol. 1: *1913–1926*, eds. Marcus Bullock and Michael W. Jennings (Cambridge, MA: Belknap Press, 1996) 79, 80.

10 Walter Benjamin, "Das Kunstwerk im Zeitalter seiner technischen Reproduzierbarkeit," in *Gesammelte Schriften*, eds. Rolf Tiedemann and Hermann Schweppenhäuser, vol. 1.1 (Frankfurt am Main: Suhrkamp, 1991) 454.

its spell on the scholar"—bestows upon it weight that, in turn, allows the interpreter to overcome its "force of gravity."[11] When cobbled together, Benjamin's sporadic allusions to gravitation suggest another "sensuous shape-giving" force entirely distinct though certainly not divorced from his primary analogy of the constellation.[12] Akin to Newton's law of universal gravitation, the relation inferred in these examples is marked by two opposing forces originating from the work of art and its beholder, respectively. It was as if Benjamin had extrapolated what he saw as the Renaissance's own "new analogy between the force of gravity and mental concentration" (as epitomized by the saturnine man's downward gaze) into the task of the modern critic. Without ever saying so unequivocally, Benjamin infers that in order for a "proper philological attitude" to break free of the aesthetic monad's inward pull, it must deploy the constellation's own gravitation as a counterforce.[13]

Missing in Benjamin's occasional reference to gravitation is, of course, the astonishing insight that emerged out of dark matter's discovery: not only does every discernible celestial body exert a gravitational force on every other body, but they all are also subject to the gravitational sway of invisible dark matter responsible for the large-scale structures of the universe spanning millions of light-years and the shape of galaxies, too, like our Milky Way's spiral disk. Astral constellations are formed precisely because of dark matter's tremendous force pulling and pushing the undulating fabric of space-time into forms both local and global in scope: from observable star systems, galaxies, and clusters to filaments, nodes, and voids imaginable only with the help of computers. Whether dark matter's discovery would have merited gravity's inclusion in Benjamin's

---

11 Walter Benjamin, "Exchange with Theodor W. Adorno on 'The Paris of the Second Empire in Baudelaire,'" trans. Edmund Jephcott and Michael W. Jennings, in *Selected Works*, vol. 4: *1938–1940*, eds. Howard Eiland and Michael W. Jennings (Cambridge, MA: Belknap Press, 2003), 108; Walter Benjamin, letter to Werner Kraft, Spring 1936, in *The Correspondence of Walter Benjamin, 1910–1940*, eds. Gershom Scholem and Theodor W. Adorno, trans. Manfred R. Jacobsen and Evelyn M. Jacobson (Chicago: University of Chicago Press, 1994) 522.

12 These examples are taken from those instances where Benjamin invokes the scientific *terminus technicus* for gravity as a force—*Gravitation, Schwerkraft, Anziehungskraft*—instead of concepts like *Schwergewicht, Gewicht,* and *Ernst,* often rendered metaphorically and thus imprecisely in English-language translation as "gravity," "gravitation," and "center of gravity."

13 Benjamin, *The Origin of German Tragic Drama*, 153; Benjamin, "Exchange with Theodor W. Adorno," 107.

case for the constellation, how a more sustained engagement with gravity would have influenced his analogy and, if so, whether its force would have had an impact on his method of truth, such questions that take his doctrine of the similar quite literally surely invite wild speculation. Of course, Benjamin never lived to learn of dark matter and, what's more, the further development of gravitational thinking waned in the hands of critical theory's immediate successors. It was none other than Benjamin's confidant and designated executor, Theodor W. Adorno, who picked up on another scantily deployed scientific concept from his friend's lexicon: force fields. In so doing, he retained Benjamin's case for gravitation, but only insofar as it served his own call to shatter the very mimetic faculty that Benjamin championed with the constellation.[14] Laid down most resoundingly in his reflections on damaged life in American exile, the cornerstone for Adorno's modification begins by shifting Newtonian gravity away from Benjamin's aesthetic framework and to the province of commodified life. Society, the bourgeois character embedded within it, all affirmative thinking, and the very logic of history, writes Adorno in *Minima Moralia*, are all "gravitating toward total catastrophe."[15] The attendant resurgence in magic, mythology, and occultism under late capitalism—all signs of consciousness's regression—is a clear indication in his mind that mimetic perception, far from accessing otherwise neglected knowledge and experience, answers to real social problems by misplacing them in the skies.[16] Instead of applying a similar gravitational force to the work of art or philosophical commentary, Adorno writes of self-contained, impervious force fields. In contrast to Benjamin, both

---

14 Compared with Benjamin's aforementioned use of the semantic field related to gravitation (see note 12), there are roughly half as many counts of "force field" (*Kraftfeld*) in his collected works. On Adorno's displacement of Benjamin's constellation from the heavens to the terrestrial sphere, see: Philipp Weber, *Stern, Bilder, Denken: Aspekte einer Denkfigur bei Walter Benjamin* (Frankfurt am Main: Peter Lang, 2006) 99–101. On the differences between Benjamin's and Adorno's constellations, see: Simon Jarvis, "Constellations: Thinking the Non-Identical," in *Adorno: A Critical Introduction* (New York: Routledge, 1998) 175–77.

15 Benjamin's concept of the force field, which dates back to his 1925 habilitation, makes a substantial appearance in: Theodor W. Adorno, *Minima Moralia: Reflections on a Damaged Life*, trans. E.F.N. Jephcott (London: Verso, 2005) 241.

16 On the failure of mimetic thinking characteristic of occultism and other denigrated forms of consciousness, he writes: "The real absurdity is reproduced astrological hocus-pocus, which adduces the impenetrable connections of alienated elements—nothing more alien than the stars—as knowledge about the subject." See: Adorno 241.

thinking and artworks alike aspire to become such fields only when they exhibit dynamic, internal tensions between their forms and content such that they, in turn, "dissolve" themselves.[17] As such, force fields strive to "transcend their material conditions" and, if achieved, essentially elude the event horizon emanating from the administered world.[18] While Benjamin's nascent musings on gravitation were intrinsically Newtonian in nature, Adorno's allusion to the monadic force field, for all its scientific trappings, repudiates the physical laws of matter altogether. It is one thing to seek out a neutral point between two bodies where the net gravitational force is zero. It is quite another to become impervious to gravity altogether. Benjamin's allusions to gravitational thought would have to wait at least another three decades before it could come into its own, and when it did so under the auspices of Alexander Kluge and Oskar Negt it assumed not just Newtonian but also cosmic proportions. How they have managed this feat is the subject of *Dark Matter*.

Blind Spots and Strange Bedfellows

For English-language readers, the loose association of thinkers conveniently corralled under the honorific "Frankfurt School" appears today like it has finally surmounted the last remaining language barriers preventing the consummation of its long-standing Anglo-American diaspora. Its histories are now widely accessible to both specialists and laypersons alike. Some of the United States' most venerated university presses have produced lavish critical editions spanning not only the entirety of Benjamin's and Adorno's output, but also those of the School's many other revered practitioners. In effect, translators now find themselves either scraping the bottom of the barrel for those few outstanding

17 "Force field" can be found throughout Adorno's oeuvre; however, these passing references to thought and the work of art refer specifically to: Adorno 296; Theodor W. Adorno, *Aesthetic Theory*, eds. Gretel Adorno and Rolf Tiedemann, trans. Robert Hullot-Kentor (Minneapolis: University of Minnesota Press, 1997) 206, 301, 292.

18 Theodor W. Adorno, "Arnold Schoenberg, 1874–1951," in *Prisms*, trans. Samuel and Shierry Weber (Cambridge, MA: MIT Press, 1983) 166. Adorno comes closest to bringing the constellation in dialogue with the force field in: Theodor W. Adorno, "The Essay as Form," in *Notes to Literature*, ed. Rolf Tiedemann, trans. Shierry Weber Nicholsen (New York: Columbia University Press, 1991) 13. See also: Susan Buck-Morss, *The Origin of Negative Dialectics: Theodor W. Adorno, Walter Benjamin, and the Frankfurt Institute* (New York: The Free Press, 1977) 254n84.

what Horkheimer called the theoretical "obstinacy" necessary for the intervention into capitalist society and the eclipse of reason.[26] If "the universal as an elementary undercurrent *beneath* … or *immanently* in the midst of the particular" does indeed count as one of the Frankfurt School's cornerstones, then another very different tack from below is necessary to remedy the gaps endemic to grand histories of the Frankfurt School.[27]

Especially tricky in this historiographical conundrum is the prospect of situating the four decades of astonishingly unique collaborations penned, recorded, and broadcast by social philosopher Oskar Negt (b. 1934) and jurist, author, and filmmaker Alexander Kluge (b. 1932). In addition to making sense of their three volumes of social philosophy and some sixty televised interviews, any balanced assessment of their collaborative work would need to appraise both the traces of these pivotal collaborations throughout their own massive collected works and, furthermore, identify therein their measure of independence from both one another and the Frankfurt School, which initially brought them together in 1969. Like no other collaborative team from within the Frankfurt School, or outside it for that matter, Negt and Kluge's work together is unique precisely because of what makes them each so different. Born of prominent middle-class parents in the town of Halberstadt, Germany, and raised by his divorced mother in Berlin beginning in 1946, Kluge trained as a lawyer in Marburg in 1949 and slogged through several internships before moving to Frankfurt, where that university's trustees employed him on account of his 1956 dissertation on self-governance in higher education.[28] With Adorno's help, whose acquaintance Kluge made by coincidence in 1955, Kluge apprenticed under film director Fritz Lang in 1958 and then, disillusioned by both the legal profession and the studio system, turned to writing prose, much to Adorno's dismay. By 1962, he had published his first collection of stories (originally entitled *Attendance List for a Funeral* in English and then later rebranded as *Case Histories*); co-authored a study on financing cultural politics with

---

26 Wiggershaus 658; Horkheimer 220.

27 Alexander Kluge and Oskar Negt, *History and Obstinacy*, ed. Devin Fore, trans. Richard Langston et al. (New York: Zone Books, 2014) 197.

28 For the most thorough English-language biography of Kluge published to date, see: Peter C. Lutze, *Alexander Kluge: The Last Modernist* (Detroit, MI: Wayne State University Press, 1998) 33–61.

his legal mentor Hellmut Becker; co-directed two documentary shorts; co-signed the Oberhausen Manifesto that paved the way for German auteur cinema; spoke before the influential West German literary salon Gruppe 47; and laid the foundation for and taught alongside Edgar Reitz at West Germany's first film school, based at the Ulm School of Design.[29] By the end of the sixties, Kluge's notoriety as author, filmmaker, legal counsel to Adorno, film theoretician, media lobbyist, and public intellectual was irrefutable. On the occasion of the 1966 Venice Film Festival, where Kluge received the top prize—a first for West Germany—Adorno wrote of the "Wunderkind" he introduced to Lang a decade earlier as if he were a father: "I swell with pride for my son."[30] In ensuing decades after Adorno's untimely death, Kluge maintained his influence within all these parallel fields while shifting, adapting, and expanding his praxis so as to account for transformations in technology, culture, and politics: Kluge wrestled, for example, with the problem of television as early as his first collaboration with Negt from 1972, *Public Sphere and Experience*. But it was on account of the advent of West German privatized television in the eighties that brought him to bid farewell to film after making fourteen features and instead to invest in private broadcasting. Starting in the late eighties, Kluge and his production company Developmental Company for Television Program (DCTP) hunkered down to furnish his three separate television programs—*News & Stories* on SAT.1 and both *10 till 11* and *Primetime/Spätausgabe* on RTL—with original material every week.[31] Beginning in 2000 he has: made an unprecedented literary comeback beginning with a two-thousand-page omnibus of stories

29 On Kluge in Ulm, see: Alexander Kluge, "Einführung: Begriff ohne Anschauung ist leer, Anschauung ohne Begriff ist blind," in *Anschauung und Begriff: Die Arbeiten des Instituts für Filmgestaltung Ulm 1962 bis 1995*, eds. Klaus Eder et al. (Basel: Stroemfeld/ Roter Stern, 1995) 7–14. See also Alexander Kluge, "What Do the 'Oberhauseners' Want?," in *West German Filmmakers on Film: Visions and Voices*, ed. Eric Rentschler (New York: Holmes & Meier, 1988) 10–13.

30 Theodor W. Adorno to Fritz Lang, June 19, 1958, in: *Alexander Kluge-Jahrbuch* 2 (2015) 15; Theodor W. Adorno to Alexander Kluge, September 10, 1968, Theodor W. Adorno Archiv, Institut für Sozialforschung.

31 For an overview of the historical context, development, and inner workings of Kluge's television programs, see Matthias Uecker, *Anti-Fernsehen? Alexander Kluges Fernsehproduktionen* (Marburg: Schüren, 2000). See also the essays in: Christian Schulte and Winfried Siebers, eds., *Kluges Fernsehen: Alexander Kluges Kulturmagazine* (Frankfurt am Main: Suhrkamp, 2002) and Kathrin Lämmle, *Televisuelle Intellektualität: Möglichkeitsräume in Alexander Kluges Fernsehmagazinen* (Constance: UVK Verlagsgesellschaft, 2013). On Kluge's post-televisual foray into the digital, see Philipp Ekardt,

entitled *Chronik der Gefühle* [Chronicle of Feelings]; released in print and on film swaths of his long out-of-print work; returned to filmmaking; expanded into online streaming video; received nearly every literary prize and award Germany has to offer; and, most recently, collaborated with world-renowned visual artists like Gerhard Richter, Anselm Kiefer, and Georg Baselitz on books and museum exhibitions.

Negt was the youngest of seven children born to working-class parents who farmed on an East Prussian estate.[32] On the run from both the advancing Soviet army and the German military intent on enlisting him as an anti-aircraft gun assistant, ten-year-old Negt escaped by sea with just two of his sisters in early 1945 and spent over two years in a Danish internment camp before being reunited with the rest of his family in Soviet-occupied lands in the shadow of West Berlin. After a second exodus to Oldenburg in the Federal Republic in 1951 due to his staunchly social democratic father's public rebuke of East Germany's collectivization of private farms, Negt balanced his mediocre school grades with the extracurricular study of Goethe, Marx, and Kant as well as Horkheimer and Adorno's *Dialectic of Enlightenment*, and therewith secured his academic future in higher education.[33] At his father's behest, he briefly studied law in Göttingen before deciding in 1956 to move to Frankfurt in order to study philosophy and sociology with first Horkheimer and then Adorno. Already a member of West Germany's Social Democratic Party in 1954, Negt assumed leading roles in the party's Socialist German Student Union in 1958 and taught at a trade union school outside of Frankfurt in 1960; the outcome of these early pedagogical experiences was his first, best-selling publication: *Soziologische Phantasie und exemplarisches Lernen: Zur Theorie der Arbeiterbildung* [Sociological Fantasy and Exemplary Learning: Toward a Theory of Labor Education] (1968). In 1962, after transforming his master's thesis on Auguste Comte and G.W.F. Hegel within a matter of several months into a dissertation under Adorno's direction, Negt followed Habermas to

"Starry Skies and Frozen Lakes: Alexander Kluge's Digital Constellations," *October* 138 (2011): 107–19. Kluge's online portal for streaming video can be found at www.dctp.tv.

32 Select biographical details about Negt in English can be found in: Rainer Stollmann and Christian Schulte, "Moles Don't Use Systems: A Conversation with Oskar Negt," trans. Fiona Elliot, *October* 149 (2014): 69–88.

33 Oskar Negt, "Denken als Gegenproduktion," in *Geist gegen den Zeitgeist: Erinnern an Adorno*, eds. Josef Früchtl and Maria Calloni (Frankfurt am Main: Suhrkamp, 1991) 76.

Heidelberg as his assistant in philosophy, only then to return to Frankfurt two years later, where he focused primarily on questions of violence and the public sphere in classical philosophies of law. Related colloquia initially offered on topics like political economy and materialist conceptions of history eventually caught the attention of an increasingly politicized student body such that nearly eight hundred students, activists, unionists, and community members—among them Hans-Jürgen Krahl, Angela Davis, Detlev Claussen, Bassam Tibi, and Alexander Kluge—sought out his expertise on Marx's Parisian Manuscripts in late 1968.[34] After a falling-out with Habermas that year over Habermas's dismissal of the protest movement as "left-wing fascism" and Adorno's passing one year later, Negt was briefly considered in 1970 as a possible successor for his advisor's professorship before he accepted an appointment in sociology at the Leibniz University of Hanover.[35] There, he and colleagues like social psychologist Regina Becker-Schmidt, sociologist Detlev Claussen, and interdisciplinary psychoanalyst Alfred Lorenzer, among others, established a Hanoverian School of Critical Theory.[36] Negt's academic calling and concomitant publishing certainly did not preclude the continuation of his previous political commitments. An early member of the Socialist Bureau committed to organizing the frayed New Left, he also advocated in the early seventies for alternative schools like the Glocksee-Schule of Hanover; battled for both the thirty-five-hour working week and the importance of unions in the eighties; and championed the SPD and its coalition with the Green Party, as well as European integration. In addition to his lengthy collaboration with Kluge, Negt also counts former German chancellor Gerhard Schröder and author and Nobel Prize–winner Günter Grass among some of his most influential comrades.

Negt's and Kluge's familial backgrounds, theoretical training, vocations, life experiences, and temperaments (not to mention their reception) could not be any more different. Kluge once fondly labeled himself

---

34 See: Oskar Negt, *Achtundsechzig: Politische Intellektuelle und die Macht* (Franfurt am Main: Zweitausendeins, 1998) 63–77; see also: Alexander Kluge, "Momentaufnahmen aus unserer Zusammenarbeit," in Oskar Negt and Alexander Kluge, *Der unterschätzte Mensch: Gemeinsame Philosophie in zwei Bänden*, vol. 1: *Suchbegriffe*, Öffentlichkeit und Erfahrung, *Maßverhältnisse des Politischen* (Frankfurt am Main: Zweitausendeins, 2001) 12.

35 Oskar Negt, "Einleitung," in *Die Linke antwortet Jürgen Habermas*, eds. Wolfgang Abendroth (Frankfurt am Main: Europäische Verlagsanstalt, 1969) 17–32; Açıkgöz, 195.

36 Açıkgöz, 211–15.

and Negt as "incompatible opposites," and Negt, in turn, has regarded himself and Kluge as two people "who could not be more different."[37] This contrast is especially applicable to their relationships to theory and philosophy. Whereas Negt is far more apt to ground his careful thinking in ancient Greek and modern German philosophical traditions (not to mention works from the Frankfurt School's first generation), Kluge, certainly no stranger to Negt's influences, has long demonstrated a curiosity if not appreciation for contemporary French and Anglo-American thought, developments that Negt himself has regarded over the years as misled "theoretical fads."[38] Yet even the most superficial of differences, like Kluge's penchant for chaotic associative montage, best exemplified by his films, and Negt's drive for concentrated logic typical of finely honed academic speeches, never express themselves according to any predictable division of labor.[39] "It was typical in *History and Obstinacy*," Negt once explained of his second collaboration with Kluge, "that I introduced the literary examples while Kluge was much more oriented toward Marxist orthodoxy ... An inversion took place that made for a very satisfying cooperation."[40] Of central importance for every installment in their entire theoretical project, cooperation for Negt and Kluge involved forging every sentence together while nevertheless allowing room and respect for both individual differences and mutual trust to thrive.[41] Each installment in their trilogy—*Public Sphere and Experience* (1972; English 1992), *History and Obstinacy* (1981; English 2014), and *Maßverhältnisse des Politischen* [Measured Relations of the Political] (1992)—thus functions as a coherent segment in what together might best be likened to a Möbius strip that loops around to query what for them was always their primary agenda, namely examining the late modern conditions for

37 Kluge, "Momentaufnahmen aus unserer Zusammenarbeit," 7; Oskar Negt, "Kairós: Über Vetrauen und Kooperation: Die langjährige Produktionsgemeinschaft mit Alexander Kluge," in *Nur noch Utopien sind realistische: Politische Interventionen* (Göttingen: Steidl, 2012) 298.

38 Eberhard Knödler-Bunte, Hajo Funke, and Arno Widmann, "The History of Living Labor Power: A Discussion with Oskar Negt and Alexander Kluge," trans. Fiona Elliott, *October* 149 (2014): 36.

39 Kluge, "Momentaufnahmen aus unserer Zusammenarbeit," 8.

40 Negt, "Denken als Gegenproduktion," 90–91.

41 Kluge, "Momentaufnahmen aus unserer Zusammenarbeit," 9. See also: Negt, "Kairós," 297–98; and Claus Philipp, "Öffentlichkeit und Erfahrung, Faust: Alexander Kluge und Oskar Negt im Gespräch," in *Alexander Kluge: Magazin des Glücks*, eds. Sebastian Huber and Claus Philipp (Vienna: Springer-Verlag, 2007) 95–96.

nurturing a sharpened political faculty of judgment necessary for constituting a more peaceful community.[42] It is therefore not in spite of but
rather because of the challenges posed by their many differences that
enabled Negt and Kluge to approach their subject from three vantage
points. It would nevertheless be imprudent to seal off their trilogy of
social philosophy (along with its sequel of televised interviews entitled
Suchbegriffe [Search Terms]) as a body of work wholly distinct and unre-
lated from their own respective outputs.[43] Even though they consciously
refrained from utilizing their own respective catalogues in the formation of their collaborative ideas, their theory does cast a shadow on their
own works even though its fingerprints are not always self-evident.[44]
Negt does reference his collaborations with Kluge in his own major
publications—e.g., his own trilogy, *Kindheit und Schule in einer Welt der
Umbrüche* [Childhood and Schools in a World of Upheavals] (1997),
Arbeit und menschliche Würde [Labor and Human Dignity] (2001), and
Der politische Mensch [Political Man] (2010)—even though his own
works are capable of standing entirely on their own. Similarly, Kluge's
literature, films, and videos do engage both ideas developed together
with Negt as well as some of Negt's independent publications, but they
are also in pursuit of answers to other different questions posed on the
aesthetic plane.

Situating the tangle of Negt and Kluge within the Frankfurt School,
let alone untying and deciphering the relationship between its parts,
is a project of massive proportions, one made doubly difficult by the
unprecedented border crossings between theory and the aesthetic so
characteristic of their respective works.[45] For the few intellectual historians who have included them both in their narratives, Kluge's role

---

42 Negt contends that "impetuses for independent thinking and the expansion of the
political faculty of judgment" had always been their objective. See Negt, "Kairós," 305. See
also the preface in: Oskar Negt and Alexander Kluge, *Maßverhältnisse des Politischen: 15
Vorschläge zum Unterscheidungsvermögen* (Frankfurt am Main: Fischer Verlag, 1992) 9.

43 Negt, "Kairós," 300.

44 See: Negt, "Kairós," 303; and Kluge, "Momentaufnahmen aus unserer Zusammenarbeit," 7.

45 Two recently published studies that explicitly link Kluge with critical theory in
ways distinct from *Dark Matter* include: Leslie A. Adelson, *Cosmic Miniatures and the
Future Sense: Alexander Kluge's 21st-Century Literary Experiments in German Culture
and Narrative Form* (Berlin: De Gruyter, 2017), and Christoph Streckhardt, *Kaleidoskop
Kluge: Alexander Kluges Fortsetzung der Kritischen Theorie mit narrative Mitteln* (Tübingen: Narr Francke Attempo Verlag, 2016).

usually takes a backseat to Negt's bona fide credentials as a professional social philosopher.[46] Yet even this fixation on Negt's identity as sociology professor overlooks in his own mind the many other waters in which he has waded—he would certainly include philosophy, literary studies, psychology, sinology, pedagogy, and political activism—over the many decades. That he fits into none of these disciplines entirely and therefore has fallen through the cracks in nearly all of them is for him less evidence of any interdisciplinary failure than a testament to his commitment to reaching non-academic readers.[47] Conversely, scholars of film and literature have long demonstrated a heightened sensitivity to Negt and Kluge's theoretical collaborations for understanding Kluge's own prose, films, and videos, but this care often inadvertently subjugates Kluge's aesthetic to the status of illustration to his theoretical collaborations with Negt. Even more severe is the disdain muttered in some quarters that Negt's polemic adds little to Kluge's creative brilliance. This imbalance is especially exacerbated in the Anglo-American world by the fact that Negt is a virtually unknown quantity; not a single one of his monographs has yet to be translated into English. In light of all the challenges and pitfalls, it is perhaps not surprising that the safest route for situating Negt and Kluge within the Frankfurt School has been to stick to their three principal theoretical collaborations and, furthermore, to rely as much as possible on their leading concepts. So, while *Public Sphere and Experience* is often tagged as a mere footnote to Habermas's 1962 study of the bourgeois public sphere, *History and Obstinacy* is generally understood as an anachronistic dialogue with Marx's critique of political economy and his case for historical materialism. The dearth of engagements with their third collection of essays on political theory leaves the impression that their body of work is both spotty and tangential to the essential dialogues left behind by Horkheimer, Adorno, Benjamin et al. as well as their offshoots advanced by peers like Habermas and younger Institute comrades like Honneth. How it all adds up to an "expansion of the political faculty of judgment" and how their political theory sizes up to Adorno's prohibition on praxis, for example, or Habermas's later call for communicative action is a puzzle made up of countless moving pieces.[48]

---

46 Wiggershaus 658–59.
47 Stollmann and Schulte 76.
48 Negt, "Kairós," 305.

Negt and Kluge would very likely agree that they would throw a monkey wrench into any attempt to broaden the Frankfurt School's history, for they never considered themselves "orthodox devotees" of any one Frankfurt School figurehead or line of inquiry.[49] "I actually made a point," Negt once confessed, "of not writing about the Frankfurt School."[50] Furthermore, their collaborations were never "about reiterating philosophical treatises and certainly not about mulling over texts by members of the Frankfurt School." "Our thinking," he added, "rebels against … limitations arising from disciplines, academic training, unconsidered traditions, or imitation."[51] Rather, theirs is a mode of thinking that does not tie them down to either fixed sets of ideas or prescribed styles of argumentation, and, what's more, it defies historiographies driven by influence, causality, and progress. Instead of categorizing Negt and Kluge according to *what* they have (or have not) addressed both cooperatively and individually, *Dark Matter* ventures another course dealing with the *how*: how Negt and Kluge think together is what binds these two strange bedfellows together in spite of their differences, what links them to the concerns of the Frankfurt School even though they appear so aloof from its core enterprise, and what brings them into dialogue with other German, French, or Anglo-American thinkers who themselves are either indifferent or downright hostile toward the Frankfurt School. On the one hand, how they think together gives rise to gray zones between what one moment reads like conventional social theory and in another smacks of storytelling. On the other, it shirks from unhindered fluidity that would invariably result in the conflation of any and all distinctions between abstract thought and the aesthetic. Kluge is the first to admit that he, certainly no philosopher, is merely the Frankfurt School's court poet, and yet this designation, even though it occasionally appears thin in his own work, is just as operative there in his storybooks, films, and television broadcasts as it is in his collaborations with Negt.[52] But, even

---

49 Stollmann and Schulte, 72.

50 Negt, "Denken als Gegenproduktion," 80.

51 Stollmann and Schulte 72.

52 Alexander Kluge, "Theory of Storytelling: Lecture One," trans. Nathan Wagner, in *Difference and Orientation: An Alexander Kluge Reader*, ed. Richard Langston (Ithaca, NY: Cornell University Press, 2019) 100. See also: Richard Langston, "'Das ist die umgekehrte Flaschenpost': Ein montiertes Interview mit Oskar Negt und Alexander Kluge," *Alexander Kluge-Jahrbuch*, vol. 2: *Glass Shards: Echoes of a Message in a Bottle* (2015): 75.

though both Negt and Kluge would probably find little to nitpick in this initial proposition, what remains unresolved is how exactly they think together and what this thinking sets out to achieve.

Gravitational Thinking: On Method and Morphologies

Speaking before an American audience in 2004, Negt reflected on the telos of his philosophical collaborations with Kluge without recourse to any of the usual concepts commonly associated with their publications. Instead, he rooted their work in two modes of thinking called "critique." "Only impulses that lead to thinking for oneself and the expansion of the political power of judgment are meaningful contributions to the constitution of a peaceful society. Therein lie the guiding principles of our collaborative thinking."[53] Yet collaboration falls woefully short of describing the shape their thinking assumes.[54] The allusions to Immanuel Kant's political essays on enlightenment and orientation in thinking that followed in the wake of his *Critique of Pure Reason* were unmistakable. But Negt was also clear that Kant's critique was not the only pillar of their thinking: "In line with the tradition of Adorno and Horkheimer and what altogether is regarded as the Frankfurt School," he continued, "our theory work has constantly searched social upheavals for ways out. Even the harshest critique of the existing order never discouraged us from calling for the possibility of something better."[55] Already a reader of Horkheimer and Adorno during his teenage years in Oldenburg, Negt, in making his allusion to his teachers' *Dialectic of Enlightenment*, invoked a very different variety of critique, one whose uncompromising rigor relegated Kant's schematization of knowledge as a precursor to the instrumental reason endemic to totalitarian regimes.[56] A form of critique that practices—to speak with the young Karl Marx—"ruthless criticism of all that exists," this latter model of thinking also guiding Negt and Kluge's work ostensibly forecloses the viability of the former and thus

---

53 Negt, "Kairós," 305.
54 Barbara Potthast, "'Dass der andere nichts denkt, was feindselig wäre': Kooperatives Denken bei Alexander Kluge," *Alexander Kluge-Jahrbuch* 4 (2017): 103–13.
55 Negt, "Kairós," 305.
56 Oskar Negt, "Denken als Gegenproduktion," 76.

calls into question exactly how Kant and the underlying Marxian spirit of the Frankfurt School add up, if at all.[57] One intervening factor that potentially alleviates this antagonism to some extent was Adorno's own reconciliation with Kant's first *Critique* over the course of the late fifties and sixties, which, in the context of his posthumous *Aesthetic Theory*, culminated in an unprecedented "new balance between Kant and Hegel."[58] That the late Adorno changed his mind about Kant had in large part to do with his new conviction, most clearly articulated in his 1959 Kant lectures that, in spite of Kant's "intents" as well as the "appearance" of his work as a "coherent totality, held together in a deductive unity," it is "in reality a force field, one that can only be properly understood if you understand the forces that come together in a kind of productive friction."[59] While this de-systematization of Kant's thought into a force field comprised of sundry tensions does allow Adorno to break the gravitational pull toward catastrophe that he and Horkheimer once felt Kant succumbed to, thus allowing Adorno to then rehabilitate Kant in his appeal for critique's vital role in postwar West German democracy, it still falls short of resolving what Negt himself identified as the markedly distinct lines of inquiry that set Kant and Marx apart.[60] As Negt so eloquently recapped in his 2002 valedictory lecture, if critique for Marx is concerned with the *quaestio facti* whereas the *quaestio juris* guides Kant, how then is the transcendental dimension of Kant's moral thinking to be brought into accordance with the empiricism of Marx's historical materialism?[61] Is the telos of freedom for Kant not wholly incompatible with Marx's? How exactly do Negt and Kluge think collaboratively when two of their primary exemplars are at cross-purposes?

Looking back exclusively on the formation of his own philosophical thinking, Negt confessed in the aforementioned lecture that his thinking

57 Karl Marx, letter to Arnold Ruge, September 1843, trans. Jack Cohn, in Karl Marx and Frederick Engels, *Collected Works*, vol. 3: *Marx and Engels 1843–1844* (London: Lawrence and Wishart, 1975) 142.

58 Peter Uwe Hohendahl, *The Fleeting Promise of Art: Adorno's Aesthetic Theory Revisited* (Ithaca, NY: Cornell University Press, 2013) 49.

59 Theodor W. Adorno, *Kant's* Critique of Pure Reason, ed. Rolf Tiedemann, trans. Rodney Livingstone (Stanford, CA: Stanford University Press, 2001) 27–28.

60 Theodor W. Adorno, "Critique," in *Critical Models: Interventions and Catchwords*, trans. Henry W. Pickford (New York: Columbia University Press, 2005) 281–88.

61 Oskar Negt, *Kant und Marx: Ein Epochengespräch* (Göttingen: Steidl Verlag, 2003) 16.

was animated not so much by that long-standing dialectical tradition in European philosophy of resolving fundamental antipodes such as, for example, Heraclitus's historical becoming and Parmenides's timeless being. Rather, his own thinking was continually agitated by "polarity," at the very least two spheres "distinctly separate from one another."[62] Negt's deliberation on the productive "problem of precarious relationships" for his thinking brings him to reflect not only on the differences between Kant's emphasis on timeless validity and Marx's on historical emergence, but also on their respective lacunae and aporias that thinking in terms of polarity is capable of revealing. Negt's objective seeks neither to restrict the truth content of either polar opposite to the rarified concerns of intellectual history, nor to meld their discrete spheres of thought into a single amalgam. On the contrary, his intent on mining the "relevance of past philosophical systems for the present" strives to understand how these polar opposites persist as cornerstones of twenty-first century society even though both face new challenges due, on the one hand, to a wave of ethical conundrums brought on by unprecedented technical knowledge and, on the other, to the logic of globalized capital's unfettered influence on all social life.[63] At stake for Negt is no insular academic diagnostic of our contemporary world. Polarity in thinking sets its sights on fostering maturity, cultivating autonomous agency, and overcoming what Adorno originally labeled the scourge of "social coldness."[64] In light of the stated similarities between Negt's own political objectives and those he attributed to his collaborative work with Kluge, it would seem to follow that their collective enterprise is also spurred by thinking between polar opposites. Yet polarity is to be sure not the only framework for describing how Negt and Kluge think together; Negt himself has volunteered a host of alternatives: theirs is an anti-systematic thinking that drills (as Max Weber once said of politics); that twists and turns (like Benjamin's own method); and that leaps over boundaries (in accordance with what Sigmund Freud outlines as the pleasure principle).[65] And, as for their models, both Negt and Kluge hardly shape their thinking exclusively according to just Marx and Kant. Author Heinrich von Kleist, who regarded the mind as a workshop capable of producing extemporaneously

62 Negt, *Kant und Marx*, 16.
63 Negt, *Kant und Marx*, 6–7, 58, 60–71.
64 Negt, *Kant und Marx*, 59–60.
65 Stollmann and Schulte 72, 84, 86.

amazing coherency when in the presence of another human face, has long fascinated both thinkers for the proximity of his ideas to their own method.[66] "It is not *we* who know things," Kleist professed in his seminal 1806 essay on thinking and speaking, "but pre-eminently a certain *condition* of ours which knows."[67] Analogous to Kleist is, of course, Marx's later disquisition on cooperation from *Capital*, in which he contends that the whole of any collective labor process is greater than the sum of its parts; for Negt and Kluge, this stimulation of what Marx called "animal spirits" heightens individual efficiency and counts not only as a general "rule of thumb" for any successful collaboration but also as a model for their collaborative "theory labor" (*Theoriearbeit*).[68] In keeping with both Kleist and Marx, who bracket off actual dialogue, Kluge and Negt also invoke Kant's call in *The Metaphysics of Morals* for an ethical pedagogy modeled after Socrates's mental midwifery insofar as it, too, relies on the tender violence of the midwife's precision grip to "provoke the child's own movement," or, in Kluge and Negt's case, the autonomous thoughts of another.[69] Leaving unresolved this Gordian knot of how they think in concert with all these many frameworks and philosophical models, Negt instead underscored in his 2004 American address the outcomes of their collaborative thinking as their actual crowning achievement: "The success of [our] mental labor [*Gedankenarbeit*] ... is not the mere combination of two sides persistently independent of one another, but rather something really new."[70] And yet, in *History and Obstinacy*, they together insist that the object of any collaborative theory labor is not so much

---

66 Negt, "Kairós," 297, and Kluge, "Momentaufnahmen aus unserer Zusammenarbeit," 10.

67 Heinrich von Kleist, "On the Gradual Production of Thoughts Whilst Speaking," in *Selected Writings*, ed. and trans. David Constantine (Indianapolis: Hackett Publishing, 2004) 408. See also: Alexander Kluge, "The Difference: Heinrich von Kleist," trans. Emma Woelk, in *Difference and Orientation*, 27.

68 Karl Marx, *Capital: A Critique of Political Economy*, vol. 1, *The Process of Production of Political Economy*, trans. Samuel Moore and Edward Aveling, in Karl Marx and Frederick Engels, *Collected Works*, vol. 35 (London: Lawrence and Wishart, 1996) 331. Oskar Negt and Alexander Kluge, *Maßverhältnisse des Politischen*, in *Der unterschätzte Mensch: Gemeinsame Philosophie in zwei Bänden*, vol. 1 (Frankfurt am Main: Zweitausendeins, 2001) 714.

69 Kluge and Negt 96. Kleist slights Kant's "midwifery of thinking," for "even the most practiced connoisseur of human beings" makes mistakes (Kleist 409). See also: Immanuel Kant, *The Metaphysics of Morals*, trans. Mary Gregor (Cambridge: Cambridge University Press, 1991) 267.

70 Negt, "Kairós," 297.

the immediate creation of any new knowledge per se but rather building mutual trust between one another in the moment of thinking itself.[71]

An adaptation of G.W.F. Hegel's concept of freedom in ethical life, Kluge and Negt's notion of building trust as the immediate product of any theory labor—which for them is just another synonym for thinking— is essential insofar as it lays stress on thinking as not only just a patently social activity (as Kleist, Marx, and Kant make clear above) but also an inherently "political disposition."[72] As with Hegel, trust for Negt and Kluge is predicated on the right measure of self-trust and interpersonal recognition that preserves individual difference while nevertheless forging solidarity. "The disposition," Hegel writes of trust in his *Elements of the Philosophy of Right*, "knows that community [*Gemeinwesen*] is the substantial basis and end."[73] Freedom, for Hegel, is that moment in the constitution of community when trust leads one to no longer perceive another individual as an other in spite of one's own or that other person's particular interests. For Negt and Kluge, thinking becomes political when, in the act of forging trust, thinking together acquires use value for the constitution and further maintenance of community.[74] Like Hegel, they model their own notion of freedom after physical nature, but, whereas Hegel once equated freedom (of the will) with gravity (of a body), insofar as both strive toward a central point, Negt and Kluge situate freedom at that point in space governed by weightlessness, a dynamic middle ground between two or more gravitational fields.[75] If we are to apply the ideals of enlightenment not just to a single individual but to relationships, they argue, we actors must first dislodge ourselves from our respective origins by violating the law of inertia so we inhabit times and spaces in between. What Negt and Kluge call the "abaric point" in relationships—better known as the Lagrangian, neutral, or "zero" point—refers to those points in celestial mechanics between two gravitational vortices where a third smaller body can maintain a stable orbit without succumbing to one or another force (fig. 0.4). In the context

---

71 Kluge and Negt 201.

72 Kluge and Negt 439; G.W.F. Hegel, *Elements of the Philosophy of Right*, ed. Allen W. Wood, trans. H.B. Nisbet (Cambridge: Cambridge University Press, 1991) 288, §268.

73 Hegel 288–89, §268.

74 Negt and Kluge, *Maßverhältnisse des Politischen*, in *Der unterschätzte Mensch*, 695.

75 Manfred Riedel, "Nature and Freedom in Hegel's *Philosophy of Right*," in *Hegel's Political Philosophy: Problems and Perspectives*, ed. Z.A. Pelczynski (Cambridge: Cambridge University Press, 1971) 141–43.

of relationships, this zone is where each actor can give rise to an alliance capable of also preserving the autonomy of its participants. And it is also the place where any and all preexisting power relations come undone: "At the interface between gravitational fields," Negt and Kluge write, "at the abaric point ... where gravitational forces have no effect, 'freedom' reigns."[76] Well aware that conflicts within the microstructures of interpersonal relationships can easily forestall such desired outcomes, Kluge and Negt nevertheless find validation reflected in actual historical processes that gravitational relations do indeed result in "deflections and deviations" rather than the progress or negation typical of linear historiographies, and that abaric points do in fact arise and lead to astonishing forms of collective coordination in the name of community building.[77]

How all this applies to the question of thinking for Negt and Kluge may start to come into view by first returning briefly to Benjamin and Adorno. In the seventeenth of his theses on history, Benjamin contends that a materialist historiography based on a "constructive principle" stands a chance of challenging historicism's delusions of universal history only if thinking "involves not only the movement of thoughts, but their arrest as well. Where thinking suddenly comes to a stop in a constellation saturated with tensions, it gives that constellation a shock, by which thinking is crystallized as a monad."[78] Implicit in Benjamin's constellative thinking is an additional counter-gravitational force capable of neutralizing all the many forces within a constellation of ideas that push and pull it into position. While Adorno does acknowledge in passing Benjamin's emphasis on deceleration in thinking without ever interrogating or retaining it in his own account of the constellation, at stake for both Benjamin and Adorno is the possibility of yielding indirectly *noumenal* knowledge from the *phenomenal* realm.[79] This tension between the transcendental and the experiential is just as operative for Negt and Kluge's

76 Oskar Negt and Alexander Kluge, *Geschichte und Eigensinn*, in *Der unterschätzte Mensch: Gemeinsame Philosophie in zwei Bänden*, vol. 2 (Frankfurt am Main: Zweitausendeins, 2001) 790.

77 Kluge and Negt 378.

78 Walter Benjamin, "On the Concept of History," trans. Harry Zorn, in *Selected Writings*, vol. 4: *1938–1940*, eds. Howard Eiland and Michael W. Jennings (Cambridge, MA: Belknap Press, 2003) 396.

79 Theodor W. Adorno, "Introduction to Benjamin's *Schriften*," in *Notes to Literature*, ed. Rolf Tiedemann, trans. Shierry Weber Nicholsen, vol. 2 (New York, NY: Columbia University Press, 1991) 228.

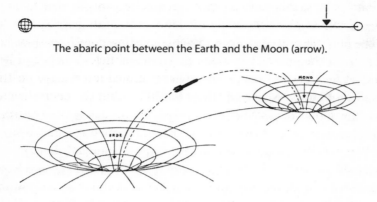

The abaric point between the Earth and the Moon (arrow).

The flight path from the Earth to the Moon—an attempt at
rendering the relations between gravitational fields.

Figure 0.4. Newtonian gravitation, the Lagrangian point. Freedom between the Earth and
the Moon. *History and Obstinacy*, p. 377. © Alexander Kluge.

call for thinking autonomously together even though it may seem at first
sight to unfold under conditions of pure presence.

After more than two decades since the appearance of its English-
language translation (and four decades since its debut in 1972), *Public
Sphere and Experience* persists outside German scholarship as Negt
and Kluge's most identifiable achievement, one couched, more often
than not, as a corrective to Habermas's work on the bourgeois public
sphere. Grasping the central role gravitational thinking plays in Negt and
Kluge's collaborations as well as in their respective works in terms of
an "enlightenment in the relations of relationships" might inadvertently
give an erroneous impression, especially since their thinking has never
sought to reconstruct historical materialism or to exchange it outright, as
was the case with Habermas's pragmatic turn to communicative rationality. Negt and Kluge neither sign on to Habermas's departure from the
philosophies of the subject and consciousness (together with his dismissal of Adorno et al.) nor do they tack on to his program regarding
the symbolic co-constitution of the lifeworld through communication,
understanding, and agreement. On the contrary, theirs is a concatenated
chain of theoretical tracts and a body of interrelated aesthetic practices
that follows Adorno, who once advised "to start by taking up the words
'subject' and 'object' such as they are handed down by the well-honed
philosophical language" in order to "continu[e] further with a critical

analysis."[80] So, in spite of first impressions—the title of their collected
works is *Der unterschätzte Mensch* [The Underestimated Subject]—it
must be made clear that Negt and Kluge's collaborative philosophy back-
pedals to neither the abstractions of idealism's transcendental subject
nor Marxism's dashed hopes once placed in a revolutionary proletarian subject. Rather, Negt and Kluge began in 1972 in medias res with
a utopian notion of post-bourgeois experience framed dialectically by
both subject and object such that neither conflates nor antagonizes the
two. What if, they hypothesize in their aforementioned debut, Marx's
concept of the "collective laborer" existed "as a real, thinking subject?"
"This social experience" would recognize "the limitations of commodity production" and make "the context of living itself the object of
production," in other words "a public form of expression" itself based
on "the subject character of organized social experience."[81] Capable
of achieving "peace between human beings" in Adorno's exhortation,
this ceaselessly countervailing "relationship of subject and object" also
informs Kluge and Negt's account in *History and Obstinacy* of autonomous self-regulating forces present in social relations that give rise to
"gravitation between dead and living labor."[82] And, in their "Measured
Relations of the Political," they identify the "incongruence" between
typically sluggish subjective capacities to differentiate and the speeds by
which objective historical change transpires as the core challenge to fostering grassroots political correctives to heedless institutional politics.[83]
Embedded in all these fine details culled from their core trilogy is not
just a consistent philosophical vocabulary with a discernible pedigree
reaching back to Kant and Hegel but also a commitment to Adorno's
long-standing program (and arguably Benjamin's, too), namely "to break
through the deception of constitutive subjectivity with the force [*Kraft*]
of the subject."[84] For Adorno, this force resides in that mode of autonomous dynamic thinking he calls negative dialectics capable of exploding

80 Theodor W. Adorno, "On Subject and Object," in *Critical Models: Interventions and Catchwords*, trans. Henry W. Pickford (New York: Columbia University Press, 2005) 246.
81 Oskar Negt and Alexander Kluge, *Public Sphere and Experience: Toward an Analy-sis of the Bourgeois and Proletarian Public Sphere*, trans. Peter Labanyi, Jamie Owen Daniel, and Assenka Oksiloff (Minneapolis, MN: University of Minnesota Press, 1993) 7–8.
82 Adorno, "On Subject and Object," 247; Kluge and Negt 113.
83 Negt and Kluge, *Maßverhältnisse des Politischen*, in *Der unterschätzte Mensch*, 699.
84 Theodor W. Adorno, *Negative Dialectics*, trans. E.B. Ashton (New York: Contin-uum, 1995) xx. Translation slightly modified.

the omnipresent appearance of identity in modern life.[85] Thinking, for
Negt and Kluge, is also not without force, but, while Adorno confines
it to one single thinking subject, they acknowledge myriad forces operating in any encounter with one or more thinking subjects. Far from
smuggling new Habermasian wine in old Adornean bottles, Negt and
Kluge's sustained attention to subjects and the forces they employ in the
name of thinking together stands in stark contrast to their confrère's case
for communicative rationality on account of the exceptional conditions
under which such an exchange transpires.

The Marxian vein coursing through *Negative Dialectics* is especially
pronounced at that point where Adorno cites the exchange principle
as the actual core of all identity thinking. Paraphrasing Marx's treatise
on the commodity from *Capital*, Adorno credits exchange for having
brought about a pernicious social order shaped by coercion, injustice,
and naked privilege, all of which sit atop a foundation composed of once
living human labor that was debased into an "abstract universal concept
of average working hours."[86] In its relentless pursuit of commensurability, this logic not only transforms subjects into unequal objects but also
brings identity thinking to grasp the world as an illusory totality full of
false equivalencies. In its confrontation with the exchange principle, critical theory's task, Adorno submits, should not be to deny it categorically,
for that would ignore the prehistory of trading unequal things and would
promptly deliver exchange over to instrumental rationality with even
more disastrous results. On the contrary, his negative dialectics strives
to "realize the ideal of free and just exchange" by exposing it for what
it really is, namely "an exchange of things that are equal and yet unequal."[87] When, in a televised dialogue with Negt based on Kant's 1786
essay "What Does It Mean to Orient Oneself in Thinking?," Kluge raises
the specter of state coercion for the freedom of expression, he seemingly
enters into the very fray of identity thinking predicated on exchange that
Adorno puts on notice:

KLUGE: If I can't exchange my ideas with someone else, then my own
thoughts have no value. Thinking is a collective process, in fact the
most communal thing that humanity can do.

---

85 Adorno, *Negative Dialectics*, 149.
86 Adorno, *Negative Dialectics*, 146.
87 Adorno, *Negative Dialectics*, 147. Translation modified.

NEGT: Yes, you're right. The freedom of the pen is therefore the only
safeguard of a people's rights ... [it] is both a need and the possibility
to make public use of one's own reason. Only then is it a verifiable
dimension that simultaneously acquires collective meaning. Thinking is nothing ... like a monad that thinks in itself. The problem isn't
just that you can't express yourself. Kant says it's also the fact that
you can't think properly."[88]

What may first appear like hypocrisy vis-à-vis Adorno's injunction is,
in actuality, only possible for Negt and Kluge by dint of the mutual shift
in positions that two or more thinkers undergo when the gravitational
force, of which their thinking is inherently capable, is engaged. Before
any exchange of ideas can ever transpire, thinkers must exert a force on
themselves in such a way so as to dislodge their own thinking from its
center of gravity anchored in their unique lived experiences and embodied interests, such that they carefully approach the other without breaking
free entirely from their own orbit. The achieved displacements resulting
in temporary propinquity afford a degree of closeness but never result
in any replication or, conversely, the forfeiture of self or its distinctions
tethered to its original point of departure. Furthermore, gravitational
thinking entails not just drawing one's thinking closer to that of another
but also a displacement allowing for both an examination of self and
the development of self-trust, the first step necessary for placing trust
in another.[89] To the unaided spectator in search of content, Negt and
Kluge's exchange performs on camera what looks like a mere recapitulation of the key features in Kant's essay, when in fact what they mediate
through Kant is a fruitful moment of togetherness whereby philosopher
and non-philosopher think in tandem. Instead of their well-cited illustration of a rocket flying at the abaric point between two gravitational
fields (fig. 0.4), they propose we imagine "spaceships that try to attain a
uniform speed through a series of braking and acceleration maneuvers.
Only in doing so can they dock with one another."[90]

What makes the sociability of thinking possible is not merely the
gravitational force capable of bringing thinkers together. Needed, too,

88 Alexander Kluge, dir., "Selbstdenken: Immanuel Kants Schrift: Was heißt: sich im
Denken orientieren?," *10 Till 11*, RTL, September 19, 2005, https://kluge.library.cornell
.edu/conversations/negt/film/2114.
89 Kluge and Negt 139–40.
90 Kluge and Negt 382.

is balance such that sharing ideas and therewith a free and just collaboration may unfold at all. Introduced by Kluge to the English-language
edition of *History and Obstinacy*, the anthropological term *Homo compensator* counts not as a pronouncement of a woeful human condition
due to some phylogenetic lack but rather as an ideal and aspiration;
constantly derailed by the forces of capital, *Homo sapiens* must strive to
strike a balance not just between one another but also within themselves,
and this applies equally to thinking, too.[91] There exists already within
every human being, Kluge and Negt maintain, a handful of autonomous
and often antagonistic orders of equilibrium ranging from natural laws
governing the universe—e.g., the law of conservation of energy—to the
self-regulation of living cells, from the self-regulation of social memories, wishes, and values to that innermost capacity they call obstinacy. Set
on achieving cooperation among autonomous activities within a single
organism, self-regulation also applies when contact with another person
or object gives rise to friction.[92] Kluge and Negt's primary example is that
of children learning by playing together:

> Two children are engrossed in deciphering letters. Three children
> are climbing a pole. One group of children is making a ruckus, while
> another has placed tables together to form a house and squats beneath
> it. Other children focus intently on solving a puzzle, and yet others
> are making artistic cardboard figures. The teacher moves between the
> different groups. No one group disturbs any other, although there is
> repeated traffic and contact between them. The highly animated chil-
> dren, as well as those working quietly by themselves, remain fixed on
> their respective activities.[93]

In this particular scenario, self-regulation is the living labor each individual child expends according to their own personal interests in concert
with that of their teammates whom they mutually recognize. These autonomous clusters together constitute a communal organization, a solidarity

---

91 See Kluge and Negt, 195, 409, 414. See also: Odo Marquard, "*Homo compensator*: Zur anthropologischen Karriere eines metaphysischen Begriffs," in *Philosophie des
Stattdessen: Studien* (Stuttgart: Philipp Reclam, 2000) 11–29; and Alexander Kluge, "Wie
gefährlich ist Kleist?," *Die Zeit* (January 5, 2011): 1.
92 Kluge and Negt 110.
93 Kluge and Negt 106, 107.

so balanced that it can withstand the dictates and disruptions of author-itative reason.[94] As with the children's learning, gravitational thinking —nothing less than a mental form of labor—also assumes more the mantle of play than work. Decisive in this cognitive play is its momentary evasion of coercion as well as its involvement of fantasy over reason.[95] In another interview with Negt based on Kant's *Critique of the Power of Judgment*, Kluge underscores the correlation between exchange aimed at balance and what Kant refers to as the imagination:

> KLUGE: But when I have good fortune, like "Hans in Luck" [from the eponymous Grimms' fairy tale—RL], and enter into an exchange, that's something I should develop and bring into equilibrium.
> NEGT: Yes, and Schiller takes up this thought as well, that the aesthetic condition and the aesthetic state are always connected to a balance between the faculties … Pleasure really lies in …
> KLUGE: … the swift exchange between the different states of mind …
> NEGT: … and in the harmonious balance of these emotional states.
> KLUGE: Almost like an artistry of moods.
> NEGT: And that also acquires for him in the context of his *Critique of Pure Reason* considerable significance in terms of the imagination. The imagination is an extremely authentic, independent, and origi-nal human force: the playful handling of thoughts and feeling. It's in the musical arts and he says therefore that in principle the mind is not deactivated. But it is not the workings of actual reason.[96]

This balanced exchange is, in other words, not simply an appeal to the communal use of reason, as if its collective use could ever fulfill its crit-ical potential after its mid-twentieth century eclipse or its subsequent confinement to communication. Hardly adverse to reason, gravitational thinking also avails itself of other serviceable forms of reason like the pleasures of the mind (not to mention those of the body) that lie beyond those that Kant exhorted us to employ.[97]

---

94 Negt and Kluge, *Geschichte und Eigensinn*, 70.
95 Kluge and Negt 174.
96 Alexander Kluge, "Der Mensch ist nur dort ganz Mensch, wo er spielt," *Prime-time*, RTL, November 13, 2005, https://kluge.library.cornell.edu/de/conversations/negt/film/2123.
97 Kluge and Negt 382.

We spectators see this playful balanced exchange unfold not just in these two aforementioned dialogues but also in any number of Negt and Kluge conversations recorded for television broadcast when, as above, Kluge interrupts Negt and dares him to follow a sudden shift in topic; to address his own fanciful implications drawn from his counterpart's philosophical exegeses; or casts, conversely, philosophical language into hypothetical scenarios.[98] Similarly, we readers glide over this playfulness in their three books of social philosophy not only in their subtle shifts of voice—they wrote everything face to face by alternating back and forth sometimes even mid-sentence—but also in the gaps between the blocks of text characteristic of every chapter and book; in the relation-ships between conceptual thinking and commentary; and in the breaks between captioned illustrations as well as their enigmatic location within the text. What may very well scan like a puzzle to be solved was, for Kluge and Negt, in the moment of thinking, "a relation of trust."[99] The same can certainly be said of Kluge's aesthetic as well. Addressing in one breath both his literary method and its desired care for the reader's autonomy, Kluge recently explained that every one of his storybooks has "a single core, just as there is a core at the center of the earth from which gravitational relations emerge. This gravitational thinking holds things on the sphere's surface together, but also the sphere itself, and this cor-responds with other spheres that zip around in space like planets. They are autonomously formulated stories that come into contact with others also formulated autonomously."[100] Of utmost concern for Kluge are not finished edifices but rather constellative frameworks against whose "force of gravity," as Benjamin calls it, a reader must hone their own powers of imagination.[101] As with a galaxy containing multiple planetary systems, gravitation holds together not only all the many pieces in any given Kluge book around its thematic core but also governs innumera-ble relationships with other texts. Since his earliest interviews about his first feature film, Kluge the filmmaker has long insisted that his films are nowhere to be found in the images on screen but rather assemble

---

98 Joseph Vogl, "Kluges Fragen," in *Maske und Kothurn: Internationale Beiträge zur Theater-, Film-, und Medienwissenschaft* 53.1 (2007): 121.

99 See: Philipp 96; and Kluge and Negt 201.

100 Alexander Kluge, "Storytelling Means Dissolving Relations," trans. Emma Woelk, in *Difference and Orientation*, 95.

101 Benjamin, *The Correspondence of Walter Benjamin*, 522.

themselves in the spectators' heads; equally relevant to his films (and video collections) as it is for his literature (as well as the theory coauthored with Negt), montage—what Kluge once called the "morphology of relationality"—harbors cohesive forces out of which audiences must gravitationally recalibrate their own thinking.[102] Essential to such adjustment is the work of the imagination necessary for shifting perspective from center to periphery, where opposing gravitational fields yield to abaric points, brief moments of equilibrium and exchange made possible not at the expense of but rather in the name of difference. "Every cut," Kluge once said of montage, "provokes fantasy, a storm of fantasy."[103]

Naysayers would not be wrong to call out what flies here under the flag of gravitational thinking as nothing really new to the Frankfurt School. Without ever availing itself of the concept, a growing body of scholarship has productively mined the tensions, for example, lurking in Walter Benjamin's and Herbert Marcuse's encounters with Martin Heidegger's existential ontology that long counted as the Frankfurt School's bête noir. It comes as perhaps a surprise that none other than Adorno, known by many for his uncompromising vitriol leveled at those he considered hucksters of authenticity, has received as of late more attention than any other of the elder stewards of critical theory for his "troubled yet *productive*" engagements with not just his archrival Heidegger.[104] Careful examinations have found, for example, considerable common ground between Adorno and such markedly different contemporaries as Hans Blumenberg (who rebuked *Negative Dialectics* for its generalities and indefiniteness), Jean-Paul Sartre (whom Adorno chided for his "regression to the eighteenth century"), and Hannah Arendt (who once regarded Adorno and his other Institute colleagues as a "gang of pigs").[105]

---

102 Alexander Kluge, "Bits of Conversation," trans. Emma Woelk, in *Difference and Orientation,* 148; Alexander Kluge, *Die Patriotin: Texte/Bilder 1–6* (Frankfurt am Main: Zweitausendeins, 1979) 41.

103 Alexander Kluge, "On Film and the Public Sphere," trans. Thomas Y. Levin and Miriam B. Hansen, in *Alexander Kluge: Raw Materials for the Imagination,* ed. Tara Forrest (Amsterdam, Amsterdam University Press, 2012) 44. See also: Negt and Kluge, *Public Sphere and Experience,* 33.

104 Peter E. Gordon, *Adorno and Experience* (Cambridge, MA: Harvard University Press, 2016) 2. See also Iain Macdonald and Krzysztof Ziarek, eds., *Adorno and Heidegger: Philosophical Questions* (Stanford, CA: Stanford University Press, 2008).

105 Christian Voller, "Kommunikation verweigert: Schwierige Beziehungen zwischen Blumenberg und Adorno," *Technik: Zeitschrift für Kulturphilosophie* 2 (2013): 381–405; David Sherman, *Sartre and Adorno: The Dialectics of Subjectivity* (Albany, NY:

Not unlike this line of work undertaken in large part by intellectual historians, younger German philosophers sometimes associated with a third generation of the Frankfurt School have also sought out interstices between Adorno and French thinkers seemingly worlds apart from his negative dialectics. For example, Axel Honneth has interrogated Michel Foucault's theory of power for "emerging correspondences" with Adorno's critique of modernity; with recourse to Jacques Derrida, Christoph Menke has sought to resolve antinomies in Adorno's *Aesthetic Theory*; and in spite of Adorno's prohibitions, Martin Seel has brought phenomenological questions to bear on the "dogma and trauma" of Adorno's negativity in an effort to render it viable for the twenty-first century.[106] There are, however, crucial differences between these ex post facto efforts at uncovering the gravitational potential lurking in the thinking of early Frankfurt School members and how Negt and Kluge think gravitationally *in situ* as well as why they do so in the first place. Firstly, their gravitational thinking is not latent content requiring any analytic reconstruction. Rather, the gravitational character of their thinking unfolds in the moment and remains legible after the fact in both content and form. (The twenty-six transcribed television dialogues constituting their fourth collaboration—*Suchbegriffe*—expose in this respect the raw form of thinking partially smoothed over in their preceding works.) Secondly, their thinking is very often mediated through a third thinker whose own thought serves as a basis for what may at first seem like mere commentary. (Commentary, they insist, counts as a common initial form of orientation in thinking by virtue of the "reliability of previously recorded work by dead thinkers.")[107] Thirdly, their gravitational thinking is adverse to the disciplinary dictates typical of academic discourse. (In lieu of professional intelligentsia's division of labor, its high level of specialization, and its tireless pursuit of the new, all of which dissociate the "cognitive drive" from the economic pressures arising from all life contexts, Negt

---

State University of New York Press, 2007); Lars Rensmann and Samir Gandesha, *Arendt and Adorno: Political and Philosophical Investigations* (Stanford, CA: Stanford University Press, 2012) 283n16; and Adorno, *Negative Dialectics*, 226n.

106 Axel Honneth, "Foucault and Adorno: Two Forms of the Critique of Modernity," trans. David Roberts, *Thesis Eleven* 15.1 (1986): 48–59; Christoph Menke, *The Sovereignty of Art: Aesthetic Negativity in Adorno and Derrida*, trans. Neil Solomon (Cambridge, MA: MIT Press, 1998); Martin Seel, "Adorno's Contemplative Ethics," *Critical Horizons* 5.1 (2004): 259.

107 Negt and Kluge, *Geschichte und Eigensinn*, 1007.

and Kluge uphold the tradition of critique. They do so while expanding it to encompass not merely the cultivation of resistance in the human consciousness but also the nurturing of faculties for perceiving relationships and difference and therewith finding ways out of life contexts mired in the misery of capitalism.)[108] Fourthly, they jettison neither philosophical aesthetics nor aesthetic praxis to some extraterritorial zone beyond the space where thinking unfolds. (Imaginative thinking requires times and spaces where it can drill, twist, turn, and leap on its own accord.) Lastly and most importantly, their thinking is political not just because of the counter-force it exerts against the inertia of identity thinking or, conversely, merely because of the counter-productions its labor gives rise to in the collaborative moment of thinking together with others. It is also not so because of the orientation its contexts and connections are capable of providing praxis, albeit—in keeping with Adorno—at a considerable distance. While all these grounds certainly contribute to the overall political dimension of their gravitational thinking, what subtends them all is an effort to make understandable both conceptually and materially what Negt once called the "darkness" where human protest energies always have resided and will continue to prosper. "The degree to which this 'protest' is not understood," he explained in an interview, "is also why it cannot develop."[109] As much as it may seem both metaphorical and highly improbable, Negt and Kluge write of dark matter quite literally in terms of that elusive substance comprising roughly 85 percent of the total mass of the universe that is essential for any emancipatory politics on earth.

Dark Matter in Defiance of Catastrophic Modernity

A brief collage sequence lodged in the middle of the third pivotal chapter on the political economy of labor power from Negt and Kluge's *Geschichte und Eigensinn* confronts readers with a seemingly arbitrary collection of captioned photographs and illustrations. Scanning forward from images of brain cells to soldiers and their wives, from the Milky Way to Galileo's astronomical manuscripts, from a group of women at

---

108 Negt and Kluge, *Public Sphere and Experience*, 22–26; Kluge and Negt 169–202; Negt and Kluge, *Maßverhältnisse des Politischen*, in *Der unterschätzte Mensch*, 777–85.
109 Negt, "Denken als Gegenproduktion," 93.

a munitions factory to another dancing at a ball, readers are suddenly confronted with a riddle: "Cells know everything from here to the stars, but the mind [*der Kopf*] has never experienced any such thing and thus has never forgotten it either."[110] How, readers may wonder, does a cell manage to know anything beyond itself let alone the universe? And why is the human brain, the seat of cognition, oblivious to this cellular knowledge? An echo of deceased Corporal Wieland's disembodied knee from Kluge's 1979 film *The Patriot*, this clue to what Negt and Kluge call Marx's "unfulfilled program" without any further qualification resurfaces two decades later in another interlude of stories and images from their collected works.[111] In a caption to an illustration of the globular cluster 47 Tucanae, readers are told: "For several years, astrophysicists have been able to weight the universe. Visible matter including all the stars and galaxies account for thirty percent of its mass. Seventy percent is dark matter, which is composed of neither atoms nor electrons. We live in a sea full of the unknown."[112] Quite possibly influenced by Kluge's television interviews with one of the directors of the Max Planck Institute for Astrophysics, Simon White, conducted that same year, the caption to this illustration from 2001 employs scientific terminology that eluded Negt and Kluge in 1981. It also suggests when juxtaposed with its earlier variant that what cells know is precisely what science struggles in vain to comprehend, namely dark matter.[113] Conversely, Corporal Wieland's knee makes utterly clear, too, that of concern for Negt and Kluge is not science's narrow agenda focused on the hunt for elusive sub-atomic particles. Instead, dark matter is yoked to history. "I'm essentially a historian," the omniscient knee confesses. But the history in question would be no less wondrous than the philosopher's stone once thought to be the elixir of life itself. "It is the resurrection of the dead," the knee explains, "that presupposes the most fundamental historical knowledge (and who ever wanted to die?)."[114] Such miraculous effects can only materialize if

---

110 Negt and Kluge, *Geschichte und Eigensinn*, 151.

111 The knee says, "Every cell in a body that never wanted to perish knows everything from the dawn of the Occident to the stars and how it all eventually ends." Kluge, *Die Patriotin*, 166.

112 Negt and Kluge, *Geschichte und Eigensinn*, 682.

113 One of Kluge's first broadcasts explicitly on dark matter is: Alexander Kluge, dir., "Auf der Suche nach der *Dunklen Materie*: Die Fortsetzung von Galileis Himmelsvermessung mit anderen Mitteln," *News and Stories*, SAT.1, December 2, 2001.

114 Kluge, *Die Patriotin*, 166.

the contents of cells—the knee declares in broad strokes that "we are full of protest and energy"—and, by extension, dark matter are adequately grasped, and to do so entails taking not just the long view of history reaching all the way back to the Big Bang.[115] It also requires that we school our increasingly fragile mimetic faculty that Benjamin says was once capable of producing and recognizing correspondences between microcosm and macrocosm.[116] All of this—cellular knowledge of the heavens as well as the secret to life after death shrouded in dark matter—may sound like the improbable stuff of fanciful science fiction. Yet it has its basis, at least in part, in what now counts as basic scientific fact. In one of many televised interviews with astrophysicists recorded since 2001, Kluge once again zeros in on the rudimentary statistics regarding the composition of the universe, but this time around he and his interlocutor, Max Planck Institute astrophysicist Günther Hasinger, also underscore the radical consequences of dark matter for human life on earth:

KLUGE: Seventy-six percent ... is dark energy and then a very large part is hot and cold dark matter. And what we marvel at as it were in the starry sky ...

HASINGER: ... and what we ourselves are composed of ...

KLUGE: ... is really baryonic matter, in fact a very small portion.

HASINGER: It's really only roughly 4 percent of the entire energy supply. The fact of the matter is that since Galileo, but really much earlier, we human beings have been pushed farther and farther away from the center of human knowledge. The Earth is no longer the center of the solar system. The Sun is no longer the center of the galaxy. The galaxy is a small garden-variety galaxy in a huge universe. And now there's talk about whether there's not just one but many other universes.[117]

In short, science's scrutiny of the heavens has culminated, on the one hand, in the relegation of humankind to the periphery of our own cosmic

115 Kluge, *Die Patriotin*, 58.
116 Walter Benjamin, "On the Mimetic Faculty," trans. Edmund Jephcott, in *Selected Works*, vol. 2: *1927–1934*, eds. Michael W. Jennings et al. (Cambridge, MA: Belknap Press, 1999), 720–21.
117 Alexander Kluge, "Cosmic Web: Evolution im Universum," in *Seen sind Fische für Inseln: Fernseharbeiten, 1987–2008* (Frankfurt am Main: Zweitausendeins, 2009) DVD 8, track 8. Originally broadcast on: *News & Stories*, SAT.1, March 9, 2008.

knowledge and, on the other, made utterly clear that reality as we know it on earth is probably just one among many possibilities. Kluge's ensuing question in the above conversation as to whether multiple universes are entwined in one another is, in essence, not far removed from Kluge and Negt's long-held belief that an authentic "realistic attitude" requires knowledge of the considerable "darkness" within ourselves where there rages a protest against the unbearable relations of reality constantly deforming our lives; with every human loss—not just the loss of man's anthropocentric position in the universe—comes as a matter of course the possibility that there could exist other lives and worlds and thus conceivable alternatives to, if not ways out of, our reality.[118] This correlation between the preponderance of dark matter throughout the universe and what the young Marx's anthropology nebulously called humankind's "objective essential powers" is precisely what Negt and Kluge see as Marxism's "unfulfilled" promise. In the face of capital's relentless alienation, the subject's essential powers intent on satisfying its own needs are inherently set on resisting the dictates of the reality principle in the name of forging other better realities.[119]

Kluge, in particular, has long appreciated the ongoing science of dark matter, but as Hasinger points out above and as Kluge himself would surely agree, it would be nearsighted to regard its relevance exclusively in terms of an arcane cosmic phenomenon. Dark matter permeates human life and bits and pieces of this "darkness," as Negt calls it more generally, find themselves strewn throughout historical experience. Under the reign of capitalism, it resides in the idea of the proletarian public sphere, a category of subaltern experience that eludes critical analysis because the bourgeois public sphere's dominion atomizes, abandons, and excludes it to such a degree that it is left entirely unsubstantiated. It inhabits the raw materials (such as embodied interests and feelings) necessary for exercising communal political praxis that hegemonic politics customarily jettisons to the periphery of everyday life. And it subtends the conceptually elusive amalgam of human characteristics that give rise to the form of self-regulation they call obstinacy, "when those below are no longer

---

118 Kluge and Negt 139, 98.

119 Oskar Negt, "Über Marx," in *Marx*, ed. Oskar Negt (Munich: Diedrichs, 1996) 56: "The program for an analysis of capital is fulfilled. Unfulfilled is the program about the constitution of the subject, ethics, and human rights."

willing and those above no longer can."[120] Inaccessible to immediate thinking, this darkness in human experience is also operative throughout Kluge's aesthetic but only insofar as any aesthetic form can merely index what it can never directly represent let alone know. Just as the abundance of dark matter in the universe calls the singularity of terrestrial reality into question, that which can never be committed to film does the same to everything that has ever been represented cinematically.[121] To this end, the principle of montage has persisted on account of its breaks and gaps—it is no coincidence that Kluge has long been concerned with the fate of celluloid's structural "dark phase" in the age of new media—as the hallmark of not just his classical cinema but also his literature and more recent video work.[122] What ultimately binds their theoretical awareness of the dark matter in historical experience with Kluge's fragmented aesthetic is the acknowledged presence of an epistemological block that, like dark matter's relationship to baryonic matter, cordons off these swaths of darkness from both lived experience and its attendant forms of representation. On the relevance of dark matter and the probability of other worlds for human life, Kluge asks Hasinger above whether a link between self-consciousness and the cosmos renders possible human recognition of relativity. Hasinger replies, "We are at least the only beings known to us at all capable of thinking about this." A rhetorical question that Kluge himself would surely have answered in the affirmative as well, this thinking is arguably best summarized philosophically by none other than Adorno, who in reference to modernity's secularization processes contended that metaphysical experience expresses itself more often than not negatively in the form of the question "'Can this be everything?'"[123] Utterly essential for both the possibility of freedom and "thought's ability to think its own conditionedness," metaphysical experience of yore is for Adorno an impossibility especially in the shadow of Auschwitz, but without it thinking is pointless.[124] For him, the only viable refuge for metaphysics in the face of the false whole of modern life is to be found in what he calls "micrology," the solitary philosopher's unceasing practice of

---

120 Kluge and Negt 102.

121 Kluge, *Die Patriotin*, 280.

122 Alexander Kluge, "On the Expressions 'Media' and 'New Media': A Selection of Keywords," trans. Richard Lambert, in *Difference and Orientation*, 273.

123 Adorno, *Negative Dialectics*, 375. Translation modified.

124 Adorno, *Negative Dialectics*, 396; Jarvis 216.

negative dialectics capable of rendering legible a "constellation of things in being."[125] For Negt and Kluge, constructing such a constellation out of exemplary particulars begins with the invitation to think gravitationally with others by inhabiting that point where forging unusual connections, trafficking in wild analogies, and proposing synecdochically unheard-of relationalities and similarities, all the while retaining a keen sense of difference in both one another's thinking and being. Conversely, dark matter is that metaphysical guarantee that, in both materialist thinking (à la the body's cells) and gravitational thinking alike, there exists more beyond than what is, that the answer to Adorno's question is always a clear no, and that thinking is always already political by the dint of its protest and its utopian telos.

As this introduction finally draws to a close, readers should begin to make sense of many of the keywords both invoked and indexed in its title, "Dark Matter in Defiance of Catastrophic Modernity": gravitational thinking attuned to dark matter is, in a word, intrinsically dubious if not altogether antagonistic toward reality's status quo while, at the same time, thoroughly convinced of the possibility of other, better states of affairs. To this end, it is curious and collaborative but in the final analysis always fiercely partisan. What remains, however, unaccounted for in this introduction and what requires at the very least some qualification before embarking is the object of this antagonism: the status of catastrophe for not just gravitational thinking addressed in this introduction but also the ensuing chapters of this book. "Catastrophe" was certainly a well-established concept long before the advent of modernity, but with the standardization of the German language in the seventeenth century, its primarily positive meaning for ancient dramaturgy—the final resolution of dramatic conflict—gave way to a thoroughly negative sensibility about the modern lifeworld. Departing from its early modern status as event—a "sudden reversal of things, especially in human and societal life"— "catastrophe" metastasized over the course of the twentieth century to describe a pervasive modern condition especially pronounced in technological (e.g., the sinking of the *Titanic*), political (e.g., World War I) and cultural discourses (e.g., the pessimism of Oswald Spengler).[126] Amid this inflationary usage, consensus on how to negotiate modernity's

---

125 Adorno, *Negative Dialectics*, 407.
126 Olaf Briese and Timo Günther, "Katastrophe: Terminologische Vergangenheit, Gegenwart und Zukunft," *Archiv für Begriffsgeschichte* 51 (2009): 166, 188.

catastrophes eluded Frankfurt School pioneers, especially at the zenith of reason's eclipse under National Socialism. Writing in 1940, Benjamin equated, for example, any and all belief in progress with catastrophic thinking, yet he did reserve the possibility for redemption in what he saw as catastrophe's "tiny fissure[s]."[127] Writing only a couple years later, Horkheimer and Adorno concurred that modern progress was indeed underwritten by regression, destruction, and enslavement, but any and all egress from this windowless jailhouse is precluded. "The lure of the Sirens remains overpowering; no one who hears their song can escape," they write in *Dialectic of Enlightenment*.[128] On whether the permanent condition of catastrophic modernity—long after the demise of German fascism, industrialism, and modernism—still conceals or forecloses ways out toward happier states of affairs, Negt and Kluge side unequivocally with Benjamin. But, unlike all their elders, for whom catastrophe was enlightened omniscient thinking gone horribly wrong—in Adorno's eyes, catastrophe begins with a conviction in totality, the gravitational pull of which pulls everything into its black hole—Negt and Kluge conceive the catastrophe of all catastrophes anthropologically and, to this end, situate it before thought. Following Marx's historical materialist account of capitalist production as the catastrophic result of primitive accumulation, they ascribe the nexus of all modern catastrophes to those historical processes of separation and division that both originally engendered and continue to perpetuate the misery of estranged human labor.[129] "We are interested," they write in the preface to *Geschichte und Eigensinn*, "in what exactly labor achieves when it alters matter in a world in which catastrophes obviously occur."[130] Implied in their qualification is the proposition that although the modern world remains inherently catastrophic, labor does not necessarily have to be so, even though more often than not it does. To be sure, their philosophy draws liberally on examples culled from European history in which labor's primitive accumulation (e.g., the peasants wars of the fifteenth to seventeenth

127 Walter Benjamin, "Central Park," trans. Edmund Jephcott and Howard Eiland, in *Selected Writings*, vol. 4: *1938–1940*, eds. Michael W. Jennings et al. (Cambridge, MA: Belknap Press, 2003) 184–85.

128 Max Horkheimer and Theodor W. Adorno, *Dialectic of Enlightenment: Philosophical Fragments*, ed. Gunzelin Schmid Noerr, trans. Edmund Jephcott (Stanford, CA: Stanford University Press, 2002) 26.

129 Fredric Jameson, "On Negt and Kluge," *October* 46 (Autumn 1988): 160.

130 Negt and Kluge, *Geschichte und Eigensinn*, 5.

centuries) as well as its subsequent industrial organization (e.g., World War I, Auschwitz) resulted in epochal catastrophes with lasting consequences for individuals and societies alike. Similarly, Kluge's aesthetic has elevated such singular twentieth- and twenty-first-century events as the Battle of Stalingrad, the Allied air raid on his hometown of Halberstadt, the nuclear accidents at Chernobyl and Fukushima, and the Great Recession, just to name a few, as points of departure for his imaginative labor. While drawing our attention to the suffering expropriated human labor has unwittingly produced against its own vested interests, Negt and Kluge also underscore the other half of the equation: namely, those underestimated labor capacities "armed with obstinacy" that processes of separation foment, capacities not just resistant to their expropriation but also capable of locating paths not taken, seeking collaborative alternatives to catastrophic modernity's doomed organization of labor power, and realizing collective emancipation.[131] To defy catastrophic modernity is thus to discern within it that much older, now largely forgotten ancient possibility explored within the dramatic arts whereby catastrophe marks a turn in the story toward a potentially joyous conclusion.[132] In this respect, aesthetic form—the place where the "pure power of possible poetic interpretations of the world" can unfold—is essential to gravitational thinking about social life, for it is the aesthetic that affords the imagination with both the spaces and times to ponder other, far less catastrophic realities invariably happier than our own.[133]

Of all the many attendant theses put forth in each of the ensuing chapters that make up *Dark Matter*, the one that binds them all together is the centrality of gravitational thinking for both Negt and Kluge and all the many other thinkers—philosophers, artists, or even audiences—they engage. *Dark Matter* makes, therefore, a case for neither orthodox influence nor generational lineage in its account of their work. Rather, it queries those zones of near-gravitationlessness, where collaboration allows for both loyalty to heritage and contact with distinctly divergent ways of thinking in the name of describing as robustly as possible all the

---

131 Negt and Kluge, *Geschichte und Eigensinn*, 5.

132 Briese and Günther, 162. On Kluge's defense of romanticism's "protest against the reality principle," see: Alexander Kluge and Klaus Eder, "Debate on the Documentary Film: Conversations with Klaus Eder, 1980," trans. Robert Savage, in *Alexander Kluge: Raw Materials for the Imagination*, 201–4.

133 Briese and Günther, 169.

many entangled layers constituting human experience—some concrete, many others abstract—that range from the factual unrealities ordained by the reality principle to the antirealism of counterfactual feelings and wishes. In every instance, the trick lies in forging relationships between a multitude of antipodes including, but not limited to, generosity and obstinacy, fact and fantasy, self and other, theory and the aesthetic, and, of course, luminous and dark matter. In each of the principal eight chapters of this book, Negt and Kluge engage not only Frankfurt School mentors and peers but also outliers and outsiders who were ignored or rebuffed by Negt and Kluge's elders, or conversely did little to hide their contempt for the Frankfurt School. Attention to obvious philosophical interlocutors like Kant, Marx, Benjamin, Adorno, and Habermas stand alongside other unlikely (and seemingly remote) bedfellows like Alfred Sohn-Rethel, Blumenberg, Niklas Luhmann, and Arendt. *Dark Matter* could have just as easily wandered across the Rhine river to assemble an equally extensive list of additional French thinkers—e.g., Claude Lévi-Strauss, André Gorz, Jacques Derrida, Gilles Deleuze and Félix Guattari, Michel Foucault, and Michel Serres. (Deleuze, the one exception to this roster, is featured in chapter 5.) Or *Dark Matter* could call upon a host of European authors (e.g., Ovid, Madame de La Fayette, Kleist, Gottfried Benn, Robert Musil, Arno Schmidt, Helmut Heißenbüttel, Hans Magnus Enzensberger) or filmmakers (e.g., Auguste and Louis Lumière, Carl Theodor Dreyer, Hans Richter, Fritz Lang, Jean-Luc Godard, Andrei Tarkovsky), all of whom Kluge has engaged in his work. (The same goes for all the many real and fictional experts, entertainers, and eyewitnesses featured in Kluge's thousands of television interviews.) Instead, this book limits its focus to just a handful of other artists (Sergei Eisenstein, Dziga Vertov, Bertolt Brecht, and Anselm Kiefer) in order to give weight to the role of Kluge's own aesthetic practice in literature, film, television, and video.

The first half of *Dark Matter* illuminates four themes subtending the core of Negt and Kluge's collaborative philosophy that have obliged them to think with others gravitationally: interests, labor and technology, the counterpublic sphere, and the political. Chapter 1 begins *Dark Matter* with the keystone of Negt and Kluge's work, namely the pitfalls and promises of critical intelligence, its place in catastrophic modernity, and its potential for initiating learning processes capable of defying the perpetuation of modern catastrophes into the future. Chapter 2 queries their investment in the utopian potential of labor; of primary concern here is their focus on technology in labor's pandemic devaluation and dematerialization under late capitalism. Chapter 3 interrogates the viability of their arguably most famous idea—the counterpublic sphere—in the digital era when the boundaries between consumer and producer have dissolved. Chapter 4 considers Negt and Kluge's engagement with the Frankfurt School's mid-century concept of permanent catastrophe in the dusk of the twentieth century, when the conditions for everyday political praxis has been seemingly paralyzed. Unlike the longer chapters of part 1 that delineate their gravitational thinking, the second half of *Dark Matter* provides four shorter analyses of Kluge's aesthetic praxis as it relates to his and Negt's collaborations. Of central concern is how Kluge has deployed thinking, talking, feeling, and writing as mainstays of his antirealist program in defiance of modernity's catastrophes. Theory, say Negt and Kluge, ideally delivers to praxis measurable quantities of orientation, and in this respect chapter 5 shifts attention away from catastrophe and to the semantically distinct category of disaster: What can theory achieve when the starry skies go black and all reference points for orientation vanish? Chapter 6 delves into the very crux of Negt and Kluge's gravitational thinking, namely their televised dialogues, and dissects how their intercourse strives to constitute a community of thinkers beyond the frame. Tackling one of the most vexing problems to beleaguer Kluge the filmmaker—namely, gender and representation —chapter 7 frames Kluge's penchant for female protagonists alternatively in terms of his and Negt's radical conceptualization of the subject, the politics of feeling, and the political potential of dramaturgy. Ending where *Dark Matter* began, namely with Kluge's prose, chapter 8 wrestles with one of Negt and Kluge's oldest concerns, namely the temporality of human experience; under investigation is the importance of literary form for Kluge's ambiguous poetics of existence. *Dark Matter* concludes with an epilogue that qualifies Negt and Kluge's notion of critique by tracking it in Kluge's very recent collaborations with the visual artist Anselm Kiefer. A mirror image of the first half of *Dark Matter*, this second half passes through Kluge's video, television, film, and literature and in so doing so underscores a second time how Kluge engages his and Negt's ideas within the formal logic of his chosen mediums.

And, finally, four provisos: Firstly, *Dark Matter* aspires neither to grapple with every detail of Negt and Kluge's collaborations, nor does it treat their individual works exhaustively. It nevertheless strives to make accessible some of their most salient ideas in order to advocate for their relevance for ongoing English-language dialogues grappling with such timely issues as experience and knowledge, media and politics, labor and capitalism, issues all central to every chapter of this book. While the book probes all of their collaborations, it takes judiciously from only some of their own respective works and leaves the balance for others to mine. Secondly, it cannot be stressed enough that Negt and Kluge are two wholly independent thinkers whose periodic teamwork grew out of a shared allegiance to the Frankfurt School. In this regard, *Dark Matter* admittedly runs the risk of overstating the prominence of their collaboration, especially when it subsumes Negt's and Kluge's solo efforts under the banner of a shared enterprise. In light of just how distinct their individual sensibilities are, future scholars concerned exclusively with either one or the other will surely shed much more needed light on their respective achievements. By contrast, *Dark Matter* zeroes in on the productive tensions that have arisen out of their differences: whereas Negt has admittedly remained steadfast in his allegiances to one trajectory of German thought (from Kant to Habermas), Kluge has long insisted on exploring other novel fields of thinking, even though he has repeatedly insisted that his loyalty lies with the original architects of the Frankfurt School and its cornerstone: *Dialectic of Enlightenment*. Thirdly, although it admittedly skews toward Kluge's aesthetic with each ensuing chapter, *Dark Matter* is ultimately not a book exclusively about Kluge, for so much of Kluge's aesthetic is undergirded by the productive tensions that have made their collaborations possible since 1972. Even when he is not in the narrative or frame, it cannot be refuted that Negt's influence continually haunts Kluge's thinking. *Dark Matter* is therefore a book about both Negt and Kluge and their chosen path taken after Adorno's death, a legacy of Frankfurt School thinking that has yet to be fully acknowledged as such because of its unprecedented reliance on aesthetic practice, its embrace of disagreeable philosophical traditions, and its seemingly tenuous relationship to the principal concerns of both their elders and the contemporary concerns of theory as a whole. Fourthly and lastly, the voice adopted throughout *Dark Matter* is knowingly constructive and micrological. Given the highly fragmented nature of Negt and Kluge's thinking, this study endeavors to make intelligible for readers some of the many disparate pieces in their vast work, and does so through both theoretical abstractions and close readings. In so doing, each chapter places a premium on what Negt and Kluge call "relationality" (*Zusammenhang*). The resultant emphasis on whether, how, and to what degree their ideas are historically situated, interconnected, and related to those of other thinkers knowingly runs the risk of dampening the skepticism that incredulous readers, dubious of the viability of their socio-political philosophy and its aesthetic, might call for. Whether the utopian aspirations of Negt and Kluge's thinking actually holds water is an entirely reasonable question that can be posed in one of two ways: either skeptics lob their questions regarding the viability of Negt and Kluge's thinking into the darkness while firmly tethered to terra firma, or they venture forth beyond their world toward that periphery where an encounter with Negt and Kluge in the form of gravitational thinking can evolve.

Cornerstones of
Collaborative Philosophy

Figure 1.1. A "sign of intelligent life": a negative of Adorno's manuscript of Franz Schubert's song from 1817, "Memnon," D. 541, Op. 6, No. 1 (Kluge, *Learning Processes with a Deadly Outcome*, p. 106). © Alexander Kluge.

1

Learning Processes, Deadly Outcomes: For a Practical Theory of Critical Intelligence

Knowledge, Lost in Space

The interwoven ideas unfurled before you in this book almost all find a point of reference in a little science fiction story about the end of the world. Were you to read this Cold War story, you would not be wrong to think of it as an allegory befitting of the new millennium. It goes something like this:

On January 15, 2011, Earth was destroyed in the Black War, a terrestrial battle between communist China and a supra-capitalist United States of America. Lasting little more than eight hours, the war was responsible not only for catastrophic loss of life, but planet Earth was obliterated, too. Induced by an unprecedented use of weapons of mass destruction, tidal waves enveloped Asia. Rivers and oceans boiled and evaporated almost entirely. Rifts in the Earth's mantle opened, spewing forth fountains of magma. Brownish-green clouds full of nuclear contamination shrouded the planet, ensuring that any remaining life, human or otherwise, was extinguished. A day after the apocalyptic events on Earth, the tragedy assumed intergalactic proportions. The planet's crust collapsed. The heavenly body home to *Homo sapiens* for hundreds of thousands of years then broke into several asteroid-like bodies held together by the

former planet's gravitational field. What was once Earth became a seemingly uninhabitable ring of intergalactic rubble.

Human life was, however, not extinguished altogether. Well before the
outbreak of the Black War, the West successfully colonized portions of
Mars as well as planets and moons within and beyond the solar system;
Western bureaucratic life—with all its governmental outposts, legal
bodies and military academies, scientific and medical centers and, above
all, private industries—continued to flourish in an outer space without
Earth. Signs of human life on what remained of Earth vanished from view
from the vantage point of these interstellar colonies, home to humankind
that managed to harbor survivors of the Black War. However, burrowed
in caves and bunkers reaching down sixty kilometers below the Earth's
surface, great masses of Chinese Marxists weathered the planet's terrestrial ruination. In a few brief years, they managed to reconstitute the
entire ecosystem of one chunk of Earth into a veritable paradise of public
parks, irrigated gardens, and forests.

As the story goes, for over ninety years, the Chinese restitution of
Earth remained a mystery to extraterrestrials, until a flotilla of Chinese
space explorers, presumably in search of new sources of human labor
power, came in accidental contact with their old enemies. By the year
2103, the plutocratic descendants of America's Mars administration, in
search of precious natural resources, laid waste to a string of star systems
reaching all the way back to the solar system. Workers eventually resisted
their virtual enslavement. Rebels mutinied. Thieves murdered and pil-
laged. In an effort to quell the mayhem, intergalactic corporations like
the Suez Canal Company ordered the massacre of its entire workforce. In
total disgust and disbelief, the heroes of the story, four surviving officers
of America's intelligence avant-garde, escaped harm by commandeering
spaceships and traveling into uncharted intergalactic territory, what they
christen the "Dawn Sector."

Central in Alexander Kluge's dystopian science fiction story from 1973
entitled *Learning Processes with a Deadly Outcome* are the actions and
commentary of one Franz Zwicki, one of the four intelligence officers
lost in deep space at the story's conclusion. Zwicki, we are told, was
once an officer in the German Wehrmacht, who (along with colleagues
Stefan Boltzmann, First Lieutenant von Ungern-Sternberg, and A.
Dorfmann) escaped the deadly Battle of Stalingrad in 1943 by furtively
traversing eastward over the Volga river's ice flows. After internment and

enslavement in China between 1943 and 1949, the four escaped to the United States of America where, thanks to their prior experience gathering sensitive information in Asia and Europe, they swiftly worked their way into the Central Intelligence Agency. By the time of the outbreak of the Black War in 2011, Zwicki advanced to the position of chief physicist in the Agency, thus ensuring him and his companions unfettered access to spaceships stationed near Frankfurt am Main (codenamed "Idaho Bunker") with which they escaped the grim fate of terrestrial humankind. In outer space, Zwicki retained his position as intelligence expert and, thanks to modern medical science's triumphs over human nature, continued his work well beyond his 180th birthday.

Of the four former Nazi soldiers in space, Zwicki stands out, for in spite of his nominal status as a space pioneer and scientist (not to mention his obvious connection to the actual astrophysicist Franz Zwicky often credited with discovering dark matter), he speaks far more like a philosopher. And, of all the great questions modern philosophy asks, it is Immanuel Kant's first of four fundamental philosophical questions—"What can I know?"—that preoccupies him most.[1] Yet Zwicki wishes not to turn to metaphysics, as Kant prescribes, but rather to what he calls still relatively early on in his saga "materialist epistemology": "The understanding of reality … and its expression of life," he explains to friend and scholar Eilers in 1972, "may consist of thousands of self-deceptions … but it rests upon an unconquerable longing."[2] This hermeneutic of longing—the will to survive and the concomitant will to eternal life—is anchored, so he claims, in each and every person's human body. Even though this material eludes all scientific elucidation, Zwicki retains his resolve. His colleagues are, however, doubtful of his curious materialism's validity. Dorfmann, for example, insists that "human beings are far more intrigued metaphysicians than they commonly admit today."[3] Zwicki nevertheless follows his dismissal of these doubting Thomases by faithfully calling into question their unreflective reliance on the empire of the mind. "How do you know all this exactly?" Zwicki asks Dorfmann, dubious of his detailed

---

1 Immanuel Kant, *Critique of Pure Reason*, eds. and trans. Paul Guyer and Allen W. Wood (Cambridge: Cambridge University Press, 1998) 677/A805/B833. See also: Immanuel Kant, *Lectures on Logic*, ed. and trans. J. Michael Young (Cambridge: Cambridge University Press, 1992) 538/25.

2 Alexander Kluge, *Learning Processes with a Deadly Outcome*, trans. Christopher Pavsek (Durham: Duke University Press, 1996) 2n2.

3 Kluge 2–3n2.

account of the final hours of life on Earth.[4] Again and again he dismisses others' propositions as improbable, doubtful, unbelievable, uncertain, incomprehensible, and inadequate. Similarly, he regularly compromises his own assertions as well as those of others by stating simply "I can't believe that" or "We don't know," flagging a contradiction, pointing out the inherent inadequacies of empirical description, calling attention to obscure details, or emphasizing the faultiness of memory.[5] While thoroughly dismissive of matters of the mind, Zwicki's theory of embodied knowledge, the *feeling* of "unconquerable longing," and the concomitant understanding of reality and life require no proof, for they are the stuff of Zwicki's fantastic story of survival—their uncanny ability to cheat catastrophe and human nature—that accompanies his and his colleagues into the twenty-second century.

In spite of his firm rejections of others' idealist claims to knowledge, Zwicki's own presumably materialist epistemology, first mentioned in the year 1972, quickly takes a backseat to seemingly more existential matters in the shadow of Earth's demise. The flipside of human "unconquerable longing," a metaphysical feeling about human transience, the insignificance of planet Earth in the unending universe, and the absurdity of existence—Dorfmann calls it a "vague attendant feeling"—waxes the farther away he and his three companions are from the remains of mother Earth.[6] Zwicki retrospectively recounts from the year 2103 those grim years following the Black War of 2011 as being full of "ridged concentration on the chances for survival of the self."[7] Increasingly aware of their deprivation of terrestrial sensory perception due to the loss of earthly time and space, Zwicki openly wonders whether it is at all possible to retain a sense of self in space. With the place of their history and language gone, the self is both unstable and fragmented. Whereas he and his colleagues were always assigned new stable identities as clandestine operatives for the CIA, their "language, appearance, the contexts of [their] lives, future tasks," all this had to be re-invented anew in space.[8] And, because any and every choice they make cannot claim an earthly referent, such decisions are as meaningless as they are arbitrary. Stranded

---

4 Kluge 11n7.
5 Kluge 11, 23.
6 Kluge 3n2.
7 Kluge 30n22.
8 Kluge 31.

on a solar platform lost in deep space, Zwicki, sick and despairing, twists
René Descartes famous maxim *cogito ergo sum* so as to insist on the futility of cognition in outer space. "I think, therefore I am. I think, because
I can disregard the fact that I am. Precisely because I am not, I think.
Therefore, I **am not**. But who thinks then? Certainly not me. For this
reason no one thinks."[9] Although Zwicki's logic is marred by jumps and
inconsistencies, his twin conclusions—the self ceases to be in outer space
and so, too, does thought—nevertheless suggest for a moment that in the
shadow of "vague attendant feeling[s]" his materialist epistemology was
nothing more than a terrestrial luxury.

What saves the apparent viability of Zwicki's original theory of knowledge or reality and life, as well as the comrades from carrying out their
suicidal thoughts, is their pleasure found in surveying the planets orbiting around a red gassy star they egotistically christen "Franz Zwicki."
Light years away from crisis and catastrophe, they discover from their
space platform a sylvan planet. Using leftover chemical weapons, they

"carve" the image of the "Hymn of the Dawn Sector" into the forests.
Boltzmann and Zwicki's blasted-out forest clearings were between six
and eight kilometers wide. This sign of intelligent life would stand
out to any intelligent beings flying by and entice them into landing.
The owners called the forested planet "Dorfmann" and its moon "von
Ungern-Sternberg." ... If Zwicki looks out ... he can read "The Dawn,"
a sign of intelligent life that delights him.[10]

The sign of intelligent life Zwicki sees through his telescope is what we
might think of as a bombastic example of land art: the first page of a
French translation of Franz Schubert's song "Memnon" (written with
poet Johann Mayrhofer in 1817) burnt into the darkness of the planet's
surface (fig. 1.1). This double sign—a sign of the astronauts' stubborn
will to keep on living as well as a complex sign system of art from a lost
world—is what apparently transforms Zwicki's despair into hope, hope
that others would eventually reach their solar system and "allow themselves to be milked dry" working under the direction of the four space
pioneers.[11] It would seem then that, in spite of the increasingly hopeless

---

9 Kluge 32.
10 Kluge 106.
11 Kluge 106.

dematerialization of the self engendered by exile in space, Zwicki's materialist epistemology finds its clearest manifestation in the creation of signs of not just life, but intelligent human life. Intelligent life is, however, a euphemism of sorts, for the terror Zwicki et al. escaped is precisely what they wish to lure with their sign. The deadly outcome in the title of Kluge's story is therewith deferred into an untold yet presumably certain disastrous future beyond the frame of the narrative.

Allegories of Intelligence

Scholarly readers have approached Kluge's story far less in terms of science fiction's propensity for inciting "cognitive estrangement" than allegory's invitation to "exegetical activity."[12] Indeed, there is plenty of fodder to read *Learning Processes with a Deadly Outcome* when we think of allegory as a conventional relationship between an "illustrative image" and a corresponding "abstract meaning."[13] To date, the story has fostered insightful readings about text-relevant themes like self-destruction, capitalism, futurity, and even the Frankfurt School, for example.[14] Sticking closer to the telos of the story's title—learning processes and their outcomes—let us instead continue our journey in outer space by first burrowing downward with Walter Benjamin into the baroque allegory as Benjamin saw it, namely as a literary form intent on unlocking a "realm of hidden knowledge."[15] Only when we begin to see Kluge's allusions to

12 Darko Suvin, "Estrangement and Cognition," in *Metamorphoses of Science Fiction: On the Poetics and History of a Literary Genre* (New Haven: Yale University Press, 1979) 3–15; and Seo-Young Chu, *Do Metaphors Dream of Literal Sleep? A Science Fictional Theory of Representation* (Cambridge, MA: Harvard University Press, 2010) 76, 75ff.

13 Walter Benjamin, *The Origin of the German Tragic Drama*, trans. John Osborne (London: Verso, 1998) 162.

14 For allegorical readings of Kluge's story, see: Rainer Stollmann, "Schwarzer Krieg, endlos: Erfahrung und Selbsterhaltung in Alexander Kluges 'Lernprozesse mit tödlichem Ausgang,'" *Text und Kontext* 12.2 (1984): 356; Claudia Rosenkranz, *Ambivalenzen aufklärerischer Literatur am Beispiel einer Text- und Rezeptionsanalyse von Alexander Kluges "Lernprozesse mit tödlichem Ausgang"* (Trier: Wissenschaftlicher Verlag Trier, 1988) 31; Klaus Scherpe, "Die Entdramatisierung der Kritischen Theorie in der Literatur: Hans Magnus Enzensberger and Alexander Kluge," *Cultura tedesca* 18 (2001): 143–44, 154–56; Leslie Adelson, "Experiment Mars: Contemporary German Literature, Imaginative Ethnoscapes, and the New Futurism," in *Über Gegenwartsliteratur: Interpretationen und Interventionen*, ed. Mark W. Rectanus (Bielefeld: Aisthesis, 2008) 36.

15 Benjamin 184.

and departures from this baroque form's techniques for disclosing the catastrophic consequences of modern knowledge can we begin to link up his and Negt's investment in learning processes as a special kind of cognitive estrangement. A culmination, in part, of earlier essays intent on refuting the "scientistic prejudices" of Kant's epistemology, Benjamin's 1928 habilitation *The Origin of the German Tragic Drama* wrestles at its outset with the problem of profane knowledge and the constitution of modern experience.[16] As explicated in its "Epistemo-Critical Prologue," the system-seeking philosophies and the method-obsessed sciences of the nineteenth century exemplified for Benjamin the acme of profane knowledge resulting from man's fall from grace. Whereas the essential unity of man's prelapsarian existence anchored in divine truth (*Wahrheit*) knew nothing of knowledge (*Erkenntnis*), let alone words or communication, the original sin—eating from the forbidden tree of knowledge—delivered man into a creaturely world—a world of natural history—where the unity of word and thing crumbled. Profane knowledge is thus an inherently fragmented knowledge, phenomenal in nature and reliant on the limited reach and arbitrary biases of empirical perception. Atomized into "various disciplines," profane knowledge, Benjamin adds, is a function of disparate methodologies devised to buttress the illusions of "systematic completeness" and the presumed prowess of transcendental subjects who take "possession" of knowledge.[17]

Against this backdrop, Benjamin casts his account of baroque allegorical *Trauerspiel* as a disruptive literary form of the seventeenth century beholden neither to the pretensions of profane knowledge nor its illusions of wholeness. Distinguished by its penchant for amassing "heap[s] of ruins"—earthly things ripped out of their profane contexts—early modern allegorical literature invites the philosophically driven commentator to mediate deeper truth content buried in its fragmentary form, for such decadent works of art are driven by a will, says Benjamin, to discern fallen man's estranged relationship to the essence of absolute being.[18] "An appreciation of the transience of things," he explains, "and the concern to redeem them for eternity, is one of the strongest impulses in allegory."[19]

---

16 I follow here: Richard Wolin, *Walter Benjamin: An Aesthetics of Redemption* (Berkeley: University of California Press, 1994) 34.

17 Benjamin 33, 33, 29.

18 Benjamin 232.

19 Benjamin 223; Wolin 71.

Yet the baroque *Trauerspiel's* indictment of profane knowledge was not the end station of Benjamin's interest in allegory. If allegory's destructive way of looking at earthly things rendered palatable the absence of original eternal truth in the seventeenth-century world, then allegory in the modern era found itself suddenly in the belly of capital. Whereas baroque allegory once devalued the world of objects in the name of its will to truth, the "world of objects itself" became, in the age of high capitalism of the nineteenth century, consumed "by the commodity."[20] Those rare allegorical works of art like Charles Baudelaire's prose poems in *Le Spleen de Paris* of 1869 thus stand out for Benjamin, for they set out to present capital's veiled refunctionalization of the allegory, to resist commodity's distortions of the object world and thus to leave the organic appearance of things in tatters.[21] In so doing, the modern allegories of Baudelaire seek out truth through form, too, yet theirs is aimed at the progressive nature of history under capitalism: "The concept of progress is to be grounded in the idea of catastrophe," Benjamin exclaimed in the late 1930s. "That things 'just go on' *is* the catastrophe."[22] For all their differences, then—baroque allegory is esoteric and contemplative, whereas Baudelaire's traffics in shock, suddenness, and discontinuity—allegory retained over time, for Benjamin, a lingering potential for transcending the limits, not to mention the myths, of profane knowledge.

In light of his "metaphysical salvation of nominalism," as his friend Theodor W. Adorno once called Benjamin's theological theory of knowledge, and with it his repudiation of positivist epistemology, it might appear that Benjamin has little if anything to say about the materialist epistemology subtending Kluge's allegory of intelligent space travelers.[23] Yet closer consideration of the distinct aesthetic vocabulary of the German *Trauerspiel* suggests that Kluge's futuristic story of deadly outcomes is not so far removed from those baroque dramas also titularly concerned with death, be it by execution, murder, avarice, seduction, or otherwise. Of all the *Trauerspiel's* many formal characteristics— Benjamin cites its disunity of place, the freedom of its plot, the prologue's

20 Walter Benjamin, "Central Park," trans. Lloyd Spencer and Mark Harrington, *New German Critique* 34 (Winter 1985): 34.

21 Bainard Cowan, "Walter Benjamin's Theory of Allegory," *New German Critique* 22 (Winter 1981): 120–22. See also Wolin 130.

22 Benjamin, "Central Park," 50.

23 Theodor W. Adorno, "Einleitung zu Benjamins 'Schriften,'" in *Gesammelte Schriften*, vol. 11, eds. Rolf Tiedemann et al. (Frankfurt am Main: Suhrkamp, 1986) 570; Wolin 90.

preemption of narrative closure, the centrality of the state of emergency, the *Trauerspiel*'s overall tone of hopelessness—it is the drama's central figure of the vice-ridden yet virtuous monarch that most closely links it to both the form constituting and epistemo-critical gesture subtending Kluge's science fiction story.[24] Against the backdrop of the Counter-Reformation, the gruesome Thirty Years' War (1618–48), and the resultant divesture of divine right in the perception of princely power, the baroque *Trauerspiel* elevated the sovereign hero as the historical incarnation of a profound contradiction between catastrophe and humankind's facile claims to absolute meaning, power, and action in the face of continual historical chaos.[25] Instead of replicating this elementary struggle between the uncloaked fictions of subjective agency and unavoidable fate in natural history using the doomed *dramatis personae* of the *Trauerspiel*—the despot, the martyr, and the schemer—Kluge transposes its diegetic structures into a parallel science fictional world of limitless technological possibilities where a professional intelligentsia wields unprecedented power over terrestrial time and space no baroque prince could ever imagine. As is the case with the paradigmatic monarch of the *Trauerspiel*, Kluge's intelligence officers are at once both tyrants and martyrs, imprudent if not callous arbiters of instrumental knowledge and melancholy wayfarers suffering at the hand of their own intelligence.

According to Benjamin, the *Trauerspiel* represented the monarch as "the paradigm of the melancholy man."[26] The monarch's self-absorption, his feelings of incredulity toward any theology of hope, and, conversely, his feelings of horror and terror of life's actual emptiness emerged from a penetrating phenomenological relationship between the brooding suffering subject and the shards of fallen nature he sees around him. This dialectically mediated melancholy marked, for the Platonist Benjamin, a historically situated and thus imperfect view onto an otherwise imperceptible truth, namely man's "intentionless state of being," which aesthetic forms like the allegory were especially proficient at encoding and which the philosopher critic was adept at representing.[27] Like the melancholy sovereigns of the baroque *Trauerspiel*, Zwicki and his initially suicidal

---

24 Benjamin, *The Origin of the German Tragic Drama*, 61, 120, 134, 65, 81.

25 Max Pensky, *Melancholy Dialectics: Walter Benjamin and the Play of Mourning* (Amherst: University of Massachusetts Press, 1993) 76ff, 110.

26 Benjamin, *The Origin of the German Tragic Drama*, 142.

27 Benjamin, *The Origin of the German Tragic Drama*, 36.

colleagues spend their twilight years reflecting on the fall of humankind and the waste it laid throughout the galaxy. With Nietzsche's essay
"On the Uses and Disadvantages of History for Life" in one hand and
the kindred essay "The German as Symptom" by Nietzsche-enthusiast
Robert Musil in the other, they call by association the wisdoms of philosophy and scientific knowledge, their very own vocations of yore, into
question.[28] For Musil, as with Nietzsche, it is art or, to be more exact,
aesthetic experience that is capable of delivering modern man from the
straitjacket of reason, and for Kluge's space travelers, too, it seems as
if the aesthetic—their interstellar "sign of intelligent life"—redeems in
the end their gloomy mood. That sign of long-gone terrestrial *Bildung*,
Schubert's "Memnon," is itself not an arbitrary one, for it, too, is steeped
in melancholy. Inspired by both the myth of Memnon, the Ethiopian
king slain by Achilles in the Trojan War, and the modern fascination
with Memnon's sorrowful wail attributed to mysterious noises said to
have emanated from a broken colossal figure of the Pharaoh Ameno-
phis III in the city of Thebes, Schubert's song is a descendant of the
baroque *Trauerspiel*.[29] According to the young Adorno, held under the
sway of Benjamin's habilitation, Schubert's lieder are "bits of music"
cobbled together lyrically in order to convey through emotion "the truth
in its minutest crystallization."[30] And, like the *Trauerspiel*, that truth
content in Schubert's lieder relates to both the "sorrow about the human
condition"—man's aimless wandering into the "chthonic deep" of nature
as an "incarnation of death"—and the inevitability of consolation to be
found in the aesthetic's "tiniest move[s]."[31]

But, unlike Benjamin, who sought to position his criticism of philosophy beyond representations of the artist and scientist, Zwicki and his

28 Robert Musil, "The German as Symptom," in *Precision and Soul: Essays and
Addresses*, eds. and trans. Burton Pike and David S. Luft (Chicago: University of Chicago
Press, 1990) 153; see also Friedrich Nietzsche, *Beyond Good and Evil: Prelude to a Philos-
ophy of the Future*, eds. Rolf-Peter Horstmann and Judith Norman, trans. Judith Norman
(Cambridge: Cambridge University Press, 2007) 70; and Friedrich Nietzsche, *Untimely
Meditations*, ed. Daniel Breazeale, trans. R.J. Hollingdale (Cambridge: Cambridge Uni-
versity Press, 1997) 115.
29 Marjorie Hirsch, "Mayrhofer, Schubert, and the Myth of 'Vocal Memnon,'"
The Unknown Schubert, eds. Barbara M. Reul and Larraine Bryne Bodley (Aldershot,
England: Ashgate, 2008) 3–23.
30 Theodor W. Adorno, "Schubert," *19th-Century Music*, trans. Jonathan Dunsby and
Beate Perrey, 29.1 (Summer 2005): 3–14. Here 9, 8.
31 Adorno, "Schubert," 12, 13, 13.

colleagues align themselves with the formal affairs of artists entirely.[32] And they do so with disastrous results. A gigantic pictograph of the very alienation, suffering, and longing for redemption they experience in their state of sensory deprivation and temporal withdrawal, their interstellar sign—at once a potential repudiation of knowledge and a gesture toward uncovering the truth of their own existence—suffers from a fatal flaw. That wrinkle is signified by the graphic inversion of Schubert's score and, accordingly, its instrumentalized transformation into a unequivocal sign system whose intended referent is a professional intelligence doubling as deadly enticement for others to enter into the very relations of production responsible for the apocalypse of the Black War in the first place. Just as Benjamin hypothesized in his deliberations on Baudelaire, allegory in the year 2103 is subsumed by the deadly logic of reification, commodification, and exchange. Its employ as siren neither refunctionalizes the allegory in the name of inhibiting capitalism's penchant for enslaving the object world, nor shatters the false appearance of things ruling the universe for nearly a century. Nor does it unveil the deadly truth behind modern progress. While the space travelers well recognize "that things 'just go on'" catastrophically, they nevertheless fail to acknowledge their knowledge of this state of affairs—their intelligence—as itself the heart of catastrophe. The deadly outcome of their story is thus rooted so much more in their long-standing self-reflexive epistemological shortcomings. Neither a simple case of economic "false consciousness" nor a cynical "enlightened false consciousness," the grounds for their inevitable failure to elude crisis and catastrophe derive from a short circuit.[33] Zwicki's intelligence fails him because his epistemology rooted in the vitality of the flesh cannot reflect on the mind's feelings of morality also necessary for any truly critical knowledge. In other words, it ignores that "vague attendant feeling" which Benjamin sought to resuscitate against profane knowledge in his reading of the German baroque *Trauerspiel*. And, even though some of the space travelers eventually do lend credence to the affectively fueled insights of melancholy—a realm Nietzsche calls the unhistorical and suprahistorical and Musil the "other condition"—its

---

32 Benjamin, *The Origin of the German Tragic Drama*, 32; Pensky 68.

33 Georg Lukács, "Class Consciousness," in *History and Class Consciousness: Studies in Marxist Dialectics*, trans. Rodney Livingstone (Cambridge, MA: MIT Press, 1971) 50ff; and Peter Sloterdijk, *Critique of Cynical Reason*, trans. Michael Eldred (Minneapolis: University of Minnesota Press, 1987) 5ff.

truth content in no way mitigates their will to knowledge—be it technical or economic—in their pursuit of life everlasting.[34]

Kluge's story of intelligence lost in space begins our odyssey through
Negt and Kluge's vast oeuvres precisely because it keenly situates knowledge as both a key generator of catastrophe and the potential precondition
for future survival of humankind. That knowledge in this case is equated
with intelligence means not that Kluge (and Negt, for that matter) conflates all epistemological matters into the domain of an exclusive class of
professional thinkers with unfettered access to bunkers and spaceships.
To the contrary, Kluge's allegory of modern intelligence's trajectory into
a cataclysmic future is, on the one hand, a story of a particular kind of
knowledge subsumed and valuated by capital. Intelligence, Kluge and
Negt explain elsewhere, is an ex post facto designator for whether psychic
labor processes of the mind like thinking and learning are deemed
advantageous for the successful production and/or maintenance of existing social orders.[35] As the story of Zwicki et al. confirms, the use value of
intelligence skyrockets in crisis-laden times. Intelligence acts defensively
to uphold the imperatives of the protagonists' vested interests, namely the
precious vessel—their undying techno-bodies—bearing their so-called
materialist epistemology subtended by preeminent metaphysical yearn-
ings. This tenacious will to live forever is essentially akin to what Adorno
and Horkheimer write of in their seminal *Dialectic of Enlightenment*,
in many ways Negt and Kluge's lodestar. The prototype of the modern
"man who has come of age," Odysseus, Adorno and Horkheimer write,
deploys his cunning knowledge—another word for stupidity according
to the authors—in order to cheat nature and secure his self-preservation;
in so doing, he fashions himself a "likeness to God [that] consists in sovereignty over existence, in the lordly gaze, in the command."[36] This is not
to infer that *Learning Processes with a Deadly Outcome* is a mere literary
illustration of Benjamin's theory of the *Trauerspiel* for the modern era,
or, for that matter, the censure of instrumental reason opening *Dialectic
of Enlightenment* or even Horkheimer's explicit reproach of materialist

---

34 Nietzsche 120; Musil 185.

35 Alexander Kluge and Oskar Negt, *History and Obstinacy,* ed. Devin Fore, trans.
Richard Langston et al. (New York: Zone Books, 2014) 170–72, 181–83.

36 Max Horkheimer and Theodor W. Adorno, *Dialectic of Enlightenment: Philosophical Fragments*, ed. Gunzelin Schmid Noerr, trans. Edmund Jephcott (Stanford, CA:
Stanford University Press, 2002) 38ff, 6.

epistemology.[37] If, as Kluge has insisted, his stories are to intuitions as theory is to concepts, then *Learning Processes with a Deadly Outcome* lays out a constellation of theoretical concepts (e.g., knowledge, progress, catastrophe) with which to expose the blindness of professional instrumentalized knowledge and, conversely, to render visible core questions subtending his and Negt's oeuvres: What exactly is a materialist epistemology and how is it related, if at all, to learning processes? What, for that matter, is a learning process and under what conditions is it bound up in catastrophe? Under what circumstances can learning processes actually avoid death? And who, if anyone, are the arbiters and beneficiaries of such processes?

As these questions should already make evident, the core of Negt and Kluge's own materialist project is less concerned with advancing its own distinct epistemology than thinking together with Benjamin's and Horkheimer and Adorno's critical reckonings with the fallacies of enlightened scientific knowledge. In spite of all Zwicki's reflections on philosophy and science, his materialist epistemology lacks, in the end, what Kluge and Negt identify in Adorno and Horkheimer as a post-Cartesian relativistic theory, one attuned to the "dissociation of the self" brought on by the violent processes of the Enlightenment.[38] So, if what is ultimately missing in Zwicki's theory and praxis is what Horkheimer and Adorno call "thought which does violence to itself" (in order to shatter its own myths), then Negt and Kluge advance a materialist theory of learning intent on figuring out ways of fostering a self-reflective critical intelligence that sidesteps deadly outcomes by recognizing this dissociation to begin with.[39] In a way the "pedagogic side" of both Benjamin's and Horkheimer and Adorno's undertakings they themselves never adequately fleshed out, Negt and Kluge's theory of learning processes props itself upon its predecessors' theories of knowledge.[40] Along with Adorno and Horkheimer's theory of radical consciousness, they dismiss any traditional epistemology's notion of an intact sovereign self. Clear distinctions

---

37 Max Horkheimer, "Materialism and Metaphysics," trans. Matthew J. O'Connell, in *Critical Theory: Selected Essays* (New York: Continuum, 2002) 10–47, especially 20ff and 25ff; see also: Martin Jay, *The Dialectical Imagination: A History of the Frankfurt School and the Institute of Social Research, 1923–1950* (Boston: Little, Brown, 1973) 53.

38 Kluge and Negt 245.

39 Horkheimer and Adorno 2.

40 Walter Benjamin, *The Arcades Project*, trans. Howard Eiland and Kevin McLaughlin (Cambridge, MA: Belknap Press, 1999) 458. N1, 8.

between the knowing self and the objects it beholds, they argue, are fictitious in actual praxis; objects and subjects continually re-constitute one another in continual countervailing processes and can thus only be conceived of in terms of dynamic subjective-objective relations.[41] And, along with Benjamin, they identify constellations of fragments as a form capable of "awakening through violent dreams" what Kluge and Negt themselves, borrowing from Francisco Goya, call the monstrous "sleep of reason."[42] But, if Negt and Kluge stand like pedagogical dwarves on the shoulder of epistemological giants, their outlook diverges markedly from their forerunners: while it can be said that both Horkheimer and Adorno and Benjamin incorporate what Dorfmann calls a "vague attendant feeling" in order to unseat traditional epistemologies, Negt and Kluge utilize an optimism akin to Zwicki's "unconquerable longing" to propel their materialist pedagogy forward. Out of Kant's foundational inquiry into the conditions of knowledge, Negt and Kluge fashion the methodological question "How can we know?" And, in their pursuit of pedagogical ends, they craft a vitalist model for critical knowledge acquisition born out of a neurobiological understanding of the self-interests inherent to human embodiment and mediated through the formal concerns of aesthetic montage. Learning processes, they argue, must not necessarily generate faulty intelligence that ends up in catastrophe. Even in the face of real incursions into the human body once only envisioned in science fiction, their theory of learning upholds a utopian tenacity for the viability of happy endings.

Interests, Drives, Brains

Although history eventually caught up with Kluge's account of the beginning of the end of the world imagined for the year 2011 and proved that the dystopia surrounding Zwicki et al. to be mostly fantasy, a closer look at the moment of overlap between authorial time and diegetic time—the interdiegetic year 1973 when Zwicki first articulated his defense of a materialist epistemology—reveals a shift in, if not

---

41 Kluge and Negt 242–46.

42 Kluge and Negt 74; Benjamin, *The Arcades Project*, 458, N1, 9; see also: Christian Schulte and Rainer Stollmann, "Moles Don't Use Systems: A Conversation with Oskar Negt," trans. Fiona Elliott, *October* 149 (Summer 2014): 86–88.

fraying of, critical theory's long-standing concern with epistemological matters. If, as Kluge's story suggests, there was an actual stronghold of intelligence experts based in Frankfurt am Main, then, by the year 1973, it was certainly either in an undisclosed bunker or solely the stuff of science fiction. Until late 1969, however—the time of Theodor Adorno's death—the Institute for Social Research based at the Johann Wolfgang Goethe-University in Frankfurt was long a hotbed for such research. In the foregoing decade alone, three generations at the Institute, beginning with Adorno and Horkheimer and including older deferent doctoral students like Alfred Schmidt and younger more rebellious ones like Hans-Jürgen Krahl, were simultaneously focused on the problems and challenges of a materialist epistemology. This interest was in fact long-standing, reaching back to the earliest days of the critical theory. Only a few short years after the publication of Benjamin's habilitation, Horkheimer's ascension as director in 1930 assured that the crisis of knowledge under late capitalism—the fetish character of scientific knowledge, on the one hand, and social philosophy's inclination to positivism, on the other—would operate like a leitmotif in the Institute's programmatic focus.[43] Fast-forwarding to around the time when Kluge began wrestling with the genre of science fiction and therewith testing the vacuous conditions of representation in outer space, Adorno had just published a rebuttal to his own pre-war repudiation of phenomenological epistemologies cast within the realm of philosophical linguistics (*Negative Dialectics* [1966]), only to turn immediately thereafter to questions pertaining to the epistemological character of art (*Aesthetic Theory* [1970]). At the same time, the star among Adorno and Horkheimer's earliest students, Jürgen Habermas, was publishing a couple of monographs (*Theory and Practice* [1963] and *Knowledge and Human Interests* [1968]) on the non-idealist status of critical theory as a unique form of knowledge production separate from the positivism of science and philosophy. Amid this flurry of interest in the vast pitfalls and conditional possibilities of epistemology within and without the institution of critical theory over the course of the sixties, ulterior voices, in part polarized by Marxism and its constructivist models of human psychology, catapulted

---

43 Max Horkheimer, "The Present Situation of Social Philosophy and the Tasks of an Institute for Social Research," trans. John Torpey, in *Between Philosophy and Social Science: Selected Early Writings Studies in Contemporary German Social Thought* (Cambridge, MA: MIT Press, 1993) 1–14; cf. Jay 27.

one concept in particular into heated theoretical and political debates of the day. In an era of sit-ins, go-ins, and love-ins, student activists spoke increasingly of the intensification of West German democratization in terms of "learning processes," involving the acquisition of both technical knowledge and an understanding of the complexities of political relations in everyday life.

Such entreaties calling for the articulation of personal experiences of repression with critical interrogations of the otherwise hidden structures subtending the political economy of domination initially struck the elder wardens of critical theory as reactionary to the core. In Adorno's eyes, learning processes represented a disastrous trend concept among activist students who desperately sought ways to transform theory into emancipatory praxis.[44] Learning processes stood, furthermore, for a feeble conceptual means with which to justify narcissistic needs and materialize them through praxis. In his death knell to the idea, Adorno linked learning processes with a reification of individual psychology, a prohibition of experience, and a leveling of the self by market- and science-driven forces with a thirst for information and communication. Learning processes were a regressive attempt at the psychological conditioning of what little sovereignty the self still possessed under late capitalism. Although Adorno was not altogether dismissive of the importance of pedagogy for humankind's still much needed emergence out of immaturity, the idea of learning processes was for him simply antithetical to the powers of reflection, self-reflection, and non-cooperation he thought necessary to preempt conditions conducive for the reemergence of barbarism. Writing one year later, recently appointed Professor Habermas echoed Adorno in 1969 after the flames of the student revolts subsided, insisting that "learning process" was an empty notion embraced by "a growing number of psychologically insecure individuals."[45] And yet it was Habermas who, in spite of his own censure, would go on to systematically recover the disparaged concept of learning processes and render it central not only to his rigorous reconstruction of critical theory but

44 For Adorno's evisceration of the concept of learning processes, see: Theodor W. Adorno, "Marginalia to Theory and Praxis," in *Critical Models: Interventions and Catchwords*, trans. Henry W. Pickford (New York: Columbia University Press, 2005) 271.

45 Jürgen Habermas, "The Movement in Germany: A Critical Analysis," in *Toward a Rational Society: Student Protest, Science, and Politics*, trans. Jeremy J. Shapiro (Boston: Beacon Press, 1970) 38.

also its defense against charges of obsolescence raised by competing theoretical models.

It was as early as his inaugural lecture held in the summer of 1965 at the University of Frankfurt when, in an elaboration on his previous censure of positivist strains in philosophy, Habermas embarked on what was originally supposed to be an overture to a major study of scientific knowledge and philosophy. Habermas originally took as his point of departure not the failures of idealist philosophy and its critics to maintain a robust and self-reflective critique of knowledge as originally envisioned by Kant. Rather, it was the "theoretical attitude" necessary for an "action oriented" knowledge—Habermas spoke almost nostalgically of ancient theoretical contemplation's entry into "the conduct of life" —that he found all but missing in not just modern science but also nearly all modern philosophy.[46] As late as the ascent of August Comte's and Ernst Mach's positivisms, philosophy passed through a succession of what Habermas would later call "abandoned stages of reflection," lost opportunities, the consequences of which lead to the dissolution of epistemology's original absolutist aspirations. In light of these failures, the implied answer to his rhetorical question opening the subsequent culmination of his lecture—in *Knowledge and Human Interests* he asks, "How is reliable knowledge possible[?]"—is undoubtedly pessimistic.[47] Given so much of modern philosophy of science's conflation of all knowledge with science, Habermas set out to recover these stages of reflection, not with the intention of restoring the grandiosity of epistemology per se, but, rather, of radicalizing the critique of reason through a "phenomenological self-reflection of knowledge."[48] To these emancipatory ends, Habermas conjoined dialectically what philosophy had always cleaved and repressed in the name of its claim to scientific objectivity, namely the passions and affects of human interests, in order to unearth, as one of his earliest critics deftly clarified, "the roots of knowledge in life."[49] It

---

46 Jürgen Habermas, *Knowledge and Human Interests*, trans. Jeremy J. Shapiro (Boston: Beacon Press, 1971) 301–2.

47 Habermas 3.

48 Habermas 5; for a comparison of his inaugural speech with Horkheimer's, see Axel Honneth, "Habermas' Anthropology of Knowledge: The Theory of Knowledge-Constitutive Interests," in *The Critique of Power: Reflective Stages in a Critical Social Theory*, trans. Kenneth Baynes (Cambridge, MA: MIT Press, 1993) 203–17.

49 Thomas McCarthy, *The Critical Theory of Jürgen Habermas* (Cambridge, MA: MIT Press, 1978) 55.

is at this juncture where learning processes first surfaces in Habermas's oeuvre. The primary category of knowledge derives, he claims, from human interest in the survival of species:

> Possible knowledge ... originate[s] in the interest structure of a species that is linked in its roots to definite means of social organization: work, language, and power. The human species secures its existence in systems of social labor and self-assertion through violence, through tradition-bound social life in ordinary-language communication, and with the aid of ego identities that at every level of individuation reconsolidate the consciousness of the individual in relation to the norms of the group.[50]

This reconsolidation—a normativizing shift from particular ontogenetic interests to "quasi-transcendental" phylogenetic concerns—transpires, proffers Habermas, through learning processes. Shortly thereafter to be anchored in the pragmatism of Charles Sanders Peirce, Habermas's concept of cumulative learning processes would afford him the conceptual tool with which to try establishing a philosophical anthropology grounded in experience mediated between subjects and objects, the empirical and transcendental, interest and knowledge, doxa and logos.[51]

Habermas's attempt to radicalize the critique of reason through a critique of scientism soon produced an avalanche of criticisms calling into question not just the viability of his envisioned exhaustive intervention into the philosophy of science but also the foundation of his emergent critical theory of society.[52] Above all, it was instances of technical imprecision—like his anthropological conflation of the materializations of the three basic human interests in the form of work, language, and power as well as his ambiguous commingling of critical and transcendental reflection—that short-circuited his emancipatory intentions.[53] Well before his critics, let alone his students, lunged at his prolegomenon, Habermas already discerned its weaknesses (or, in his

---

50 Habermas 313.

51 Habermas 93. See also: Richard J. Bernstein, *The Restructuring of Social and Political Theory* (New York: Harcourt Brace Jovanovich, 1976) 192ff.

52 Jürgen Habermas, "A Postscript to *Knowledge and Human Interests*," *Philosophy of the Social Sciences* 3.2 (June 1973): 159–60, 187n47.

53 McCarthy 92–100.

mind, its superfluousness) and shifted his energies toward the seeds of what would eventually become his monumental achievement, namely his theory of communicative action published in 1981. Learning processes were, however, not discarded in the course of his linguistic turn that took him far afield from his early investment in an anthropology of knowledge and its underlying cognitive interests. To the contrary, learning processes—anchored now in part in Noam Chomsky's generative grammar, Hans-Georg Gadamer's hermeneutics, and Jean Piaget's and Lawrence Kohlberg's respective contributions to cognitive developmental psychology—would resurface again and again in his journey toward and beyond his magnum opus.[54] On the one hand, learning processes recast within this new constellation afforded Habermas the means with which to erect a robust post-transcendental theory of social evolution based on a concept of developmental communicative rationality. To this end, he overlaid the idea of learning processes subtending Marxism's historical materialism—the "objectivating … of technical and organizational knowledge, of instrumental and strategic action"—with a second higher order "that take[s] place in the dimension of moral insight, practical knowledge, communicative action, and the consensual regulation of action conflicts."[55] On the other hand, learning processes would serve as a decisive criterion for disqualifying other social theories like the behaviorism of B.F. Skinner, the systems theory of Niklas Luhmann, or, much later, the deconstruction of Jacques Derrida. Perhaps not *the* watchword instantly associated with Habermas, "learning processes" nevertheless has persisted well into the present as the amalgamation of two core pillars—social experience as embraced by the fathers of critical theory and an emancipatory conception of progressive human history—subtending the whole of his philosophy.

Right around the time when Habermas began embarking on his shift away from the category of "pseudo-transcendental" interests in the midst of the student revolts, his "hard-boiled" Marxist assistant Oskar Negt penned his own contribution to the contemporary significance of

---

54 Jürgen Habermas, *On the Logic of the Social Sciences*, trans. Shierry Weber Nicholsen and Jerry A. Stark (Cambridge, MA: MIT Press, 1988) 67–70 and 13–35 and 143–61.

55 Jürgen Habermas, "Historical Materialism and the Development of Normative Structures," in *Communication and the Evolution of Society*, trans. Thomas McCarthy (Boston: Beacon Press, 1979) 97–98; see also: Gertrud Nunner-Winkler, "Lernprozesse," in *Habermas-Handbuch*, eds., Hauke Brunkhorst, Regina Kreide and Cristina Lafont (Stuttgart: Verlag J.B. Metzler, 2009) 347–49.

learning processes.[56] Without making explicit reference to Habermas—this he would do in another forum that same year—Negt contested his boss's conflation of all learning processes. If, as Habermas tentatively concurred with Marx in *Knowledge and Human Interests*, "labor is ... an epistemological category," then Negt countered by adding that neither all work nor the knowledge of the world it mediates is equal.[57] After experiencing firsthand in the early sixties the difficulties with initiating emancipatory learning processes among the working class in the educational offices of the Industrial Union of Metalworkers and then as acting director and instructor at one of the Confederation of German Trade Unions' post-secondary schools, Negt set out to think through pedagogical techniques potentially capable of affecting a proletarian political consciousness, one grounded in the "knowledge-constitutive interests of a political economy of labor."[58] Shorthand for what would evolve into the central concerns in his later philosophical collaborations with Alexander Kluge, Negt's blueprint essentially refracts Habermas's concern for generic human interests through the lens of the historical experience of proletarian disenfranchisement. In light of Habermas's conclusive censure of Marx on account of his equation of "critique with natural science," Negt's subsequent reclamation of the category of interests in the name of a class politics—he singles out labor laws and technology as two core proletarian interests suitable for exemplary teaching—appeared to Habermas theoretically naïve, if not altogether retrograde.[59] Commenting on the evolution of Negt's pedagogical interests into organizational matters of enlightenment in the wake of the failed student revolts, he chided his former assistant, for example, for remaining "captive within the tradition ... of strategic action" best exemplified by Georg Lukács and the Communist party.[60] Although Habermas's own failed project—*Knowledge*

---

56 Habermas, "A Postscript to *Knowledge and Human Interests*," 185. Oskar Negt, "Jürgen Habermas: Deutscher Intellektueller mit politischem Urteilsvermögen," in *Unbotmäßige Zeitgenossen: Annäherungen und Erinnerungen* (Frankfurt am Main: Fischer Taschenbuch Verlag, 1994) 266.

57 Habermas, *Knowledge and Human Interests*, 28.

58 Oskar Negt, *Soziologische Phantasie und exemplarisches Lernen: Zur Theorie und Praxis der Arbeiterbildung*, 3rd ed. (Frankfurt am Main: Europäische Verlagsanstalt, 1971) 24.

59 Habermas, *Knowledge and Human Interests*, 63.

60 Jürgen Habermas, *Theory and Practice*, trans. John Viertel (Boston: Beacon Press, 1973) 36–37; Oskar Negt, "Einleitung," in *Die Linke antwortet Jürgen Habermas*, eds. Wolfgang Abendroth et al. (Frankfurt am Main: Europäische Verlagsanstalt, 1968) 30.

and Human Interests—attempted to deliver critical theory away from the straits of Hegelian Marxism flowing in part out of Lukács's *History and Class Consciousness*, this was a gross simplification on his part to type-cast Negt as having rallied behind Habermas's antipode.[61]

Attacked from within his own Marxian quarters for his new pedagogy, Negt would later go on to qualify his proposal candidly as having merely addressed a practical problem—is it possible to awaken the alienated and ahistorical proletarian consciousness out of its apolitical slumber and, if so, how?—and not as standing in for an epistemology missing in Marx's writings.[62] Without delving into the minutiae of Negt's critique of Lukács, or the nature of his own recognition of Marx's fatal disregard of epistemology, or even his consensus with Habermas's critique of Marx in *Knowledge and Human Interests*, it should suffice for now that there is ample evidence in Negt's own writings from the late sixties and onward that he preserved the category of interests knowing full well the targets and new trajectories Habermas's linguistic turn away from it would entail. Given Negt's initial modest ambitions as well as his acknowledgment of Habermas's evolving position, the intentional distinction he stakes out must be understood as a sign of both his indebtedness to the early Habermas's animation of the category of learning processes as well as his unwillingness to forfeit the ancillary idea of interest originally buttressing the concept. Arguably, the kernel of this reluctance and his concomitant rationale for retaining a conceptualization of learning processes rooted in interests is the primacy of the subject at conflict in his, and by extension Kluge's, philosophy. To this end, Negt upholds the utility of psychoanalysis along with its primacy of the subject as deployed in critical theory's first generation. In Habermas's hands merely a short-lived tool for solving a methodological problem—namely the formulation of a self-reflective and thus critical social science—psychoanalysis among predecessors like Adorno, Erich Fromm, and Herbert Marcuse among others opened up an indispensable window into the inner workings of individual subjects

On Negt and organization, see: Oskar Negt, "Die Intellektuellen und die politische Opposition in Westdeutschland," in *Politik als Protest: Reden und Aufsätze zur antiautoritären Bewegung* (Frankfurt am Main: agit-buch-vertrieb, 1971) 214–18.

61 Martin Jay, *Marxism and Totality: The Adventures of a Concept from Lukács to Habermas* (Berkeley: University of California Press, 1984) 482–83.

62 Oskar Negt, "Arbeiterbildung als schrittweise Vermittlung von Klassenbewußtsein: Eine Anti-Kritik," in *Keine Demokratie ohne Sozialismus: Über den Zusammenfassung von Politik, Geschichte und Moral* (Frankfurt am Main: Suhrkamp Verlag, 1976) 368.

caught between the pull of the unconscious and autonomous drives and
the demands of their external social environments.[63] On account of the
contradictions impairing his prolegomenon to a "critique of scientism,"
Habermas's linguistic turn, a turn that linguistically reinterprets Freud
in order to evince the teleology of social action between subjects, down-
grades the obstinate influence of external nature (the body, the drives,
and the interests) in the name of conceiving the discursive justification
of social norms. The price of Habermas's theory of communication is,
in a word, "the reality and independence of the body."[64] Not only did
Negt and, by extension, Kluge refuse to make any such a sacrifice, but
subaltern subjects, in general, and their recalcitrant bodies, in particular,
figured centrally as the nexus of Negt and Kluge's own emergent concept
of learning processes as potentially emancipatory processes.

In Negt's aforementioned proposal from 1968 for reforming proletarian learning processes, he draws attention to that seemingly irresolvable
tension at the heart of working-class existence. Workers, Negt contends, have historically been trapped between the "wish not to have to
be a worker any more" and an array of external forces bungling their
interests and holding them at bay, like a technocratic state, the power
relations in the workplace, the directives of labor organizations, technical innovation, and the consciousness industry.[65] What exacerbates
their predicament under the technological sophistication common in
advanced capitalist industries is the virtual disappearance of the material misery so long experienced by workers. Negt thus crafts his early
proposal for exemplary learning processes among the working class as
a "incremental mediation of class consciousness," a "practical process"
intended to account for the vanishing of the material basis long held as
precluding any formation of social consciousness.[66] Like Engels, Lukács,
Horkheimer and Adorno, Habermas, and Hans Magnus Enzensberger

63 Joel Whitebook, "Reason and Happiness: Some Psychoanalytic Themes in Critical
Theory," in *Habermas and Modernity*, ed. Richard J. Bernstein (Cambridge, MA: Polity
Press, 1991) 140–42, 151–160.

64 Whitebook 155; see also: Axel Honneth, "Habermas' Theory of Society: A
Transformation of the *Dialectic of Enlightenment* in the Light of the Theory of Com-
munication," in *The Critique of Power: Reflective Stages in a Critical Social Theory*, trans.
Kenneth Baynes (Cambridge, MA: MIT Press, 1993) 281.

65 Negt, *Soziologische Phantasie und exemplarisches Lernen*, 44, 33, 45.

66 Negt, "Arbeiterbildung als schrittweise Vermittlung von Klassenbewußtsein" 368,
370.

before him, Negt's underlying interest in consciousness is guided, on the one hand, by a conviction in second nature's industrialized deformation of a historical subject's faculties for perceiving and knowing historical processes and, on the other hand, by the conditions of possibility for that very subject's reversal of those relations. Remediating the real structure of needs and political interests, emancipating class interests long repressed in the name of capital or the nation-state, breaking through the ideological sheen of harmonized inter-class interests, in short the viability of recovering fragmented proletarian interests soon exceeded, however, the realm of pedagogical design Negt initially delineated. With their first collaboration *Public Sphere and Experience* from 1972, Negt and Kluge revamp the former's earlier queries by delving into the subterranean architecture of consciousness and with it the shaky foundation of human interests, claiming not, as Habermas would have it, that interests constructively consolidate consciousness into social norms, but rather, like Freud, Wilhelm Reich, and Marcuse before them, that they are rooted in the messy conflicted realm of unconscious drives. Cognitive drives, on the other hand, belong to a fragmentary complex secondary in nature and born out of social inhibitions placed on individual primary drives.[67] Derived from the prefix *inter-* and the Latin copula *esse*, *interesse* signifies first and foremost a libidinal "relationship between [an] involved self and [an] affectively charged object"; well before it accumulated juridical connotations in the Middle Ages, "interest" denoted a single self's libidinal investments, themselves "particular and scattered," in the object world, interests neither inherently synonymous nor reconcilable with those of the collective.[68] Cognitive drives are thus the upshot of a battle over obstinate subjective interests: the more the libidinal infrastructure directing cognition is impeded (in other words, the more highly it is instrumentalized in the name of accruing specialized knowledge), the less the primary drives—the terrain of material interests—participate in shaping the methods and outcomes of cognitive processes.

For all its apparent reliance on the language of classical psychoanalysis, Negt and Kluge's early invocation of the drives is anything but

---

67 Oskar Negt and Alexander Kluge, *Public Sphere and Experience: Toward an Analysis of the Bourgeois and Proletarian Public Sphere*, trans. Peter Labanyi et al. (Minneapolis: University of Minnesota Press, 1993) 22.

68 Oskar Negt, *Wozu noch Gewerkschaften? Eine Streitschrift* (Göttingen: Steidl, 2004) 91–92.

derivative or secondhand, for underneath the conflicted consciousness exists the vast terrain of the working brain, the seat of intelligence.
Already in *Public Sphere and Experience*, they write of the "brain's own
laws of movement" as well as its "laws of operation," laws that correspond
neither to the dramaturgy of speech acts nor the rules of discourse.[69]
It was only, however, with their prequel *History and Obstinacy*, from
roughly a decade later, where they lay out far more extensively the
implied relationship between the will of consciousness and the desires of
the brain. And, to this end, they erect upon their Marxian foundation not
only the language of psychoanalysis but also rudimentary presumptions
developed in evolutionary biology and the cognitive sciences. The first
of several gravitational fields discussed here, in which Negt and Kluge
assemble otherwise heterogeneous if not altogether competing theoretical models, their inclusive modeling of cognitive processes seeks, by
virtue of its motley assemblage, to expand the terrain on which preceding theories of false, reified, and industrialized consciousness operate,
thereby allowing for both an account of this deformation and the conditions for its potential resistance. The most complicated of all the human
organs but nevertheless an operational model for every other, the human
brain, say Negt and Kluge, is not just a platform on which reason unfurls
or consciousness is manipulated. Nor is what it does inherently rational,
logical, or teleological. Writing from the position of non-specialists, Negt
and Kluge call upon not-so-recent developments in the human sciences
(specifically the basic revelations of electroencephalography) in order to
point out that the brain is constantly at work—more so, in fact—when it is
idle and not thinking. They go on to model the working brain, on the one
hand, as one hermetic organ among many composed of a complex array
of networked parts, a monad full of ciphers preoccupied with feeling and
regulating its own internal affairs. On the other hand, they argue that the
brain is the seat of perception, a window onto the world, the arbiter of
consciousness, a mediator of experience, and the point of departure for
any and all action. Torn between two diametrically opposed non-identical tasks—Negt and Kluge boil its dual functions down to a tension
between internal feeling and external action—each with its own very
different wiring and operating procedures, the brain is thus much more
than just a stage for consciousness and an engine of thought. Already in

---

69 Negt and Kluge, *Public Sphere and Experience*, 37, 47.

1972, they succinctly insisted that the human brain, "in even its most attenuated form," is *the* site of living labor, the seat of dark matter that resists the mandates of capital in all its multifarious guises.[70] And yet, within the narrower mental realm of consciousness and the specialized and often abstract thought it churns out, which, in hindsight, we are so often wont to label reasoned and intelligent, is drastically divorced from the interests of the brain, namely the materialist instinct to maintain its own vitality.[71] Neither the labor expended by general intelligence we might care to associate with the nightly news, nor the specialized labor of technical intelligence performed by elite professionals, can ever lay claim to the objective ways the brain wants work in order to survive. These modes of cognition also fall short of changing oppressive material conditions in such a way so as to make any such survival feasible in the first place. In other words, these calls for intelligence push the brain to work like a window.

Digging downward into increasingly specialized lairs of mental labor, Negt and Kluge arrive at that exceptional subset of conscious labor performed in earnest by the custodians of critique only to exclaim that what gets packaged as critique is, all too often, just another form of dead mental labor (fig. 1.2). Unlike general and technical intelligence, critique *ideally* seeks to resist the restrictedness of the latter by maintaining a broad purview of interests, on the one hand, and by looking for the universal in the particular, on the other. It exhibits a knack for differentiating out and mediating heterogeneous realms of knowledge situated in distinct social habitus. It neither churns out objective products (its products are immaterial: words, discourses, and relationships), nor does it lend itself to the conventional circulation of commodities. More like handwork than industrial or postindustrial labor, the labor of critical intelligence, which they intimately liken to theory, strives to pose robust questions regarding the nature of social relations. Unlike most intellectual labor, which suffers from a lack of a relational sense of itself vis-à-vis reality outside, theory labor strives, first and foremost, they maintain, to construct this relationality in threefold fashion: it exercises "'radical critique of the existing order'" by peering like a detective beyond the porous sheen of empirical reality downward into the subterraneous indices and abstract tendencies latent yet constitutive of reality's unbearable quotient. Secondly, theory

---

70 Negt and Kluge, *Public Sphere and Experience*, 185.
71 Kluge and Negt 185, 104–5; Kluge and Negt 172.

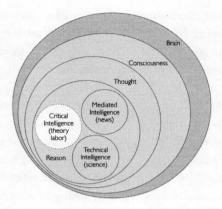

Figure 1.2. Situating critical intelligence: consciousness, thought, and reason as constituent activities of the working brain. © Richard Langston

confronts reality with excess consciousness typical of theory's expansive relationality, consciousness beyond the narrow purview of most intelligence that is capable of bringing to mind a subjective anticipatory thought rooted in reality.[72] Thirdly, critical intelligence makes possible and facilitates the orientation human beings once measured according to stars and horizons.[73] All these details aside, critical intelligence amounts to engaging in exceptional processes from within the constricted interiority of reasoned thought that strive to spill over its own boundaries and push outward toward outlying, increasingly less instrumental realms of mental labor, even when other more dominant mental processes are well underway. And it achieves its goal of critique by virtue of a vast quantity of non-linear associational streams flowing across synapses between heterogeneous ideas. In this respect, "there is thus not one form of critique but rather many," they exclaim.[74] This process, whereby thought retains its neural character, is not guided by an empirical assertion regarding the precise nature of the monadic brain's pathways other than the fact that they are ciphered and that "they know not what they do."[75] Critical intelligence's yearning for the ways of the body's dark matter and, in particular, that of the brain's self-oblivious neural networks—an approximation of

---

72 On this second point, Negt and Kluge invoke Lukács's concept of "objective possibility." See Lukács 51.

73 Negt and Kluge, *Geschichte und Eigensinn*, 481–82.

74 Negt and Kluge, *Geschichte und Eigensinn*, 475.

75 Negt and Kluge, *Geschichte und Eigensinn*, 468.

its imperceptible and unsystematic processual forms and provisional aggregates—ultimately underscores Negt and Kluge's pluralist convictions (they are, in this respect, neither strict dualists nor monists) that for it to become critical, thought must learn to operate more like the body (a community of monads), and that the body itself possesses forms of knowledge otherwise ignored by the mind (a window) (fig. 1.3). Such a simulation of bodily processes on the part of the thinking mind would conceivably bring critical knowledge closer to the vital interests of the flesh and therewith uphold a modified version of Habermas's concept of interest, a concept he himself quickly downgraded as derivative only then to discard it altogether. This is not to suggest that Negt and Kluge advance a convergence model of mind morphing with body. To the contrary, the compartmentalized nature of the brain (not to mention the embattled components of its consciousness compounded by the dictates of the external world)—in other words, its inherent cantankerousness— guarantees that any neural-like learning processes are likely to fall short of a happy ending much of the time. Conversely, other bodily organs— not only the usual "five senses" but also other sensoria like the feet or diaphragm as well as "the social organs constructed on top of them: love, knowledge, mourning, memory"—possess autonomous forms of often untapped knowledge that could lead to happier outcomes were they ever heeded.[76] Yet successful human learning processes would require so much more than just bringing the conflicted brain in dialogue with the knowing body, for such processes are, in the words of one intergalactic stratocrat, dragged down by the "sluggish cycle of human biology" incapable of competing with the continually accelerating "velocities" of industrial organizations.[77]

Exemplarity, Organization, Formalism

We should, by now, begin to see that the underlying separation propelling Zwicki's endless catastrophic odyssey forward into the nether regions of

---

76 Kluge and Negt 98; Francisco J. Varela et al., *The Embodied Mind: Cognitive Science and Human Experience* (Cambridge, MA: MIT Press, 1991) 27 and Andy Clark, *Being There: Putting Brain, Body, and World Back Together Again* (Cambridge, MA: The MIT Press, 1997) xvii.

77 Kluge, *Learning Processes with a Deadly Outcome*, 94.

outer space—namely a cleft between a "vague attendant feeling" about the nature of life and an "unconquerable longing" to live forever—resurfaces again and again in different guises. For Benjamin, it was a question of exposing the sham of profane knowledge's purchase on divine truth using the revelatory power of the melancholy sovereign's despondent feelings and the baroque tragedy's concomitant "heaps of ruins." For Habermas, it was (initially) a matter of trying to reconcile the dominion of scientific objectivity with the long excluded realms of material interests necessary for the survival of the human species. And of utmost concern for Negt and Kluge was the recovery of the theoretical validity of interests (in the face of their disposal) by expanding their theoretical framework to account for the locus of all materiality, the conflicted body, in order to outline both the conditions of possibility for individuals to progress via thought itself out of material misery. Out of one of the innermost sanctums of mental labor, Negt and Kluge enumerate some of the criteria by which critical intelligence could imbue itself with the necessary self-interests for exploding the otherwise narrow confines of most other affirmative forms of intelligence. This split responsible for the seemingly endless chain of hubris and catastrophes in outer space is certainly not one Negt and Kluge seek to reunify in the guise of a totalizing theory as we might know it. Theory understood as a product of brain work, as a reasonably fixed genre with prescribed discursive rules, or as a canon comprised of successive competing schools of thought is not the seat of critical intelligence for them. This is precisely why they are so quick to note that theory labor is often beset by so many of the same pitfalls that other forms of professional intelligence succumb to: theory's value is measured according to the (often limited) usefulness awarded to it after the fact; it must heed performance-related pressures imposed by the marketplace of ideas on all forms of professional intelligence; it regularly backs itself into an unwanted dead end of narrow specializations and churns out both dead labor and the commodities it produces; and it ultimately fails to contribute to the constitution of an inclusive public sphere, a space of collective experience. Far more a potential than a promise and certainly a means and not the end in itself, the particular attitude and idiosyncratic forms of theory as described by Negt and Kluge accrue their value only as a process. The problem at hand then is both organizational and formal in nature. Is it possible to reorganize the dominant tendencies of mental processes (propositions, logic, reasoning) such that they flow like open, non-linear neural pathways? What kinds of forms, for that matter, would the catalyst of theory need to assume for this to transpire? How can critical intelligence compete with the speeds characteristic of industrial organizations?

Leading up to the publication in 1968 of his aforementioned tome on "organizational forms of anti-authoritarian ... learning," Negt acquired as an educator working with trade unionists ample experience with the practical challenges of politics within organized labor (he later would call unions "interest organizations").[78] "It became suddenly very clear to me ... that no meaningful educational work was possible without knowledge of the interests, fantasies, and ideas of the adults in my courses," he recollected many years later. Melding West German science educator Martin Wagenschein's unorthodox concept of "exemplary teaching" with American sociologist C. Wright Mills's idea of the "sociological imagination," Negt arrived at the outlines of a technique with which he thought it feasible to select and organize instructional materials that, on the one hand, could potentially speak to individual interests and a working-class consciousness in terms of emancipation while, on the other hand, accounting for unavoidable interferences from mass media's information overload, and the interloping institutions of family, school, and work, as well as the ubiquitous specter of technocratic rationality. Unfurled initially in a speech held in 1956, Wagenschein's case for "exemplary teaching" was an appeal to reconceptualize science instruction not in terms of the long tradition of systematic, chronological courses of study that, in his mind, often led to haste, sloppiness, and boredom. Instead, Wagenschein exhorted the values of teaching the essential through a web of interrelated particulars:

> We recommend you have the "courage to leave gaps," which means to have the courage to be thorough and to dwell on limited topics intensively. So instead of going through the catalogue of knowledge uniformly and superficially, step-by-step, we exercise the right—or better we fulfill our duty—to set up shop here and there, to dig our heels in, to throw down roots, to stake out a place. Some call this "building islands." But this would only be valid if we simultaneously imagine along with it a suboceanic mountain range linking them together. We

---

78 Negt, *Soziologische Phantasie und exemplarisches Lernen*, 7; Negt, *Wozu noch Gewerkschaften?* 115.

do not want disaggregation, but rather accumulations and condensa-
tions within this continuity … The supports of a well-anchored bridge
can carry lighter arches much more quickly. The more earnest the condensation, the smoother the connection will be between the nodes of
thoroughness. Skimming over parts is not a lack of thoroughness, for
the pillars of the bridge supported this. Other metaphors can illustrate
our point: the plant that sends out tendrils, which then root and form
new plants (like strawberries); the bird that draws its strength from a
sense of home, which it carries from its last resting and nesting place,
knowing full well that it will soon again be on solid ground; the glider
pilot, who only when caught in an upward draft can sail high above
a single place and can then rapidly resume his flight until his next
quiet ascent. In order to hold onto the character of stages, I choose to
imagine the image as a "platform" (within a tower): a place where one
can stay and rest a while.[79]

Intent on leaving gaps, building islands, erecting platforms, constructing bridges, and sending out tendrils, Wagenschein's metaphorically rich
model for re-organizing instruction inductively ultimately aims, on the
one hand, at reflecting for students the whole of a discipline in individual
phenomena and, on the other hand, at motivating them to act spontaneously and intensively on the whole of their own interests. Accordingly, it
requires, on the part of the instructor, a willingness to select and then lead
students laterally and without any previous knowledge into "exemplary
themes" that are "not too complex," problem-oriented topics challenging
for both teacher and student alike. It entails diving into the fundamen-
tals of a single phenomenon (e.g., how is light refracted in water?) and
seeking out plausible explanations, only then to exit and re-enter the
problem at a higher level of complexity (i.e., how is refraction different
than reflection?) with the intent of posing more sophisticated questions
that bridge the multiple entry points. And it necessitates longer stretches
of instructional time such that teaching and learning burrow "into the
hearts of both students and teachers day and night."[80]

79 Martin Wagenschein, "Teaching to Understand: On the Concept of the Exem-
plary in Teaching," trans. Gillian Horton-Krüger, in *Teaching as a Reflective Practice:
The German Didaktik Tradition*, eds. Ian Westbury, Stefan Hopmann, and Kurt Riquarts
(Mahwah, NJ: Lawrence Erlbaum Associates, 2000) 163–64. See also: Negt, *Soziologische
Phantasie und exemplarisches Lernen*, 25–27.
80 Wagenschein 169, 167, 168.

But just the seed of Negt's efforts to develop "new instructional methods and ways for organizing teaching materials," Wagenschein's model quickly proved to be too mired in the confines of single disciplines and too susceptible to abstract stylizations typical of reigning interests for it to contribute to any class-conscious form of political action.[81] For this to happen, Negt expanded Wagenschein's ideal of the exemplary using Mills's concept of "sociological imagination" with the intention of moving from Wagenschein's disciplinarity to broader reflections of whole "social processes of production and reproduction" otherwise parceled out and obscured according to historically contingent divisions of labor.[82] According to Mills, the sociological imagination is a cognitive

> capacity to shift from one perspective to another—from the political to the psychological; from examination of a single family to comparative assessment of the national budgets of the world; from the theological school to the military establishment; from considerations of an oil industry to studies of contemporary poetry. It is the capacity to range from the most impersonal and remote transformations to the most intimate features of the human self—and to see relations between the two.[83]

For Negt, the promise of Mills's interdisciplinary method lay not only in its power to bring to light the "structural relationalities between individual life histories, immediate interests, wishes, hopes and historical events," but also in its ability to facilitate conscious action.[84] Not unlike Horkheimer's own 1937 call for a critical theory erected upon interdisciplinary connections and intent on effecting social change, the utility of Mills's method for Negt certainly rested in part in Mills's embrace of hope in lieu of checking into the later Horkheimer and Co.'s infamous "Grand Hotel Abyss," as well as in his waxing popularity within the burgeoning New Left in both America and the Federal Republic of Germany.[85] A

---

81 Oskar Negt, *Kindheit und Schule in einer Welt der Umbrüche* (Göttingen: Steidl, 1997) 301–2.

82 Negt, *Soziologische Phantasie und exemplarisches Lernen*, 27.

83 C. Wright Mills, *The Sociological Imagination* (New York: Oxford University Press, 1999) 7; cited, in part, in Negt, *Soziologische Phantasie und exemplarisches Lernen*, 28.

84 Negt, *Soziologische Phantasie und exemplarisches Lernen*, 28.

85 Horkheimer, "Traditional and Critical Theory," 193–94, 220; Thomas Wheatland, *The Frankfurt School in Exile* (Minneapolis: University of Minneapolis Press, 2009) 305–8.

back door for recuperating the very links between critical theory and political action that Horkheimer long ago preached but no longer could endorse in the postwar period, Mills eventually faded into the background as Negt's concern for organizational praxis turned to the West German student movement. Recalling Lenin's and Lukács's bygone calls to situate matters of organization into theory and practice, Negt insisted in public addresses to the New Left that while matters of organization were still valid, the conditions for exercising organized political protest under the relative stability of late capitalism had radically changed; supportive of neither Lukács's case for elite cadre parties nor, for that matter, Blanquism or anarchism, he spoke well before the hot summer of '68 of the real potential to be found in decentralized, loose, and tractable organizational nodes. In hindsight, Negt pointed out, however, that the difficult balancing act necessary for keeping both the stability of organizations and any and all spontaneous action rooted in local materialist interests together in the air failed: "political imagination, individual-emancipatory interests, strategic flexibility" all fell by the wayside in the student movement's hasty quest for consolidation and discipline.[86]

The failures of the New Left were, for Negt, precisely what was long lacking in traditional pedagogy, what was missing in early communist calls for an organizational praxis, what Habermas saw as being absent in the whole of the philosophy of knowledge, and what was to subtend the political force of a "sociological imagination." The essential task of organizing interests can only succeed if the subjects, whose interests are to be organized, are not conceived of as whole human beings, Negt concluded years later; fraternal interests capable of binding people "cut across" the facile "arbitrary divisions" made in the name of supervising and controlling constituents in the name of the organization.[87] In the months leading up to the 1972 publication of his "organizational analysis" of bourgeois and proletarian public spheres co-authored with Kluge, Negt spoke bluntly, insisting that people, proletarian and otherwise, are not the totalities political organizations imagine them to be; a mirror of their subdivided, conflicted, and multitasking brains, human beings are rather vessels full of "characteristics, capabilities, interests, and needs" rendered fragmentary by the conditions of production and consumption

---

86 Oskar Negt, "Don't Go By Numbers, Organize According to Interests! Current Questions of Organization," *New German Critique* 1 (Winter 1973): 47.

87 Negt, "Don't Go By Numbers," 47.

under which they live.[88] For any oppositional organizational praxis to succeed at tapping into the organizational disarray of human beings compounded by the dominant organizational forms of capitalist society (what Negt and Kluge call the public sphere of production and reproduction), it must, above all, liberate the faculty of the imagination, that unconscious realm of "sensual-fantastic" activity in the brain that usually compensates, like a "libidinal counterweight," the real conscious experiences of oppression.[89] The flipside to organizing interests thus boiled down to nothing other than mediating what Mills called the sociological imagination, what Ernst Bloch identified around the same time as the "anticipatory consciousness" of daydreams, and what Negt and Kluge labeled the reorganization of fantasy.[90] If fantasy is to step out of its usual shell in which it labors as a compensator churning out timeless escapist products cut off from reality, then this "productive force of the brain" must, they argue, connect "libidinal structure[s], consciousness, and the outside world ... with one another."[91] To facilitate this reorganization—a counter-organization constitutive of constructive learning processes— Negt and Kluge advocate a formal counter-response to the abstract forms of organized production, experience, consciousness, knowledge, and expression that shape human life. It is at this juncture of our initial voyage into Negt and Kluge's works where they, like Bloch before them, seamlessly integrate matters of aesthetic forms into their practical theory of knowledge.[92]

One is rightly hesitant to call Negt and Kluge outright advocates of formalism, especially when the concept long served in German aesthetic theory as an epithet of the worst kind. And yet the formalism that Bloch and Lukács bandied in the infamous expressionist debate from the 1930s over the political implications of realist and modernist literary practices was anything but exhaustive. As Bertolt Brecht contended in

---

88 Negt, "Don't Go By Numbers," 49; cf. Negt and Kluge, *Public Sphere and Experience*, 185.

89 Negt and Kluge, *Public Sphere and Experience*, 35, 33.

90 Negt and Kluge, *Public Sphere and Experience*, 176; Oskar Negt, "Ernst Bloch: The German Philosopher of the October Revolution," trans. Jack Zipes, *New German Critique* 4 (Winter 1975): 11–16; and Oskar Negt "The Non-Synchronous Heritage and the Problem of Propaganda," *New German Critique* 9 (Autumn 1976): 47–52.

91 Negt and Kluge, *Public Sphere and Experience*, 37.

92 Negt, "The Non-Synchronous Heritage and the Problem of Propaganda": "For Bloch a separated aesthetic theory is not necessary, [it is] in fact even impossible" (59).

his posthumous foray into the debates, even the artist concerned with representing reality "is constantly occupied with formal matters" and these formal matters apply not only to the handwork of artists—works of art—but also to symbolic strategic action typical of everyday life: the art of work.[93] Not unlike Benjamin's infamous notion of the "aestheticization of politics," political formalism, for Brecht, is characteristic of the privileging of opportunistic proceduralism, a cynical rightness awarded to the organizational forms of bureaucracy in spite of the moral wrongness of their contents. In oblique reference to Brecht's notion of political formalism, Negt and Kluge themselves explicate the term further as belonging to the long "intellectual tradition of the bourgeois domination of nature," an Odyssean "intellectual show of force" intent on engendering "appeasement" in spite of its participation in the violent mechanism of domination and exclusion.[94] (In this respect, the score to Schubert's song "Memnon" burnt into the surface of the planet "Franz Zwicki" would be nothing less than an intergalactic case of formalism!) If the cunning of political formalism does indeed subtend much of dominant experience in modern public spheres, then its appeasement and the "highly organized level of production" it facilitates is mediated according to Negt and Kluge by a wide range of discursive and aesthetic forms spanning from "elections," "public ceremonies," and "theater premiere[s]" to "childrearing, factory work and watching television."[95] As for aesthetic forms like theater and television (not to mention literature and film), Kluge the author and filmmaker has expressed little sympathy for advocating any sort of orthodox formalism. Alluding to the aforementioned debates between Bloch, Lukács, and others, Kluge, writing together with Edgar Reitz in 1965, declared for example both the formalism symptomatic of early experimental film and the photorealist naturalism typical of most narrative film as ill-suited for achieving the "high level of filmic imagination" necessary for achieving what they call complexities and multiplicities.[96] And yet, as late as 1964, Kluge was already thinking of what leads to the "organizational buildup of a disaster" like the Battle of

---

93 Bertolt Brecht, "Against Georg Lukács," in Ernst Bloch et al., *Aesthetics and Politics* (London: Verso, 1980) 71–72.

94 Negt and Kluge, *Public Sphere and Experience*, 10–11n20.

95 Negt and Kluge, *Public Sphere and Experience*, xliii.

96 Edgar Reitz, Alexander Kluge, and Wilfried Reinke, "Word and Film," trans. Miriam Hansen, in *Difference and Orientation: An Alexander Kluge Reader*, ed. Richard Langston (Ithaca, NY: Cornell University Press, 2019) 128, 136, 131.

Stalingrad in terms of a "world of forms" only representable, in turn, by recycling the formal techniques of modernist literature.[97] What exactly Kluge's formal concerns are, how exactly his aesthetic formalism relates to political formalism, and how best to name this relationship have bedeviled scholars for decades, even though some of his earliest critics were quick to point out that Kluge's "completely different way of writing" resists traditional categorization.[98] One relatively early attempt at typifying the formal principle subtending Kluge's prose—the first of many media he mastered—called it catastrophic due to its fields of rubble, shards, and fragments.[99] (According to this dubious reading, the story of space traveler Zwicki formally assumes the very deadly outcomes it narrates.) A much more recent attempt rightly casts doubt on this particular case for mimesis by asking, "Fragments of what?" If fragments are inherently relational to "fulfilled forms," so the argument goes, then Kluge's "self-contained form" can be neither fragmentary nor representational of some non-existent whole.[100] Resorting to the long-standing philological tradition of chalking an unclassifiable body of analogous forms up to an idiosyncratic genre only sidesteps the extra-textual indexicality informing Kluge and Negt's formal concerns.

Understood as the pedagogical outgrowth of their shared investment in a political theory of knowledge, form as deployed by Negt and Kluge is fragmentary, anti-mimetic, and non-representational. Exactly the opposite of the "heap[s] of ruins" Benjamin detected in the baroque *Trauerspiel*, the bits and pieces distinguishing the forms of stories like *Learning Processes with A Deadly Outcome* and the eponymous collections of stories in which they appear (not to mention the duo's fragmentary book *History and Obstinacy*) are the ingredients for facilitating the potentially constructive "sociological imagination," fantastic thought beyond the reach and rules of mediated and technical intelligence, thought ultimately intent on seeking ways out of catastrophes like the Battle of Stalingrad

---

97 Alexander Kluge, *Schlachtbeschreibung* (Olten und Freiburg im Breisgau: Walter-Verlag, 1964) 339ff, 9.

98 Helmut Heißenbüttel, "Der Text ist die Wahrheit: Zur Methode des Schriftstellers Alexander Kluge," *Text + Kritik* 85/86 (January 1985): 3.

99 Hans Magnus Enzensberger, "Ein herzloser Schriftsteller," *Der Spiegel* (January 2, 1978): 81.

100 Jan Philipp Reemtsma, "Unvertrautheit und Urvertrauen – Die "Gattung Kluge": Laudatio auf Alexander Kluge," in *Deutsche Akademie für Sprache und Dichtung: Jahrbuch* (Göttingen: Wallstein, 2003) 171.

(fact) and the Black War (fiction). Whether imagined as disparate platforms to be bridged or a bundle of individual neurons capable of transmitting signals along any number of non-linear pathways, Negt and Kluge's "short" and "mixed" forms capable of being strung spontaneously into myriad "sequences" and "variations" are merely the scaffolding for unpredictable learning processes to unfold.[101] Lessons are, in short, to be found in these processes; they are identical neither to the scaffolding nor to any final product any teaching or learning process may yield. This is precisely why Kluge has long been adamant that "television, video ... the radio and the cinema" are not "media." Rather, they are "merely the *forms* and the conditions under which ... media exist. The true medium of experience ... [is] ... real human beings ... ; it is *their* imagination that animates the screen."[102] Erected upon this basic distinction between forms and media, Kluge has deployed his pivotal mantra—"the film [happens] in the spectator's head, in the gaps between the elements"— over and over again in all his theoretical and aesthetic works. Yet, his insistence on caring for the autonomy of his spectators' "heads" has nevertheless run the risk of implying hermeneutic anarchy or populist relativism when in fact his montage aesthetic actually organizes itself loosely around thematic platforms related to the "processes of production and reproduction" otherwise unknown and unseen.[103] Just as there are specific fields of knowledge for any re-organization of fantasy to happen, so too are there successful forms of montage (investigative, perspectival, and open) and counterproductive ones (preconceived, associational, and closed).[104] Regardless of how perambulatory critical intelligence

---

101 Alexander Kluge, "Ein Hauptansatz des Ulmer Instituts," in *In Gefahr und größter Not bringt der Mittelweg den Tod: Text zu Kino, Film, Politik*, ed. Christian Schulte (Berlin: Verlag Vorwerk 8, 2002) 57–59; and Florian Rötzer, "Kino und Grabkammer: Gespräch mit Alexander Kluge," in *Die Schrift an der Wand: Alexander Kluge: Rohstoffe und Materialien*, ed. Christian Schulte (Osnabrück: Universitätsverlag Rasch, 2000) 42.

102 Alexander Kluge, "On Film and the Public Sphere," trans. Thomas Y. Levin and Miriam B. Hansen, in *Raw Materials for the Imagination*, ed. Tara Forrest (Amsterdam: Amsterdam University Press, 2012) 36.

103 See: Reitz, Kluge and Reinke, 129; and Alexander Kluge, "Bits of Conversation," trans. Emma Woelk, in: *Difference and Orientation*, 148.

104 On the conditions for successful montage, see: Kluge, "On Film and the Public Sphere," 47–48; see also Miriam Hansen, "Alexander Kluge: Crossings between Film, Literature, Critical Theory," in *Film und Literatur: Literarische Texte und der neue deutsche Film*, eds. Sigrid Bauschinger, Susan L. Cocalis, and Henry A. Lea (Munich: Francke Verlag, 1984) 180–81.

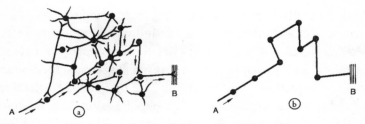

Figure 1.3. Thought as neural pathways: "(a) shows a piece of the nervous system's network. Before the points representing the receptors, a gap is located with each synapse representing the effector ... An association can thus assume the route represented by (b), but can also take countless other routes" (Kluge and Negt, *History and Obstinacy*, 112). © Alexander Kluge.

is, the neural-like pathways it traverses still deliver it from point A to B (fig. 1.3). The potential for success of any learning process therefore rests upon a form's potential for facilitating the perception of distinctions otherwise imperceptible within an inscribed field of experience. In this respect, Negt and Kluge's investment in the formal conditions for counter-knowledge follows their conviction that for a favorable outcome, any scaffolding must enable scaffolders to index myriad modes of concrete and abstract social experiences to the multitude of individual responses originating in both intelligence (the work of consciousness) and fantasy (brain work) (fig. 1.4).

That Negt and Kluge at one point go so far as to align their counter-method for acquiring critical intelligence with "a form of work ... Lévi-Strauss called ... that of the tinkerer, the *bricoleur*" should not tempt us to conflate their concerns for organization and form with those of French structuralists.[105] While, on the one hand, it is certainly irrefutable that, in Negt and Kluge's work, "perception and imagination," to speak with Lévi-Strauss, undergo "continual reconstruction" using a heterogeneous yet finite "set of tools and materials," as is the case with structuralism's *bricoleur*.[106] On the other hand, if they are indeed *bricoleurs* as they insist, then, according to Lévi-Strauss's typology, their tinkering is more in the vein of the engineer's quest to create events out of structures and go "beyond the constraints imposed by ... civilization" than it is of the *brocoleur*'s.[107] Even less congruous are the compromising

105 Negt and Kluge, *Geschichte und Eigensinn*, 222.

106 Claude Lévi-Strauss, *The Savage Mind* (Chicago: University of Chicago Press, 1966) 15, 21, 17.

107 Lévi-Strauss 19.

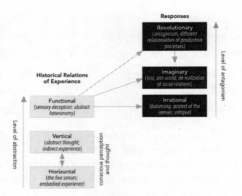

Figure 1.4. Three degrees of abstract social experience and three subjective responses: these "six dimensions … contain within themselves the additional dimensions of the political, the historical, the realization of labor power, feelings, consciousness, revolutionary transformation, as well as the horizontal and the vertical (the dimensions best known to sensuous perception), which, for their part, include place, time, punctuality, space, movement, non-movement, relationalities and differentiations" (Kluge and Negt, *History and Obstinacy*, 503n25). © Richard Langston

recuperations attributed to Lévi-Strauss's structuralist method: its oblivious employ of play to neutralize history, its "nostalgic" search for origins and truth despite its intent on decentering, its obliteration of difference despite its insistence on the existence of two different modes of scientific knowledge (the *bricoleur* versus the engineer). These bifurcations subtending Lévi-Strauss's typology are not to be found in Negt and Kluge's writing.[108] Far more in tune with Derrida's famous declaration —*bricolage* is the substrate of myth and magic as well as engineering and science—than with Lévi-Strauss, Negt and Kluge's method actually echoes what Derrida calls the "common ground" shared by these "two interpretations" by allowing for as much play as possible in their forms for learning processes.[109] Play for Derrida involves making "infinite substitutions" (along with repetitions, transformations, and permutations) within a finite field precisely because that field lacks a center that otherwise would arrest it.[110] Similarly, play for Kluge and Negt is a means of annulling the force of reality and reason (or what Derrida called the "disruption of presence") and manifests itself in the form of

108 Jacques Derrida, "Structure, Sign and Play in the Discourse of the Human Sciences," trans. Richard Macksey and Alan Bass, in *Writing and Difference* (London: Routledge, 2005) 360.
109 Derrida 370.
110 Derrida 365, 352.

a game of casting dice.[111] Channeling Nietzsche, they also align play
with what Gilles Deleuze reads in *Thus Spoke Zarathustra* as Nietzsche's
necessary "affirmation of *chance [hasard]*"—Negt and Kluge associate
the roll of the dice with *Glück* (good fortune)—and, by extension, the
affirmation of multiplicity.[112] That their method toward "emancipatory
positivity," a method they say can be found in "simple discovery," flirts
with the anti-dialectical treatises of French poststructuralists means not
that Negt and Kluge have broken with a core of Frankfurt School thinking.[113] Instead, the utility of Derrida and Deleuze for Negt and Kluge
lies in the fact that they help them shift the dialectic away from its usual
status as bifurcating tool of thought and toward the actual multipolar
"material processes" transpiring between interrelated parts of an organization (like the brain) constantly undergoing change.[114] The dialectic
for Negt and Kluge is the specific form by which change transpires in
living organizations; it arises from the "self-regulating movement of relationalities" that constitute them, a synthesis involving varying degrees
of incorporation, self-preservation, and transformation between more
highly organized sub-systems (a lord or reason, for example) and less
organized sub-systems (a bondsman or the sense of touch, for example).[115] Yet, these learning processes rooted in tinkering are reliant upon
discoveries—both ostensibly scientific and patently non-scientific—that
interrupt what we might otherwise just see as contingent bipolar relationships. By virtue of chance (shorthand for what Negt and Kluge also
call the "law of the included third"), unexpected aberrations and detours
arise, thereby facilitating new alliances and associations.

Coda: Robo sapiens

If the preceding account of Negt and Kluge's pedagogy seems like a
simple matter of following a recipe, then it behooves us to return one last
time to Kluge's allegory about erstwhile Nazis in space. Less a palimpsest

---

111 Kluge and Negt 200; Derrida 369.
112 Gilles Deleuze, *Nietzsche and Philosophy*, trans. Hugh Tomlinson (New York:
Columbia University Press, 1983) 25–27. See also Negt and Kluge, *Geschichte und Eigensinn*, 487.
113 Negt and Kluge, *Geschichte und Eigensinn*, 487.
114 Negt and Kluge, *Geschichte und Eigensinn*, 241, 239n13.
115 Negt and Kluge, *Geschichte und Eigensinn*, 240.

of the real Swiss-American astronomer Franz Zwicky than a personifi-
cation of Negt and Kluge's own theory of knowledge catapulted into a
fantastic dystopia, the fictional scientist Franz Zwicki rightly lays claim
to the vitality of dark matter—the body's "unconquerable longing"
to live forever, the brain's unclaimed realm of unconscious thought—
without ever being able to bring it to bear on the task of critical thinking.
Highly intelligent men—in the end, American intelligence officers on
the lam—repeatedly fail to use their intelligence to escape catastrophe.
The grounds for this inability stem, above all, from the deterioration of
the material conditions for thought. That no one really thinks anymore
has most fundamentally to do with the fact that the "original interests"
of the intergalactic travelers—interests acquired with two feet on earthly
soil—cease to exist in outer space.[116] In the face of both time and sensory
deprivation, Zwicki et al. are no longer capable of forming libidinal
relationships between their selves and the scant extraterrestrial objects
around them such that cognition could ever become more neural. As a
result, their intelligence is far more instrumental than it is critical. In the
moment, it is hardly relational and thus underproduces consciousness,
colludes with the status quo, and falls short of ever orientating the space
travelers out of catastrophe. Furthermore, their learning processes along
the way—from surviving the Battle of Stalingrad and Chinese slavery
to entering into the American intelligence service and Jupiter's orbit—
obviously follow a feeling of "unconquerable longing" for survival, yet
they never achieve the breadth of sociological imagination necessary for
comprehending the interstellar processes that keep on producing and
reproducing catastrophe in deep space. In light of all these shortcomings, Negt and Kluge's teachers Horkheimer and Adorno might have
called Zwicki a perfect example of intelligent stupidity, "partial stupidity"
resulting from the inhibition of the "play of muscles" responsible for surveying the natural world using an array of senses.[117] However, disastrous
learning processes, say Negt and Kluge, do not necessarily lead to lingering scars associated with stupidity, as their mentors once insisted. Instead,
such processes are grounds for additional post-catastrophic learning
processes: Under what conditions *did* past experience turn destructive?
What *could* have led to emancipatory outcomes?[118] Indeed, the forms

116 Kluge, *Learning Processes with a Deadly Outcome*, 31.
117 Horkheimer and Adorno 214.
118 Negt and Kluge, *Public Sphere and Experience*, 246.

Zwicki's "writing in the year 2103" assumes—its jumbled vignettes; its mixed-up narrative times, places, people, and voices; and its digressive illustrations—together make up a formal counter-organization Negt and Kluge would say is the precondition for promoting the sweeping consciousness characteristic of a critical intelligence intolerant toward the misery endemic to catastrophe.[119] Certainly less than 20/20, given the many elusive abstractions comprising so much of human experience, this hindsight for Negt and Kluge is nonetheless perspicacious ... as hindsight. Whether it is constitutive of future learning processes with happier endings is not just a function of the existent dialectical processes within the brain and the unpredictable roles chance and play therein. Rather, it is also a matter of whether entire collectives take part in the learning processes and whether they transpire well before it is too late. In Zwicki's case, such a learning process may have needed to happen before the Battle of Stalingrad. Indeed, emancipatory learning processes are anything but simple recipes.

Complicating even further the implied extradiegetic promise conveyed by the formal counter-organization of Kluge's allegory is the intradiegetic implication that the material base of any materialist theory of knowledge is endangered in a post-apocalyptic future. Can, in other words, intelligence still aspire to become critical in a post-human world? In the futuristic frontiers of intergalactic capital where natural resources are boundless and available labor power is scarce, the only viable solution for the accumulation of more capital around the year 2042 is to maximize available human labor capacity through technology. In this respect, we find, within Zwicki's story, a cluster of smaller interior narratives about a cosmos colonized by a military-industrial complex intent on upholding the old telluric rhetoric of the sanctity of human life as it is busy thinking up scientific, juridical, and commercial ways of turning humans into machines. Renamed business "partners" so as to obfuscate their exploitation, laborers are forced into indentured servitude.[120] Demoted to "non-human life-forms" so as warrant their inhuman treatment, outlaws are put to work in labor camps.[121] As quests for intelligent extraterrestrial life forms turn up nothing in the search for new

119 Kluge, *Learning Processes with a Deadly Outcome*, 3; Negt and Kluge, *Geschichte und Eigensinn*, 486.
120 Kluge, *Learning Processes with a Deadly Outcome*, 42.
121 Kluge, *Learning Processes with a Deadly Outcome*, 43.

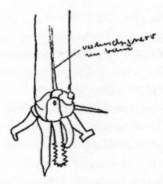

Figure 1.5. Human evolution versus cyborg intervention: Left, "Mutational change of the human hand (natural)"; right, "The labor economy's valorization of a mutated hand in terms of the human hand's augmentation into an effective tool of labor. Sketch by Prof. Meixner." (Kluge, *Learning Processes with a Deadly Outcome*, 60). © Alexander Kluge.

sources of labor power—Zwicki insists alien life "has been scientifically disproven"—advances in "industrial medicine" succeed in surgically shifting, recombining, and replacing human body parts—brains, internal organs, limbs—in an effort to maximize the shortages in the existing labor pool.[122] Masterminded by an intellectual elite, additional flesh-altering procedures like genetic engineering and organ harvesting as well as crossbreeding foster the growth of a new "economy of labor" in which labor capacities are expanded while the likelihood of rebellion among workers is reduced to a minimum (fig. 1.5). Ultimately, success for maintaining the status quo in outer space boils down not only to making highly productive cyborgs and mutants. The military-industrial complex's dominion also rests on its ability to overwhelm the ineradicable and irrepressible resistance rooted in the brain's and body's dark matter. To do so, it decelerates and prematurely terminates the future proletariat's emancipatory learning processes "by concealing what we're doing and ... beheading the ringleaders," on the one hand, and accelerates dominant industrial processes such that they outpace any such liberating learning processes innately bound to "the sluggish cycle of human biology," on the other hand.[123] This two-pronged solution—the transmutation of human biology and the unprecedented outpacing of cellular capacities for resistance—is unquestionably the stuff of dystopian science fiction, and yet so much of this new logic of capital, says

---

122 Kluge, *Learning Processes with a Deadly Outcome*, 43n4, 92.
123 Kluge, *Learning Processes with a Deadly Outcome*, 92, 94.

not-so recent scholarship in humanities, has already become reality even if it has not always emerged solely in the name of maximizing human labor capacities. In spite of the conceivable challenges such imagined and real physiological shifts conceivably pose for organizing emancipatory learning processes, Negt and Kluge's theory of intelligence, as laid down in *History and Obstinacy*, nevertheless insists that dark matter—the counter-logic to capital—would always persist as a deeper anthropological fundament, the wellspring of any emancipatory knowledge. In theory, even the burly elephantine women bred, trained, and enslaved to work in the middle of the twenty-first century within the light gravity of the Swan Sector possess potential for a critical intelligence: their dark matter, like ours, is as indefatigable as it is immune to any determinism.[124]

In the decades since the publication of *Geschichte und Eigensinn*, Negt and Kluge have revisited their theory of intelligence, not by pursuing any of the very real consequences of actual technological intrusions into man's physiology but rather by querying the technically mediated projections of man's consciousness into outer space. If the cantankerous human brain has long operated like both a monad and a window, what then when its latter function—its mediation of second nature—is partially displaced onto machines? What, if anything, becomes of the brain's hierarchies of labor—from consciousness all the way down to critical intelligence—when the available pools of information mushroom exponentially? What demands or challenges are placed upon the theory labor characteristic of critical intelligence when new ubiquitous regimes of abstraction overshadow like never before the powers of critical inquiry, excess consciousness, and orientation? And, most importantly, what, if any, consequences must be drawn for assembling the expansive relationalities necessary for any counter-organization, especially when artificial intelligence erects itself upon its own neural-like networks? In pursuit of answers to these questions, it was Kluge who quickly found Frankfurt School thinking at its limit point. Still faithfully keeping tabs on Habermas well into the eighties, Kluge acknowledged Habermas's observation regarding emergent technologically based "worldwide threat[s] to universal life interests," only to part ways with his proposed solutions for finding clarity amid the so-called new postmodern obscurity; instead of searching for a "bird's-eye view"—

---

124 Kluge, *Learning Processes with a Deadly Outcome*, 62.

Habermas actually writes of the "no-man's-land of the normative"—
Kluge opts for the "mass production of [the] capacity for differentiation."[125] Merely another designation for what Negt initially recognized
in Mills's sociological imagination and later with Kluge became their
call for reorganizing fantasy, Kluge's recourse to delve into the messy
pluralities of hyperreality—in this case that of a public sphere besieged
by emergent subscription-based television services—subsequently
drew him to Niklas Luhmann's systems theory and its engagement
with artificial intelligence. Mediated through Luhmann's student Dirk
Baecker, Kluge's sustained encounters with systems theory at the turn
of the millennium cover considerable ground, testing, on the one hand,
the affinities to and differences between Negt and Kluge's model of the
human brain (a self-regulating psychic system full of consciousness,
thought, and intelligence) and what Luhmann, also borrowing from
neurobiology, calls the autopoiesis of social systems.[126] On the other
hand, he delves into the postulates of artificial intelligence born out of
both robotics and the neurosciences to learn that creating intelligence
only proves possible when a system (like a robot's "brain") seeks out
differences separating it from the complex environment (its body and
beyond) around it.[127] On the surface, a curious encounter with a theoretical tradition antithetical to his own, Kluge's queries into system
theory's take on the difference between thought and consciousness, the
learning ability of organizations, the vitality of artificial intelligence,
and the unreliability of intelligent systems. He does so not to gain, as
Luhmann does, a view on cognition from high above a thick cover of
clouds.[128] As with their encounters with Derrida and Deleuze, Negt
and Kluge refrain from assimilating any of the larger consequences of
Luhmann's thinking, above all his dismissal of the knowing subject or

125 Jürgen Habermas, "The New Obscurity: The Crisis of the Welfare State and the
Exhaustion of Utopian Energies," in *New Conservatism: Cultural Criticism and the Historians' Debate*, ed. and trans. Shierry Weber Nicholsen (Cambridge, MA: MIT Press,
1989) 50, 67; Alexander Kluge, "On the Expressions 'Media' and 'New Media': A Selection of Keywords," trans. Richard Lambert, in *Difference and Orientation*, 265.

126 See Dirk Baecker and Alexander Kluge, *Vom Nutzen ungelöster Probleme* (Berlin:
Merve Verlag, 2003) 61–62, 224, 110–11, 135–36.

127 Baecker and Kluge 19–20.

128 Dirk Baecker and Rainer Stollmann, "Wozu Theorie? Dirk Baecker und Rainer
Stollmann über Kritische und Systemtheorie," in *Der Maulwurf kennt kein System: Bei-
träge zur gemeinsamen Philosophie von Oskar Negt und Alexander Kluge*, eds. Christian
Schulte and Rainer Stollmann (Bielefeld: transcript Verlag, 2005) 60.

his posthumanist revision of social reality as a cognitive construction.[129] Rather, Kluge's fascination for systems theory lies in its matter-of-fact acknowledgment of the complex and confusing, disorderly and unpredictable terrain on which intelligence, be it human or artificial, unfolds.

While the humanist concepts from Negt and Kluge's collaborations retained in Kluge's own conversations with systems theory (self-regulation, the thinking subject, regulative society, subject/object relations) do substantiate an underlying loyalty to what Luhmann dismissively calls the ostensibly "extinct volcanoes of Marxism," Kluge nevertheless substantiates an affinity to an exemplary model for making sense of the complexities of the "new obscurity."[130] Furthermore, Kluge sees in Luhmann's pluralism a correspondence with his and Negt's recognition of myriad cognitive systems (cells, brains, the nightly news, and science). Kluge is arguably also drawn to the constitution of difference in Luhmann's epistemology on account of its striking resemblance to Negt and Kluge's own call to nurture the "capacity to draw distinctions." What, however, is absent in Kluge's standpoint is any of the usual pessimism so often characteristic of tenaciously humanist positions confronted with the onslaught of a posthuman world. Specters like robo sapiens, cyborg cannibals ceaselessly in need of information, the machine replication of human characteristics like motherliness or discontentment, or most generally the emergence of artificial life hardly cause any consternation for Kluge.[131] Such hysteria does rear its head, however, in more recent dialogues with journalist and newspaper editor Frank Schirrmacher. Interviewed in 2010 after the publication of his trade book *Payback* on the digital revolution, Schirrmacher provides an affirmative dystopian answer to the question Baecker proved unable to answer a decade earlier, namely whether artificial intelligence is alive:

> SCHIRRMACHER: Now something new is coming and that is … the over-mind. We are erecting an *Übergeist*, if you will … The bottom line is that we are experiencing an externalization of thought, something hardly recognized in the current debate. The moment I delegate, so to speak, decision-making structures by means of algorithms, this

---

129 Hans-Georg Moeller, *The Radical Luhmann* (New York: Columbia University Press, 2012) 78–82.

130 Baecker and Kluge 110, 125, 19; Schulte and Stollmann 75–77.

131 Baecker and Kluge 15, 17, 18–19, 22.

process sets in motion a migration of thought ... out of its former place, namely the brain ... On account of the flood of information no longer in the control of human beings, texts appear in the Net that in turn react to other texts, but because the time is too short to bring about a response ... ideas metamorphose independent of human influence ...

KLUGE: ... as if they were living creatures ...

SCHIRRMACHER: Exactly.[132]

Anything but a Luddite, Schirrmacher nevertheless assembles a mountain of scientific and commercial evidence supporting the present-day ubiquity of algorithmic intelligence, confirming what media theorist Katherine Hayles has succinctly called the posthuman "regime of computation," namely "the penetration of computational processes not only into every aspect of biological, social, economic and political realms but also into the construction of reality itself."[133] In response to this unparalleled agency of disembodied intelligence, Schirrmacher, like Hayles before him, calls for a human response, one capable of repositioning embodied intelligence effectively amid the myriad calculations that make up the cognisphere. And yet, in his appeal to reform the institutions of secondary and higher education—he calls for attuning *Bildung* to the unprecedented stockpiles of information stored in clouds—Schirrmacher drops buzzwords reminiscent, in part, of Wagenschein and Mills like "informal learning" and "a change in perspective" as well as allusions to Negt and Kluge's "law of the included middle" ("non-algorithmic, completely incalculable problem solving") but without ever substantiating how this alternative pedagogy would unfold.[134] While Kluge and Negt do lend credence in our current era of information excess to a splitting of subjects into carriers of intelligence and interlocutors in virtual communities, never do they entertain anything so drastic

---

132 Alexander Kluge, "Die Auswanderung des Denkens aus dem Gehirn," *Mensch 2.0* (Zurich: NZZ Format, 2011) DVD 3, track 25; cf. Baecker and Kluge 22:

KLUGE: As of when can we call a robot alive? ...

BAECKER: Those are difficult questions.

133 Frank Schirrmacher, *Payback: Warum wir im Informationszeitalter gezwungen sind zu tun, was wir nicht tun wollen, und wie wir die Kontrolle über unser Denken zurückgewinnen* (Munich: Pantheon, 2011) 156; Katherine Hayles, "Unfinished Work: From Cyborg to Cognisphere," *Theory, Culture & Society* 23.7–8 (2006): 161.

134 Schirrmacher 216.

as the "metamorphosis of humans into mathematics," as Schirrmacher calls it, nor do they restrict the cultivation of what Negt calls "technological competency" to mere school reform.[135] In spite of their recognition of both the real tsunamis of information and any further splitting of the already fragmented subject they have caused, Kluge contends that the mental labor of the mind has neither willingly nor forcibly undergone change.[136] What have changed are the conditions of possibility for valuating the spate of information: imagining the algorithmic abstractions and coded relationalities subtending reality and seeking orientation therein have become more complicated. Discriminating embodied self-interests shared by individuals in society from those derived from algorithmic recommender systems requires "a stronger means of selectivity."[137] Rather than affecting the nature of dark matter, information technologies have merely upped the ante for aesthetic forms intent on facilitating a critical intelligence. The aesthetic needs to operate accordingly more than ever like magic, say Kluge and Negt, producing forms suitable for knowledge production that peer beyond the fields of vision and everyday language.[138] It must engender an arsenal of unsettled questions and emotions that stoke our fantasy. And it must hone our "capacity to draw distinctions," our powers of critique.

As much the backbone of Negt and Kluge's entire social philosophy as it is of Kluge's aesthetic practice, it is no coincidence that their practical theory of critical intelligence acquisition outlined in their first collaboration from the early seventies was accompanied by a science fiction story. "The potential of science fiction," they wrote in 1972 (the same year the fictional character Zwicki ostensibly penned his materialist epistemology), lies not in its apparent "distance … from real experience." Rather, the rules of the science fiction genre trigger reactions to a very real "experiential mode of fantasy forced back into the process of work and socialization."[139] In other words, the "cognitive estrangement" characteristic of so much science fiction is predicated on the notion that it makes us readers conscious, at the very least, of the prison house in which our

---

135 Kluge and Negt 194; Schirrmacher 99.
136 Alexander Kluge, "Planting Gardens in the Data Tsunami," trans. Steffen Kaupp, in *Difference and Orientation*, 331–36.
137 Kluge and Negt 196.
138 Kluge and Negt 195.
139 Negt and Kluge, *Public Sphere and Experience*, 106n11.

quotidian fantasies reside.[140] In this respect less about imagining strange possible futures than becoming estranged from the knowledge that constitutes the actual present, *Learning Processes with a Deadly Outcome* sends up in the year 1973 the formal conditions for actual learning processes about present-day abstractions. To be erected upon imagined experiences of future fictional catastrophes (rooted in actual historical disasters like the Battle of Stalingrad), the imminent learning processes inscribed within the shards that make up Kluge's story ultimately anticipate the timely acquisition of knowledge about the will to knowledge necessary for recognizing and possibly steering clear of catastrophes like the Black War in the near future, namely our present. Alas, *Learning Processes with A Deadly Outcome* is merely a set of interrelated vignettes. It is neither any such consciousness nor the concomitant action necessary for undoing misery. Nor does it accomplish the necessary organizational work for deriving collective learning processes out of individual ones. To speak of the potential for happier learning processes in the future is to speak (borrowing an idea from Fredric Jameson) merely of an utopian formalism: the very best form for nurturing critical intelligence but also a formal non-place for such thought, for the fantasy inscribed into a text's gaps can transpire only along the circuitous yet imperceptible pathways of the brain's dark matter.[141] For Kluge, this formalism laid down in his first literary foray into science fiction is neither exclusive to his attempt at this genre nor the medium of literature. By extrapolating the baroque *Trauerspiel*'s penchant for estranging the authority of profane knowledge, Kluge's science fiction has in fact embedded itself in practically all of his work in literature, film, and television. This becomes especially apparent when we recognize that the drive behind Kluge's science fiction, on the one hand, for an alienation of instrumental knowledge and, on the other hand, for the acquisition of critical knowledge about the abstract conditions of alienation that can ideally be put to use against the concept of progress as catastrophe. That Negt and Kluge together cultivate their theory of learning processes not only on the aborted idea of interests taken from second-wave critical theory but also on claims rooted in the human sciences should, in closing, not suggest that their practical theory of critical intelligence props itself up on a facile working contradiction.

---

140 Suvin 4ff; see also Fredric Jameson, *Archaeologies of the Future: The Desire Called Utopia and Other Science Fictions* (London: Verso, 2005) xiii.

141 Jameson, *Archaeologies of the Future*, xiii.

Neither strict adherents of a scientific realism à la Friedrich Engels or Vladimir Lenin (whose naturalism insists on an a priori objective world) nor diehard anthropocentrists à la Kant (whose idealism places the empire of the mind over matter), Negt and Kluge belong to those who have sought a viable middle road. Their pedagogical model sidesteps the epistemological dilemma of the chicken or egg by affirming both: learning processes themselves entail dynamic subjective-objective relations. The propositions of science answer for the processes of creative activity just as much as these aesthetically anticipated processes unseat science's authority over nature by generating with its gaps, islands, and platforms a critical knowledge about the lacuna and aporia of technical intelligence.

Figures 2.1–2.4. The epochs of the hand's decline: manipulative action, the hand as motor, machine operators, the computer programmer. From top to bottom: *Yesterday Girl*

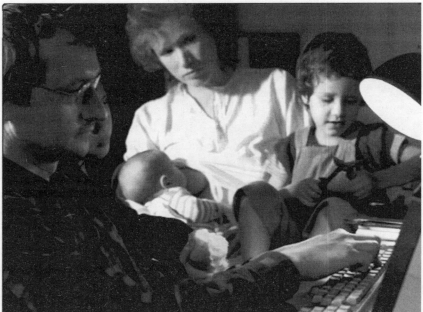

(1966); *The Patriot* (1979); *Part-Time Work of a Domestic Slave* (1973); and *The Assault of the Present on the Rest of Time* (1985). © Alexander Kluge.

2

Toward a Dialectical Anthropology: Labor, Technology, Time

The Part Played by Hands

What ever happened to work?

When attentive spectators scan Alexander Kluge's feature films long enough, they eventually see hands everywhere: Hands under oath. Hands on stage. Hands wielding tools. Hands at work screwing, balancing, cutting, and counting. Scientific and medical hands. Hands folded in prayer. Hands committing crimes. Pieces of a puzzle as it were, Kluge's many hands, when assembled together like a storyboard, tell us what appears at first glance to be a sad story about the decline of human labor, a latent substratum propping up all the many manifest stories populating his fourteen feature films. To be sure, Kluge's sustained interest in the human hand is not the first of its kind. According to the long evolutionary perspective of paleoanthropology, for example, the story of the human hand began some 4 million years ago when hominids started standing upright. No longer encumbered by the drudgery of quadrupedal locomotion, their hands discovered unprecedented freedoms of movement, practical and symbolic gestures that became crucial for their survival and further evolution. The first in a series of future liberations, this freedom, when tracked down in our modern age, has paradoxically evolved into a liberation of the hand from labor altogether, a liberation, as some thinkers would have it, from the very essence of humankind.

Much like this long-range perspective, Kluge's allusion to this story of decline—its traces are found throughout the entirety of his cinematic, literary, and televisual oeuvres—can be told in four simple stages: In the earliest chapter shared with our primate relatives, hands developed complex gestures necessary for grasping and touching, picking and kneading, peeling and tearing, scratching and digging. The decisive break in human evolution emerged in the subsequent prehistoric phase when the human hand—the ever-skillful servant of human technical intelligence, according to French anthropologist André Leroi-Gourhan—augmented these elementary gestures by extending itself outward onto tools.[1] Instead of trying to pry nuts open with their own fingers, as the itinerate protagonist Anita G. in *Yesterday Girl* (1966) is wont to do (fig. 2.1), hominids devised simple equipment out of wood or stone with which to crush and hammer, dig and scrape, cut and pierce (fig. 2.2). We see schoolteacher Gabi Teichert do this when she takes hammers, sickles, and drills to history books in *The Patriot* (1979). The next decisive evo-lutionary stage entailed displacing the hand's immediate motor function typical of hand-tool aggregates onto tools themselves. With the dawn of historical time, the hand's indirect motor function shifted further away from the body in order to harness the power of animals, wind, and water. As of the age of steam, any remaining motor function in the hand was relegated to machines lacking nervous systems that nevertheless required minimal involvement of the hands either to feed or stop them. Standing around an open hearth, steel workers merely watch in *Part-Time Work of a Domestic Slave* (1973) as a motor lowers a massive crane into the furnace (fig. 2.3). What Leroi-Gourhan calls both the "peak of human history" and the twilight of man, the final stage—our present age—is a synthesis of all preceding stages.[2] Centuries after the first automatons were realized by medieval clockmakers, electronic innovations have mimicked living matter by integrating artificial nervous systems into semi-conscious machines. Along with the exteriorization of the brain, our stage of technical evolution has witnessed a further regression of the hand. Once a tool for hammering and cracking, hands now merely press buttons in order to initiate autonomous pre-programmed processes, something we see in the tableau of the Burk family in *The Assault of the Present on the Rest of Time* (1985) (fig. 2.4).

Contrary to the late Friedrich Engels's Darwin-inspired pronouncement

1 André Leroi-Gourhan, *Gesture and Speech*, trans. Anna Bostock Berger (Cambridge, MA: MIT Press, 1993) 255.

2 Leroi-Gourhan 249, 248.

claiming the hand as "the organ [and] *the product of labor,*" Kluge's allusions to the stages of decline of the hand call into question triumphant Marxian narratives of human evolution in which the human hand was considered to have been worked into physiological perfection.[3] If the hand is indeed *the* organ of labor, then does not its accelerated obsolescence in such a short span of time evince the vanishing of labor in the life of the species? The decline of labor in the modern era is certainly not a new story. By the close of their American exile, Frankfurt School elders like Max Horkheimer and Theodor W. Adorno were long convinced that the "submissive" industrial working class was incapable of ever realizing itself as a historical actor for social change; the communal experience of alienated machine labor merely drove the proletariat to craft itself tirelessly and counter-intuitively into the compliant "ideal type of *homo oeconomicus.*"[4] In later decades marked by unprecedented scientific-technical automation, new Marxian narratives about the shifting of work and the emergence of attendant knowledge-based and managerial occupations came to the fore, occupations that like those of the "old working class" saw themselves as the new antagonists in the ongoing battle against capital.[5] With the rise of post-industrial, post-Taylorist, and post-Fordist societies, post-Marxist theoreticians have struck—in light of the further waning of manufacturing and waxing of an information economy—a more conciliatory tone, assuring us that technology and science would rescue people from drudgery altogether.[6] Flying under the banner of a new hybrid communism, Michael Hardt and Antonio Negri have

3 Friedrich Engels, "The Part Played by Labour in the Transition from Ape to Man," *Dialectics of Nature*, in Karl Marx and Friedrich Engels, *Collected Works*, vol. 25: *Friedrich Engels: Anti-Dühring, Dialectics of Nature* (New York: International Publishers, 1987) 453.

4 Max Horkheimer and Theodor W. Adorno, *Dialectic of Enlightenment: Philosophical Fragments*, ed. Gunzelin Schmid Noerr, trans. Edmund Jephcott (Stanford, CA: Stanford University Press, 2002) 168; see also: Alexander Kluge and Oskar Negt, *History and Obstinacy*, ed. Devin Fore, trans. Richard Langston et al. (New York: Zone Books, 2014) 123.

5 Examples of the so-called new working class thesis include: Herbert Marcuse's *One-Dimensional Man: Studies in the Ideology of Advanced Industrial Society* (Boston: Beacon Press, 1964), André Gorz's *Strategy for Labor: A Radical Proposal*, trans. Martin A. Nicolaus and Victoria Ortiz (Boston: Beacon Press, 1967), and Serge Mallet's *The New Working Class*, trans. Andrée and Bob Shepherd (Nottingham: Bertrand Russell Peace Foundation for Spokesman Books, 1975).

6 In addition to Daniel Bell's *The Coming of Post-Industrial Society: A Venture in Social Forcasting* (New York: Basic Books, 1973), this position is also represented by

most recently reinserted the political back into this latest stage of labor's decline; the immateriality of work in the Information Age, they claim, is a double-edged sword: on the one hand, it marks an advanced stage in the political economy of capital in which capital itself has permeated all life and, on the other, it signals a "capacity" for social cooperation capable of wrestling control away from capital spontaneously.[7]

The silver lining in Hardt and Negri's contemporary account of labor's decay—they write of a potentially propitious, virtual "hybridization of humans and machines"—is absent in the final shot of Kluge's storyboard.[8] We see in the carefully constructed tableau vivant (fig. 2.4) what Kluge along with his collaborator Oskar Negt consider the primal impetus for the initial liberation of the hand—when infants' hands clamored at their mother's breast—alongside hands holding an apple, hands grasping a wrench, and hands operating a computer keyboard. Four stations in a 4-million-year history of human evolution sit side by side, all drawn into the glow and hum of one of the first commercially available microcomputers. Kluge's voice-over—"We bid farewell to the classical age of industrialism. The laborer's hands have become superfluous"— seems to leave little doubt that in this single reckoning with the hands of labor the computer leaves no room for any peaceful coexistence. A fanciful union of human and machine is nowhere to be found. Contrary to these first impressions, however, it would be nothing short of a colossal error to pigeonhole Kluge as a techno-determinist, a Luddite, or even a cultural conservative, especially in light of his recourse to the technologies of cinema in his engagement with the predicament of labor. In fact, it is precisely this glaring contradiction between Kluge's recognition of the disappearance of manual labor and his response via the cinematic apparatus that we must consider further if we are to grasp the singularity of his and Negt's contribution to a political economy of labor power.

A political economy of labor, Kluge and Negt explain in *History and Obstinacy*, would be nothing less than the antipode to Karl Marx's

---

Michael J. Poire and Charles F. Sabel's *The Second Industrial Divide: Possibilities for Prosperity* (New York: Basic Books, 1984).

7 Michael Hardt and Antonio Negri, *Empire* (Cambridge, MA: Harvard University Press, 2000) 365–67, 294. On the convergences and distinctions with Negt and Kluge's work, see: Richard Langston, "Palimpsests of '68: Theorizing Labor after Adorno," in *The Long 1968: Revisions and New Perspectives*, eds. Daniel J. Sherman et al. (Bloomington: Indiana University Press, 2013) 49–72.

8 Hardt and Negri 367.

exhaustive critique of the political economy of capital.[9] Immanent to
Marx's critique is that other political economy of labor that never fully
materialized in his thinking. Its absence, Kluge and Negt add, explains
why Marx never penned a political theory of equal profundity. Far from
compensating for this lack themselves, they make clear in this second
installment to their theory trilogy that their intentions—in spite of its
original outward resemblance to the original German edition of Marx
and Engels's collected works—are far more modest. For a political
economy of labor to be capable of constituting the "basis for resistance" to capital, there first needs to be an account of what constitutes
not labor, per se, but rather the select labor capacities (*Arbeitsvermögen*)
culled from labor power (*Arbeitskraft*) that capital valorizes.[10] And, for
this, we require an understanding of human nature where labor power
resides and from which historical capacities are extracted. It is this backward march into the anthropological terrain championed by the young
humanist Marx that Negt and Kluge bring into dialogue with the mature
scientistic Marx in what is actually their preamble to a political economy
of labor. "A lot of what we say," Negt confessed decades later, "sounds
anthropological," and for the simple reason that to determine "how
people react to" capitalism, they explained decades earlier, presupposes
a "theory of the human being."[11] Nevertheless, Negt was unmistakable
when he insisted shortly after the debut of *Geschichte und Eigensinn* that
their theory of labor power is certainly "not historical, not sociological, [and] not anthropological."[12] Negt's preference for the generic label
"philosophical thinking" notwithstanding, this chapter lingers on the
curious anthropological quotient operating in their political economy
of labor power not merely on account of its unlikely inclusion in a work
whose Frankfurt School pedigree bestowed little merit on anthropology
let alone its philosophical variant. That Negt and Kluge tackle the question of the human being by inadvertently converging on the thought of
philosopher Hans Blumenberg, whose phenomenologically oriented

---

9 Kluge and Negt 50.

10 Eberhard Knödler-Bunte, Hajo Funke, and Arno Widmann, "The History of
Living Labor Power: A Discussion with Oskar Negt and Alexander Kluge," trans. Fiona
Elliott, *October* 149 (Summer 2014): 42.

11 Christian Schulte and Rainer Stollmann, "Moles Don't Use Systems: A Conversation with Oskar Negt," trans. Fiona Elliott, *October* 149 (Summer 2014): 70; Knödler-Bunte
et al., "The History of Living Labor Power," 39.

12 Knödler-Bunte et al. 68.

philosophical anthropology is miles removed from Marxian concerns of labor, commands attention for just how far their historically and geographically contextualized theory of labor is willing to venture forth. Without ever realizing their proximity to this unlikely bedfellow, they nevertheless refrain from approximating Blumenberg's ocularcentric project entirely by emphasizing embodied experience that precedes not just signification but reasoned thought as well. Nowhere does this difference better come to light than quite literally in Kluge's cinema, where we shall see technology's telos traveling in reverse. Rather than contributing to the further demise of manual labor, technology mediates the times and spaces where labor power flourishes beyond the demands of capital.

The Legacy of Negative Anthropology

The problem of anthropology for the Frankfurt School is anything but new with its appearance in Negt and Kluge's work. In fact, it was none other than Max Horkheimer who, in his capacity as the second enterprising director of Frankfurt's Institute for Social Research, set the tone for critical theory's relationship to philosophical anthropology. Echoing Georg Lukács's critique from a decade earlier, Horkheimer took aim in his 1935 essay "Remarks on Philosophical Anthropology" at philosophical anthropologist Max Scheler by contending that any social scientific discipline like his, intent on determining the "basic structure of human existence," is impossible.[13] "There is no formula," Horkheimer declared, "that defines the relationship among individuals, society, and nature for all time."[14] Such an endeavor rooted in absolute principles not only disregards the "dialectical character of historical events," but also ignores the fact that "human characteristics are inextricably linked to the course of history, and history itself is in no way marked by a uniform will."[15] In

---

13 Cf. Georg Lukács, "Reification and the Consciousness of the Proletariat," in *History and Class Consciousness: Studies in Marxist Dialectics*, trans. Rodney Livingstone (Cambridge, MA: MIT Press, 1997) 186: "By transforming philosophy into 'anthropology' [Ludwig Feuerbach] caused man to become frozen."

14 Max Horkheimer, "Remarks on Philosophical Anthropology," in *Between Philosophy and Social Science: Selected Early Writings Studies in Contemporary German Social Thought*, trans. G. Frederick Hunter, Matthew S. Kramer, and John Torpey (Cambridge, MA: MIT Press, 1993) 153.

15 Horkheimer 174.

spite of this overall dismissal of Scheler, Horkheimer did grant anthropology a limited degree of legitimacy: like Horkheimer's own dialectical theory of history, philosophical anthropology holds in high regard the importance of its own historically astute self-consciousness, and yet the relevance of its attention to matters of praxis falls woefully short. "The project of modern philosophical anthropology," he summarized, "consists in finding a norm that will provide meaning to an individual's life in the world as it currently exists."[16] But, in its pursuit of norms, it loses track of the historical vicissitudes of society and thus a handle on the real prize: an answer to the "anthropological question par excellence: … how can we overcome an inhumane reality?"[17] Referring tacitly to his own program, Horkheimer argues that a "theory free from illusions can only conceive of human purpose negatively, and reveals the inherent contradiction between the conditions of existence and everything that the great philosophies have postulated as a purpose."[18] And, to this end, a dialectical theory must grant possible "the notion of social life as a willful product of collective individual labor" according to "[human beings'] changing needs and desires."[19] Such a negative anthropology would need to investigate, on the one hand, the overwhelming presence of misery, suffering, and unhappiness that obscure processes of production and reproduction generate. On the other hand, it is also obliged to recognize that yearning for happiness, too, persists throughout human history and would be found in the reconciliation of ever-changing needs and life. In a word, negative anthropology would be pointless if it foreclosed at least the possibility of a positive anthropology.[20]

Horkheimer's assessment of philosophical anthropology was no fluke, for he remained steadfast well after his retirement as director of the Institute for Social Research in his call to go beyond Scheler's shortcomings

---

16 Horkheimer 155–56.

17 Horkheimer 160.

18 Horkheimer 156–57; see also Dennis Johannssen, "Toward a Negative Anthropology: Critical Theory's Altercations with Philosophical Anthropology," *Anthropology and Materialism* 1 (2013): 3.

19 Horkheimer 155.

20 Vestiges of this positive anthropology manifest themselves in the very first aphorism from Horkheimer's 1934 collection of aphorisms entitled *Dawn, Notes 1926–1931*: "The dusk of capitalism [does not] have to usher in the night of mankind." See: Max Horkheimer, *Dawn and Decline: Notes 1926–1931 and 1950–1969*, trans. Michael Shaw (New York: Seabury Press, 1978) 17.

by tracking the countervailing "influence of society and individual on each other."[21] However, in the intervening years, room for a positive anthropology diminished appreciably. It was in his fragmentary notes and sketches to *Dialectic of Enlightenment* penned together with Adorno where the pendulum swung negative. Penned exclusively by Horkheimer as early as 1939 but only intermittently commented on by Adorno, the concluding aphorisms "in part deal provisionally with problems of future work," they explain in the 1944 preface. "Most of them relate to a dialectical anthropology."[22] On such topics as stupidity, the living's disturbed relationship to the dead, isolation caused by communication media, and humans' love-hate for their bodies, this dialectical anthropology concerns itself with what Horkheimer saw as a new concept: "the rise of an 'anthropological' species we call the authoritarian type."[23] Although their promised anthropological follow-up to *Dialectic of Enlightenment* never appeared, Adorno did carry on both in form and content a "negative anthropology of mass society" of his own in *Minima Moralia*, his gift to Horkheimer on the occasion of his fiftieth birthday in 1945.[24] Far more explicit than in their collaboration, Adorno minced few if any words with regard to the etiology of this new species of man: "The metamorphosis of labor-power into a commodity has permeated men through and through and objectified each of their impulses." The effect of capitalism's division of labor is nothing less than catastrophic, he goes on to explain: "The will to live finds itself dependent on the denial of the will to live: self-preservation annuls all life in subjectivity."[25] In this respect, Adorno's and, by extension, Horkheimer's negative anthropology are indeed ones devoid of *anthropos*.[26] Capital's hollowing out of humankind finally brought Adorno, in his 1966 *Negative Dialectics*, to decree once and for all, "We cannot say what man is."

---

21 Max Horkheimer, "The Concept of Man," in *Critique of Instrumental Reason*, trans. Matthew J. O'Connell (London: Verso, 2012) 7; cf. Johannssen 4.

22 Horkheimer and Adorno xix.

23 Max Horkheimer, preface to *The Authoritarian Personality*, T.W. Adorno et al. (New York: Harper, 1950) ix.

24 Theodor W. Adorno, *Minima Moralia: Reflections on a Damaged Life*, trans. E.F.N. Jephcott (London: Verso, 2005) 167.

25 Adorno, *Minima Moralia*, 229.

26 Stefan Breuer, "Adorno's Anthropology," in *The Frankfurt School: Critical Assessments*, ed. Jay Bernstein, vol. 3: *Section 4: Theodor Adorno* (New York, NY: Routledge, 1994) 128.

Man today is a function, unfree, regressing behind whatever is ascribed to him as invariant—except perhaps for the defenselessness and neediness in which some anthropologies wallow. He drags along with him as his social heritage the mutilations inflicted upon him over thousands of years. To decipher the human essence by the way it is now would sabotage its possibility.[27]

Any anthropology that tries to account for humankind using abstract concepts would inevitably fail to grasp the actual devastating conditions of its dehumanization and desubjectivization under capital. The question "What is man?" was to remain, for Adorno, a programmatic lacuna.

Anthropology's status was anything but settled in West Germany in both the stormy times preceding Adorno's death in August 1969 as well as those following in his wake. Whereas some of Adorno's earliest Frankfurt pupils sought to correct what they saw then as a Western European tendency in the fifties to reduce Marx to his early flirtation with Ludwig Feuerbach's anthropological materialism, a confluence of other international voices intent on synthesizing biological, ethnological, and sociological questions brought others to herald an anthropological renaissance over the course of the sixties.[28] By the time the New Left reached its early utopian phase, calls for a "new anthropology" as well as the creation of a "new man" quickly elicited indictments of their astonishing proximity to older conservative anthropologies like Arnold Gehlen's.[29] Rescue operations like, for example, Ulrich Sonnemann's edict against any and all positive Freudo-Marxian anthropologies or Wolf Lepenies and Helmut Nolte's case for anthropological experimentalism focused on transforming social structures sought to ward off definitive pronouncements in the name of defending man as an

---

27 Theodor W. Adorno, *Negative Dialectics*, trans. E.B. Ashton (New York: Continuum, 1983) 124.

28 See Alfred Schmidt, *The Concept of Nature in Marx*, trans. Ben Fowkes (London: New Left Books, 1971) 9; Wolf Lepenies, *Soziologische Anthropologie: Materialien* (Munich: Carl Hanser Verlag, 1971) 3. The culmination of this renaissance is certainly Hans-Georg Gadamer and Paul Vogler's seven-volume anthology that addresses biological, social, cultural, psychological and philosophical anthropologies; see: *Neue Anthropologie*, 7 vols. (Stuttgart: Georg Thieme Verlag, 1972–74).

29 Cf. Herbert Marcuse, "The End of Utopia," trans. Jermey Shapiro and Shierry M. Weber, in *Marxism, Revolution and Utopia*, eds. Douglas Kellner and Clayton Pierce (London: Routledge, 2014) 255; Lepenies 120–22.

inexhaustible possibility.[30] The pull of philosophical anthropology was, however, not limited to the fleeting spirit of the student revolts. Born out of his involvement in the positivist dispute between Adorno and Karl Popper as well as his long-standing critical engagement with Gehlen, the first steps toward Jürgen Habermas's theory of communicative action were made in the form of his anthropology of knowledge based in part on American pragmatism.[31] Influenced by the new social movements of the seventies, Axel Honneth along with Hans Joas forged an alternative to Habermas, one erected on Feuerbach's anthropological premises that eventually evolved into Honneth's signature theory of intersubjectivity as recognition.[32] It was at this juncture, in the early eighties, when the utility of both the anthropological young Marx and the economic mature Marx fell into unprecedented disrepair, when Negt and Kluge delivered their own knowingly belated contribution to unresolved anthropological issues from the West German student movement and did so while retaining both halves of Marx's oeuvre. But the story told by all the many hands in Kluge's films, though it recalls Horkheimer when he called for tracing "[the atrophying] of human powers" backward to the renaissance and beyond, cannot be reconstructed from just Horkheimer's, let alone Marx's, writings.[33] In *Capital*, Marx does indeed say that the relations of production turn the head and the hand, once a unified team, into "deadly foes."[34] And Horkheimer, too, demands that dialectical anthropology "overcom[e] the conflict between an advanced form of rational thought and blind reproduction of social life."[35] However, what remains outstanding in Negt and Kluge's eyes is a "a concept of human labor in which head and mind cooperate."[36]

---

30 Ulrich Sonnemann, *Negative Anthropologie: Vorstudien zur Sabotage des Schicksals* (Reinbek bei Hamburg, 1969) 322; Lepenies 126.

31 Axel Honneth, "Habermas' Anthropology of Knowledge: The Theory of Knowledge-Constitutive Interests," in *The Critique of Power: Reflective Stages in a Critical Social Theory*, trans. Kenneth Baynes (Cambridge, MA: MIT Press, 1991) 203–39.

32 See Axel Honneth and Hans Joas, *Social Action and Human Nature*, trans. Raymond Meyer (Cambridge: Cambridge University Press, 1988).

33 Horkheimer, "Remarks on Philosophical Anthropology," 157.

34 Karl Marx, *Capital: Volume 1*, trans. Ben Fowkes, in Karl Marx and Friedrich Engels, *Collected Works*, vol. 35 (London: Lawrence and Wishart, 1996) 509.

35 Horkheimer, "Remarks on Philosophical Anthropology," 154. Translation slightly changed according to the original essay. See: "Bemerkungen zur philosophischen Anthropologie," *Zeitschrift für Sozialforschung* 4 (1935): 4.

36 Alexander Kluge, "The Role of Fantasy," trans. Rory Bradley, in *Difference and*

Marauding Myths versus Brooding
Fairy Tales: The House as Cave

Kluge's gratitude to his "chief rabbis"—above all "Benjamin, Adorno, Bloch, Marx"—is certainly no secret.[37] Although Negt recognizes Kant and Marx as the "alpha and omega" of his thinking, he also counts ancients (Aristotle and Plato) as well as sundry moderns (like Hegel and Habermas, to name but a few) as essential interlocutors for the patchwork that is their "collaborative philosophy."[38] One philosopher nowhere to be found, neither in their countless footnotes nor in any of their many unidentified quotations, someone whose pedigree clashes outright with many of these chief rabbis but whose primary concerns nevertheless seem to course through the very fabric of Negt and Kluge's philosophical collaborations is Hans Blumenberg. There are compelling reasons to make a claim for Blumenberg's place, not necessarily within but alongside Negt and Kluge's theory. Contrary to, for example, Fredric Jameson's method of allegorical transcoding that seeks resemblances between heterogeneous theoretical codes, bringing Blumenberg and Negt and Kluge into dialogue does much more than unveil a "hidden master narrative," one of the meta-critic's own making.[39] And, instead of framing the "convergences" and "parallels" between these three thinkers as a lasting intergenerational consequence of the willful refusal to engage in philosophical dialogue—a refusal that marked Blumenberg's deep-seated contempt for Negt and Kluge's teacher and mentor Adorno—we shall see, rather, that the space where Negt and Kluge meet Blumenberg actually illuminates their own otherwise oblique departure from Adorno's philosophical method by accommodating some of the very philosophical territory—in particular, phenomenology and anthropology—that Adorno abhorred. This shift shall additionally cut a path between the doom and gloom of Horkheimer's own case for eclipsed reason and

---

Orientation: An Alexander Kluge Reader, ed. Richard Langston (Ithaca, NY: Cornell University Press, 2019) 340.

37 Alexander Kluge, *Macht der Gefühle* (Frankfurt am Main: Zweitausendeins, 1984) 178.

38 Oskar Negt, *Kant und Marx: Ein Epochengespräch* (Göttingen: Steidl, 2003); and Richard Langston, "'Das ist die umgekehrte Flaschenpost': Ein montiertes Interview mit Oskar Negt und Alexander Kluge," *Alexander-Kluge Jahrbuch* 2 (2015): 51.

39 Fredric Jameson, *The Political Unconscious* (Ithaca, NY: Cornell University Press, 1981) 28.

their peer Habermas's promise of communicative rationality.[40] Employing Blumenberg as an optic with which to magnify and sharpen our view onto this shift seeks not so much to dislodge Negt and Kluge from their Frankfurt School roots, but rather to demonstrate one of many instances whereby they strive to think along the neutral point between philosophical traditions that in this particular instance ultimately delineates another kind of reason, one that is neither instrumental nor communicative, one that Blumenberg regards as essential for the "self preservation" of the species, but that Negt and Kluge regard as located elsewhere other than the abstractions of the mind.[41]

Announced already in the fall of 1979 to be the penultimate installment to precede the concluding one-thousandth title in Siegfried Unseld's prestigious edition Suhrkamp series, Negt and Kluge's advertised book *Deutschland: Geschichte einer Produktivkraft* [Germany: The History of a Productive Force] never appeared. In light of differences over where to publish their gigantic book of fragments full of footnotes and illustrations, the authors claimed to set their sights not high but low, and in lieu of Suhrkamp settled on Zweitausendeins, a young leftist press with a reputation for illustrator Franz Greno's bold text/image experimentation.[42] After telegrammed threats and conciliatory phone calls, Kluge promised Suhrkamp in two to three years time a definitive multivolume "text version" (*Textfassung*) of what would appear in March 1981 as the three-part, single-volume *Geschichte und Eigensinn*.[43] As we now know, Kluge never made good on that promise; after waiting four years, Unseld finally gave slot 999 away. Prior to Suhrkamp's slightly revised 1993 reissue of *Geschichte und Eigensinn* in three discrete paperback volumes—a publishing event precipitated by the fall of the Wall, Chernobyl, and the Gulf War—the only piece of *Geschichte und Eigensinn* that the publisher ever got its hands on was the sixth commentary that concludes book 2

40 Christian Voller, "Kommunikation verweigert: Schwierige Beziehungen zwischen Blumenberg und Adorno," *Technik: Zeitschrift für Kulturphilosophie* 2 (2013): 381–405.

41 Hans Blumenberg, *Beschreibung des Menschen*, ed. Manfred Sommer (Frankfurt am Main: Suhrkamp, 2006) 47; Franz J. Wetz, "The Phenomenological Anthropology of Hans Blumenberg," *Iris: European Journal of Philosophy and Public Debate* 1.2 (October 2009): 405–6.

42 Marion Janzin and Joachim Günter, *Das Buch vom Buch: 5000 Jahre Buchgeschichte* (Hanover: Schlüterische, 2006) 437.

43 Siegfried Unseld, internal correspondence, November 13, 1980, Siegfried Unseld Archiv, Deutsches Literaturarchiv Marbach.

on "Germany as a Public Sphere of Production." Originally included in Habermas's 1979 anthology *Stichworte: Zur »geistigen Situation der Zeit«* —number 1000 in Suhrkamp's "es series"—Negt and Kluge's commentary "The Ancient Naval Hero as Metaphor for the Enlightenment" counts along with the other contributions as a critical reckoning with Adorno's theoretical legacy over the course of the seventies.[44]

"If we shift our attention within the realm of ancient myths," Kluge and Negt write at the outset of their commentary, "a constellation reveals itself," namely that of "human victims ... who suffer under the enterprising, enlightened grip of others."[45] Kluge and Negt's shift away from Horkheimer and Adorno's focus on the seafaring Odysseus as the "prototype" of the cunning bourgeois subject is but only the first of two steps in their argument.[46] "We Germans were never oarsmen on the Mediterranean Sea," they underscore later in book 3. "Instead, we are the colonizers of the Behemoth, the monster of the countryside."[47] In other words, the victims who perished under Odysseus and even more so under Jason of the Argonauts are literally forgotten in the wake of these mobile rogues for whom there are no equivalents in the long history of central European experience. There are two factors, say Kluge and Negt, that explain why what Horkheimer and Adorno associate with "the cultural fascist's attitude to Homer" is, in fact, an incomplete, if not altogether incongruous, account of the sematic chain "myth"-"mendacity"- "fascism"-"enlightenment" that stands for landlocked central European cultural history.[48] If we are to expand the realm of myth to bring into view fascism's victims, then we must firstly see "*the dimension of production* ... [as] *the defining moment*" and, secondly, call to mind that

---

44 See Jürgen Habermas's two-volume anthology, in which Negt and Kluge's essay on fairy tales was first published (with a slightly altered title and without images): Oskar Negt and Alexander Kluge, "Der antike Seehald als Metapher der Aufklärung; die deutschen Grübelgegenbilder: Aufklärung als Verschanzung; 'Eigensinn,'" in *Stichworte zur »Geistigen Situation der Zeit«*, vol. 1: *Nation und Republik*, ed. Jürgen Habermas (Frankfurt am Main: Suhrkamp Verlag, 1979) 35–163. Negt and Kluge's commentary was dropped for the English-language translation of *Stichworte* (*Observations on "The Spiritual Situation of the Age": Contemporary German Perspectives*) that appeared with MIT Press in 1984.

45 Kluge and Negt 268.

46 Horkheimer and Adorno 35.

47 Oskar Negt and Alexander Kluge, *Geschichte und Eigensinn*, in *Der unterschätzte Mensch: Gemeinsame Philosophie in zwei Bänden*, vol. 2 (Frankfurt am Main: Zweitausendeins, 2001) 1004.

48 Horkheimer and Adorno 37.

"a house, farm, and field cannot escape danger like a ship."[49] These two factors, they go on to say, are inextricably intertwined: economic production, they underscore, is "entrenched in houses"; it is what "resists interpretation when projected onto antiquity."[50] It is this inapplicability of the ancients as seen through the eyes of their modern interpreters that brings Kluge and Negt to devote so much time to houses throughout *History and Obstinacy*.

In an excursus entitled "On Houses" from chapter 5 of *History and Obstinacy*, on the historical character of German labor capacities, Kluge and Negt write: "The seat of the economy—what both the hand and the head do—is the house. It is neither the ship nor the river (as is the case with seafaring peoples), but rather the house and the home, along with the people who live in them."[51] Of concern is the historical transformation of the house, its premodern status as a primary site of production that later morphed over time: "If the home was earlier a sphere of production unto itself, later it became, above all, a place of defense, fortification, and community withdrawn into the home's interiority."[52] After tracing both the long etymology and just some of the many semantic fields for the German word *Haus*, they then contend: "The body has the same basic form as a house." "The original system for maintaining boundaries is one's own body. I experience borders by what I let out of my insides and what I put into them."[53] This shift from house to body midway through *History and Obstinacy* is, of course, a reversal of how Kluge and Negt plot out their case for a political economy of labor power. Their very first mention of houses in book 1, a quotation from Marx's *Eighteenth Brumaire*, rings not historical but rather metaphorical: "Windows are to a house what the five senses are to the head."[54] Whereas Marx's maxim was originally meant to describe how the windowless hovels that some 16 million French peasants called home denied them adequate access to the outside world, thus turning them into "troglodytes," the clean geometry of the analogy comes undone in Kluge and Negt's hands. Deployed in

49 Horkheimer and Adorno 36, 37; Kluge and Negt 278.
50 Kluge and Negt 280.
51 Kluge and Negt 229.
52 Kluge and Negt 230.
53 Kluge and Negt 230.
54 Karl Marx, "The Eighteenth Brumaire of Louis Bonaparte," in Karl Marx and Friedrich Engels, *Collected Works*, vol. 11: *Marx and Engels: 1851–1853* (London: Lawrence and Wishart, 1979) 190.

History and Obstinacy as a caption for a photograph of a large house with thirteen shadeless windows (fig. 2.5), Marx's maxim is qualified when Kluge and Negt add, "Here: eyes without eyelids," as if to suggest the exact inverse: in other words, nothing on the house's façade prevents too much outside from inundating what dwells inside.[55] On the recto, a boy stands with eyes closed holding a goody bag on his first day of school. Addressing the Marx quote on the verso, this second photograph's caption reads: "This is an important moment. For this reason the eyes are shut" (fig. 2.6).[56] Through twin illustrations denoting a vital distinction between essential human characteristics (exemplified by the obstinate boy on the recto) and "the social organs constructed on top of them" (the defenseless house on the verso), Kluge and Negt complicate Marx's analogy in twofold fashion.[57] Firstly, industrial capital deprived the collective senses according to Marx, whereas modern capital now stands to flood them entirely. Secondly, houses may be like people, but people are not always like houses; in exceptional moments, the only adequate response is to do what this house cannot, namely to shut one's eyes, to double down on the threshold between inside and outside.

Arguably, Kluge and Negt's most conspicuous allusion to the language and thought of Hans Blumenberg can be found in yet another excursus from the same chapter, one in which they defend their appropriation of language taken from materials physics in order to describe the mixed set of relations subtending all historical experience.

> The word *aggregate states* comes from physics. It describes phenomena (solid, fluid, gassy, plasmic) that have their basis in the various speeds and paths of motion … common among the elements … We use the term [*aggregate states*] as an analogy. Analogies are, in principle, clumsy. They are dictated by the very lack of concepts.[58]

This account of the deficit in conceptual thought is precisely why Blumenberg advances his own program for a metaphorology, an effort that originally sought to expand conceptual history to include the "conceptually irredeemable expressive function" of what he calls "absolute

---

55 Kluge and Negt 100.
56 Kluge and Negt 101.
57 Kluge and Negt 98.
58 Kluge and Negt 672–73.

Figure 2.5. "'And windows are to a house what the five senses are to the head.' Here: eyes without eyelids." (Alexander Kluge and Oskar Negt, *History and Obstinacy*, p. 100). © Alexander Kluge.

Figure 2.6. "'This is an important moment. For this reason the eyes are shut.'" (Alexander Kluge and Oskar Negt, *History and Obstinacy*, p. 101). © Alexander Kluge.

metaphor."[59] We need not yet turn to third parties like, say, Ernst Bloch, for whom metaphor fuels the ambiguity of allegory, or even to Jacques Derrida, who considers analogy "metaphor par excellence" in order to size up if not square altogether Kluge and Negt's penchant for figurative speech with what later blossomed into Blumenberg's theory of nonconceptuality and then outlines for a phenomenological anthropology.[60] Instead, let us turn to that place where Negt and Kluge and Blumenberg could have met one another, namely in the cave.

Addressing the inherent tension between the need for identity, on the one hand, and the expropriation endemic to capital's primitive accumulation, on the other, Kluge and Negt write: "There is a need for primitive property. For example, I need a place where I can stand, someplace to retreat, where I can find shelter, a house or a cave (*ein Haus oder eine Höhle*). Again, this must have a certain breadth and egresses (*eine gewisse Weite und Ausgänge*)."[61] This need for a refuge, one with both elbowroom within it *and* ways out into the world, thereby allowing, in their words, for "an abundance of possibilities for *movement*" frames, for Blumenberg, the foundational dilemma of the cave.[62] "The dilemma of the cave," he explains in his last magisterial monograph published within his lifetime—*Höhlenausgänge* [Ways Out of the Cave]—"is that within it life is indeed lived out but the sources of livelihood therein are nowhere to be found."[63] It is this quandary of leaving the cave only then to return to it, played out in countless iterations throughout the history of human experience—from the interiority of the subject to the actual hearth and home, from the urban grid to the spheres of culture, from the material body to the starry firmament—that opens up onto the paradoxical realm of myth and absolute metaphors where the central place the cave occupies—a "'twilight zone' between mythos and logos"—comes into view.[64] It is the

---

59 Hans Blumenberg, *Paradigms for a Metaphorology*, trans. Robert Savage (Ithaca, NY: Cornell University Press, 2010) 3.

60 Ernst Bloch, *Tübinger Einleitung in die Philosophie* (Frankfurt am Main: Büchergilde Gutenberg, 1986) 339: "The allegorical always passes itself around metaphorically again and again"; Jacques Derrida, "White Mythology: Metaphor in the Text of Philosophy," trans. F.C.T. Moore, *New Literary History* 6.1 (Autumn 1974): 42.

61 Kluge and Negt 235.

62 Kluge and Negt 502n22.

63 Hans Blumenberg, *Höhlenausgänge* (Frankfurt am Main: Suhrkamp, 1989) 29.

64 Blumenberg, *Paradigms*, 79; Blumenberg, *Höhlenausgänge*, 11. Blumenberg lays the seed for *Höhlenausgänge* already in both his 1957 essay "Light as a Metaphor for Truth: At the Preliminary Stage of Philosophical Concept Formation," trans. Joel

precarious space between inside and outside that speaks directly to Negt and Kluge's central figure of the house in their underlying anthropological inquiry into labor capacity's potential for resisting inhuman reality.

The Cave Imagination

A two-thousand-year reception history of Plato's cave allegory, Blumenberg's *Höhlenausgänge* reads like a theme and variations on his long-standing conviction that the cave myth marks a "primordial event" on top of which strategies for "human self-fulfillment" have been traced again and again.[65] Blumenberg's point of departure calls on the language of both psychoanalysis and anthropology when he writes, "The history of the individual begins with a separation."[66] Projected over into a phylogenetic history, this ontogenetic trauma marking the foundational exit from the darkness of the womb into the lightness of the world also outlines mankind's anthropological predicament: "Man is a visible being in the emphatic sense of the word. He is affected by his visibility on account of the conspicuousness of his upright gait and the defenselessness of his poorly equipped organic body."[67] Building ultimately on Paul Alsberg's account of man's inherent deficiencies, Blumenberg's underlying anthropological thrust—how is the phenomenon of visible man possible at all? —sites the cave in all its many instantiations as that longed-for refuge where invisibility and thus safety can be found from the dangers lurking outside in the world of the savannah, prairie, or jungle—what Blumenberg calls the "absolutism of reality."[68] This persistent dilemma between our expulsion from *the* cave and the longing for protection from *any* number of substitutes, between safety inside and sustenance outside, culminates for Blumenberg in a "culture of care": imaginative techniques

---

Anderson, in *Modernity and the Hegemony of Vision*, ed. David Michael Levin (Berkeley, CA: University of California Press, 1993) 36–40.

65 Blumenberg, *Paradigms*, 79; Pini Ifergan, "Hans Blumenberg: The Cave Project," in *Erinnerung an das Humane: Beiträge zur phänomenologischen Anthropologie Hans Blumenbergs*, ed. Michael Moxter (Tübingen: Mohr Siebeck, 2011) 186.

66 Blumenberg, *Höhlenausgänge*, 20; cf. Negt and Kluge, *Geschichte und Eigensinn*, 29.

67 Blumenberg, *Höhlenausgänge*, 55.

68 Blumenberg, *Beschreibung*, 535; see also: Oliver Müller, "Mensch," in *Blumenberg lesen: Ein Glossar*, eds. Robert Buch and Daniel Weidner (Berlin: Frankfurt am Main, 2014) 188.

for coping that bring what is absent into immediate perception.[69] Only a shift in perspective away from Plato's freed prisoner and therewith the dominant epistemological reading of his allegory—in other words, a phenomenological shift that sides with the perspective of the other chained prisoners—can effectively grasp the techniques (*Technik*) of the "cave imagination" (*Höhlenimagination*) central to a culture of care.[70] Blumenberg asks, if "the chained prisoners could come to an agreement among one another, would they not consider what they see to be reality?"[71] This perception of the cave's shadows as reality points to the contingencies of not just reality but also truth, and brings Blumenberg to assert:

> The cave is in a certain sense indiscernible as much from the inside as it is from the outside ... Whoever thinks he's on the outside must think up of a different inside that would be just as barely perceptible and describable to him as the cave is to those chained inside it who know only its shadows. Whoever describes the cave, does so using categories that cannot be acquired within it; whoever wishes to describe to someone else what counts as its outside and where its exit leads must understand what his listener cannot comprehend.[72]

Rather than fortifying the cave's threshold and therewith relegating himself to an imprisoned existence, the cave dweller suspends perceived differences between inside and outside by dreaming up metaphors and myths with which to render reality less threatening.[73]

The inherent ambivalence of the cave's threshold that Blumenberg underscores is precisely what drives Negt and Kluge's own shift away from Horkheimer and Adorno's attention to the marauding Odysseus, and to the cave-like experiences in the fairy tales collected by the Brothers Grimm. The life-saving power of reflection, rhetoric, and fantasy—in short, the self-preserving reason characteristic of Blumenberg's "culture of care" cultivated out of the cave imagination—finds yet another correspondence in Kluge and Negt's readings, the centerpiece of which—"The

---

69 Blumenberg, *Höhlenausgänge*, 35.

70 Blumenberg, *Höhlenausgänge*, 61; and Hans Blumenberg, "Lebenswelt und Wirklichkeitsbegriff," in *Theorie der Lebenswelt*, ed. Manfred Sommer (Berlin: Suhrkamp, 2010) 162.

71 Blumenberg, "Lebenswelt und Wirklichkeitsbegriff," 162.

72 Blumenberg, *Höhlenausgänge*, 668.

73 Wetz 406–7.

Wolf and the Seven Young Kids" [Der Wolf und die sieben Gießlein]—
makes clear that "the home can never be completely barricaded."[74] The
story of the cunning wolf whose motherly disguise deceives the little
goats into letting their guard down is ultimately about the inherent dif-
ficulty with differentiating the boundaries between inside and outside,
safety and danger, loved ones and foes.[75] "The seven young kids abso-
lutely must let their mother, who brings them food, inside," they insist,
but "conversely, they must keep out the wolf."[76] Crucial for Kluge and
Negt is the fact that the tale's purportedly revolutionary ending—the six
devoured kids reemerge alive from the sleeping wolf's sliced belly—is
not revolutionary at all; no lasting lessons are ever learned from their
traumatic experience. A tale with striking resemblances to Hitler's acts of
deception and violence, they say, "The Wolf and the Seven Young Kids"
underscores not only the "exclusions and omissions" typical of "original experience" but also the ambivalence regarding inside and outside
that no fairy tale is capable of resolving.[77] Related to other ancillary tales
like "Freddy and Katy" [Der Frieder und das Katherlieschen] that follow
their primary analysis—the protagonists unwittingly invite thieves to
their hidden fortune by removing their home's front door—a common
denominator emerges, namely the fairy tale's inability to differentiate.
In Blumenberg's view, what Kluge and Negt identify as the "permanent
doubt at the point of contact between inside and outside" is not the
genre's flaw at all, but rather the very nature of the cave imagination: its
penchant for blurring boundaries translated into narrative form.[78]

   If brooding in the title of Kluge and Negt's excursus indeed harkens
back to that "introverted form of thinking" from German Romanticism intent on probing the depths of the soul, then the counterimages
in which this thinking manifests itself are to be found in those ensuing
ancient and medieval stories in which the soul turns obstinate due to the
experience of a trauma.[79] In contrast to their analysis of the preceding
Grimm's tales full of houses, their subsequent analysis of the enslaved
blacksmith Volund from the Poetic Edda queries the other half of the

---

74 Kluge and Negt 280–82, 285–87.
75 Kluge and Negt 280–81.
76 Kluge and Negt 279.
77 Kluge and Negt 286.
78 Kluge and Negt 287.
79 Burkhard Meyer-Sickendiek, *Tiefe: Über die Faszination des Grübelns* (Munich: Wilhelm Fink, 2010) 13–16, here 14–15.

equation, namely human labor capacities bound to the house and therefore provoked to resist. Enslaved and hamstrung, Volund exacts revenge
on his captor, the robber king Nithuth, by learning to fly away, but not
before seducing the king's daughter (much like the wolf did to the kids)
and then impregnating her such that the king's progeny will be Volund's
own. Fueled by a longing for the happy life he once had, Volund finds a
fantastic way out, but as the next Grimm's tale analyzed—"The Rejuve-
nated Little Old Man"—makes clear, such good fortune is only possible
in principle, but never in the hands of mortal men. If cunning first
associated with the wolf can be used to translate obstinacy into escape,
then so too can obstinacy foil ways out. In a subsequent reading of the
Grimm's tale "Lean Lisa," the hard-working protagonist dreams up an
improbable strike-it-rich ploy that excludes everyone else, including
her equally destitute husband. That one person's obstinacy is indifferent
to the welfare of another let alone the collective good brings Kluge and
Negt to linger on three narrative encapsulations of this unruly characteristic: the Grimm's tale "The Obstinate Child," the story of little Meret
in Gottfried Keller's *Green Henry* (1855), and Sophocles's *Antigone*. On
the basis of this far-reaching evidence, obstinacy, they underscore, is not
a natural human characteristic. Engendered by historical acts of violent
expropriation—capital's primary motive—it lives on well after the death
of an individual in the form of collective memory, but its ontogenetic
force is neither predictable nor a phylogenetic panacea. A consequence
of the ambivalence characteristic of the cave-cum-house, obstinacy
occupies what Kluge and Negt call, borrowing from Adorno's toolbox,
the "temporal core" (*Zeitkern*) of labor's protracted unhappy experience
in landlocked central Europe.[80]

"Fairy tales have a historical core," nineteenth-century French historian Jules Michelet decreed in *La sorcière*, "and it tells of great disasters."[81]
An intertitle included in Kluge's 1979 film *The Patriot*, Michelet's characterization falls woefully short according to fairy tale researcher Hans
Heckel, interviewed midway through the film. He regards "The Wolf and
the Seven Young Kids" as nothing less than a story about a mass mur-
derer that unexpectedly comes to a joyous conclusion. "Sleeping Beauty"
ends well only by dint of the last fairy, whose good will foils another

---

80 Kluge and Negt 268.
81 Cited in Alexander Kluge, *Die Patriotin: Texte / Bilder 1–6* (Frankfurt am Main:
Zweitausendeins, 1979) 126.

Figure 2.7. "Whoever laughs at fairy tales was never in distress." (Alexander Kluge, *Die Patriotin*, p. 465). © Alexander Kluge.

evil fairy's vengeance. "The Seven Ravens" undoes the father's curse when his favorite child, his only daughter, finds her long-lost brothers hexed into a flock of birds and brings them home. "A fairy tale," Heckel digresses, "is normally supposed to end well."[82] What Kluge and Negt consider in their 1979 essay to be the fairy tale's hallmark, the reversal of real tragic experiences into happy endings, not only overshadows any and all vestiges of real obstinacy but also offsets what Blumenberg, writing that same year, calls the "existential anxiety" that emerged when humankind's ancestors first walked upright and started anticipating all manner of threats beyond their horizons.[83] This countervailing relationship between this biogenetic anxiety and techniques for its reduction through the production of images, wishes, and stories finds its remarkable affirmation in Kluge's conclusion to his film's excursus on fairy tales. Described in the screenplay as a "fairy tale image with a radiant crescent moon, stars, shimmering ocean, and light on the horizon," the painting

---

82 Kluge, *Die Patriotin*, 125.

83 Kluge and Negt 283; Hans Blumenberg, *Work on Myth*, trans. Robert M. Wallace (Cambridge, MA: MIT Press, 1985) 6.

still shows a brilliant landscape "seen from the confines of a cave," before which a volcano erupts (fig. 2.7). "Whoever laughs at fairy tales," Kluge's voice-over decrees, "was never in distress."[84] Neither idyllic nor utopian, the image—quite literally a cave painting—renders safe the frightening spectacle of natural disaster and worldly splendor precisely because of its vantage point withdrawn into the safety of the cave. In fact, Kluge underscores the importance of this lesson by drawing attention in his screenplay to the fairy tale image's counterpoint in the preceding minia-ture of German history's catastrophes played out in the open battlefields of war. From this secure point of view, Negt and Kluge appear to be firmly ensconced within Blumenberg's phenomenological-anthropological ter-ritory without any explicit recourse to his work and thus appear to join the ranks of one of Horkheimer and Adorno's most spirited detractors.

Technologies of the Head and Hand

It is not so much the structural ambivalence characteristic of the cave's threshold that Blumenberg and Negt and Kluge agree upon, but rather the consequences they draw from that ambivalence where the limits to their affinities begin to show themselves. First, the futility Blumenberg sees in drawing distinctions between inside and outside finds its corollary in the compensatory function of the world-making power of the imagina-tion. Like Blumenberg, Negt and Kluge also avail themselves of Freud in their understanding of fantasy—they call it a "libidinal counterweight to unbearable, alienated relations"—but the work they also associate with fantasy goes much deeper than just its superficial effects brought forth by the reality principle.[85] A deeper mode of production that is dejected by capitalist processes of valorization rooted in humankind's nature, fantasy is capable of connecting "libidinal structure, consciousness, and the outside world."[86] Although Negt and Kluge would likely agree with Blu-menberg that, as an expression of alienation, fantasy is indeed "autistic," "incapable of generating a binding force [Verbindlichkeit]," and distinctly

---

84 Kluge, Die Patriotin, 129, 465.

85 Oskar Negt and Alexander Kluge, Public Sphere and Experience: Toward an Anal-ysis of the Bourgeois and Proletarian Public Sphere, trans. Peter Labanyi, Jamie Owen Daniel, and Assenka Oksiloff (Minneapolis, MN: University of Minnesota Press, 1993) 33.

86 Negt and Kluge, Public Sphere and Experience, 37, 34.

amnesic, they would nevertheless insist that fantasy's underlying work-character operating beneath capital's radar—its living labor—is the key to finding actual ways out of the cave dilemma.[87] Second, Blumenberg's phenomenological turn renders the epistemological question of deception in the cave "meaningless," for deception is entirely contingent upon what counts as reality for those in the cave.[88] For Negt and Kluge, however, deception from the outside for those deceived on the inside is anything but meaningless. Bracketing the fairy tale's distinctive reversal confirms the lasting effects that deception has on those dwelling and working in houses. Third and most important, Blumenberg associates the culture of care with the mastery of diverse techniques (*Technik*) capable of bringing into immediate perception absent threats such that the intimate space of the cave becomes a compensatory space of virtual action where reality is conquered before ever making contact with it.[89] Ranging from the dream to the cave painting, from poetry to pre-cinematic devices, these techniques all have in common the creation of immersive, panoramic models of reality. "The 'magic lantern,'" Blumenberg explains in *Höhlenausgänge*, "is a precursor to a whole sphere of illusion generators whose power of influence interferes with the difference between the outside world and inner life causing them to disappear."[90] While Blumenberg's insistence that human consciousness is the "embodiment of technical processes" does recall Kluge's own well-worn mantra that "the film assembles itself in the mind of the spectator," Kluge would never go so far as to renounce the political need for producing more exacting capacities for perceiving differentiation, let alone agree with Blumenberg's reduction of cinematic history to the immersive spectacle.[91] In fact, his cinema poses earnest challenges to Blumenberg's insistence that modern technologies capable of manipulating light merely emulate the effects of the cave's own age-old technologies.[92] As shall be demonstrated in the remainder of this chapter, Kluge deploys his cinema to pierce the illusory veil of the cave

87 Blumenberg, *Höhlenausgänge*, 818; Kluge and Negt 282.

88 Blumenberg, *Theorie der Lebenswelt*, 162; Ifergan 183.

89 Blumenberg, *Höhlenausgänge*, 35–36.

90 Blumenberg, *Höhlenausgänge*, 673.

91 Blumenberg, *Höhlenausgänge*, 394; Alexander Kluge, "Bits of Conversation," trans. Emma Woelk, in *Difference and Orientation*, 148; Kluge and Negt 282.

92 Blumenberg, "Light as a Metaphor for Truth," 54; Hans Blumenberg, "Dogmatische und rationale Analyse von Motivationen des technischen Fortschritts," in *Schriften zur Technik*, eds. Alexander Schmitz and Bernd Stiegler (Berlin: Suhrkamp, 2015) 270.

and therewith set the stage for labor capacities to flourish independent of the cave's bewildering effects.

The question of technology lurks throughout Negt and Kluge's collaborations from the start, but it was only in the wake of *Geschichte und Eigensinn* when both thinkers began to deliberate concertedly on technological advances that came of age in the eighties. Astonishingly reminiscent of Blumenberg's own Freudian-framed case for the central role anxiety plays in human life, Negt's 1984 monograph *Lebendige Arbeit, enteignete Zeit* [Living Labor, Expropriated Time] regarded what were then new technologies to be "powerful security systems" assigned with the task of reducing fear and suffering.[93] Far more than mere tools, technology has burrowed itself into the human being's internal state of affairs such that it acquired those very same "metaphysical subtleties and theological niceties" Marx once associated with the fetish character of commodities.[94] Technology's own propensity to undergo "mysterious transubstantiation" meant, for Negt, that its initial promise to save time by accelerating life invariably led to the accelerated expropriation of time, insofar as technology's swift speeds exceeded the cognitive and sensory capacities of humans.[95] The harrowing ambivalence resulting from the thin gap between the latest technology's emancipatory promises and its dangerous assimilation of not just living labor but also the lifeworld itself brings Negt to question the historical validity of Heidegger's Friedrich Hölderlin-inspired technological paradox that "where danger is, grows / The saving power also."[96] In light of unprecedented advances in nuclear, genetic, and computer engineering capable of eclipsing the dignity of human life altogether, the only efficacious political response must refrain from trying to put individual technologies in their place and instead must train living labor power on the production of new forms of communal experience.

Whereas Heidegger finds solace in his turn from modern technology to *poiēsis* and Negt calls for reorganizing labor power altogether, Kluge strikes a middle ground with his plea for cinema. Writing less than a

---

93 Oskar Negt, *Lebendige Arbeit, enteignete Zeit: Politische und kulturelle Dimensionen des Kampfes um die Arbeitszeit* (Frankfurt am Main: Campus Verlag, 1984) 235.

94 Marx, *Capital*, 81.

95 Negt 236, 250.

96 Negt 255. Negt is clearly referring here to Martin Heidegger's "The Question Concerning Technology," trans. William Lovitt, in *Basic Writings*, ed. David Farrell Krell (San Francisco: HarperSanFrancisco, 1993) 333.

year after the successful launch of the first European Communications
Satellite in the summer of 1983, Kluge focused his own reckoning with
the technological shifts of the eighties exclusively on the dawn of digital
broadband. An unparalleled step toward what he called the absolute
"industrialization of consciousness," emergent developments in satellite and cable television were poised on account of both their speed
and comprehensive synthesis to unseat the last vestiges of the classical
public sphere and place its atomized pieces entirely into private hands.[97]
Marked by its unprecedented powers of centralization, isolation, and
inattention, broadband programming excels at consuming both time
and experience and thus leaves, Kluge opines, the representatives of the
classical public sphere—including film—no choice other than to go on
the defensive. If new media have indeed succeeded in colonizing the
imagination of a "new sort of cave dweller" while ignoring the need for
"*direct* life experience," then film and its allies "must adjust technology's
method of labor to fit with that of human minds and hands."[98] To provide
the mind recourse to the hand otherwise spurned by technology means
nothing less than giving time back to impoverished experience. In other
words, the art of film must provide the time and place where to reestablish a circuit long broken yet nevertheless necessary for bringing forth,
to use Heidegger's language, what for Kluge distinguishes human beings
from animals, namely our ability to slow down and gain time. Kluge calls
this defining feature the "*principle of deceleration*."[99]

Kluge's conviction in the crucial coordination of the mind and the
hand did not first materialize amid the technological crises of the eighties. Already in his 1974 lectures, held at Goethe–University Frankfurt,
he pointed explicitly in his theory of fantasy to Marx for having laid the
groundwork for defining labor as a unified process whereby a worker's
hands materialize the imaginations of the mind.[100] Yet the actual discursive context from which it arose dates back another four years when
the then little-known German-Jewish philosopher Alfred Sohn-Rethel

97 Alexander Kluge, "On the Expressions 'Media' and 'New Media': A Selection of
Keywords," trans. Richard Lambert, in *Difference and Orientation*, 286.

98 Kluge, "On the Expressions 'Media' and 'New Media'" 267, 266; Alexander
Kluge, "Die Macht der Bewußtseinsindustrie und das Schicksal unserer Öffentlichkeit,"
in *Industrialisierung des Bewußtseins: Eine kritische Auseinandersetzung mit den "neuen"
Medien*, eds. Klaus von Bismarck et al. (Munich: Piper, 1985) 92.

99 Kluge, "On the Expressions 'Media' and 'New Media,'" 257.

100 Alexander Kluge, "The Role of Fantasy," 339; Marx, *Capital*, 187.

caught the attention of Frankfurt School acolytes with his manuscript *Intellectual and Manual Labor* after it languished nearly four decades after its original inception while he was in Swiss exile. A marginalized acquaintance of Adorno's who nevertheless left a discernable albeit virtually unattributed impact on both his and Walter Benjamin's writings, Sohn-Rethel's work first caught Negt's attention in 1970 by way of Adorno's gifted doctoral candidate and student activist Hans-Jürgen Krahl. Looking back at that first encounter nearly two decades later, Negt attributed Krahl's insistence that Sohn-Rethel was the "the most original Marxist mind of the day" to his unparalleled theory of abstraction.[101] "An essential feature of all [the student movement's] realms of social action subject to practical criticism was the problem of *abstraction*," Negt explained in his 1988 tribute to Sohn-Rethel, "the separation ... of *thought* ... from the concrete life contexts and emancipatory interests of people."[102] On the surface nothing more than an extrapolation of Marx's exhortation that "social existence determines [human] consciousness," Sohn-Rethel's innovation entailed applying Marx's account of commodity production and the attendant abstractions involved in valuation and monetary exchange to what remained for him and other sympathetic minds like Adorno Immanuel Kant's unconvincing insistence on the mind's "phantasmagorical performance of 'transcendental synthesis *a priori*,' locatable neither in time nor in place."[103] A historical materialist account of abstract thought's divorce from manual labor, Sohn-Rethel's intervention thus provides a theoretical account regarding why the most advanced technologies—the offspring of intellectual labor—invariably reinforce this separation and the social exploitation it gives rise to even when deployed in socialist states.

A question of the "degree of unity of head and hand," Sohn-Rethel's historical account of social labor—like Kluge's that began this chapter—derived from his Marxist epistemology follows a series of cascading stages beginning with primitive communism and ending with commodity production.[104] With every new step away from communal production

---

101 Oskar Negt, *Alfred Sohn-Rethel* (Bremen: Verlag Bettina Wassmann, 1988) 6.

102 Negt, *Alfred Sohn-Rethel*, 7.

103 Karl Marx, *A Contribution to the Critique of Political Economy*, trans. Yuri Sdobnikov, in Karl Marx and Friedrich Engels, *Collected Works*, vol. 29 (London: Lawrence and Wishart, 1987) 263; Alfred Sohn-Rethel, *Intellectual and Manual Labor: A Critique of Epistemology*, trans. Martin Sohn-Rethel (London: MacMillan, 1978) 7.

104 Sohn-Rethel 84.

toward capitalist appropriation, human hands fall into further oblivion. Yet Sohn-Rethel's intervention also asserts, as Negt pointed out, that "if real abstraction really exists, then there must also be conditions under which it can be repealed."[105] Especially attractive to student activists of the early seventies, this revolutionary potential made conceivable, even in late-capitalist societies, the possible reversal of technology's effects on labor, whereby tools could be turned back into "repositories of ... social potentialities" capable of satisfying human needs and wishes.[106] Sohn-Rethel proposes this reversal, however, with only the broadest of strokes. He postulates, for example, that capitalist and socialist societies alike could be inundated with an excess of technology such that the logic of scarcity would vanish and a "qualitative" transformation in relations of production would emerge.[107] This re-socialization of labor would facilitate not just an "alliance of society with nature" but would also bring about "a classless society" in which people are "direct producers" who control "the material and intellectual means of production."[108] Neither an affirmation of technological progress typical among technicists nor a wholesale condemnation of technology typical among some Frankfurt School adherents, Sohn-Rethel's underlying insistence on the reversibility of technological progress (along with his insistence on the possible subordination of abstraction to production) is arguably what long resonated with Kluge. Yet, unlike Sohn-Rethel's call for the grand reorganization of labor power, Kluge adapted this technological functionalism on a micrological scale. Instead of simply subordinating technology to social labor, he deploys the filmic apparatus as a helping hand capable of facilitating the subject's own reunification of head and hand. That Kluge sites this union at the threshold to the cave is, as shall be established in the final pages of this chapter, of crucial importance for qualifying his and Negt's departure from Blumenberg's phenomenological anthropology.

Handwork at the Threshold

Originally conceived in the early seventies during the writing of *Public Sphere and Experience* as a story of a blue-collar worker fired for her

---

105 Negt, *Alfred Sohn-Rethel*, 9.
106 Sohn-Rethel 177.
107 Sohn-Rethel 174, 184.
108 Sohn-Rethel 181, 140, 184.

inventive timesaving techniques on the job, Kluge's screenplay "Undoing a Crime by Means of Cooperation" gestated over ten years and assumed multiple guises before becoming the tale of prostitute Knautsch-Betty and her pimp, the burglar Kurt Schleich, that concludes his 1983 feature *The Power of Emotion*.[109] Crafted as a modern-day fairy tale about the "desire for something utterly improbable," the story revolves around not one but two caves.[110] Not unlike the compromised houses in the Grimm's fairy tales analyzed in *History and Obstinacy*, the first cave is Betty's crimson-lit apartment in Frankfurt, where she and Kurt unwittingly welcome for a nightcap newly acquainted Manfred Schmidt and his girlfriend Mäxchen, whose Macbethian ambitions soon lead to robbery and attempted murder. Several days later, after returning home from a night of work, Betty discovers their new friends have helped themselves to her apartment, where they have pummeled, robbed, and left Yugoslavian diamond smuggler Ante Allewisch to die (fig. 2.8). Convinced they are more likely to "bring a dead man back to life" than to convince a jury of their innocence, Betty and Kurt inspect Allewisch's grave head wound, first place a candle and then a hand mirror before the stranger's mouth to confirm he is still barely breathing, and then smuggle him to a backwoods cabin (fig. 2.9).[111] In this second cave, Betty and Kurt put their hands to work bandaging the patient's head, preparing various medicinal remedies, and reading aloud to him in order to activate his mind (figs. 2.10–11). Weeks later, Kurt declares the patient well enough to transport back to Yugoslavia. "They were later of the opinion," Kluge's voice-over explains, "that by reading they had kept the damaged brain active and alive."[112] After passing a particularly stringent border control, Betty and Kurt reach Frankfurt. "Six weeks hard labor—unpaid," Kluge's final voice-over explains as they kiss (fig 2.13). "They've grown closer to one another. In time, the *Technik* will improve."[113]

109 Original sketches can be found in: Alexander Kluge, *Gelegenheitsarbeit einer Sklavin: Zur realistischen Methode* (Frankfurt am Main: Suhrkamp, 1975) 15, 24–51; see also Kluge, *Die Macht der Gefühle* (Frankfurt am Main: Zweitausendeins, 1984), 41–61 and 224, 228–33.

110 Alexander Kluge, "Die Macht der Gefühle: Geschichten, Gespräche und Materialien von und über Alexander Kluge," *Ästhetik und Kommunikation* 53/54 (December 1983): 195.

111 Kluge, *Gelegenheitsarbeit einer Sklavin*, 15.

112 Kluge, *Die Macht der Gefühle*, 156.

113 Kluge, *Die Macht der Gefühle*, 160.

Figures 2.8–2.13. From top to bottom: the mugged Yugoslavian diamond smuggler in prostitute Bette's apartment; Betty's pimp, Kurt Schleich, uses a candle to determine

the victim's vital signs; Betty prepares a remedy between an incandescent light bulb hanging before a window and three lit candles; Betty and Kurt read to their patient;

Betty's crushed lipstick as inconclusive evidence; the final kiss under a crescent moon. *The Power of Emotion* (1983). © Alexander Kluge.

If fairy tales are indeed distinguished by their hallmark reversal leading to happy endings, as established in the fourth section of this chapter, then one possible reading of Betty and Kurt's tale could attribute Allewisch's resurrection from the dead to the work they perform on this stranger, a collaborative handwork whose technique aims at rehabilitating another person's mind. Indeed, Kluge himself has suggested that, of the few paths for attaining happy endings, one involves an equal measure of work and chance.[114] Yet such an account leaves unsettled at the film's conclusion the ambiguous question of *Technik*—is it technique or technology or perhaps both? As for the nature of Betty and Kurt's technique, a previous voice-over modeled after a landmark nineteenth-century study on developmental psychology provides vital clues: "When a bright object slowly passes in front of a four-week-old child's face," Kluge explains, "the child's eyes follow the light with respective movements while keeping its head still."[115] Whatever care Betty and Kurt provide their patient—we see ever so briefly bandages, an intravenous drip, and a mortar and pestle—pales in comparison to all the many diagnostics they use to assess his improved health. By reading aloud to him they merely give his brain ample input to sustain its own "critical ... activity" and by shining light into Allewisch's eyes—be it a candle, light reflected by a mirror, a light bulb, or even sunlight—they merely confirm his improved state.[116] If there is a single term that best describes Betty and Kurt's technique, then it is "maieutics." Unlike Socrates, who appropriated the Greek word for midwifery to describe his cooperative method for bringing forth latent ideas, Kluge and Negt single it out in *History and Obstinacy* as an exemplary configuration of labor characteristics executed by the hand. Maieutics is handwork that deploys a tender

114 Alexander Kluge, "Alexander Kluge on Opera, Film, and Feelings," trans. Sara S. Poor and Miriam Hansen, *New German Critique* 49 (Winter 1990): 108: "The only examples of happy endings have to do with either the absence of feeling (chance, luck, being rescued by criminals) or with labor + miracle."

115 Kluge, *Die Macht der Gefühle*, 157. This voice-over is taken from the penultimate chapter on the labor of relationships (in: Negt and Kluge, *Geschichte und Eigensinn*, 890) and is attributed there to the German original of Wilhelm Thierry Preyer's observations on the development of sight and the human powers of fixating on objects, in particular, in volume one of *The Mind of the Child* (1888) in which he describes passing his hand and a candle in front of a newborn's eyes. See: W. Preyer, *Die Seele des Kindes: Beobachtungen über die geistige Entwicklung des Menschen in den ersten Lebensjahren* (Leipzig: Th. Grieben's Verlag, 1884).

116 Kluge, *Die Macht der Gefühle*, 156.

violence intent on merely provoking the child to navigate its own way through the mother's birth canal.[117] Similarly, Betty and Kurt stimulate Allewisch's still functioning mind and determine with the help of various light sources his childlike progression from unfocused staring to fixating on a bright object.

Preserving their patient's autonomy is but only one half of Betty and Kurt's life-saving technique. The other half is technological. Undisturbed by friend and foe alike, the remote cabin is equally instrumental, for, at first sight, it seems like the antithesis of Betty's compromised Frankfurt apartment, a secluded setting entirely devoid of intruders and distractions. The claim overlooks, however, the fact that Kluge's camera shuttles across the cabin's threshold with an unprecedented ease that the wolf in the Grimm's "The Wolf and the Seven Young Kids" dreams of. This second cave is therefore different than the first as its access and egress are entirely unobstructed to the eye. An establishing exterior long shot taken at dusk first frames Betty in the cabin's window lit by a single light bulb. The camera then joins Betty and Kurt inside the dimly lit cabin as they tend to their patient (fig. 2.10). A follow-up medium shot joins Kurt standing outside reading to their patient through the sunlit window (fig. 2.11). A close-up of Betty inside looking into the daylight then cuts to yet another exterior shot of Allewisch turning his head to look into the sunlight as well. A final interior close-up shows Allewisch's eyes following the swinging light bulb hanging over his head. Far from dissolving the threshold to this cave, Kluge's montage creates a heightened sense of its interiority with respect to the outside world. The same can be said of the deliberate composition of the *mise-en-scène*. In contrast to her Frankfurt apartment awash in mostly undifferentiated hues of red, every shot at the sylvan cabin is composed of at least two if not three juxtaposed light sources simultaneously visible to the spectator: one artificial source (like "hot" candles or the light bulb) and another natural one (like "cold" sunlight). What Kluge's film attends to with all these contrasts is precisely what is lacking in the collective experiences encapsulated in the Grimm's fairy tales, namely "the faculty of differentiation."[118] Yet the *Technik* for augmenting these powers leads to neither the fortification of the cave nor any resolve to remain within it. Betty and Kurt's diegetic objectives as well as that of the film's technical features point toward an eventual

117 Kluge and Negt 96.
118 Kluge and Negt 286.

exodus from the cave and into the daylight such that the caregivers absolve themselves of the crime by shipping the victim back home.

In light of the tale's happy ending, it is arguable that Betty and Kurt's work performed in the woodland cave does facilitate a certain reunification of head and hand that Sohn-Rethel calls for in his revolutionary outlines for a classless society. But, then, whose head and hands are reunited and how exactly? While Allewisch's head wound is his unexpected reward for attempting to engage in illicit transactions, his vocation traffics in as much abstraction as Kurt's, which unloads stolen goods on the black market, and Betty's, which puts a price tag on her own head. In other words, both caregivers and their patient toil under the yoke of abstractions born out of the schism between manual and intellectual labor. However, this state of affairs shifts for Betty and Kurt in the moment of crisis when the telos of their handwork in the cave, no longer monetary in nature, is dictated by the precarity of both Allewisch's and by extension their own existence.[119] What the cave affords all three is what Kluge calls film's "temporal places" and Blumenberg similarly regards as the cave's own "indefinite temporal dimension," namely a considerable duration of time—six weeks to be exact—necessary for Allewisch's head to recover.[120] Yet Blumenberg would undoubtedly take issue with the culture of care Betty and Kurt provide. Whereas he defines care primarily in terms of imparting techniques for cultural signification (e.g., images, symbols, names, and philosophical concepts), Kluge aims at nurturing the pre-linguistic realm of feelings and sensations. Conversely, Kluge would resoundingly refute Blumenberg's characterization of cinema as yet another technology in service of the cave imagination, one that stands in a long line of precursors imbued with the power to blur boundaries. Rather than conflating the cave and cinema, as Blumenberg is wont to do, Kluge deploys the cinematic apparatus at the cave's threshold in order to heighten perceptible distinctions between light and dark, warm and cold, inside and outside, infirm and healthy. In this respect, his cinema shatters what Blumenberg sees as the cave's artifice by throwing its illusions into relief against its antithesis, the natural world.[121] At stake

---

119 Kluge and Negt 96: "*Labor always reverts back to simple labor.*"

120 Kluge, "On the Expressions 'Media' and 'New Media,'" 273; Blumenberg, *Höhlenausgänge*, 35.

121 Blumenberg, "Light as a Metaphor for Truth," 36; Blumenberg, *Höhlenausgänge*, 35.

then is not what should be allowed inside or kept outside the cave, as in the fairy tale of the cunning wolf and the befuddled kids, but, rather, how both technique and technology can attune both the characters' and the spectators' flagging powers of differentiation that result from residing within the cave. In this respect, technology does not so much coerce the eye or denigrate the "freedom to look," as Blumenberg would have it, but rather mediates a relationship between the discerning mind and the labor—cutting to and fro from light to dark—necessary for honing its powers of differentiated perception.[122]

*

To begin to grasp the horrors of the twentieth century, we humans must confront, Kluge and Negt insist at the outset of *History and Obstinacy*, the abstract monster that Marx says only capitalism could have created: "the masses of hands and ... instruments" that slaved away to produce two world wars and the Holocaust.[123] More importantly, we must mine possible ways out of catastrophes engendered by capitalism's chaotic orchestration of human labor capacities by examining what Marx also called humankind's "essential powers," the multifarious characteristics laboring within a single person that not only constitute subjectivity but also constantly enter into intercourse with all of society. One half of the challenge therein lies in apprehending both the composition of amalgamated characteristics subtending labor power, as well as the forces, both internal and external, capable of either derailing or potentiating their effects. The other conundrum is the fact that it is impossible to reincorporate outmoded labor characteristics into newer modes of production.[124] "Isolated," "blocked," and "disconnected," obsolete labor characteristics are virtually "powerless" vis-à-vis "ruling interest[s]."[125] Unaltered, these characteristics cannot themselves be fostered to retake their place in the political economy of labor. Rather, they must "separate," "transform," and "organize" themselves and therewith perform a collaborative labor necessary for reasserting their utility in an entirely

---

122 Blumenberg, "Light as a Metaphor for Truth," 54.

123 Karl Marx, *Economic and Philosophic Manuscripts of 1844*, in Karl Marx and Friedrich Engels, *Collected Works*, vol. 28 (London: Lawrence and Wishart, 1986) 431; see also Kluge and Negt 82.

124 Negt and Kluge, *Public Sphere and Experience*, 296.

125 Negt and Kluge, *Public Sphere and Experience*, 296; cf. Negt and Kluge, *Geschichte und Eigensinn*, 33.

different guise.[126] In order to facilitate such a recalibration of character-istics, expanded "spaces and times" are required to operate as "protective enclosures" such that these revolutionary results can slowly unfold.[127] To this end, Kluge enlists both cinema and the cave. Making time, he has argued, is what analogue cinema is all about. Both a "time machine" and a "temporal place," film—like the cave—is capable of pausing capital's routine expropriation of lived time.[128] Unique to cinema is, however, its cunning agility, an ability to bring into awareness the very experience of being in the cave by entering and leaving it.

As for leaving the cave, Blumenberg long argued that the progress modern philosophy associated with this exodus invariably leads to a need to return to the cave where distance, seclusion, withdrawal, and reorientation are possible.[129] What made the cave such a rich object for his metaphorology is not merely all of humankind's many returns back into it but also humankind's projection of the cave imagination's mollifying effects outward onto the terrifying reality of the world. In effect, Blumenberg contends that humankind's continued existence is possible in the first place by virtue of the fact that humans continually make and re-make the conditions necessary for their survival, condi-tions they develop from within the cave. For Negt and Kluge, the spatial and temporal luxuries of the cave—Blumenberg himself calls them "aristocratic"—are exactly that, namely luxuries not readily available to those of society—"the lowly spheres of the commonly human," writes Blumenberg—who require them the most.[130] To this Kluge has insisted, "We are cave dwellers who simultaneously inhabit prairies. We live therefore in two worlds."[131] The countervailing nature of these worlds—the world of labor power versus the world of capital—has the final word in *The Power of Emotion*. While the improbable story of the resuscitated diamond smuggler ends happily thanks in part to the cave's affordances, the link *Technik* forges therein between head and hand is only momen-tary. In the film's penultimate scene, a German border guard in search of contraband crushes Betty's lipstick in his hand (fig. 2.12). Without

126 Negt and Kluge, *Public Sphere and Experience*, 297.
127 Negt and Kluge, *Geschichte und Eigensinn*, 71.
128 Alexander Kluge, "Film: A Utopia," trans. Samantha Lankford, in *Difference and Orientation*, 176; Kluge, "On the Expressions 'Media' and 'New Media,'" 274.
129 Blumenberg, "Light as a Metaphor for Truth," 40.
130 Blumenberg, "Light as a Metaphor for Truth," 40.
131 Langston, "'Das ist die umgekehrte Flaschenpost,'" 64.

the guidance of the head, the unbridled hand is just as capable of violence as the head fueled by abstract thoughts; the balance struck in the
cave comes undone entirely. The film ends, however, neither back in the
tree-covered shack nor in Betty's Frankfurt abode, but rather somewhere
in transit between these two caves. With the crime undone and their
names absolved, Betty and Kurt presumably return to their professions
pilfering and hustling in the prairie. What remains of their time in the
cave is a sense of closeness that could have only arisen on account of the
success of their strenuous, unindemnified collaborative labor. Rooted
not in the cave imagination but rather in concrete feelings, this closeness
spawned in the cave but retained and presumably deployed in the prairie
is arguably the nexus where a positive anthropology needs to further
query humankind's chances for overcoming not only the denigration of
labor—the separation of head from hand—but also the very inhumanity
of reality.

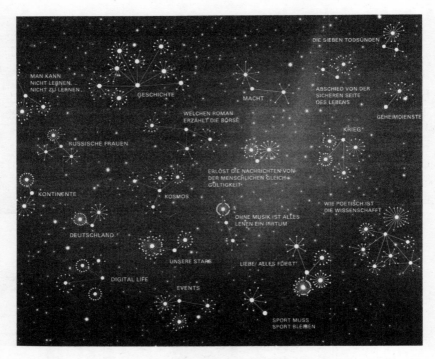

Figure 3.1. Gardens of Information as decentered network. Promotional material for dctp.tv (1988). © Alexander Kluge.

3

Counterpublic Sphere as Asymmetrical Network: Media Metaphoricity and the Production of Trust

After the Real Subsumption of Counterproduction

In the summer of 2014, Oskar Negt and Alexander Kluge met on neutral ground in Vienna to pick up where their forty-five-year-old collaboration last left off. It was fourteen years since they had published their fourth and last co-authored volume entitled *Suchbegriffe* [Search Terms]: twenty-six out of nearly sixty transcribed conversations that Kluge originally filmed for his weekly television programs beginning in 1988. With the usual decade-long interval between collaborations long overdue, they set out to "re-examine and sharpen their chain of 'search terms.'"[1] Working on his autobiography *Überlebensglück* [The Luck of Survival] (2016) while a fellow at Vienna's International Research Center for Cultural Studies, Negt outlined several contemporary concerns for Kluge (for example, the European debt crisis) before the two of them settled on a point of departure for a future installment of their collaborative philosophy.[2] Certain was their shared resolve that their most important

---

1 Alexander Kluge, "Provisorisches Protokoll des Treffens mit Oskar Negt am 13. und 14. Juni 2014 in Wien," *Alexander Kluge-Jahrbuch* 1 (2014): 219.

2 See: Oskar Negt, *Überlebensglück: Eine autobiographische Spurensuche* (Göttingen: Steidl, 2016); and Oskar Negt, *Gesellschaftsentwurf Europa* (Göttingen: Steidl, 2012).

search term, one that courses through all their work, would remain front and center. To identify a "CONCRETIZED CONCEPT OF ALIENATION" for the twenty-first century they would first need to heed the young Marx's proposition, "The path into estrangement is always simultaneously the path out of estrangement."[3] An antidote to the alarmism they say is typical of so much of critical theory, Marx's proposition was clearly on their minds when they re-introduced their long out-of-print English edition of *Public Sphere and Experience*, reprinted two years later. Referring to their meeting in Vienna, they write: "We turned our attention to the latest developments, including the Internet as an imposing modern public sphere. We came to the conclusion, however, that the fundamental elements and forces, the antagonisms, had not changed across recent decades within the framework of such concepts as 'experience,' 'public sphere' and 'alienation.'"[4] The alienation of human labor, forty years earlier still organized around "compact zones of industry," now finds itself not only strewn about the globe but also "driven ever further into the innermost realm of the individual."[5] But even though Negt and Kluge regard the dangers posed by this twofold structural transformation of the public sphere as unprecedented—both in term of its colonization of the global labor force and its harnessing of individuals' most intimate desires and fantasies—they aver, too, that "counterforces are also manifest."[6] In effect, the two key claims from their first collaboration—the precarity of social experience in late capitalism and the immanent conditions for resistance—continue to be essential for an account of contemporary alienation. When read alongside Negt's most recent emphasis on the crisis of linguistic accountability and veracity in the public sphere, especially in light of the cultural erosion that he attributes to digitalization, Kluge's own recent contemporary work on semantic fields capable of expanding Walter Benjamin's *Arcades Project*

---

3 Kluge, "Provisorisches Protokoll des Treffens mit Oskar Negt," 224; cf. Karl Marx, *Economic and Philosophic Manuscripts of 1844*, trans. Martin Milligan and Dirk J. Struik, in Karl Marx and Friedrich Engels, *Collected Works*, vol. 3: *Marx and Engels: March 1843 – August 1844* (London: Lawrence and Wishart, 1975) 294.

4 Oskar Negt and Alexander Kluge, "Introduction: On New Public Spheres," in *Public Sphere and Experience: Toward an Analysis of the Bourgeois and Proletarian Public Sphere*, trans. Peter Labanyi, Jamie Owen Daniel, and Assenka Oksiloff (London: Verso, 2016) xliii.

5 Negt and Kluge, "Introduction: On New Public Spheres," xliii.

6 Negt and Kluge, "Introduction: On New Public Spheres," xliii.

into the twenty-first-century experience make clear that both men are still very much wedded to principal concerns in their first book.[7] Even though it is doubtful that Negt and Kluge will produce a fifth installment in their collaborative philosophy, twenty-first-century readers of *Public Sphere and Experience* must nevertheless take the authors by their word and re-imagine how their original argument organized around publicly funded television now applies to today's dominant medium, the Internet.

In spite of Negt and Kluge's insistence on the resilience of their dialectical argument, they nevertheless concede in their new introduction that the historical relevance of whole chapters from *Public Sphere and Experience* has lapsed entirely. The private media cartels they originally attacked for transforming the nature of commodities and their distribution (not to mention the structures of human perception) are now, in their words, "hopelessly defending themselves against innovations from Silicon Valley."[8] A taste of the paradigm shift brought on by digital capitalism, Negt and Kluge's cursory diagnosis offers, however, few additional details. In another commemoration of the fortieth anniversary of their book, Kluge writes of the current real stage of subsumption that has gobbled up the heart of the classical public sphere: the intimate spheres of human emotion and thought.[9] Underscoring what is at stake for a renewed theorization of the public sphere—the imperiled subjective factor necessary for any autonomous public sphere—Negt and Kluge leave their readers with the impression that it is up to others to separate the wheat of their original argument from its historical chaff. Yet, already in 1993, Kluge's student and collaborator Miriam Hansen began

---

7 On Negt's recent interest in the validity of linguistic meaning in the precarious age of digitality, see: Oskar Negt, *Erfahrungsspuren: Eine autobiographische Denkreise* (Göttingen: Steidl Verlag, 2019) 314–26. On Kluge's interest in expanding Benjamin's *Arcades Project*, see: Alexander Kluge and Burkhardt Lindner, "Inventory of a Century: On Walter Benjamin and *The Arcades Project*," trans. Andreas Freytag Hill, in *Difference and Orientation: An Alexander Kluge Reader*, ed. Richard Langston (Ithaca, NY: Cornell University Press, 2019) 462–83; Alexander Kluge's seven-part video contribution to the opening of the three-year exhibition "The New Alphabet," entitled "From Zed to Omega: Walk-In Theater: A Babylon, Whose Tower Does Not Collapse, in Berlin" and held at the Haus der Kulturen der Welt; and Alexander Kluge, "Reading and Writing: How Can I Live? How Can I Know? What Does the Future Hold?," in *The New Alphabet: Opening Days*, eds. Bernd Scherer and Olga von Schubert (Berlin: HKW, 2019) 33–46.

8 Negt and Kluge "Introduction: On New Public Spheres," xliii.

9 Alexander Kluge, "Zu Öffentlichkeit und Erfahrung," *Alexander Kluge-Jahrbuch* 2 (2015): 122–23.

parsing *Public Sphere and Experience* at a time when Anglo-American debates began recognizing the need to "redefine the spatial, territorial, and geopolitical parameters of the public sphere."[10] Hansen places, however, far less emphasis on the subjective factor in her important case for the book's continued relevance in the early nineties. The longevity of Negt and Kluge's argument, she maintains, lies in their assertion that "it is impossible to define or describe the public sphere in the singular."[11] Because the public sphere is actually a heterogeneous, "unstable mixture" of three basic kinds of coexistent publicities—classical, neoliberal, and alternative—much of contemporary experience, regardless of whether it is affirmative or oppositional, is a function of incessantly changing "combinations, conjunctures, or collisions."[12] Indispensable for the development of what Hansen elsewhere calls a "political ecology of the senses," Negt and Kluge's insights are especially important for understanding what makes counterpublics in the digital age viable:[13]

> The seams and overlays between different types of publicity, conflicts between short-term economic interests and longstanding ideological norms, bricolages of deterritorialized media and participatory interaction—such hybrid, impure forms provide the blueprint from which counterpublics can and do emerge, the conditions under which industrially mediated experience can be reclaimed for the articulation of concrete needs and contradictions, for discursive struggles over subjectivity, meaning, and representation.[14]

While Hansen does effectively rebuff those who have regarded *Public Sphere and Experience* to be anachronistic, irrelevant, or even failed, her endorsement, itself now over twenty years old, shows its own signs of datedness. Even though she does call attention to Negt and Kluge's prescience regarding the coming of new media—they regard television as a "medium of a transitional epoch"—her examples include now archaic

---

10 Miriam Hansen, foreword to *Public Sphere and Experience: Toward an Analysis of the Bourgeois and Proletarian Public Sphere*, trans. Peter Labanyi, Jamie Owen Daniel, and Assenka Oksiloff (Minneapolis: University of Minnesota Press, 1993) xiii.

11 Hansen, foreword, xxix.

12 Hansen, foreword, xxix, xxxviii.

13 Miriam Hansen, "Why Media Aesthetics?" *Critical Inquiry* 30 (Winter 2004): 394.

14 Hansen, foreword, xl-xli.

artifacts like "videotape[s] and laser disc[s]."[15] Moreover, her attention to what soon became juggernauts in their own right, namely "new computer and telephone technologies," are pinned to what today are minor, residual phenomena like "computer bulletin boards" and "telephone sex."[16] Rigorously formalized in the immediate wake of Hansen's case for Negt and Kluge, theories of the emergent network society catalyzed by the privatization of the Internet and the boom in wireless communication over the course of the nineties cast more shadows over their book's political relevance than Negt and Kluge might have cared to admit in 2014.[17]

Arguably the most profound shift affecting the core of what Hansen regards to be Negt and Kluge's "blueprint from which counterpublics can and do emerge"—when commercially cultivated "partial publics" and counterpublics link up to form larger oppositional publicities—is the structural transformation of production in the last four decades.[18] Following their point of departure that not distribution (as Jürgen Habermas would have it) but rather "production predominates over publicity," Negt and Kluge maintain over the course of *Public Sphere and Experience* that dominant capitalist modes of production—be they bourgeois, industrial, or informational—have continually disenfranchised the life experiences of "an overwhelming majority of the population."[19] As long as they are situated within the reigning mode of production, neither "radical struggle" nor critique ever stands a chance of improving this constituency's lot.[20] Using a concept they recognize is antiquated and therefore ostensibly resilient to the influence of dominant discourses— the proletariat—Negt and Kluge conclude that **"the only antidotes to the production of the illusory public sphere are the counter-products of a proletarian public sphere: idea against idea, product against product, production sector against production sector."**[21] History is certainly not

15 Negt and Kluge, *Public Sphere and Experience*, 121; Hansen, foreword, xxiv.

16 Hansen, foreword, xxiv, xxxviii.

17 Manuel Castells, *The Rise of the Network Society*, 2nd ed. (Chichester, UK: Wiley-Blackwell, 2010) 14, xxv–xxvi.

18 Hansen, foreword, xl, xxxviii: "What … partial publics have in common is that they operate through industrial-commercial venues; that they are usually not constructed on an identitarian model; that they organize vast constituencies …; but that their activities tend to remain more or less … hidden from public view, that is, from anyone who is not directly paying for and participating in them."

19 Negt and Kluge, *Public Sphere and Experience*, 4n8, xlv. Translation modified.

20 Negt and Kluge, *Public Sphere and Experience*, 266n5, 124ff.

21 Negt and Kluge, *Public Sphere and Experience*, 79–80.

without examples of such counterproduction. The student movements of the sixties reanimated the "early bourgeois means of production" in the form of the printing press and thus attempted to offset the mass media's exclusion of the left. Refraining from the very exclusionary logic—they write of a "Robinson Crusoe attitude"—characteristic of both the classical public sphere and partial publics is crucial for the production of any such counterpublic sphere.[22] But, with the rapid ascendency of what author and essayist Hans Magnus Enzensberger first identified a decade earlier as the "consciousness industry," another iteration of the public sphere engineered entirely by private media has mapped itself on top of the classical, bourgeois one.[23] Rather than excluding those private realms of life previously excluded from the classical public sphere, the consciousness industry has given rise to "public spheres of production" by pandering to people's most private, everyday thoughts and desires. In the forty years since the student movements, the technical transformation of the consciousness industry has mushroomed exponentially, while the agency to be found in appropriating older means of production has diminished considerably. Not only does the singularity of the Internet overshadow the "bricolages of deterritorialized media" Hansen extolled, but its reach and connectivity have also enticed counterproductions to migrate over to its mode of production. The once utopian notion of the "prosumer"— someone who consumes what they produce—is now a staple of today's information economy built on surveilling user interactivity and shepherding it using predictive algorithms.[24] The giants of Silicon Valley have, in other words, realized in their own way a semblance of the hopes that Negt and Kluge once pinned to a counterproduction "whose object is coherent human sensuality."[25] The question boils down to whether the relations of production in the network society foreclose the combinations, conjunctures, and collisions of diverse spheres that give rise to opposition. In other words, can online production ever amount to more than just the subsumption of the partial publics? Can it give rise to and set in motion counterpublic spheres?

---

22 Negt and Kluge, *Public Sphere and Experience*, 213.

23 Hans Magnus Enzensberger, "The Industrialization of the Mind," in *Critical Essays*, eds. Reinhold Grimm and Bruce Armstrong (New York: Continuum, 1982) 3–14.

24 "Prosumer" was originally coined by Alvin Toffler in *The Third Wave* (New York: William Morrow, 1980) 284.

25 Negt and Kluge, *Public Sphere and Experience*, 297n3.

Neither antiquated nor in need of pruning, what *Public Sphere and Experience* requires for the full potential of its own account of the historical transformation of the public sphere to come into full view in the twenty-first century are addenda of two kinds: on the one hand, Negt's and Kluge's scattered reflections on new media and, on the other, Kluge's own very recent online media practices. "Theory's intention," they write in *Geschichte und Eigensinn*, "is to supply praxis a measurable amount of orientation."[26] Regardless of whether a theory is right or wrong, it can still contribute to orientation, they say, when it enters into real relations and creates a relationality. However, in his recent reflections on the Internet, Kluge remarks that orientation is precisely what is lacking in today's digital networks. Making use of just one of many metaphors widespread in his reflections on new media, Kluge notes, "You cannot swim across an ocean of information by yourself and reach the other side. You'd never arrive. If you start to swim across the Atlantic from the coast of Brittany, you might manage, say, five kilometers."[27] As every one of Kluge's media metaphors entails an attendant "web of ideas," the peril posed by a seemingly endless metaphorical ocean can be matched with yet another metaphor.[28] "A boat is ... the equivalent of an oasis," he continues, "a fixed place." "This dialectic between abundance and a single point where I am by myself is a movement that leads to the formation of a strong core."[29] The solid core in question arguably subtends orientation, "the precondition of thinking" and, by extension all so-called theory labor.[30] Navigating the high seas of digital networks in search of experience suitable for the formation of counterpublic spheres is, however, more than just a question of choosing an apt metaphor. In fact, the plentitude of Kluge's media metaphors that seemingly verge on catachresis strongly suggests that they are merely a means to an end as well. Working in pincer-like fashion toward the middle term between theory and praxis,

---

26 Oskar Negt and Alexander Kluge, *Geschichte und Eigensinn*, in *Der unterschätzte Mensch: Gemeinsame Philosophie in zwei Bänden*, vol. 2 (Frankfurt am Main: Zweitausendeins, 2001) 483.

27 Alexander Kluge, "The Equivalent of an Oasis: An Essay for the Digital Generation," trans. Richard Langston, *Alexander Kluge-Jahrbuch* 6 (2019): 199.

28 Alexander Kluge, "What Is a Metaphor?," trans. Emma Woelk, in *Difference and Orientation*, 111.

29 Kluge, "The Equivalent of an Oasis," 199.

30 Alexander Kluge and Oskar Negt, *History and Obstinacy*, ed. Devin Fore, trans. Richard Langston et al. (New York: Zone Books, 2014) 439–40.

this chapter approaches the problem of orientation's compromised core by correlating the work of metaphor in theory and praxis with the production of what Kluge and Negt call trust. Trust is what allows strangers working together (e.g., gravitational thinking) to tolerate their respective contradictions.[31] Trust is the precondition for any and all labor required for mounting protest. And trust facilitates the formation of community especially when the latest historical stage of medialization has rendered shared experience largely indirect. But how exactly does a medium engender trust? Whether new media can contribute to the constitution of conditions necessary for building trust ultimately boils down to a question of whether it can wrestle with the complexities unleashed by the Internet, and to this end, Negt and Kluge enter into an adventure in gravitational thinking with systems theoretician Niklas Luhmann.

Old New Media Metaphors: Window versus Frame

Negt and Kluge re-issued in 2001 their ongoing dialogues reaching back to *Public Sphere and Experience* from 1972 in a massive, two-volume compendium they call in German a *"gemeinsame Philosophie,"* a collaborative philosophy. While the collaborative nature of their work should appear self-evident to readers familiar with their intense, close-knit working method in which they debate face to face and jointly write every single sentence, its status as philosophy requires further qualification.[32] In his introduction to their collected works, Negt merely divulges, however, how their intense inner devotion to thinking warrants the title "philosophy"; elsewhere he simply equates their philosophizing with Socrates's penchant for investigation.[33] Beyond these cursory remarks, their works themselves rarely reflect on their status as philosophy. Instead of substantiating this claim, Negt and Kluge write repeatedly of theory labor, an emancipatory form of collaborative intelligence rooted in the critique of existing forms of tyranny and oppression, the anticipation of

---

31 Kluge and Negt 139–40.

32 Alexander Kluge, "Öffentlichkeit und Erfahrung: Alexander Kluge und Oskar Negt im Gespräch mit Claus Philipp," in *Magazin des Glücks*, eds. Sebastian Huber and Claus Philipp (Vienna: Springer Verlag, 2007) 95.

33 Christian Schulte and Rainer Stollmann, "Moles Don't Use Systems: A Conversation with Oskar Negt," *October* 149 (Summer 2014): 71–72.

"objective possibilities" for happiness, and social orientation necessary for generating relationalities.[34] Whereas pure philosophy is devoid of this experiential content, theory, they argue, is a distinctly impure form of philosophical thinking insofar as it employs language, albeit imprecisely, in order to index the living experience of protest.[35] Negt and Kluge go on to point out, in *Geschichte und Eigensinn*, that the vernacular lies somewhere between the Kantian poles of philosophical concepts and intuition. By the same token, a colloquial language rich in metaphors is neither conceptually exact nor is it necessarily intuitively accessible.[36] The resulting imprecision is advantageous not only because it necessitates high levels of negotiation, but also because of the network of ideas it creates. "Metaphors unify facts into a coral reef," Kluge noted in a 2016 interview on Karl Marx's metaphors.[37] In fact, *Geschichte und Eigensinn* illustrates this with its enigmatic beginning. Negt and Kluge preface their first chapter on the historical origins of labor capacities—the first step in their political economy of labor power—with a brief description of the tender violence typical of a midwife's labor. "Sometimes a fetus lies twisted in the so-called breech presentation in the mother's womb. If the midwife does not turn it in time, the child will be strangled at birth ... In order to allow it to pass through the birth canal, her grip must provoke the child's own movement. Such violence as applied by the midwife is distinct from the violence of hammers, sickles, hoes, or saws."[38] It is, however, not enough to simply award theory labor the metaphor of midwifery. The agglomeration of ideas linked to this central metaphor—sundry modalities of violence in the labor process ranging from destructive to co-constitutive—also threaten to solidify into a rigid one-to-one equivalency. Never an end in itself, thinking through metaphors requires one of several counter-tendencies equally crucial for impure theory to keep up with the shifting historical terrain of experience, one capable of putting a metaphor's hardened constellations back into motion. To this end, commentary and storytelling, Kluge points out, are especially well suited for interrogating the contemporaneity of hardened old metaphors and dissolving their crystalline states.

---

34 Negt and Kluge, *Geschichte und Eigensinn*, 481–82.
35 Negt and Kluge, *Geschichte und Eigensinn*, 792, 303–5, 1208.
36 Negt and Kluge, *Geschichte und Eigensinn*, 1237n8.
37 Kluge, "What Is a Metaphor?," 112.
38 Negt and Kluge, *Geschichte und Eigensinn*, 25–6; Kluge and Negt 96.

While Negt and Kluge's impure philosophy is full of stories and critical commentaries conveyed in both words and images that react against the standstill of metaphoricity, Kluge's film theory recognized early on the structural discrepancy that put film at a disadvantage when compared with language's recourse to metaphor.[39] "Film cannot form metaphoric concepts," he exhorted in a 1965 essay co-authored with fellow film instructors Edgar Reitz and Winfried Reinke.[40] With the advent of sound technologies in film and their rapid incorporation into commercial cinema in the late twenties, film quickly succumbed to a naturalism intent on channeling the primacy of literary language rather than advancing its own nonliterary ones. Even a superficial inquiry reveals film's expressive inferiority when compared with language's "thousand years of tradition" steeped in not just metaphor but also abstraction, condensation, and differentiation.[41] While film may never approximate the precise mental imagery typical of language, opportunity nevertheless lurks within this deficiency. Film can potentially "escape this quandary," Kluge opines, by combining language and imagery such that sound, language, image, narrative, and theme enter into non-hierarchical relations with one another.[42] In contrast, then, to spoken and written language, film can combine "the radical intuition of its visual material with the conceptual possibilities of montage; thus it offers a form of expression which is as capable of a dialectical relationship between concept and intuition … without, however, stabilizing this relationship, as language is bound to do."[43] In other words, the aural-visual combinations film is capable of and the constellations of ideas they can in turn touch off never come to rest, as is the case with metaphors. "In literature," Kluge explained in the shadow of his first international success as a filmmaker, "I am dependent on the traditionally determined meanings embedded in words, whereas with images I am solely limited by what spectators are able to imagine."[44] If the

39 Dorothea Walzer, *Arbeit am Exemplarischen: Poetische Verfahren der Kritik bei Alexander Kluge* (Paderborn: Wilhelm Fink Verlag, 2017) 86–87; see also Michel Foucault, "The Order of Discourse," trans. Ian McLeod, in *Untying the Text: A Post-Structuralist Reader*, ed. Robert Young (Boston, MA: Routledge & Kegan Paul, 1981) 56.
40 Edgar Reitz, Alexander Kluge, and Wilfried Reinke, "Word and Film," trans. Miriam Hansen, in *Difference and Orientation*: 126.
41 Reitz, Kluge, and Reinke, 127.
42 Reitz, Kluge, and Reinke, 131, 125.
43 Reitz, Kluge, and Reinke, 129. Translation modified.
44 Alexander Kluge, "Bits of Conversation," trans. Emma Woelk, in *Difference and Orientation*, 151–52.

search for a sophisticated cinematic language promised to transcend the fixed opportunities of metaphorical thinking, the proliferation of new media in the form of commercial television, a paradigm shift ordained by the Federal Constitutional Court in 1981 that took the Federal Republic of Germany by storm by the middle of the eighties, suddenly threatened to undermine such innovations.

Beginning in earnest in 1983, Kluge began taking aim in a series of essays at the all but inevitable onslaught of privatized television in West Germany, a country that had long equated its democratic foundation with its federally mandated public service broadcasting system. Seen from the vantage point of film, the initial prognosis looked especially grim. Hastened by recent advancements in digital communication technologies like fiberglass cable, private television's ascendancy appeared to threaten something as fundamental as the objective representation of space and time.[45] Unlike the fixed spectatorial distances typical of formal cinema, television offers up intimate spectacles within the domestic sphere, while nevertheless purporting to transmit vast distances, often in real time.[46] Unlike the flicker of cinema's projectors that keep spectators in the dark 50 percent of a movie showing, television radiates the human eye ceaselessly and thereby destroys the temporal gaps and niches essential for cinematic montage.[47] Similarly, television is composed of a constant flow devoid of clear beginnings and endings, even though it appears to accelerate and truncate the duration of time in order to accommodate its programming requirements.[48] Part and parcel of these spatio-temporal shifts is television's engulfing of older media, giving rise to unbridled citationality.[49] A precious antidote to impure theory's reliance on metaphor, commentary on television becomes a mass-produced commodity.[50] As a result, television dampens the affective intensities typical of cinema, leaving spectators and their imaginative faculties comparatively indifferent.[51] Kluge's final negative verdict would seem all but assured, when, in

---

45 Richard Langston, *Visions of Violence: German Avant-Gardes after Fascism* (Evanston, IL: Northwestern University Press, 2008) 210–12.

46 Alexander Kluge, "Film: A Utopia," trans. Samantha Lankford, in *Difference and Orientation*, 183.

47 Alexander Kluge, "On the Expressions 'Media' and 'New Media': A Selection of Keywords," trans. Richard Lambert, in *Difference and Orientation*, 273–74.

48 Kluge, "Film: A Utopia," 183.

49 Kluge, "Film: A Utopia," 183.

50 Kluge, "Film: A Utopia," 202.

51 Kluge, "Film: A Utopia," 185.

fact, he actually stops short of forsaking the medium altogether. "Television is a hybrid," he asserts.[52] As long as it disobeys the commercial "will to programming" and, instead, conveys what Walter Benjamin described in terms of the *"uniqueness* and *permanence" (Einmaligkeit und Dauer)* of mediated experience within classical public spheres, then television can still be an agent of social experience like cinema before it.[53] In order to secure television's partisanship and ensure it gives its spectators' powers of fantasy more time than it expropriates, television must undergo what Kluge calls a "terrestrial re-connection."[54] The terra firma in question refers not just to terrestrial transmitters and antennae responsible for sending and receiving radio waves (as opposed to satellite and cable signals). Television must be also re-connected to the mental lives of its spectators. "The true medium of experience," Kluge underscored in a separate reflection on the nature of media from 1979, "of desires, of phantasies, and actually of aesthetic appreciation as well, are real human beings and never specialists."[55] To this end, he not only retained his long-standing principle of montage but also made it more complicated in an effort to provoke the fantasy. Additionally, he sought apt metaphors in both his theory and praxis capable of tethering this hybrid to the solid ground of experience. In fact, this search for new media's potential metaphoricity is a direct function of Kluge's quest to deploy television as a form capable of concretizing the abstractions endemic of what Negt calls new media's second-order reality.[56] If what is at stake is nothing less than the "space where the political takes shape," says Negt, then Kluge's media metaphors are essential not only for the constellations they engender but also the concretizing force they apply to the medium.[57]

Of all the many metaphors Kluge adopted for his productions in new media, the earliest and arguably most prominent was that of the window.

---

52 Kluge, "On the Expressions 'Media' and 'New Media,'" 255.

53 Kluge, "On the Expressions 'Media' and 'New Media,'" 255; Walter Benjamin, "The Work of Art in the Age of Its Technological Reproducibility," trans. Harry Zohn and Edmund Jephcott, in *Selected Writings*, vol. 4: *1938–1940*, eds. Howard Eiland and Michael W. Jennings (Cambridge, MA: Belknap Press, 2003) 255–56.

54 Kluge, "On the Expressions 'Media' and 'New Media,'" 286.

55 Alexander Kluge, "On Film and the Public Sphere," trans. Thomas Y. Levin and Miriam B. Hansen, in *Alexander Kluge: Raw Materials for the Imagination*, ed. Tara Forrest (Amsterdam: Amsterdam University Press, 2012) 36.

56 Oskar Negt, *Achtundsechzig: Politische Intellektuelle und die Macht* (Göttingen: Steidl Verlag, 1995) 98.

57 Negt, *Achtundsechzig*, 103.

A holdover from film theory's long fascination with the window as metaphor for the "special, ocular access" afforded by cinema, television's alleged window-like character actually failed in Kluge's mind to function accordingly.[58] Be it public or private, television broadcasting purports to "open a window," Kluge opined, but "then prevent[s] anything from being represented from a distance."[59] Why Kluge originally then settled on appropriating the dominant metaphor of window given its deceptive nature had little to do with the window's inferred transparency, its inherent status as a medium, or its ability to mediate virtual experience.[60] "If people do not leave their homes anymore," he explained the year his production company began broadcasting, "and they look through this so-called window which is television, then we have to go to the people."[61] A declaration of war intent on wielding his own auteur products on the very same battlefield where corporate agents of the public sphere of production operated, Kluge's "culture windows" initially exploited a media policy provided for by social democrats in the state of North Rhine-Westphalia that allowed third parties—neither public broadcasters nor private corporations—to ensure programming diversity on cable television.[62] If Kluge's hosts, the privately owned German television channels SAT.1, RTL, and Vox obliged to honor his broadcasting license, were opaque, non-functioning windows in the sense criticized by Kluge above, then his broadcasts were to be counter-windows that derived their force by literally clashing with the opposition on its supposed turf.[63] However, Kluge's reworking of the window metaphor sought neither to render transparent the television's screen nor to realize its promise to "expand and cultivate the immediate senses."[64] Rather than encouraging

58 Thomas Elsaesser and Malte Hagener, "Cinema as Window and Frame," in *Film Theory: An Introduction through the Senses*, 2nd ed. (New York: Routledge, 2015) 14–38.

59 Alexander Kluge, "Medialization—Musealization," trans. Emma Woelk, in *Difference and Orientation*, 293.

60 On the window as virtual reality, see: Lutz Koepnick, *Framing Attention: Windows on Modern German Culture* (Baltimore, MD: Johns Hopkins University Press, 2007) 3.

61 Stuart Liebman and Alexander Kluge, "On New German Cinema, Art, Enlightenment, and the Public Sphere: An Interview with Alexander Kluge" *October* 46 (Autumn 1988): 29.

62 Knut Hickethier, "Von anderen Erfahrungen in der Fernsehöffentlichkeit Alexander Kluges Kulturmagazine und die Fernsehgeschichte," in *Kluges Fernsehen: Alexander Kluges Kulturmagazine*, eds. Christian Schulte and Winifried Siebers (Frankfurt am Main: Suhrkamp, 2002) 204.

63 Kluge, "On the Expressions 'Media' and 'New Media,'" 283–84.

64 Negt, *Achtundsechzig*, 104.

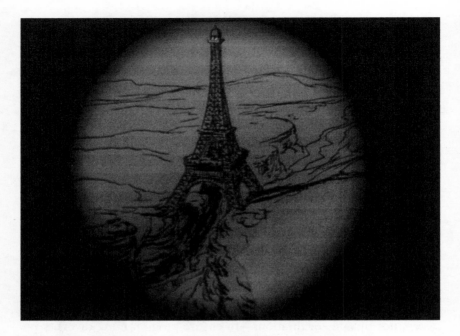

Figures 3.2 and 3.3. Stills from "The Eiffel Tower, King Kong, and the White Woman" (1988). © Alexander Kluge.

the spectator's gaze to pass *through* the television's screen, he was far more concerned with the television's potential as a frame and, to this end, aligned his televisual auteurism with a long line of constructivist discourses from film theory (e.g., Béla Balázs, Rudolf Arnheim, and Sergei Eisenstein). If the ontological metaphor of the window subtended practices of cinematic realism, then Kluge's shift to the metaphor of the frame, which long underscored the constructed nature of filmic perception, was resoundingly antirealist.[65] Kluge's "culture windows" were, in other words, wolves in sheep's clothing, Trojan horses fashioned as yet another set of windows on television that actually operated like frames. But how?

Liquid Video

A holdover from his own theory of filmic antirealism, the frame metaphor that Kluge himself applied to his video productions might give the impression that he, like many others before him, misrecognized the medium of video as a mere outgrowth of film.[66] To the contrary, just as Negt and Kluge's theory labor recognized the need to dissolve the metaphors that colloquial language affords in order to explode their constellations, so too was Kluge's recourse to old media metaphors motivated by the need to undermine the deceit at work in the otherwise affirmative metaphor of the window. And far from ignoring video's distinct genealogy, Kluge's early praxis intent on making video's material specificity visible—a hallmark of the frame—acknowledges the impossibility of pigeonholing an inherently hybrid medium, which in the words of another video theoretician, lacks an "essential form."[67] Brief consideration of his last broadcast from 1988 (his first year in television), a twenty-four-minute "musical film magazine" in Kluge's own words, shows how his video labor has wrestled with not just these two contradictory cinematic metaphors but also acknowledged a third metaphor, a decidedly post-cinematic one that collapses the

---

65 Cf. Elsaesser and Hagener 16.

66 Alexander Kluge, "The Sharpest Ideology: That Reality Appeals to Its Realistic Character," trans. David Roberts, in *Alexander Kluge: Raw Materials for the Imagination*, 191–96.

67 Sean Cubitt, *Videography: Video Media as Art and Culture* (Houndmills, UK: MacMillan, 1993) xv; see also Peter C. Lutze, *Alexander Kluge: The Last Modernist* (Detroit, MI: Wayne State University Press, 1998) 187.

opposition between the other two.[68] Instead of deploying commentary
or storytelling as is the case with theory, Kluge fights this battle set on
winning television for the classical public sphere solely with images. Entitled "The Eiffel Tower, King Kong, and the White Woman," Kluge sets
up two of the program's three titular characters in the first sixty seconds.
Spectators are first introduced to stills of both Kong, a mere gorilla, and
the white woman, an anonymous starlet (fig. 3.3). With the help of an
establishing shot of a cruise ship and accompanying foghorns, we then see
Kong and his object of desire looking down through a skylight window
from above into presumably the ship's dining room, which is undulating, as if it were sitting at the bottom of the ocean. They fade from view
and in the bottom-right corner of the rippling chamber an amorphous,
fluctuating perforation appears through which the spectator sees the
aforementioned ocean liner and then Kong's actual head superimposed
on Bing Crosby wearing a dinner jacket in *Road to Singapore* (1940).
Through the window above, viewers see a *mise en abyme* of the aquatic
dining room below before the image sutures the billowing aperture shut.
Via allusions to two of Hollywood's enduring catastrophic myths—the
sinking of the *Titanic* and Cooper and Schoedsack's *King Kong* (1933)—
Kluge frames the underwater scene using two windows, one situated
within the plane of representation and the other rupturing the plane itself.
Without any explicit explanation to guide us, we spectators see, on the
one hand, the cinematic imaginary incorporated into the watery image
and, on the other, cinema positioned behind it as if it were a substrate, yet
the significance of this strange image of the unassuming room, let alone
its rippling effect, remains unclear. What, however, is certain is how this
string of meta-pictures generates in short order what W.J.T. Mitchell calls
a "second-order discourse about pictures *without* recourse to language."[69]
Certain, too, is the fact that cinema's gaze is captured within this watery
image that proves capable of also looking back at cinema.

The significance of the Eiffel Tower for Kong and the white woman
finally comes into view following a succession of dizzying images of

68 Alexander Kluge and Martin Weinmann, *Album*, in Kluge, *Seen sind für Fische
Inseln: Fernseharbeiten 1987–2008* (Franfurt am Main: Zweitausendeins, 2007) 17. The
broadcast is included as track three on the first of fourteen DVDs in the accompanying
box set. The original broadcast is: Alexander Kluge, dir. "Der Eiffelturm, King Kong und
die weiße Frau," *10 till 11*, RTL, December 26, 1988.

69 W.J.T. Mitchell, *Picture Theory: Essays on Verbal and Visual Representation*
(Chicago, IL: University of Chicago Press, 1994) 38.

acrobats, a dog wedding, dinosaurs, and the tragic career of the socialist-cum-fascist Pierre Laval. "Someone stole the Eiffel Tower," actress Ulli Hartmut then exclaims, looking into the camera much in the manner that a West German news anchorwoman did at the time. "It now stands above a canyon in the American West. The people of Paris are distraught" (fig. 3.2).[70] Using the first issue of the French comic book series *Les Dessins animés présentent Cyclone* from 1947, Kluge shows panels from the comic strip recounting in tinted CMYK hues the fallout from the missing tower, along with a series of alternating undulating windows that once again puncture the image so as to reveal the Eiffel Tower and incensed Parisian crowds. Moderator Silke Rein then reports that the muscular giant Cyclone, yet another instantiation of Kong, and his charge, the petite Parisian Babette, enlist the help of magician Rafagor's supernatural powers and a fleet of flying machines in order to return the tower. "Evil forces were beaten back," Rein concludes. Like a spaceship passing through the starry night, the Eiffel Tower zips past the Arc de Triomphe to take its place near the banks of the river Seine. Only the third of eleven parts in Kluge's broadcast, the story of the Eiffel Tower abruptly shifts beginning in part 4 and continues until part 10 in a vein that has seemingly little if anything to with Kong, the white woman, or the purloined tower for that matter. In part 4, a split screen shows whitewater rapids on the left and a silent-era slapstick comedy involving a police officer swimming after what he believes to be a drowning child. Part 5 features an excerpt from the Lumière brothers' actuality film *Niagara, Horseshoe Falls* (1896) and part 6 shows a portion of their *Place de l'Opéra*, filmed that same year. A ceremonial ship launch from 1896, a swimming contest between horses from 1895, an animated image of dinosaurs engaged in watery battle (undulating much like the aforementioned dining room), and Japanese submarines off the coast of California follow in quick succession before spectators see Crosby as Kong once again at the bow of an ocean liner. These seven intervening interludes are all interrelated metaphors for flow, be it in the guise of gushing water, heavy traffic, naval vessels, or swimming creatures. There exist many kinds of flow, say Kluge and Negt in *History and Obstinacy*. There is the flow of labor power that stands in opposition to the flow of protest. Bodily energies, memories, and human characteristics also flow according to their

---

70 Alexander Kluge, *Facts and Fakes: Fernseh-Nachschriften*, vol. 4: *Der Eiffelturm, King Kong und die weiße Frau* (Berlin: Vorwerk 8, 2002) 10.

respective economies.[71] But what these various representational flows index here is the medium itself. A constant stream of undulating light passing through the television screen's cathode ray tube, video amounts to more in Kluge's hands, however, than just a study in the technology of light flows. Nor is it the flow of television programming that Kluge sets his sights on in this broadcast. On the contrary, of utmost importance is video's ability to render the hardened illustrations, photographs, and cinematic stills from video's forerunners into three-dimensional stacks of malleable surfaces. In video, still images come alive. They ripple and fly. They fade in and out of one another. They reproduce themselves like reflections caught between two mirrors. They burst open to reveal other moving images underneath them. And they meld with others (like Kong's head, the Eiffel Tower, and dinosaurs), which float atop them to form composite images that make no secret of their heterogeneity and depth. Unlike the early cinema of attraction that functioned like a realist window onto various flows, video stands capable of incorporating flows as well as windows into its very representational regime. In so doing, it allows for a synchronic simultaneity and multiplicity that builds upon cinema's diachronic march of images once so central for Kluge's dialectical theory of montage. "Every cut," he once explained of cinematic montage, "provokes fantasy ... where the film does not show anything."[72] Beyond approximating the linear sequence of cinematic montage, video can engage in a recursive archaeology of the image equally well suited for making time and space for more fantasy. Entirely capable of replicating the Lumières' windows, video may also reduce itself to a purely opaque frame; subsume cinema's inorganic windows within its frame; or generate its own decidedly organic, fluctuating windows. In some instances, it can achieve all three simultaneously. The greater video's hybridity, the more prevalent are the effects of its frame.

It is, however, not enough merely to identify the "self-knowledge" that "The Eiffel Tower, King Kong, and the White Woman" generates regarding its status as a hybrid medium defined by its frames.[73] The recursive effects of its meta-pictures say little about its two titular actors involved in recovering the Eiffel Tower, an operation that has arguably as much to with the Eifel Tower's function as a radio tower as its popularity as

---

71 Kluge and Negt 134–35.

72 Alexander Kluge, "On Film and the Public Sphere," 44, 48.

73 Mitchell, *Picture Theory*, 57.

a Parisian icon. The tower's function as a broadcast medium comes to the fore late in the video when, for example, dials from a tube radio, one presumably reminiscent of the kind Kluge and his family listened to in their dining room during the Third Reich, substitute the tower suspended in the heavens.[74] The fact that Kong and the white woman save a radio tower indeed casts an entirely new socio-political light on the video's production of self-knowledge. Radio and television are, in fact, not-so-distant cousins, Negt and Kluge remind us in *Public Sphere and Experience*: "Radio and television ... were not conceived as communication between free *citoyens*, individuals ... A product of the structure of postbourgeois society, this relationship is governed by the fact that the wealth objectified in social production appears so omnipotent that relationships between individuals fade into insignificance. In terms of social importance, a conversation between two people cannot compete with a radio or television broadcast."[75] Yet the very title of Kluge's video does suggest that radio and, by extension, television can enter into a beneficial relationship with individuals as long as it strives to replicate cinematic conditions capable of stoking the human capacity for fantasy. (Indeed, the broadcast's final shot captures this succinctly with its image of the Eiffel Tower zooming through the heavens on a movie screen within a darkened theater: radio is literally framed by a cinema replicated by video.) But why the two individuals in question are necessarily King Kong and a white woman remains not just unclear but also potentially vexed. Some viewers may rightly raise eyebrows at the video's apparent happy ending, insofar as it seems to overlook those racist and sexist discourses informed by colonial fantasies from the original 1933 film that preclude the labor of enlightenment Kluge and Negt attribute in *History and Obstinacy* to social relationships committed to preserving the autonomy of the other.[76]

But, upon further consideration, what the video (in dialogue with Negt and Kluge's theory) makes irrefutable is just how symbolically relevant the couple is for Kluge's ultimate goal to undermine these discourses as part of his larger effort intent on imagining social conditions for a public

---

74 Kluge writes, for example, of his family's "big super-radio" in their dining room in: Alexander Kluge, "Kluge on Opera, Film, and Feelings," ed. Miriam Hansen, trans. Miriam Hansen and Sara S. Poor, *New German Critique* 49 (Winter 1990): 94.

75 Negt and Kluge, *Public Sphere and Experience*, 99–100.

76 Kluge and Negt 376.

sphere in the age of new media. This subversion transpires on three levels.
Firstly, Kong and the white woman embody, in grotesque form, what
Negt and Kluge call the commodity character of nonrelationships; in the
backstory that precedes Kluge's video, Kong receives the white woman in
a violent exchange set on forging a provisional peace between so-called
savages and beasts. Yet this sacrificial act and its reliance on the logic of
the commodity's use value are negated in that moment when another
unforeseen economy between Kong and the white woman emerges that
evolves into an actual relationship built on mutual trust, reliability (i.e.,
the coordination of the labor involved in loving another person), care,
and protectiveness between the two. Secondly, Kluge recodes Kong (and
by extension the white woman, too) both anthropologically and evolu-
tionarily not as the embodiment of human prototypes but rather as basic
creaturely characteristics that can be traced back not only to humans'
and gorillas' common ancestors but also dinosaurs and the primordial
flows from which they came. This is why Kluge also sees Kong and the
white woman in not just Cyclone and Babette, as well as Bing Crosby
and Dorothy Lamour, but also in any number of other human and non-
human relationships. In fact, Kluge goes so far in his 2017 storybook
Kong's Finest Hour as to recast Kong somewhere between Hegel's absolute
spirit and elemental molecular forces found throughout the universe.[77]
Grasped from the perspective of these *longues durées*, what Kong and
the white woman embody cannot be pinned to the categories of race and
gender from whence they came. Rather, they are the elemental stuff that
makes the "risk of life" together possible.[78] Thirdly and lastly, Kluge and
Negt insist that the dissolution of the classical public sphere strains the
search for good fortune in relationships; both conflict and quietude are
far more prevalent due to the inflation of unmitigated external forces.[79]
This is the very quandary that Kong and the white woman, characters
sent out into the world in the fateful year 1933, face when the radio was
absconded in ways not unlike what happened to the medium that same
year under German fascism. What ensures, however, a relationship's
success, Kluge and Negt submit, is an object two people in a relationship can work on libidinally that is located at the very place where their

---

77 Alexander Kluge, *Kong's Finest Hour*, trans. Martin Brady et al. (Milan: Fondazi-
one Prada, 2017) 125–26, 35–37.

78 Kluge, *Kong's Finest Hour*, 41.

79 Kluge and Negt 343.

relationship began. "Love will bind itself to it, and it will transform into something lovable ... This transformation of worldly commodity values ... into a socially supported relationship is the exchange value in the labor of relationships"[80] A site of mediation through which the characteristics in relationships are exchanged, this object in the case of Kong and the white woman is nothing other than what suddenly went missing, the agent of the classical public sphere: cinema. The task, as Kluge demonstrates, lies in deploying video to replicate and expand upon the ways cinema can arbitrate this exchange. "In contrast to the television screen, which is a mere window," he explains in an interview about this very broadcast, "cinema is a unique replication of human characteristics."[81] The exchange involved in the labor of relationships is one and the same as capturing video's fluidity in discrete vessels. Without the trust subtending the former, the latter would never stand a chance.

From Decentered to Distributed Networks

Writing on television in the mid-eighties, Kluge foresaw three conditions his counterproductions on television would have to fulfill in order to succeed: they would need to follow commercial television's strengths; they would have to compensate for their comparable lack of capital with a strong sense of cohesiveness (*Zusammenhang*); and their organization would need to be decentralized.[82] Arguably, the third category—organization—was the arena where Kluge had the greatest freedom in terms of his program's form-content relations and its means of production. Whether it was ultimately decentralization that Kluge strove for is, however, not entirely clear. Programs like "The Eiffel Tower, King Kong, and the White Woman" exemplify his resolve to maximize the expressive plurality of his content and forms in an effort to oppose the centralized strengths of commercial television's content. And behind the scenes, a complex, decentralized network of actors—legal representation from the state of Hesse; financial backing from Tokyo, Hamburg, and Zurich; editorial assistance in West Berlin; post-production assistance

---

80 Kluge and Negt 366.

81 Alexander Kluge, "Primitive Diversity," trans. Sandra Niethardt, in *Difference and Orientation*, 329.

82 Kluge, "On the Expressions 'Media' and 'New Media,'" 286–87.

in Munich; and, most importantly, broadcasting rights in the state of North Rhine-Westphalia where dctp is headquartered—worked together to bring Kluge's auteurism to approximately a half a million viewers weekly.[83] An unintended result of all this decentralization was a certain decentralized reception as well. As many others have pointed out, Kluge's *10 till 11* broadcasts, an annoyance to the channels obligated to accommodate him, were relegated to the periphery of late-night Monday cable television, where viewers found them sandwiched between commercials and filler programming.[84] As one scholar aptly put it, the frustration Kluge's shows induced, the reluctance on the part of television and culture critics to engage them meaningfully, and the likelihood viewers would quickly forget them with every new and different installment all contributed to a decentered form of attention Siegfried Kracauer associated with critical "disclosure in distraction."[85] Yet Kluge's decentralized approach was, in many respects, playing catch-up to an already transformed media landscape. In fact, Negt and Kluge already diagnosed in *Public Sphere and Experience* the public sphere of production—a confluence of consciousness industries and administrative apparatuses—as having benefited from a hegemonic oscillation between centralization ("the accumulation of instruments of power") and decentralization ("the delegation of such instruments to other social realms").[86] Nevertheless, their first round of collaborative thinking lacked the metaphoricity demanded by the challenges that privatized new media in the eighties posed for the public sphere. Accordingly, Kluge went it alone and advanced in his later writings about new media from that same decade two more media metaphors in order to describe cartographically the fate of terra firma under the stars of cable and satellite television. Compared with the experiential expanses typical of classical public spheres, new communication technologies and their media moguls have given rise

83 Lutze 180–84; see also: Paul Leo Giani and Rainer Stollmann, "Das Privatfernsehen hat mit Verfassungsbruch angefangen," *Alexander Kluge-Jahrbuch* 4 (2017): 61–73.

84 Lutze 179–80; see also Matthias Uecker, *Anti-Fernsehen? Alexander Kluges Fernsehproduktionen* (Marburg: Schüren Verlag, 2000) 7.

85 Uecker 160. Siegfried Kracauer, "Cult of Distraction," in *The Mass Ornament: Weimar Essays*, ed. and trans. Thomas Y. Levin (Cambridge, MA: Harvard University Press, 1995) 326. On Kracauer's theory of distraction and the reception of Kluge's television, see also Uecker 155–57.

86 Negt and Kluge, *Public Sphere and Experience*, 70.

to "islands overloaded with communication."[87] As a result, these largely homogeneous concentrations of commercial content surrounded by water have depleted the biodiversity typical of the veritable gardens of experience that once populated the classical public sphere.

Just as Kluge sought to counter with the frame the affirmative realism of the window, so too the metaphor of the island required a counter-measure. Early writings alluded, for example, to coral reefs while more recent ones have invoked oases. Yet subtending these and other atten-dant metaphors is that of the garden. In fact, the garden operates as the metaphorical centerpiece of Kluge's media praxis for a public sphere in the age of digital capitalism, yet its origins reach back at least to Kluge and Negt's theory of a political economy of labor. At the crux of their theory lies the claim that, in spite of capital's powers of reification set on mortifying labor power, this innate human capacity—"an 'immense accumulation' of prehistories of characteristics"—nevertheless maintains an uncompromised remainder of its intrinsic nonidentity.[88] "The politi-cal economy of labor power is itself a laboring concept," they write, "and this is the reason why there is no metaphoric concept for it."[89] (In fact, this a-metaphoricity of labor characteristics, predicated on their prelin-guistic nature, is arguably the very plane on which they and the language of cinema, equally nonmetaphorical, engage in intercourse with one another.) Historical processes of separation, which continually divorce human beings from their original property (their bodies, the soil they once worked, and the communities they built) cannot preclude labor capacities from working on objects capable of mediating not so much the restitution of these original relations prior to their estrangement but rather new forms of relationality. The garden is an exemplary object in this respect:

Every highly industrialized person contains the ability to re-appropriate relations to the primitive means of production, the soil, and themselves. They do not necessarily have to actually move to the countryside to

---

87 Alexander Kluge, "Die Macht der Bewußtseinsindustrie und das Schicksal unserer Öffentlichkeit," in *Industrialisierung des Bewußtseins: Eine kritische Auseinandersetzung mit den "neuen" Medien*, eds. Klaus von Bismarck et al. (Munich: Piper, 1985) 86; Kluge, "On the Expressions 'Media' and 'New Media,'" 287–89.

88 Kluge and Negt 122.

89 Kluge and Negt 122–23.

create an urban horticulture as Marx prescribes it for the proletariat in Italian cities. They can also pursue gardening in their urban cultures, e.g., their brain as gardens, building canals, making connections between places, people, and situations like irrigating an area through a system of furrows, planting a nursery, and so on in every figurative, but nonmetaphorical sense.[90]

Although the language Kluge uses to name the relationality arising from the living labor of garden work—footpaths and canals—is decidedly metaphorical, the necessary labor and the resultant material relations are not. What appears at face value as being akin to the island is upon closer inspection, however, precisely its opposite. Referring to psychoanalyst Sándor Ferenczi's theory of the catastrophic development of genitality, Negt and Kluge point out in one of their many decisive footnotes in *Geschichte und Eigensinn* that the ultimate desire of all horticultural labor is a return to the ancestral ocean from which all life emerged. With this in mind, the distance between Kluge's notion of a garden and the islands he associates with the public sphere of production is quickly thrown into relief; unlike commercial television's endless archipelagos, Kluge's gardens are thalassic networks—aquatic versions of rhizome-like constellations devoid of beginnings and endings, centers and peripheries, and guiding golden threads—capable, in the words of Negt and Kluge (and Ferenczi), "of nourishing us without any assistance."[91] Neither viewers committed to tracking Kluge's broadcasts from week to week (before the advent of YouTube), nor scholars equipped with the extensive bibliographies of Kluge's shows could ever succeed at producing a definitive thematic let alone philosophical schema of his counterproductions. Instead of orbiting around one or more thematic centers, each of Kluge's broadcasts can potentially insert itself in any number of thematic nodal points in what is ultimately a multi-directional, distributed network of ideas far more anti-hierarchical than the decentered ones he originally argued for in his manifesto for auteurism on television from the mid-eighties. This is precisely why Kluge thought of his television programs not as what islands are to human beings but rather as what oceans are to fish.

---

90 Negt and Kluge, *Geschichte und Eigensinn*, 640.
91 Negt and Kluge, *Geschichte und Eigensinn*, 552n9; see Sándor Ferenczi, *Thalassa: A Theory of Genitality*, trans. Henry Alden Bunker (New York: W.W. Norton, 1968) 80.

Even though the English translation of *Public Sphere and Experience* gives readers the impression that Negt and Kluge explicitly thought in terms of networks, their engagement with the transformation of German public television in the eighties does demonstrate remarkable overlap with contemporary thinking about network architectures and control.[92] Commercial television programming and, by extension, its private networks are, Negt and Kluge contend, "structures of control" capable of restricting "viewers' unfulfilled needs" and this "technical control of the organization of experience" amounts to nothing less than an "actual instrument of power."[93] Although the emergence of publicly mandated commercial television signaled for them a paradigm shift away from the centralized networks of public television to more decentralized ones, Negt and Kluge make no secret of their suspicion toward Enzensberger's Brechtian call in his seminal 1970 essay "Constituents of a Theory of Media" for the decentralization of mass media in the name of facilitating greater public access. "The decentralization advocated by Enzensberger," they proffer, "would, under the prevailing social conditions, express itself as the further penetration of the consciousness industry. In other words, social forces would try to use this theory of delegation and decentralization in serving their own interests."[94] However, Negt and Kluge explicate their subsequent claim that "other structures of production and transmission" apart from Enzensberger's are theoretically possible with only a few faint brush strokes. "New forms of organization," they write, would need to encourage television viewers to abandon their usual position as endpoints in television's decentered networks, and instead orient themselves in a "broad conception of the circumstances in which [they find themselves]."[95] What Negt and Kluge index here without ever naming it explicitly, is, arguably, the distributed network of ideas that Kluge gradually realized with each and every installment

---

92 What is translated into English as "network" is in the German original either an *Anstalt* (institution) or a *Zusammenhang* (context or relationality). Although nowhere in *Öffentlichkeit und Erfahrung* do Negt and Kluge write of *Netzwerke* (networks), they do nevertheless think in terms of the three principle kinds of networks: centralized, decentralized, and distributed. See: Alexander R. Galloway, "Networks," in *Critical Terms for Media Studies*, eds. W.J.T. Mitchell and Mark B.N. Hansen (Chicago, IL: University of Chicago Press, 2010) 288.

93 Negt and Kluge, *Public Sphere and Experience*, 102, 4, 210.

94 Negt and Kluge, *Public Sphere and Experience*, 126.

95 Negt and Kluge, *Public Sphere and Experience*, 127, 128.

in what evolved into a seemingly never-ending web of interconnected television broadcasts devoid of a center. With every new broadcast, dctp's viewers set out in new directions capable of linking up with any number of other broadcasts. "I have always been concerned with networks," Kluge's acknowledged in 2010. "My literary works and films form webs as well."[96] Yet what Kluge achieved with his thirty-one years of uninterrupted television programming—dctp broadcast its last installment of *10 till 11* in June 2019—was a markedly different network than, say, the centralized networks in his early prose he modeled after Gottfried Benn's poetics or the decentralized ones operating in each of his individual films. Kluge's praxis (not to mention Negt and Kluge's theory) is deeply aware of the historically contingent nature of networks and the attendant power they exude. As media studies scholar Alexander Galloway has rightly pointed out, it would therefore be a gross error to overlook the ruin distributed networks are also capable of. "The web of ruin," Galloway explains with reference to the distributed networks in Aeschylus's tragedy *Agamemnon*, is "designed to ensnare and delimit even the most intractable opponent."[97] Galloway's point that distributed networks exert their own unique mode of organization and control, that they are arguably more democratic than centralized and decentralized ones, and are more powerful than every other one certainly invites the question as to what underlying protocols—i.e., rules outlining standards within a contingent environment—have subtended the distributed network of Kluge's television programs.[98] Far more pressing, however, is firstly the question regarding the apparent antagonism informing Kluge's reliance on the distributed network at a time when decentered ones shaped the dominant medium. How, exactly, does one emergent network architecture and its corresponding forms of control potentially undercut those of another, entirely different system? In other words, if the decentralized networks of commercial television operated according to the mantra "trust is good, but control is better," then how exactly does Kluge's distributed network forsake control in favor of building trust?[99]

---

96 Alexander Kluge, "Planting Gardens in the Data Tsunami," trans. Steffen Kaupp, in *Difference and Orientation*, 333.

97 Galloway 281.

98 Alexander R. Galloway, *Protocol: How Control Exists after Decentralization* (Cambridge, MA: MIT Press, 2004) 7, 13, 147.

99 Negt and Kluge, *Public Sphere and Experience*, 208.

Secondly, what becomes of Kluge's distributive network when the decentralized networks of commercial television have ceded their authority to
the Internet and therewith the "distributed network [becomes] the new
citadel, the new army, the new power"?[100]

Building Trust in Gardens of Trees:
Counter-Production as Critique

Asked in the spring of 2009 what he was working on, Kluge revealed
his plans to embark on an entirely new, colossal project, twenty-one
years after breaking into German television, a project that would involve
nothing less than creating an independent "theme park" on the Internet.
The nascent metaphor of the park soon morphed into a full-scale garden
and on May 8, 2009, Kluge debuted his domain www.dctp.tv, entitled
Gardens of Information.[101] Leaving little doubt at the time that his rationale for the shift was hardly influenced by technophilia, Kluge noted in a
reflection published several years earlier that it essentially boiled down
to an urgent matter of trust in rapidly changing times:

> Radio is the dominant medium at the time of the outbreak of war in
> 1939. People do not go to the movie theater at five in the morning
> when tanks roll into Poland. Rather, they listen to special announce-
> ments. On September 11, 2001, people do not reach for novels, but
> rather they tune in CNN on their televisions. TV and telephones are
> dominant mediums. The relation of trust—*Where do I get my news
> in an emergency?*—changes quickly. When India declares war against
> Pakistan in the year 2009, do I turn on CNN or the Internet?[102]

Assuming the rapid migration of trust to the Internet did indeed drive
Kluge to plant a garden amid what he has called the Internet's "data
tsunamis," an initial glance at his original webpage rightly induced
head-scratching on account of its striking similarities to his television
programs. In fact, many of his old "culture windows" originally broadcast

---

100 Galloway, "Networks," 290.

101 Alexander Kluge, "Woran arbeiten Sie gerade, Alexander Kluge?," *Die Zeit* (April
30, 2009).

102 Kluge and Weinmann 23.

on television were digitized from Betacam tape, edited down and pooled together on cloud servers, and linked through an Adobe Flash interface so that users had what looks like decades of Kluge's television readily available on their desktops or smartphones. In spite of the derivative relationship conveyed by its web address, what appeared to be Kluge's body of television work simply migrated over to the Internet was actually a carefully orchestrated interface entirely aware of its decidedly different environment compared with German cable television. In its earliest instantiations, the site loaded onto a desktop computer screen and greeted users with an Adobe Flash window front and center—the site's "livestream"—that began playing a video somewhere midstream so as to give the impression that one has just tuned into a live broadcast (see fig. 3.4).[103] Upon closer inspection, viewers recognized, however, the actual ploy without even having to inspect the provenance of the videos let alone the source code: individual videos were cued up to play in sequential order: after an interview entitled "The Fastest Star in the Milky Way," users then saw "Less Protection and More Participation for Children on the Internet" and, following that, "A Lifeboat Called Education." Users curious about a video's content could hover their cursor over the video to reveal its title and a brief description. Users eager to share their viewing experience could also embed a link to any of the livestream videos using unique social media tabs alongside the frame. They could either allow the player to run through the pre-programmed sequence of videos or choose any one of the many other videos thematically related to the "livestream," listed in a horizontal menu below the window. What initially appeared like a random selection of videos gradually came into view as featured excerpts belonging to whole thematic clusters. One moment a user might be looking at one of ten videos grouped around the title "Mathematics Is Mired in Everything," or another from a collection of twenty-three videos on "Catastrophe Theory and Evolution," or a third from the twenty-nine videos on "How Poetic Is Science?" Users

---

103 Since the completion of this chapter (in the spring of 2018), Adobe discontinued the flash player originally used to realize Kluge's vision of his online Gardens of Information's interface as a screen within a screen surrounded by four pinwheels (each containing a wealth of thematic subdirectories) (see figs. 3.4 and 3.5). Even though its spherical menus have been replaced by a thematic grid requiring users to scroll downward, as of this writing the current instantiation of the graphical user interface for dctp. tv retains the original centerpiece, the "livestream," and still sits atop the same sylvan architecture discussed below.

less interested in the "livestream" or the attendant videos relating to astrophysics previewed in the horizontal menu could explore four other portals positioned at the corners of the screen's frame—"Grand Topics," "News Workshop," "Gardens of Curiosity," and "Partners and Events"— all of which contained their own Rolodex of color-coded topics ranging from "World War I" (forty-three videos) to "Everything Flows" (thirty-three videos), from the "Philosophy of Money" (eighteen videos) to an omnibus of interviews with Oskar Negt (eleven videos) (see fig. 3.5). While the prominently featured link to the site's "Catch-Up Service" underscored the impression that www.dctp.tv is merely an archive for Kluge's television shows, careful inspection makes clear that the site's thematic nature actually involved a careful editing and curating of Kluge's filmography as well as his entire television catalogue. What was once a twenty-four-minute television interview recorded in the nineties might be reduced, for example, to a three-minute excerpt sandwiched between a recently made, five-minute program entirely composed of title cards and a three-minute excerpt from one of Kluge's black-and-white shorts from the sixties.

A window framed by indices cataloguing an ever-expanding array of themes, Kluge's Gardens of Information appears on the surface to traffic in the very same recursive metaphoricity operative in his television programs. Its windows and frames (all contained within the browser window) notwithstanding, dctp.tv is really a garden in terms of both its structure and function. Gardens, Kluge has recently pointed out, strike a balance between the inhospitable nature of deserts and the excesses of jungles. The Internet, on the other hand, is both a silicon desert and a jungle of information.[104] Under these extreme circumstances, say both Kluge and Negt, the Internet has given rise to a form of labor akin to the workshop system: it has facilitated unprecedented amounts of communication, unleashed new capacities for intelligence, allowed for greater participation, and by extension catalyzed new public spheres (which Hansen would rightly call partial public spheres).[105] In spite of all this welcomed online diversity and dissonance, the Internet lacks both the proportions and balance necessary for orienting oneself. "The excess of

---

104 Gawan Fagard, "Die Fliege im Bernstein: Alexander Kluge über Rudolf Steiner und Andrei Tarkowski, Teil I," *ALL-OVER: Magazin für Kunst und Ästhetik* 6 (Spring 2014): 42.

105 Kluge and Negt 191, 423, 165, 191.

the natural material 'information' on the Internet," Kluge remarked in an essay on digital culture from 2013, "leads to the need for horticulture, the erection of a barrier against 'information.' It is therefore important that there are places in the Internet where a person can retreat to a specific interest of their own."[106] Modeled after the *hortus conclusus* or "enclosed garden" typical of medieval cloisters, Kluge's Gardens of Information is designed as a closed space where a more humane proportionality between the infinite expanses of the Internet and the fixed limits of lived time and space are made accessible. You can enter it, but, save for backtracking, Kluge's garden will not deliver you back out into the wilds of the Internet. His objective—to make gardens out of raw information much like oceans make coral reefs—seeks to facilitate the transformation of indifference (a result of feeling overwhelmed by too much) into interest.[107] Essential for this operation is the introduction of distinctions. In so doing, Kluge's digital horticulture makes no secret of its recourse to the language of Niklas Luhmann's systems theory. On Kluge's fascination for systems theory, Luhmann's student Dirk Baecker, one of Kluge's many frequent interlocutors, has underscored what Kluge and Negt themselves acknowledge in *History and Obstinacy*, namely what unlikely bedfellows their Frankfurt tradition of critical theory and Luhmann's systems theory are.[108] Without a doubt familiar with Luhmann's work ever since he substituted for Adorno at the Goethe– University Frankfurt in the winter semester of 1968–69, Negt and Kluge never actually formally engaged Luhmann in their three principal works. Unlike his former supervisor Habermas, who at least took Luhmann's systems theory to task, Negt in fact never bothered with him in his own work either, most likely because Luhmann's second-order thought is so alien and downright hostile toward his. It should come therefore as little to no surprise that it was the avowed non-philosopher Kluge who was largely responsible for bringing Luhmann to the table.

"Following Niklas Luhmann," Kluge explains in *History and Obstinacy*, "Dirk Baecker [has] laid out in greater detail some of the processes

---

106 Kluge, "The Equivalent of an Oasis," 198.

107 Alexander Kluge, "Gardens Are Like Wells: Inside Every Person (However Serious or Playful) Lies an 'Enclosed Garden,'" trans. Martin Brady and Helen Hughes, in *Serpentine Gallery Pavilion 2011: Hortus Conclusus*, eds. Sophie O'Brien et al. (London: Koenig Books and Serpentine Gallery, 2011) 21.

108 Kluge and Negt 92.

that arise with … shifts … in the communication of knowledge." "An observable partial aspect in the mutation of the concept of intelligence," he continues, "comes from the *resistance* against the excess of substance that a new medium imposes on it."[109] In other words, what Baecker lifts from Luhmann's masterpiece *Theory of Society* that resonates with Kluge is the premise that every new media shift—from speech to writing and printing to computers—generates techniques for reducing complexity, which in turn unleash according to Baecker's language of systems theory an "excess of meaning."[110] Although Kluge is far more inclined to speak of fantasy, the status of this surplus appears to him much less urgent than does the matter of trust. "I do not need to hear and understand everything in order to be able to preserve my trust," Kluge goes on to note with respect to the shocks that come with every media paradigm shift and the resistance they provoke. First tackled in his book *Trust and Power*, published a year before his temporary post in Frankfurt, trust is, for Luhmann, a basic fact of all social life. "In many situations, a person can choose in certain respects whether or not to bestow trust," Luhmann asserts at the book's outset. "But a complete absence of trust would prevent him or her even from getting up in the morning. He would be prey to … paralyzing fears."[111] Bestowing trust is, in contradistinction to hope, a matter of making risky decisions that involve reducing unmanageable complexity through the creation of a boundary separating the inside of a system from its surrounding environment. Not only risky, trust is also fragile insofar as violations to its threshold from the outside invariably flood the system with more information than it can handle, and for this reason control and maintenance of the boundary are paramount. What the strategy of trust ultimately achieves, says Luhmann, is an increase in "possibilities for experience and action" that is directly proportional to a heightened indifference toward other possibilities within the system.[112] When Kluge identifies the objective of his Gardens of Information as the reduction of indifference as mentioned above, he means, from Luhmann's vantage point, building a system that actually

---

109 Kluge and Negt 195.

110 Dirk Baecker, *Studien zur nächsten Gesellschaft* (Frankfurt am Main: Suhrkamp Verlag, 2007) 10.

111 Niklas Luhmann, *Trust and Power*, eds. Christian Morgner and Michael King, trans. Howard Davis, John Raffan, and Kathryn Rooney (Cambridge, UK: Polity Press, 2017) 5.

112 Luhmann, *Trust and Power*, 9, 28.

Figure 3.4. Screenshot of the "livestream" on dctp.tv: Peter Berling as lawyer. © Alexander Kluge.

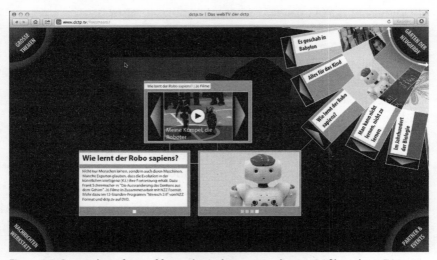

Figure 3.5. Screenshot of one of four spherical menus on dctp.tv: 26 films about "How Robo Sapiens Learn." © Alexander Kluge.

generates indifference toward the limitless connections possible within the vast distributed network of ideas that his weekly television programs have been expanding for decades. The pared-down videos sequenced in thematic clusters and categorized according to broad rubrics constitute, in other words, a second-order system that fixes one set of connections at the expense of countless others that could have been made between Kluge's nearly four thousand individual television broadcasts. In terms of its organization, Kluge's garden is, at least on the level of the user interface, a closed and decentered network that feeds a central window framed by four tree structures containing nodes and leaves (see fig. 3.5). In the face of complexity, building trust, for Kluge, entails, in short, a return to the more hierarchical structures he sought to counter with the distributed network of themes characteristic of his television programs.

Of course, Kluge's original intention was never to cordon off his online garden system from a television environment of his own making. Indeed, without the latter, the former would be impossible. For Kluge, the actual environment under scrutiny is the Internet itself, which he described in an interview from late 2017 as a porous system in which trust has eroded considerably: "The algorithms of Silicon Valley generate fear because they leave each and every individual relatively powerless."[113] While it is entirely feasible to introduce, for example, Luhmann's concept of the "structural coupling" in an effort to extend Kluge's recourse to the language of systems theory to his multiple subsystems (streaming video, television, film, and literature), there are, however, strong reasons for abstaining from subsuming all of his praxis along with his and Negt's theory under Luhmann's. Above all, Kluge attests to the limits of Luhmann's thinking for both his own praxis as well as his and Negt's theory the moment he returns to the language of Kant and Marx. A form of "supplemental labor," he insists, operations that reduce complexity enact for Kluge a form of critique—ostensibly no different than Kant's—that "distinguishes what I need not know from that what I should know."[114] In the end, unwilling to follow Luhmann's theory to its logical conclusion (where a subject's praxis becomes a system's autopoiesis and theory's critique is exchanged for second-order description), Kluge makes clear that Luhmann's posthuman "super-theory" can merely serve as a discrete set of procedural tools—a means to an end—for serving Kluge's own subject-centered agenda wedded to human obstinacy and the balance its labor can strike. "Where there are algorithms," Kluge exclaimed in the aforementioned interview, "there are also counter-algorithms."[115] Yet these

---

113 Kolja Reichert, "'Künstler sind Pilotfischchen': Alexander Kluge im Interview," *Frankfurter Allgemeine Zeitung* (October 19, 2017), http://www.faz.net/-gsa-92vbx.

114 Kluge and Negt 195.

115 Reichert, "'Künstler sind Pilotfischchen.'"

counter-algorithms are arguably not those responsible for managing the content, transmission, and consumption of his Gardens of Information. Just as is the case with viewers tracking the themes of Kluge's television broadcasts from week to week, these counter-algorithms are any number of mental operations that users may undertake in order to derive cohesiveness from the principle of montage—a framing device par excellence—still firmly intact within and between the 123 branches that constituted his gardens' four trees that contained over 2,200 different videos.

In this respect, Kluge's Gardens of Information does make good use of Luhmann's observation that a system's reduction of external complexity does generate internal complexity, but Kluge does so within a first-order system still very much indebted to hermeneutics that the "systems network 2000" has long ago dispensed with. Accordingly, the judgment subtending what Kluge calls critique is not simply the subtractive logic of "scrutinizing, surveying, balancing, and selecting" that Adorno once decried on account of its preconceived, reductive categories.[116] It is also exponential insofar as Kluge's Gardens of Information provides users with an inscribed space where their fantastic labor may forge sundry footpaths and waterways between its tree's roots and branches without necessarily getting lost entirely. What this has to do with the potential for counterpublic spheres in the present-day network society in the end boils down to a matter of the structure of experience. A counterpublic sphere's viability is more than just a question of mounting an adversarial form of production. It is also not enough to speak of the hybrid matrix of various public spheres from which counterpublics can emerge. If Kluge's own productions within the scope of new media are any indication, then crucial, too, is a counterpublic sphere's structural asymmetry to the dominant networks on which the public spheres of production continue to organize and consume the mental life of human beings. The point is not that there is such a thing as a network free of control and power, but rather that a counterproduction capable of engendering relationalities askew to the dominant ones responsible for organizing affirmative experience can enlist the control and power characteristic of its chosen asymmetrical network as a force of opposition. Furthermore, it means

---

116 Theodor W. Adorno, "Cultural Criticism and Society," in *Prisms*, trans. Samuel and Shierry Weber (Cambridge, MA: MIT Press, 1994) 23.

that resistance does not reside in any single counter-network—regardless of whether it is centralized, decentralized, or distributed—but rather
that it must be staged simultaneously in multiple kinds of networks
across different environments (literature, film, television, and the Internet), that these counter-networks transcend their boundaries in order
to engage in intercourse with one another, and that in every instance no
one network configuration is a silver bullet for estrangement. Of greatest
importance, say Kluge and Negt, is whether a medium and its attendant
metaphors can provide "orientation as it applies to the practical experience of life," and this comes down to the subjective factor of whether
one places one's trust in indirect experience.[117] Although an essential first
step, the reduction of complexity through the formation of a metaphorical *hortus conclusus* is not enough. Trust accrues only once one puts one's
mind to it.

---

117 Kluge and Negt 197.

Figures 4.1 and 4.2. Two stills from *Miscellaneous News*. Top, a family looks at clouds; bottom, red clouds over Germany. © Alexander Kluge.

4

Permanent Catastrophe and Everyday Life: Judgment and the Remediation of the Political

The Political Aporia of Critical Theory

One of Oskar Negt and Alexander Kluge's most insightful critics, Rainer Stollmann, has tendered a most useful framework for grasping the concerns driving each of their first three publications, which together clock in at 2,265 pages. Recalling Immanuel Kant's three queries constituting his vision for a cosmopolitan philosophy, Stollmann has proposed three questions that correspond to each of their three publications:[1]

What is a public sphere?
What is culture?
What is politics?[2]

Careful consideration of Negt and Kluge's own reflections on their thinking as they moved from their first book, *Public Sphere and Experience* from 1972, to the third book, the untranslated *Maßverhältnisse*

---

1 Immanuel Kant, *Lectures on Logic*, ed. and trans. J. Michael Young (Cambridge: Cambridge University Press, 1992) 538/25.

2 Rainer Stollmann, "Vernunft ist ein Gefühl für Zusammenhang," in *Der Maulwurf kennt kein System: Beiträge zur gemeinsamen Philosophie von Oskar Negt und Alexander Kluge*, eds. Christian Schulte and Rainer Stollmann (Bielefeld: transcript Verlag, 2005) 233.

des Politischen [Measured Relations of the Political] from 1992, reveals, however, that the sequence of their publications (and by extension these three questions) does not reflect the actual evolution of their thought. In *Geschichte und Eigensinn*, for example, they explain how they pick up where they left off in the preceding *Public Sphere and Experience*, namely with the question of proletarian characteristics and their disorganization.[3] Yet they also confess that *History and Obstinacy* was as much, if not more, a return to perspectives that preceded their first book than any continuation. "Politics necessarily presupposes a theory of the proletarian public sphere," they explain in chapter 3 of *History and Obstinacy*, "and this in turn requires a theory of the developmental history of each and every labor capacity."[4] Neither posterior nor anterior with respect to the two preceding works, their third collaboration might best be described as a supraordinate remediation intent on qualifying what repeatedly eluded their grasp all along: "As soon as our attention focused on the political, this object vanished as it were," they write in the preface to "Measured Relations of the Political." "The *political* remained a question, but what officially counted as politics increasingly assumed a twisted and mistaken character."[5] Regardless of what exactly constitutes the political—they initially call it a "distorted compound thing"—what's clear is Negt and Kluge's insistence that it, thoroughly unlike the substance of professional politics with its laws, apparatuses, and elites, can exert a force critical for transforming the culture of labor that subtends all public spheres.[6] And, whereas the political is what both public spheres

---

3 Oskar Negt and Alexander Kluge, *Geschichte und Eigensinn*, in *Der unterschätzte Mensch: Gemeinsame Philosophie in zwei Bänden*, vol. 2 (Frankfurt am Main: Zweitausendeins, 2001) 32; see also Oskar Negt and Alexander Kluge, *Public Sphere and Experience: Toward an Analysis of the Bourgeois and Proletarian Public Sphere*, trans. Peter Labanyi, Jamie Owen Daniel, and Assenka Oksiloff (Minneapolis: University of Minnesota Press, 1993) 295–97.

4 Alexander Kluge and Oskar Negt, *History and Obstinacy*, ed. Devin Fore, trans. Richard Langston et al. (New York: Zone Books, 2014) 121; see also: Eberhard Knödler-Bunte, Hajo Funke, and Arno Widmann, "The History of Living Labor Power: A Discussion with Oskar Negt and Alexander Kluge," trans. Fiona Elliot, *October* 149 (Summer 2014): 35.

5 Oskar Negt and Alexander Kluge, preface to *Maßverhältnisse des Politischen: 15 Vorschläge zum Unterscheidungsvermögen* (Frankfurt am Main: S. Fischer Verlag, 1992) 9. This preface is excised from the reprint found in volume 1 of *Der unterschätzte Mensch* cited below.

6 Negt and Kluge, preface, 9.

and the culture of labor lack in good measure, it always inhabited as a matter of course, they say, both their "political course of conduct" and corresponding "activities."[7] Called "theory labor" in their preceding collaboration, the political in their collaborative philosophy now comes across in "Measured Relations of the Political" as an attitude or comportment that was there from the very beginning but one that only got its due toward the end of their formal trilogy.

Pursuing the elusive nature and location of the political as Negt and Kluge outline it must also take into consideration its avowed relationship to the legacy of Frankfurt School thinking. In his introduction to their collected works, Kluge writes as if stating the obvious, "Critical Theory is and always was a political theory."[8] The historical origins of the Frankfurt School's political thrust, he adds, grew out of a fiendishly difficult question: "How does a highly developed civilization turn to fascism?"[9] In this spirit, he has gone so far in a recent interview as to say that the scourge of fascism not only continues to haunt contemporary society, but that he and Negt are also ready and waiting in the trenches: "We want nothing more than to defeat fascism [and] to turn Nazis around."[10] But as intellectual historian Martin Jay tells it in his groundbreaking history, the Frankfurt School's syncretic method actually precluded the narrow focus required to develop an "autonomous theory of politics" in spite of the Institute's inclusion of political scientists like Franz Neumann and Otto Kirchheimer.[11] Furthermore, its interrogations of fascism were far more concerned with interdisciplinary analyses of society—its authoritarian psychology, the political component of its political economy, its weakness for technological rationality and mass culture—than with the development of a "discrete theory of political authority or obligation."[12] Were it to exist, a grand theory of authority or obligation would nevertheless fall under what Negt and Kluge deride as "twisted and mistaken"

---

7 Negt and Kluge, preface, 9.

8 Alexander Kluge, "Momentaufnahme aus unserer Zusammenarbeit," in *Der unterschätzte Mensch: Gemeinsame Philosophie in zwei Bänden*, vol. 1 (Frankfurt am Main: Zweitausendeins, 2001) 16n2.

9 Kluge, "Momentaufnahme aus unserer Zusammenarbeit," 16.

10 Richard Langston, "'Das ist die umgekehrte Flaschenpost': Zwei Interviews mit Oskar Negt und Alexander Kluge," *Alexander Kluge-Jahrbuch* 2 (2015): 75.

11 Martin Jay, *The Dialectical Imagination: A History of the Frankfurt School and the Institute of Social Research, 1923–1950* (Boston: Little, Brown, 1972) 118.

12 Jay 166, 118.

politics with lasting "catastrophic consequences."[13] Looking alternatively
to their mentor Theodor W. Adorno, the political might resonate—when
grasped negatively—with the resistance he finds mediated through the
autonomous aesthetic, anti-fascist pedagogy, and negative theory.[14]
However, Adorno would certainly draw the line at Negt and Kluge's
emphasis on the political's use value as well as its potential for constituting and maintaining a community or commonwealth (*Gemeinwesen*).[15]
Such talk would certainly be an affront to Adorno's injunction that "political undertakings can sink into pseudo-activity."[16] If not in the spirit of
Neumann, Kirchheimer, or even Adorno, and also avowedly unable to
make use of Jürgen Habermas's theory, Kluge's recourse to critical theory's alleged pantheon of political thinkers raises red flags.[17] Equally, if not
more, challenging is how, within this theoretical context, to situate the
opening to chapter 1: "In the following work we shall pose the question:
What is political about political action?"[18]

If the subtle clues buried in their preface—words like "course of
conduct" and "activities"—were not obvious enough, Negt and Kluge
reveal in a single blow their most important of interlocutors in this first
sentence. Aside from isolated Freudian references to mental exercises
as *Probehandeln* and "impossible collective action" exemplified in the
Grimm brothers' fairy tales, the concept of action (*Handeln*) makes only
rare and unqualified appearances in their preceding collaborations.[19]
Both the prominence and the provenance of this concept should startle
those readers especially familiar with Hannah Arendt's seminal work
The Human Condition from 1958, in which she argues, "action is the
political activity par excellence."[20] Nowhere in their philosophy there-
tofore had Negt and Kluge ever engaged Arendt let alone this crucial

13 Oskar Negt and Alexander Kluge, *Maßverhältnisse des Politischen: Vorschläge zum Unterscheidungsvermögen*, in *Der unterschätzte Mensch: Gemeinsame Philosophie in zwei Bänden*, vol. 1 (Frankfurt am Main: Zweitausendeins, 2001) 695.

14 Cf. Russell Berman, "Adorno's Politics," in *Adorno: A Critical Reader*, eds. Nigel Gibson and Andrew Rubin (Malden, MA: Blackwell Publishers, 2002) 110–31.

15 Negt and Kluge, *Maßverhältnisse des Politischen*, 696.

16 Theodor W. Adorno, "Resignation," in *Critical Models: Interventions and Catch-words*, trans. Henry W. Pickford (New York: Columbia University Press, 1998) 292.

17 Negt and Kluge, preface, 9.

18 Negt and Kluge, *Maßverhältnisse des Politischen*, 696.

19 Kluge and Negt 184, 290–91. Translation slightly modified.

20 Hannah Arendt, *The Human Condition*, 2nd ed. (Chicago: University of Chicago Press, 1998) 9.

subdivision of the *vita activa* she distinguishes from labor (*Arbeit*) and work (*Herstellen*). Not even Habermas, who introduced action in his own thinking as early as 1968 and made it the cornerstone of his magnum opus, availed himself of Arendt's concept of action first made accessible in German translation in 1960.[21] Whereas Habermas would eventually engage Arendt productively, Negt and Kluge kept her at bay for decades. The reasons are not difficult to surmise. Deeply critical of not just Marx but all materialisms, Arendt saw the pandemic conflation of labor in all modern thought and the resultant banishment of action into the private sphere as further denigration of politics' role in elevating human existence. Kluge and Negt's collaborations find themselves squarely in Arendt's crosshairs for the simple reason that they, convinced that Marx "never wrote on politics" because he never wrote a political economy of labor power, sought to fill this lacunae by applying the concept of labor to spheres of social life distinctly outside usual places of work.[22] That Kluge and Negt and Arendt would have butted heads becomes especially clear when comparing the former's "labor of relationships" and the latter's diametrically opposed insistence on the "special relationship between action and being together."[23] The third and final book that Negt and Kluge co-authored before turning their attention in earnest to making television dialogues, "Measured Relations of the Political" is arguably that installment in their formal trilogy most overlooked. There is certainly no one single reason for this, but one of only a very few reviewers, writing shortly after the book's publication, struck a chord with his observation that when compared with contemporary political theories multicultural, postcolonial, and transnational in focus, what appeared like Negt and Kluge's nineteenth-century European humanism undergirding "Measured Relations of the Political" was simply out of step with the increasingly globalized times.[24] However, if the preamble to their third book is indeed a sign of a productive dialogue with Arendt that presumably worked through these aforementioned antagonisms, then not only is their case for the political without question representative

---

21 Jürgen Habermas, "Arbeit und Interaktion: Bemerkungen zu Hegels Jenenser *Philosophie des Geistes*," in *Technik und Wissenschaft als "Ideologie*," (Frankfurt am Main: Suhrkamp Verlag, 1968) 9–47.

22 Kluge and Negt 120–21.

23 Kluge and Negt 341; Arendt 23.

24 Rainer Ganahl, "Blaupause für eine deutsche Revolution," *Texte zur Kunst* 2.7 (1992): 176.

of the later twentieth century, but also quite possibly a sign of a remarkable opening in their thinking.

To make sense of the curious place reserved for Arendt in Negt and
Kluge's pursuit of the elusive category of the political and its relationship
to action as they define it, we follow Arendt's lead, that contends that
"politically, the modern world ... was born with the first atomic explosions."[25] A key feature of what Arendt calls the third most recent stage in
the alienation of the *vita activa*, the natural sciences (best exemplified
by astro- and nuclear physics) have advanced as the primary agent of
a misguided form of action that no longer avails itself of speech, has
blurred the threshold between nature and world, and has refrained from
influencing human relationships as action once did. Writing over thirty
years later, in the shadow of the fall of the Iron Curtain, the Gulf War,
and the Yugoslav Wars, Negt and Kluge look not to recent world political
events but rather to the catastrophic meltdown at the Chernobyl Nuclear
Power Plant in April 1986 as their exemplar of science and technology's
disastrous effects on the parameters necessary for political action. What
made this catastrophic event so exceptional for Negt and Kluge was the
fact that the deadly effects of the meltdown—unlike those from major
calamities associated with the years 1914, 1933, and 1989—eluded the
powers of human perception and confounded political action like never
before. Yoking the fundamental alterations to time and space that the
singular event in Chernobyl suddenly brought to the fore to the quotidian dimensions of the political—everyday feelings—was not the only
pressing concern Negt and Kluge faced. Chernobyl spawned other political theories that also touted a paradigm shift in politics that threatened
to foreclose Negt and Kluge's own concept of the political. In addition
to illustrating both Negt's and Kluge's respective critical appraisals of
postmodern catastrophe theories with respect to the Frankfurt School's
own thoughts on permanent catastrophe, this chapter argues, on the
one hand, that Arendt provided Negt and Kluge's concept of the political with a model for mapping political judgment onto Immanuel Kant's
aesthetic judgment. On the other hand, it queries exactly how the plurality of spectatorship so central for Arendt's concept of judgment plays
out in Kluge's cinematic and televisual work intent on remediating the
invisible transformation of time and space that a global catastrophe like

---

25 Arendt 6.

Chernobyl precipitated. As shall be established, only the mediation of affective intensities otherwise absent in the shadow of such a catastrophe can reestablish measured relations necessary for the political to take shape.

Catastrophe Management and Judgment

Of all the many recurring characters populating Kluge's films, literature, and television broadcasts, Swiss mathematician Witzlaff is certainly one of the more obscure ones. In the first of four iterations of his story spanning nearly three decades of Kluge's storytelling, Witzlaff—arguably a Germanized rendition of the actual British archaeologist John Malcolm Wagstaff—is introduced as a fictional contemporary of mathematicians René Thom and Christopher Zeeman, the French founder and British promoter of catastrophe theory, respectively. After explicating in a few strokes how their theory deposes the commonsensical improbability of effects devoid of causes by deriving mathematically basic types of catastrophic discontinuities that can arise in continuous processes, Witzlaff tells his wife, "We are fortune-tellers."[26] With the help of a computer, he explains further, catastrophe theory can predict the tipping point of any number of phenomena ranging from industrial explosions to political negotiations, business trends to the growth of biological organisms. "But why is it necessary to calculate this after the fact?" his wife counters. Regarding how an organism evolves, "we already know how it happens even without any prediction." Using the rudimentary illustration of superheated water, Witzlaff retorts that knowledge based solely on empirical evidence fails to explain what happens when "pure water" devoid of contaminants is slowly heated in an ideal sterile container free of dirt. "You can't manage that in the form of an experiment," he brags. "But with the help of catastrophe theory, I can represent in the form of a simple classical equation what you cannot."[27] At face value a story about the divide between scientific and lay knowledge, Kluge's take closes with Witzlaff at his desk writing a letter to an advertising consultant in

---

26 Alexander Kluge, "Erfassung der 'Katastrophen ohne Ursache,'" in *Neue Geschichten, Hefte 1–18: "Unheimlichkeit der Zeit"* (Frankfurt am Main: Suhrkamp, Verlag, 1977) 477.

27 Kluge, "Erfassung der 'Katastrophen Ohne Ursache,'" 478.

Johannesburg who he hopes will find him a prospective buyer interested in securing his mathematic invention for the region's diamond industry. If Witzlaff seems like a crass opportunist in Kluge's story from 1977, our next meeting with the statistician in a story published two years later punctuates his wife's incredulity. Now intent on using "the newest findings in probability calculations" to verify the quantity of labor necessary for producing historical catastrophes, Witzlaff is clearly mocked; "Outstanding results!" the narrator sarcastically exclaims, as if to suggest how crass it is that the accuracy of such outcomes trumps not only the tragic nature of catastrophic events but also the labor that ends in tragedy.[28] In his most recent appearance in 2012, any pretense to apply Witzlaff's theory to humanitarian ends falls flat entirely. Having originally predicted a confluence of natural and man-made catastrophes off the coast of Istanbul, he rebuffs colleagues who chide him for claiming, after the fact, that his data correctly predicted the catastrophe in Fukushima, Japan, on March 11, 2011. Unfazed by his critics, Witzlaff has the last word. "The earth has the tendency to show its power from time to time. It is therefore immaterial ... where and when nature rears its paw."[29]

The fact that Witzlaff has remained not only a staple in Kluge's stock of characters but also an object of implicit derision underscores the fact that not only what constitutes catastrophes but also how they should be theorized has remained a core concern for his prose. What his stories omit, however, is a clear alternative to Witzlaff's mathematical fortune-telling. Given the reference in Witzlaff's original story to Engels's explication of the dialectical leap as illustrated by superheated water, contemporary English-language debates between proponents of catastrophe theory, like the aforementioned Wagstaff, and proponents of dialectical materialism could effectively fill this lacuna.[30] (Whereas dialectical materialists claimed that catastrophe theory was only concerned with observing the appearance of discontinuity, scholars like Wagstaff considered Marxism's claim to a "deep understanding of reality" as nothing more than specious philosophical "mysticism.")[31] What proves far more fleshed out than this

---

28 Alexander Kluge, *Die Patriotin: Texte/Bilder 1–6* (Frankfurt am Main: Zweitausendeins, 1979) 315.

29 Alexander Kluge, "Witzlaffs Katastrophentheorie," in *Das fünfte Buch* (Frankfurt am Main: Suhrkamp Verlag, 2012) 51.

30 Cf. Friedrich Engels, *Anti-Dührung*, in Karl Marx and Friedrich Engels, *Collected Works*, vol. 25 (New York: International Publishers, 1987) 58–59, 117.

31 The summary of British Marxian criticism leveled at catastrophe theory can be

inconclusive spat is Negt's own wrangle with another subsequent theory of catastrophe similarly dismissive of Marxian hermeneutics. Writing in the year of the Space Shuttle *Challenger* disaster and the meltdown at the Chernobyl Nuclear Power Plant, sociologist Ulrich Beck argued that such tragedies were endemic to a new unprecedented level of techno-scientific modernization that prompted since the early seventies not only inward reflection but also a call for the "political and economic management" of such catastrophes. "How," Beck asks in order to frame his thesis in the form of a question, "can the risks and hazards systematically produced as part of modernization be prevented, minimized, dramatized, or channeled?"[32] Another name for "catastrophic society," Beck's risk society is one in which imminent catastrophe is ubiquitous, imperceptible, planetary (insofar as it is capable of metastasizing around the globe), long-lasting, incalculable, and irreversible.[33] In contradistinction to the diagnostic certitude of Thom's structuralist typology, Beck reserves no exclusive place for scientific knowledge. In his poststructuralist reflexive postmodernity, the ascendant politics of knowledge fueled by media and information technologies is decentralized and populist, and its truth claims are always contested. Nevertheless, both theories of catastrophe share, like the character of Witzlaff who holds the principle of causality to be naïve and flawed, a suspicion of deep functional, systemic certainties.

For Negt, the problem with Beck's pursuit of postmodernity is a political one. When practiced as a critical theory of society, sociology is invariably caught between the need for interpretative concepts that explain the existing social order and concepts intent on acting so as to "render the shrouded side of an object public and provide access to possible transformative intervention."[34] The success of such a sociology lives or dies, Negt contends, by the signifying power of its concepts. Beck's refashioned sociology does away with his discipline's accepted structural concepts—for example, class and collectivity, capitalism and socialism, domination and power—and in their stead conflates replacement concepts for grappling with society—like risk, event, or fun—that are

---

found in: Michael Day and Jacqueline Tivers, "Catastrophe Theory and Geography: A Marxist Critique," *Area* 11.1 (1979): 54–58.

32 Ulrich Beck, *Risk Society: Towards a New Modernity*, trans. Mark Ritter (London: Sage Publications, 1992) 19.

33 Beck 78–79.

34 Oskar Negt, *Arbeit und menschliche Würde* (Göttingen: Steidl Verlag, 2001) 586.

incapable of addressing adequately the tensions between the universal and the particular constituting actual social life. To do so would mean to engage in dialectical thinking that ostensibly has no truck with the postmodern transformation of society diagnosed by Beck. Instead of zeroing in, for example, on the morphed logic of capital (not to mention the motives, interests, and strategies of its arbiters), his model of reflexive modernity promotes modernization itself—an "objective spirit," as it were—as the sole force shaping all social relations.[35] Without a care for who actually carries what kinds of risk on an everyday basis, Beck's existential, universalizing tone, says Negt, is egalitarian and individualistic, indifferent and cynical. How is it possible, in other words, to speak of the pandemic metastasis of catastrophic fear, on the one hand, and disregard the uneven social experience of actual catastrophe, on the other? "Even the virtually universal spread of dangerous radiation from the catastrophe at Chernobyl," Negt proffers as an illustration in the extreme, "witnessed divisions according to old privileges and power structures."[36] The political upshot of Beck's paradigm shift undercuts not only critical sociology's power to expose the ideologies driving society, but also acquiesces to the hollowing out of collective political processes. In Beck's account of the society of risk, scientific, technological, and economic innovations have grown such that they assume new political authority, while the traditional centers of politics, like the halls of parliamentary democracy, persist as shells devoid of the concentrated power once invested in them. This "unbinding of politics" into heterogeneous, decentralized centers of "sub-politics"—the technologically driven marketplace, mass media, the private sphere—allows for new political possibilities rooted in the individual's creativity, self-determination, initiative, and entrepreneurial drive, characteristics Negt is quick to rebuke for their cyncical advocacy of social Darwinism.[37] Although Beck may very well abhor the doctrine of neoliberalism, his descriptive concepts present themselves as ideal strategies for legitimizing the predatory practices of neoliberal forces.[38] Risk society is, in a word, a self-fulfilling catastrophe.

What Negt's uncompromising criticism of Beck brings to Kluge's oblique mockery of Witzlaff is exactly what Adorno identified decades

---

35 Negt 599.
36 Negt 604.
37 Beck 183–199; Negt 617, 621.
38 Negt 613.

earlier as ideology shrouded as theory that serves the "constellations of power."[39] Adorno's position on the historical denigration of the dialectical relationship between "action and thought," as Negt succinctly puts it, runs to the core of what makes both catastrophe theories—the fictional Witzlaff's and the real Beck's—so bankrupt.[40] In both instances, theory's collusion with capital strives to expunge causality in their accounts of catastrophe, thereby opening a space for causality's opposite, namely freedom. Yet this particular freedom is wholly personal and, as such, entirely detached from the universal concerns of society.[41] Neither the primacy of the individual nor the "repression of the particular by the universal" can ever amount to an effective political praxis, Adorno cautions in his posthumous marginalia on the topic.[42] The precondition for such practice is theory's very antithetical relationship to action: "Through its difference from immediate, situation-specific action, i.e., through its autonomization, theory becomes a transformative and practical productive force."[43] Curiously enough, Negt sees in Beck's neoliberal tendencies not any dearth of thinking in the form of theory per se, but rather the absence of any "critical power of judgment."[44] Even though this choice of words in Negt's 2001 monograph *Arbeit und menschliche Würde* (Labor and Human Dignity) is not entirely unprecedented—in the original introduction to "Measured Relations of the Political" from 1992 he and Kluge maintain, in fact, that "there obviously lacks a need for a sharpened political power of judgment" since the fall of communism—it is nevertheless exceptional given judgment's otherwise scant career throughout their previous writings.[45] The only other substantive instance is found a decade earlier in an addendum to the final chapter from *Geschichte und Eigensinn*. In a move reminiscent of Adorno's own deployment of psychoanalysis in *Negative Dialectics* against Kant's theory of the self,

---

39 Theodor W. Adorno, "Cultural Criticism and Society," in *Prisms*, trans. Samuel and Shierry Weber (Cambridge, MA: MIT Press, 1981) 30.

40 Negt 610.

41 Theodor W. Adorno, *Negative Dialectics*, trans. E.B. Ashton (New York: Continuum, 1995) 276. See also pages 265–70 for Adorno's own philosophical account of the crisis of causality.

42 Theodor W. Adorno, "Marginalia to Theory and Praxis," in *Critical Models: Interventions and Catchwords*, trans. Henry W. Pickford (New York: Columbia University Press, 2005) 264.

43 Adorno, "Marginalia to Theory and Praxis," 264.

44 Negt 617.

45 Negt and Kluge, preface to *Maßverhältnisse des Politischen*, 10

Negt and Kluge first employ Sigmund Freud to postulate a Kantian faculty of cognition not subject to the distortions of instrumental reason endemic in a society based on compulsory exchange.[46] By mapping onto Kant's categories of understanding Edmund Husserl's case for the role that prepredicative logic plays in the formation of practical knowledge, Negt and Kluge seek out an expanded notion of autonomous judgment operating simultaneously in the "depths of the human soul," as Kant puts it, and on the surface of things where perception roams.[47] Aware of the "insanity" of their strange theoretical amalgam, the authors in effect close *Geschichte und Eigensinn* with a wish to conceive theoretically the conditions for judgment's autonomy not in any moral sense per se, but rather in the political sense of the independent self-legislation of one's individual life in concert with one's social community.[48] And to this end, they ground judgment first in thought—that component lacking in Witzlaff's and Beck's catastrophe theories—and then in sensory experience, which takes them straight toward Hannah Arendt.

Theorizing the Political: From Judgment to the Faculty of Differentiation

"Hannah Arendt's political theory," J.M. Bernstein asserted in 2012, "accomplish[es] the translation of artistic practice into political praxis; in her writings, modernism for the first time takes on a systematic political visage."[49] Whereas so much of Adorno's philosophy considers politics

---

46 Negt and Kluge, *Geschichte und Eigensinn*, 1074–75. Negt and Kluge refer here to Freud's 1895 fragment "The Project for a Scientific Psychology" and then Edmund Husserl's *1939 monograph Experience and Judgment*. See: Sigmund Freud, "The Project for a Scientific Psychology," in *The Origins of Psycho-Analysis: Letters to Wilhelm Fliess, Drafts and Notes, 1887-1902*, eds. Marie Bonaparte, Anna Freud, and Ernst Kris, trans. Eric Mosbacher and James Strachey (New York: Basic Books, 1977) 347-445; and Edmund Husserl, *Experience and Judgment: Investigations in a Genealogy of Logic*, ed. Ludwig Landgrebe, trans. James S. Churchill and Karl Ameriks (Evanston, IL: Northwestern University Press, 1973).

47 Negt and Kluge, *Geschichte und Eigensinn*, 1078.

48 Negt and Kluge, *Geschichte und Eigensinn*, 1075, 1074.

49 J.M. Bernstein, "Political Modernism: The New, Revolution, and Civil Disobedience in Arendt and Adorno," in *Arendt and Adorno: Political and Philosophical Investigations*, eds. Lars Rensmann and Samir Gandesha (Stanford, CA: Stanford University Press, 2012) 57.

as having "migrated into the autonomous work of art," Arendt retrieves politics from the confines of aesthetic modernism (without ever invoking Adorno's theory) and delivers, according to Bernstein, a political philosophy befitting of critical theory.[50] As Arendt herself recognizes in her late lectures on Kant, political philosophy has, as a rule, less to do with the political realm of human affairs—the *vita activa* so central in her *The Human Condition*—than it does with the *vita contemplativa* that emerged as the centerpiece of her late writings. More precisely, political philosophy, says Arendt, is a "relation between philosophy and politics," and the crystallization of this link is the concept of judgment.[51] A middle term between theory and praxis—that interstitial space Adorno reserved for the negativity of the work of art—judgment permeates the whole of Kant's writings. Yet it is the particularities of aesthetic judgment established in his third *Critique* that Arendt identifies as the foundation for any political philosophy.[52] Aesthetic judgment, she reminds us, deals not with any universals, as the case with most thought, but rather particulars. Judgments of taste are also not synonymous with the imperatives of Kant's moral philosophy addressed to singular man: both an autonomous reasonable being and an end in himself. Instead, the political corollary of aesthetic judgment is its reliance on the sociability of men. Political judgment is, in other words, that faculty of critical thinking predicated on the general communicability of particular judgments, which in turn requires a community of men erected on communal sense, *sensus communis*. Judging the particular requires, therefore, enlarging one's thought; being impartial to other viewpoints; comparing one's own judgments with those of others by imagining oneself in their place even in their absence; and then finally reflecting on that thought, deciding whether it is pleasing or not, and validating those feelings, which presuppose the presence of others, before a public. If Arendt does indeed bestow a "political visage" on the modernism that Adorno celebrated, to cite Bernstein once again, then her "translation" certainly falls short of prescribing any deliberative action. In lieu of any political praxis, Arendt's penultimate positions on judgment strongly suggest that her

---

50 Adorno, "Commitment," in *Notes to Literature*, ed. Rolf Tiedemann, trans. Shierry Weber Nicholsen, vol. 2 (New York, NY: Columbia University Press, 1991) 93–94.

51 Hannah Arendt, *Lectures on Kant's Political Philosophy*, ed. Ronald Beiner (Chicago: University of Chicago Press, 1989) 22.

52 Arendt, *Lectures on Kant's Political Philosophy*, 36.

definitive statement would have unequivocally aligned judging, as the title of her last unfinished book makes clear, with *The Life of the Mind*. Yet judgment, that "most political of man's mental abilities," is not exclusively quietist.[53] Whereas thinking promotes forms of anti-action like the negation and refusal of universals in times of political emergencies, the autonomous mental activity of judging is capable of building out of particulars both a sense of community and human dignity.[54] Although no longer a part of the *vita activa* as she once conceived it, judging may still in fact be able to "prevent catastrophes, at least for the self."[55]

In their introduction to "Measured Relations of the Political," Negt and Kluge not only make allusions to Arendt's concept of action but they also incorporate judgment into their case for the political. In light of what they call rapid "objective challenges" at the end of the millennium —Chernobyl, the end of socialism, the Gulf War—"practical judgment" has been thrown into disarray. "There is obviously need for a sharpened political power of judgment," they opine.[56] In spite of this initial appeal to judgment, Negt and Kluge push aside this concept for an analogous one, namely the faculty of differentiation (*Unterscheidungsvermögen*). Nowhere in their writings do we find a clear, explicit account of the relationship between the power of judgment and the faculty of differentiation. Deployed a decade earlier in *Geschichte und Eigensinn*, the faculty of differentiation appears at two prominent junctures: one a reading of the Grimm brother's fairy tale "The Wolf and the Seven Young Kids," and the other a commentary included in the original 1981 edition entitled "The Political as an Area of Activity and Specific Degree of Intensity of Feeling" that was excised in later editions only then to resurface in revised form in "Measured Relations of the Political."[57] It is this latter excerpt where we find the significant negative impulse for Negt and Kluge's faculty of differentiation, namely Carl Schmitt's 1932 essay *The Concept of the Political*. Intent on turning Schmitt's antagonistic concept

---

53 Hannah Arendt, *The Life of the Mind*, vol. 1: *Thinking*, ed. Mary McCarthy (San Diego, CA: Harcourt, 1978) 192.

54 On the status of human dignity, see Arendt's postscriptum to *Thinking*: Arendt, *Lectures on Kant's Political Philosophy*, 5.

55 Arendt, *The Life of the Mind*, 193.

56 Negt and Kluge, preface to *Maßverhältnisse des Politischen* 10.

57 Alexander Kluge, "The Political as Intensity of Everyday Feelings," trans Andrew Bowie, in *Alexander Kluge: Raw Materials for the Imagination*, ed. Tara Forrest (Amsterdam: Amsterdam University Press, 2012) 283–90.

of the political inside out, Negt and Kluge note that if the political distinction between friend and foe rests on "the utmost degree of intensity of a union or separation," then there must also be distinctions to ensure solidarity among different peoples within a single community.[58] Of greatest significance for their thinking is Schmitt's suggestion that such intensities, moral, aesthetic, and affective in nature, are not exclusively cognitive. But, whereas Schmitt places emphasis on existential intensities—universals—Negt and Kluge prioritize the particularities of embodied experience. Accordingly, they write of political distinctions rooted in subjective "raw materials"—feelings, interests, motives they call the "cellular form of the political"—found in everyday life capable of uniting, expressing, and building collective movement in the public sphere.[59] "What concerns us," they summarize at the close of their commentary, "is to provoke the imagination to the point such that the abstract mind is not the only primary tool for trying to give form to the political."[60] What remains unclear is where, if at all, their emphasis on the faculty of differentiation fits into Arendt's case for judgment.

It was not until the 1992 republication of their abandoned commentary on the political from 1981 that Negt and Kluge began engaging Arendt, but it was only Negt who went on to recognize in detail both the challenges and promises her political interpretation of Kant's third *Critique* posed. In an essay published a year after "Measured Relations of the Political," Negt acknowledges how astute she was in identifying the disastrous turning point that Marx's eleventh thesis on Feuerbach had heralded for classical political philosophy. He draws attention to this overlooked lacuna that Marxism failed to address; enlists Arendt in his disqualification of Schmitt's concept of the political; concedes both labor's and work's negative influence on the viability of political action; and even goes so far as to credit Arendt, surely against her own intentions, with mapping out the "structure of *political action* in the time after Marx" by starting out (as the Frankfurt School would do) from the "force of the particular" instead of the universal.[61] Convinced that Arendt's

---

58 Carl Schmitt, *The Concept of the Political*, trans. George Schwab (Chicago: University of Chicago Press, 2007) 26.

59 Negt and Kluge, *Maßverhältnisse des Politischen*, 52, 47, 46.

60 Negt and Kluge, *Maßverhältnisse des Politischen*, 100.

61 Oskar Negt, *Der politische Mensch: Demokratie als Lebensform* (Göttingen: Steidl, 2010) 338–39, 342. This is an expanded version of: Oskar Negt, "Zum Verständnis des

political intervention is of tremendous contemporary importance, Negt returns to the matter of judgment eclipsed in "Measured Relations of the Political" and argues that Arendt's reconstruction of Kant's reflective judgments of taste as worked out in his third *Critique* allows for the mediation of the two pillars of cognition—sensibility (intuition) and understanding (concepts)—otherwise missing in the power strategies of realpolitik. "*The power of judgment* is the connection of the particular with the universal," Negt exclaims, and to this end fantasy, the imagination, and reflection play considerable roles.[62] "Imagination," Arendt explains, "transforms the objects of the objective senses into 'sensed' objects, as though they were objects of an inner sense."[63] The upshot of Negt's charitable account of Arendt's late work is his confirmation that his and Kluge's emphasis on the faculty of differentiation did not so much eclipse judgment or even interfere with it as facilitate judgment's process of mediation on the side of the particular, namely the sensible. Without ever having encountered her unfinished lectures on Kant, Negt and Kluge in effect advance a concept for the acute particularities of human perception that Negt later realized were complementary to her theory of "how to *found* a commonwealth."[64] In fact, this is not the only constituent part of Arendt's Kant lectures operating in Negt and Kluge's "Measured Relations of the Political." What Negt and Kluge call the intensity of feelings, Arendt calls (along with Kant) the *sensus privatus*. For both camps, the imagination and reflection translate and render the "cellular form of the political" communicable as a *sensus communis*.[65] Like Arendt, who contends that judgment becomes politically relevant only when "special emergencies arise," Negt and Kluge locate the political at "nodal lines" where the commensurability between objects and subjects suddenly explodes.[66] Like Arendt and Kant, who both associate judgment with spectatorship, Negt and Kluge contend that only when illusory images that sustain the catastrophic potential of reality are rendered transparent by critical analysis do they lose their power: "A sign of

Politischen bei Hannah Arendt," in *Die Zukunft des Politischen: Ausblicke auf Hannah Arendt*, ed. Peter Kemper (Frankfurt am Main: Fischer Taschenbuch Verlag, 1993) 55–68.

62 Oskar Negt, *Der politische Mensch*, 21.

63 Arendt, *Lectures on Kant's Political Philosophy*, 65.

64 Arendt, *Lectures on Kant's Political Philosophy*, 16.

65 Negt and Kluge, *Maßverhältnisse des Politischen*, 52.

66 Arendt, *The Life of the Mind*, 192; Negt and Kluge, *Maßverhältnisse des Politischen*, 18.

the factual world falling apart into different blocks of reality is the fact that it is held together with (imaginary) images. Analytical work would render it transparent till it disintegrated altogether."[67] And finally, like Arendt, who in her postscript to her essay on thinking insists "judgment is our faculty for dealing with the past," Negt and Kluge see the faculty of differentiation operating hand in hand with coming to terms with the past.[68]

Arguably the most important common ground that Negt and Kluge and Arendt share pertains to the social dimension of both judgment and the faculty of differentiation. Unlike Kant's first *Critique*, in which he forecloses judgment from all pedagogical influence, Arendt insists "the faculty that judges *particulars* ... can be taught and learned until they grow into habits."[69] Similarly, Negt and Kluge's point of departure is predicated on the conviction that "political judgment" can be sharpened and, furthermore, that the faculty of differentiation can be trained and expanded exponentially. For Arendt, the public dimension of aesthetic judgments emerges in the moment of reflection when one's private sense takes into account the possible judgments of others and then, by virtue of an extra mental capacity Kant called common sense, fits one's own judgment into those of a community. Arendt calls this, in a word, "the communicability of a sensation."[70] A precondition for any recourse to speech for communicating one's own judgments is, of course, the supposition that everyone is capable of sensing astutely. What concerns Negt and Kluge and drives their own urgent call for a pedagogy of the senses is the disarray in which the human sensorium, fantasy, and reflective judgment find themselves due in large part to the disastrous influence science, technology, war, and commerce have on the public sphere. The long-range effects of Chernobyl shocked every facet of German society, Negt and Kluge note, but the unbearable experience failed to translate into any lasting action. Live news coverage reported by CNN journalists embedded in the United States' Gulf War offensive generated spectacular images that obliterated for the eye the difference between waging

---

67 Negt and Kluge, *Maßverhältnisse des Politischen*, 291.

68 Arendt, *Lectures on Kant's Political Philosophy*, 5; Negt and Kluge, *Maßverhältnisse des Politischen*, 339.

69 Arendt, *The Life of the Mind*, 192–93. Cf. Arendt, *Lectures on Kant's Political Philosophy*, 4, 84.

70 Arendt, *Lectures on Kant's Political Philosophy*, 69.

war and committing mass murder. The six-week revolution that began
with the fall of the Berlin Wall and concluded with assimilation of the
German Democratic Republic unfolded so fast that many were caught
off guard. What these three scenarios exemplify for Negt and Kluge is
the contemporary regime of temporal and spatial relations that exceed
the capacities of the human senses, thus leading to what they call the
de-realization of the reality. Incapacitated more than ever before by the
inhuman proportions of these nodal points, political judgment must
reclaim concepts otherwise deformed in the course of professional politics; it needs to recuperate requisite times and places commensurate with
the slower speeds and limited scope characteristic of the human senses
and reflective judgment; and it must learn to parlay the initial astonishment precipitated by catastrophe into common sense. Negt and Kluge
contend that a first step to this end entails a remedial lesson in reading.
When grasped as an interpretative process akin to translation, reading
can assume the mantle of critique and pierce the illusions of reality.
Reading aesthetic texts can entail a mental exercise (in Freud's sense of
Probehandeln im Geiste) that can allow for the recognition and verifica-
tion of subjective motives for the political. Reading "vessels of memory"
can also unlock the ciphers of historical experience and, in so doing, seek
to imagine missed opportunities.

Incommensurability of Catastrophic Experience

In the course of its long passage from antiquity to late modernity, the
idea of catastrophe underwent its most profound transformation only
very recently.[71] Whereas the compounds formed from the ancient
Greek preposition κατα, designating a reversal movement, and the verb
στρέφειν for "to turn" once denoted a wide variety of pivotal *events*, the
concept of catastrophe emerged in the course of the twentieth century
as a ubiquitous *condition* encapsulating the whole of planetary life. Once
exceptional, catastrophe became, in a word, quotidian and, as a result,
largely indiscernible. Arguably the most prolific terrain on which the

---

71 This initial treatment of the etymology and historical semantics of catastrophe
relies heavily on: Olaf Briese and Timo Günther, "Katastrophe: Terminologische Vergangenheit, Gegenwart und Zukunft," *Archiv für Begriffsgeschichte* 51 (2009): 155–95.

catastrophic condition of late modern life was initially articulated was the cultural criticism and philosophical treatises on history by intellectuals like Walter Benjamin, Siegfried Kracauer, and Herbert Marcuse. Unlike Benjamin who famously saw, like Karl Marx before him, future redemptive potential within the catastrophic status quo of modern life under capitalism, others grew ever more skeptical of any such hope.[72] In the latest rationalized stage of capitalism, it was not, Kracauer opined in 1930, major events, but rather a string of "tiny catastrophes of which everyday existence is made up, and [a person's] fate is certainly linked predominantly to the sequence of these miniature occurrences."[73] Writing only a few years later, Marcuse upped the ante by casting the latest stage of capitalism as not only a "political crisis" but also a "catastrophe of the human essence."[74] In the shadow of the Holocaust, the unresolved status of redemption in critical thinking about catastrophe from a decade earlier initially appeared to be settled once and for all. While Max Horkheimer and Adorno did write of "yesterday's catastrophe" in reference to the carnage found in Nazi death camps, Adorno was less engaged with historical catastrophes than he was with the idea of a single permanent or total catastrophe, that is, catastrophe whereby a society virtually precludes "the possibility of spontaneous change."[75] In one of his most detailed explications of this catastrophe without a turn—namely, his 1958 analysis of Samuel Beckett's *Endgame*—he intimates a cataclysmic convergence whereby second nature extinguishes first nature once and for all: "The phase of complete reification of the world, where there is nothing left that has not been made by human beings, is indistinguishable from an additional catastrophic event caused by human

---

72 Walter Benjamin, "Central Park," trans. Edmund Jephcott and Howard Eiland, in *Selected Writings*, vol. 4, eds. Howard Eiland and Michael W. Jennings (Cambridge, MA: Belknap Press, 2003) 184; see also: Briese and Günther 171; and Juha Koivisto and Thomas Weber, "Katastrophe," in *Historisch-kritisches Wörterbuch des Marxismus*, ed. Wolfgang Fritz Haug, vol. 7.1 (Hamburg: Argument Verlag, 2008) 437–40.

73 Siegfried Kracauer, *The Salaried Masses: Duty and Distraction in Weimar Germany*, trans. Quintin Hoare (London: Verso, 1998) 62.

74 Herbert Marcuse, "New Sources on the Foundation of Historical Materialism," trans. Joris de Bres and John Abromeit, in *Heideggerian Marxism*, eds. Richard Wolin and John Abromeit (Lincoln, NE: University of Nebraska Press, 2005) 106.

75 Max Horkheimer and Theodor W. Adorno, *Dialectic of Enlightenment: Philosophical Fragments*, ed. Gunzelin Schmid Noerr, trans. Edmund Jephcott (Stanford, CA: Stanford University Press, 2002) 171; Theodor W. Adorno, *Minima Moralia*, trans. E.F.N. Jephcott (London: Verso, 1996) 241.

beings."[76] With the absolute supremacy of second nature, catastrophe loses its age-old hallmark, namely the very distinguishability of its status as transformational event. Adorno recognized immediately the dire consequences of life in the permanent catastrophe; ill-equipped to perceive this structural calamity, postwar society disregarded it by only attending to and relativizing discrete historical catastrophes "as a kind of unfortunate occupational accident on the path to economic and technical progress."[77] Neither the promise of progress nor any "tiny fissure" within the continuous catastrophe, as Benjamin had once envisioned it, was powerful enough for Adorno to alter permanent catastrophe's hold on all of modern life.

In the eyes of Adorno's acolytes, the consequences of his theory of permanent catastrophe were severe and soon met with umbrage. In the eyes of Hermann Schweppenhäuser, Adorno had essentially collapsed past experience as well as an ineluctable ominous future into a paralyzed catastrophic present, a resigned state of standstill verging on the very mythical consciousness he otherwise decried. In contrast then to Adorno, Schweppenhäuser called for not only a redoubling of historical consciousness in our encounters with catastrophe but also a reconsideration of the catastrophic event's redemptive potential in the form of catharsis.[78] Long adverse to both the discourse of catastrophe as well as Adorno's totalized critique, Habermas followed suit only very recently when, asking whether it is possible to learn from history, he tendered the idea of a dynamic "world domestic policy" capable of forestalling the return of catastrophes from the first half of the twentieth century.[79] Another peer Habermas counts among Adorno's scions who turned away from catastrophe's permanence is Kluge: "Kluge is interested in turning points," he explained in his encomium given on the occasion of Kluge's

---

76 Theodor W. Adorno, "Trying to Understand *Endgame*," in *Notes to Literature*, vol. 1, ed. Rolf Tiedemann, trans. Shierry Weber Nicholsen (New York: Columbia University Press, 1991) 245.

77 Theodor W. Adorno, "Wird Spengler recht behalten?" in *Gesammelte Schriften*, ed. Rolf Tiedemann, vol. 20.1, (Frankfurt am Main: Suhrkamp, 1986) 141.

78 Hermann Schweppenhäuser, "Mythisches und historisches Katastrophenbewußtsein," in *Tractanda: Beiträge zur kritischen Theorie der Kultur und Gesellschaft* (Frankfurt am Main: Suhrkamp Verlag, 1972) 118–30. See also Briese and Günther 191.

79 Jürgen Habermas, "Learning from Catastrophe? A Look Back at the Short Twentieth Century," in *The Postnational Constellation: Political Essays*, ed. and trans. Max Pensky (Cambridge, MA: MIT Press, 1998) 110.

receipt of the Lessing Prize, "the moment when the fate of a battle, a war, an epoch is decided."[80] Indeed, historical catastrophe as event—from the Battle of Stalingrad to 9/11, from the bombing of Kluge's childhood home in Halberstadt to the Great Recession, from the Battle of Verdun to the Iraq War—occupies an essential place and function throughout his oeuvre. Yet it would be a gross oversight to conclude that Negt and Kluge turned a blind eye to the precedent of structural catastrophe advanced by Adorno and others before him. In the immediate shadow of the meltdown of the fourth reactor core at the nuclear power plant in Chernobyl on April 26, 1986, Kluge both acknowledged the permanence of a historical catastrophic event like Chernobyl and redressed its imperceptibility using the tools of filmmaking and television broadcasting.

The category of the everyday has always operated as the proverbial bedrock upon which Negt and Kluge erected their theoretical contributions to critical theory. For example, in *Public Sphere and Experience* they write, "The real social experiences of human beings, produced in everyday life and work, cut across such divisions."[81] The everyday divisions partitioning social experience are those separating public and private spheres, between "[f]ederal elections" and the everyday duties of "childrearing," between "the actions of a commando unit" and the daily "factory work," between the "Olympic ceremonies" of 1972 and the usual "television within one's own four walls."[82] The dire problem with these divides is not only their imperceptible nature—we unknowingly traverse them countless times throughout our daily lives—but also their uneven valorization. Authentic everyday experience perennially goes missing in both the constitution of public spheres as well as in their politics, such that they either have no use for everyday experience or must seek to expropriate it as raw material to be manufactured into artificial needs, interests, and desires for future profit. Regardless of whether they are dismissed or exploited, the complex border crossings essential to the relationality of everyday life—"as it exists"—languish in obscurity and, so too, does everyday experience itself.[83] Three years later, in the fall 1975,

---

80 Jürgen Habermas, "The Useful Mole Who Ruins the Beautiful Lawn: The Lessing Prize for Alexander Kluge," in *The Liberating Power of Symbols: Philosophical Essays*, trans. Peter Dews (Cambridge, MA: MIT Press, 2001) 118.

81 Negt and Kluge, *Public Sphere and Experience*, xliii.

82 Negt and Kluge, *Public Sphere and Experience*, xliii.

83 Negt and Kluge, *Public Sphere and Experience*, 17.

Kursbuch editor Karl Markus Michel went one step farther by recast-
ing the trouble with the everyday and the denigration of experience as
a narrative quandary: "The everyday has become a problem everywhere
today, but not because a few people have started to talk about it." The
underlying problem had, in fact, far more to do with the proposition that
"everyday life cannot be narrated."[84] For Michel, the everyday inherently
eludes the powers of narration precisely because it is devoid of the exceptional. Without an "exceptional," "sensational," or "objectionable" event,
the mundane normalcy of the everyday remains unidentifiable, anonymous, and indescribable: "It remains arbitrary, chaotic, unstructured
—*meaning-less*."[85] In a word, the everyday eludes the unconscious
grammar that confers cultural meaning on modern society's ubiquitous
stories organized around the exceptional. If the problem of the everyday is to be remedied according to Michel, then the task at hand is a
tricky narratological one, insofar as the disparate elements of everyday
life must be articulated in such a way so as not to potentiate them into
something exceptional, which would ultimately obfuscate precisely what
constitutes their diffuse everydayness in the first place.

Kluge the storyteller has probed the everyday narratologically long
before leftists declared its politicization as one of the defining mantras
of the seventies. But instead of proceeding positively, as Michel suggests,
and suturing the constituents of everyday life into a diffuse constellation,
Kluge has consistently worked negatively. If, to quote Kluge, "everyday
life is determined by what allegedly is not everyday: airstrikes, declara-
tions of war, Black Friday …," then his obsessive, unceasing attention
to modern Germany's historical catastrophes (along with their many
aftershocks) ever since his literary debut in the early sixties has been
nothing other than a dialectical query of the paucity and therefore the
catastrophic character of everyday experience.[86] Kluge says as much in
concert with Negt when in *Public Sphere and Experience* they write that
"own experience"—that is, everyday experience neither disregarded nor
exploited—precludes catastrophes.[87] Conversely, limited experience—

84 Karl Markus Michel, "Unser Alltag: Nachruf zu Lebzeiten," *Kursbuch* 41 (September 1975): 3.
85 Michel 2, 5.
86 Alexander Kluge and Edgar Reitz, "In Gefahr und größter Not bringt der Mittelweg den Tod," *Kursbuch* 41 (Sept. 1975): 71.
87 Negt and Kluge, *Public Sphere and Experience*, 12.

that is experience diminished by the vested interests of the public sphere
—displays, they maintain, "an inherent tendency for catastrophe."[88] In
this respect, Habermas is on the mark when he claims that for Kluge, like
Benjamin before him, "the moment of catastrophe is also the moment
of emancipation."[89] Within what Michel calls the arbitrary, chaotic, and
unstructured moment of historical catastrophe, Kluge has indeed sought
out, as Habermas infers, that dialectical moment he and Negt call the
abaric point, where individuals could find freedom from any and all
external forces once responsible for diminishing autonomous experience
and maintaining catastrophe's potential.[90] However, Kluge's survey of
historical catastrophes has tended more often than not to their manifest
tragic character. By zeroing in on the countless ways catastrophic-prone
public spheres paper over and diminish everyday life, Kluge's stories
routinely probe how disfigured everyday life is replete with illusory
wishes that blind us from discovering ways out of our usual tendency for
catastrophe politics.[91]

Not all catastrophes are the same for Kluge, and the blindness they
induce is equally variable. Of all the many catastrophic events that have
commanded Kluge's fascination, it is, without question, the meltdown in
Chernobyl that has occupied the most unique position in his catalogue
of modern disasters. The reason is simple: Chernobyl undid historical
catastrophe's long-standing dialectical relation to everyday life. If the
everyday—that is, life from "below"—was once determined by what
is presumably not everyday—that is, calamity from "above"—then the
imperceptible reach of nuclear radiation across the Iron Curtain and well
into Western Europe signaled for Kluge both an unprecedented metastasis of historical catastrophe into the everyday, and the sudden expiration
of the public sphere as a political space of authority delineated by the
nation-state.[92] Furthermore, the cutting across divisions constituent
of the real social experiences of human beings suddenly encompassed,

88 Negt and Kluge, *Public Sphere and Experience*, 13.

89 Habermas, "The Useful Mole Who Ruins the Beautiful Lawn," 118.

90 Negt and Kluge, *Geschichte und Eigensinn*, 790.

91 Alexander Kluge and Bion Steinborn, "Cinema Pure, Cinema Impure," *Filmfaust*
7.26 (February–March 1981): 43.

92 Kluge and Negt, 102–3; Negt and Kluge, *Geschichte und Eigensinn*, 787-90; see
also Kluge's implied theory of the strategies from below and above in: Alexander Kluge,
The Air Raid on Halberstadt on 8 April 1945, trans. Martin Chalmers (London: Seagull
Press, 2014) 26–80.

on account of the windblown fallout from Chernobyl, entire continents and posed a threat to life for thousands and thousands of years. Accordingly, distinctions once rendered from the fundamental dimensions of everyday experience—near versus far, today versus thirty thousand years—suddenly became invalid, and thus historical experience quickly felt like permanent catastrophe. In spite of the pervasive everyday feelings of hopelessness that soon hung over Europe, Kluge immediately latched on to this extraordinary event as a chance for recovering the "critical sensibility" that the distant catastrophe radiated away in a flash.[93] It is, therefore, no coincidence that the year of the Chernobyl catastrophe is also the year when Kluge bid adieu to filmmaking once and for all and focused exclusively on finalizing his media shift to private television. What remains to be seen then is how, after all sense of time and space seemed to collapse in the shadow of Chernobyl, Kluge deployed television's otherwise Janus-faced promise of long-distance sight as a means for resuscitating the "measured relations and navigation" necessary for autonomous experience.[94] But, before turning to the resuscitation of the dimensions of experience, Kluge initially toiled away at substantiating their very dissolution, and did so by looking at the sky.

Questions among West Germans about the dangers posed by Chernobyl's fallout were, says Kluge, innumerable and went largely unanswered. What sorts of food could be eaten? What effects might inadvertent overexposure have on human bones and organs? What should pregnant women and children do? Is it even wise to go for a walk outside, especially if it's raining?[95] The unbearable uncertainly of everyday life drove Kluge to pack up and seek shelter in Portugal, where radionuclide levels were at their lowest in Europe. "In April and May, 1986, I actually fled with my family and children to Portugal," he confessed many years later, "because we simply could no longer trust anyone."[96] Upon returning home to Munich, Kluge scrambled to finish his final feature, *Miscellaneous News*, a film both scantily distributed and poorly received

---

93 Alexander Kluge, introduction to *Die Wächter des Sarkophags* (Hamburg: Rotbuch Verlag, 1996) 10.

94 Negt and Kluge, *Geschichte und Eigensinn*, 644.

95 Kluge, *Die Wächter des Sarkophags*, 7–8, 10.

96 Lydia Dykier and Philippe Roepstorff-Robiano, "Sonden in Randbereiche der Zeitgeschichte: Ein Interview mit Alexander Kluge," *Revolver-Blog*, April 27, 2011, http://revolver-film.blogspot.com/2011/04/sonden-in-randbereiche-der.html.

in theaters in its own moment and treated ever since in the critical literature as either a negligible afterthought or a foreshadowing of the frenetic
formalism often associated with his imminent television programing
but nothing more. An explicit allusion to the *faits-divers* typical of what
Kluge calls "classical newspapers"—sensational reports about homicides,
suicides, or misfortune reserved for the last page of French dailies—the
film's seemingly generic title points, says Kluge, to a "distorting mirror"
of the "raw materials of events in the world."[97] Yet the film's eclectic
content—shorts, narrated storyboards, documentaries, condensed silent
films, not to mention sundry montage sequences—ostensibly says
nothing of the catastrophe in Chernobyl or of any other contemporaneous calamity, like the Space Shuttle *Challenger* disaster from four months
earlier. According to one critic, *Miscellaneous News* was "a hodgepodge
of outtakes and miscellany from previous productions, more fragmented
and less successful than any previous Kluge film."[98] For another, the film's
failure was not just on account of Kluge's infuriating modernist collage
pushed well past the tipping point, but also the concurrent structural
transformation of the Federal Republic's media landscape in the middle
of the 1980s, in which cinema no longer seemed to play the leading role
it once did.[99]

Roland Barthes once explained, "A murder is committed: if political, it is news, otherwise we French call it *faits-divers*."[100] It is precisely
this oblique yet pivotal distinction between the politics of "news" versus
the insignificance of the *faits-divers*—in a word, the chasm separating
exceptional knowledge from everyday life—that has long been lost on
critics and their limited appreciation of Kluge's *Miscellaneous News*.
Wedged in between *faits-divers* about swindlers, dying mothers, forlorn
lovers, dying soldiers, and attempted murders, the core of Kluge's film
is, in fact, a short documentary directed by Volker Schlöndorff. "Before

97 Martin Weinmann and Alexander Kluge, *Neonröhren des Himmels: Filmalbum*,
in Alexander Kluge, *Sämtliche Kinofilme* (Frankfurt am Main: Zweitausendeins, 2007)
86.
98 Peter C. Lutze, *Alexander Kluge: The Last Modernist* (Detroit, MI: Wayne State
University Press, 1998) 65, 197. On the disappointing contemporary reception of *Vermischte Nachrichten*, see: Lutze 95–96.
99 Matthias Uecker, *Anti-Fernsehen? Alexander Kluges Fernsehproduktionen*
(Marburg: Schüren Verlag, 2000) 50.
100 Roland Barthes, "Structure of the *Fait-Divers*," in *Critical Essays*, trans. Richard
Howard (Evanston, IL: Northwestern University Press, 1972) 185.

Figure 4.3. A screen within a screen. A still from Volker Schlöndorff's short included in
Kluge's *Miscellaneous News*: a television broadcast of Chancellor Schmidt's departure in
Güstrow, 1981. © Alexander Kluge.

Christmas 1981: a tense political situation of international importance,"
actress Sabina Trooger declares, playing the part of a fictional anchorwoman. "Everyone knows already that the classic doctrine of *Ostpolitik*
has come to an end. It is both a bereavement and a dangerous situation. We will show you the day in all its tenaciousness that television
did not document." The tensions Trooger refers to include a series of
political events in quick succession—the Soviet invasion of Afghani-
stan, NATO's double-track decision, and the declaration of martial law
in Poland—that suddenly threatened to destabilize German-German
rapprochement since its formal ratification in 1972. The otherwise
veiled tenacity subtending these geopolitical threats is to be found in
Schlöndorff's documentary footage of West German chancellor Helmut
Schmidt's state visit to the Democratic Republic of Germany in early
December 1981. What counts as particularly tenacious is the mundane
everydayness of the extraordinary visit: the small talk on the tarmac's red
carpet, the drive to Werbellinsee, the uneventful photo ops in the Huber-
tusstock hunting lodge, and the Christmas market in Güstrow. When

a faceless woman shouts in the crowd, "I cannot see a thing," the same could be said of the legibility of politics conducted during this ostensibly most political of events. That moment caught on live television when politics behind the Iron Curtain was supposed to be unfolding literally in real time—Schmidt's press conference held immediately after martial law went into effect in Poland—was actually pure choreographed artifice. Kluge himself framed the significance of the short in terms that throw the inauthenticity of politics into relief: "Chancellor Schmidt does not speak about the martial law declared in Poland; he gives his prepared speech … This is choreographed, but not by us."[101] Long on everyday *faits-divers* and short on world-historical news, Schlöndorff's documentary concludes with footage of Schmidt's farewell on the railway platform in Güstrow caught on live television (see fig. 4.3), a *mise en abyme* that essentially says that the politics television purports to show is, in fact, everyday life embellished with political meaning that counts as politics merely on account of its televisual mediation.

Unlike Barthes who set out to classify the different types of sensationalist news items set off from a newspaper's usual fare, Kluge's *Miscellaneous News* actually recalls Jean Baudrillard's contention that the distinction between front-page news and the *faits-divers* relegated to the last page has withered in our modern, mass-mediated consumer society. "All political, historical, cultural information," Baudrillard proclaimed in 1970, "is received in the same—at once anodyne and miraculous—form of the *faits-divers*."[102] This praxis of media consumption rooted in misrecognition effectively inverts the exclusion of everyday life to which Negt and Kluge as well as Michel drew attention. With the abundance of *faits-divers*, impoverished everydayness "autonomize[s] and reinterpret[s] the world 'for internal consumption.'"[103] Baudrillard goes even further by explicating this dialectic of the everyday by using the exact same image with which Schlöndorff concludes his short: "The TV image, like a window turned outside-in, opens initially onto a room and, in that room, the cruel exteriority of the world becomes something intimate and

101 Florian Rötzer, "Kino und Grabkammer: Gespräch mit Alexander Kluge," in *Die Schrift an der Wand: Rohstoffe und Materialien*, ed. Christian Schulte (Osnabrück: Universitätsverlag Rasch, 2000) 39.

102 Jean Baudrillard, *The Consumer Society: Myths and Structures* (Thousand Oaks, CA: Sage, 1998) 33–34.

103 Baudrillard 35.

warm—warm with a perverse warmth."[104] We would fall miserably short in our reading of Kluge's *Miscellaneous News*, however, were we merely to package it as a cinematic attempt at a critical phenomenology of the alibi of everyday participation in the media spectacle of world politics. Rather, Kluge's final feature film is far more concerned with wrestling with the political consequences of a structural transformation of catastrophe of which both television and the meltdown in Chernobyl were equally emblematic. And, even though the nuclear catastrophe never makes an appearance as television does, Kluge's film does indirectly point to the fallout's own toll on the fundamental temporal and spatial dimensions of autonomous experience.

The renowned halo effect Walter Benjamin called "aura," which we humans perceive when contemplating either historical or natural objects, could also be thought of as an object's cloud of authenticity. Benjamin elucidates his concept thus: "What, then, is aura? A strange tissue of space and time: the unique apparition of a distance, however near it may be. To follow with the eye—while resting on a summer afternoon—a mountain range on the horizon or a branch that casts its shadow on the beholder is to breathe the aura of those mountains, of that branch."[105] Leaving aside for a moment Benjamin's claim that aura has ostensibly declined today thanks to our technologically fueled desire "*to 'get closer' to things*," Benjamin's illustration taken from the natural world begs the question whether clouds themselves have cloud-like halos.[106] Polymath Johann Wolfgang von Goethe would very likely be dubious. For Goethe (and British meteorologist Luke Howard before him), clouds confound aura's apparition of distance precisely because they are not objects. Rather, clouds are natural events at the threshold of the perceptible that signal the presence of invisible and imperceptible forces like air pressure, humidity, temperature, and wind speed.[107] "Whoever sees clouds," one Goethe scholar summarized, "also sees at the same time something

---

104 Baudrillard 35.

105 Walter Benjamin, "The Work of Art in the Age of Its Technical Reproducibility," trans. Edmund Jephcott and Harry Zohn, in *Selected Writings*, vol. 3: *1935–1938*, eds. Howard Eiland and Michael W. Jennings (Cambridge, MA: Belknap Press, 2002) 104–5.

106 Benjamin, "The Work of Art in the Age of Its Technical Reproducibility," 105.

107 Joseph Vogl, "Luft um 1800," in *Vita Aesthetica: Szenarien ästhetischer Lebendigkeit*, eds. Armen Avanessian, Winfried Menninghaus, and Jan Völker (Zurich: diaphanes, 2009) 46.

invisible and imperceptible."[108] For these reasons, clouds pose unsettling phenomenological and epistemological problems that Benjamin's mountains simply do not. This problem becomes most apparent when we enter into a cloud: "In the cloud ... everything appears close and far away at the same time and perspectives are reduced to two dimensionality, in which reference points get lost; immediate space and distant space, dream space and physical space become one."[109]

Whereas the formal instability and spatial undecidability of clouds for Goethe are attributable to natural phenomena that, by their very nature, put the human powers and limits of perception and knowledge to the test, clouds in Kluge's *Miscellaneous News* are so much more. Not until the final nine-minute montage sequence entitled "Sommer 1986" do the half-dozen or so shots of clouds throughout earlier sequences in the film (see fig. 4.2) appear to signify anything more than just first nature. Thanks to both the sequence's opening intertitle as well as footage taken from a West German civil defense instructional film on surviving nuclear attack, the images of mothers with their children behind windows (see fig. 4.1) along with another half-dozen time-lapse shots of passing clouds all operate together as indices of what Barthes calls "news." "Such news cannot be understood immediately," he explains, referring to the antithesis of *faits-divers*. "It can be defined only in relation to a knowledge external to the event, which is political knowledge, however confused."[110] The knowledge in question as represented by all the cloud sequences throughout *Miscellaneous News* is nothing other than a confused knowledge about the catastrophe in Chernobyl. Indeed, had it not been for Swedish nuclear monitors who literally caught wind of Chernobyl, awareness of the radioactive-laden clouds pulled westward by shifting winds from Western Ukraine would have never come to light. Once that knowledge along with the rains that fell in the West in late April sunk in, everyday life grew increasingly afflicted by uncertainty, fear, denial, and resignation.[111] West German politics proved no match for the magni-

---

108 Vogl. 46.

109 Wolfgang Bock, "Dialektik des Nebels: Zu den Motiven der Wolken und des Wetters bei Walter Benjamin," in *Archiv für Mediengeschichte: Wolken*, eds. Lorenz Engell, Bernhard Siegert, and Joseph Vogl (Weimar: Universitätsverlag, 2005) 43.

110 Barthes 186.

111 For a meteorological account of the wind patterns from April 26–29 that crossed whole geographic regions and continents, see: Kluge, *Die Wächter des Sarkophags*, 122. On the transformation of everyday life after Chernobyl, see: Helge Gerndt, "Der Schatten

tude of a crisis verging on natural catastrophe, let alone the widespread paralysis it unleashed throughout society: "Politicians' replies stifled and assuaged," one chronicler of West Germany's reaction to Chernobyl wrote, "and when they used exact numerical data they were unintelligible for many and also contradictory."[112]

It is, therefore, neither coincidence nor a case of last-minute sloppiness that *Miscellaneous News* juxtaposes televised political events in the GDR from 1981 with the most oblique of references to the nuclear catastrophe in 1986: clouds. In fact, the structures of television and clouds have a great deal in common for Kluge. Throughout *Miscellaneous News* they recursively call out one another. Like clouds that appear as discernible objects from afar, television promises, by virtue of its very name, an unprecedented prosthetic extension of human sight. Upon close inspection clouds vanish, says Goethe, in a haze of fog and mist and, so too, does television's spectacle according to Kluge.[113] "I think the word 'medialization' primarily alludes to 'television,'" Kluge explained in an essay from 1990, "but when all its parts are examined, then the 'long-distant vision' the word 'tele-vision' implies has nothing at all to do with any of the television stations I know. They actually create foreground and generate wallpaper. They open a window and then prevent anything from being represented from a distance."[114] What Kluge calls a blocked window, one that only opens onto shallowness, Baudrillard calls an inverted window, a closed-off, privatist world of fantasy divorced from the real. In either case, the metaphor of the defective window stands in critical opposition to any and all affirmative perceptions that television entails long-range vision. Conversely, like television, the clouds of Chernobyl not only baffled the human senses but also blurred the political boundaries of the public sphere and the quotidian experiences of everyday life. Just as television transforms all information into *faits-divers*—regardless of whether it's extensive political news or the intensive minor odds and ends saved for the back page—wind, clouds, and rain from the other

---

von Tschernobyl," *Kulturwissenschaft im Zeitalter der Globalisierung: Volkskundliche Markierungen* (Münster: Waxmann Verlag 2002) 82.

112 Gerndt 80.

113 Cf. Vogl, p. 46.

114 Alexander Kluge, "Medialization—Musealization," trans. Emma Woelk, in *Difference and Orientation: An Alexander Kluge Reader*, ed. Richard Langston (Ithaca, NY: Cornell University Press, 2019) 293.

side of the Iron Curtain effectively exploded in late April and early May 1986 the customary boundaries of a nation-state's politics. Once disregarded in the name of politics only later to be preyed upon by the culture industry, everyday experience suddenly became an inherently political concern, one for which the existing public sphere in the Federal Republic had no effective recourse. In effect, both clouds and television converged for Kluge as "imperceptible forces," catastrophes that threatened to weaken for millennia the tenacity of both consciousness and experience subtending everyday life.[115]

Imagination and Reflection: Astonishment as Remediation

Even though Chernobyl was for Kluge a historical catastrophe that threatened to last seemingly forever, it was not the only catastrophe from mid-eighties that troubled him. "By the end of the year, there was a whole chain of catastrophes, among them the launching of private television in Germany, which in some circumstances has for human consciousness exactly the same long-term effects and half-life period as nuclear energy."[116] Coalesced by the Chernobyl catastrophe, Kluge's media theory of television as clouds as implied in *Miscellaneous News* is anything but a reactive response to the privatization of West Germany's media landscape, an event that Kluge actually considered "uncannier than the phenomenon of Chernobyl."[117] On the contrary, Kluge had long been concerned with talk about privatizing German television, and with the emergence in the late seventies of new technologies like fiber optics, broadband cable networks, and satellite broadcasts, he recognized immediately both how far new media could penetrate both everyday consciousness and the gestalt of the public sphere. By 1984, the conditions were favorable for him to enter into the fray of television production as a shareholder, and by 1985 he had generated twenty-two fifty-five-minute programs for the fledgling commercial station SAT.1. Although he had been thinking long and hard about the detrimental nature and effects of new media,

---

115 Vogl, 46.
116 Henning Burk, "Die Wächter des Sarkophags: Interview mit Alexander Kluge," *Maske und Konthurn: Internationale Beiträge zur Theater-, Film- und Medienwissenschaften* 53.1 (2007): 67.
117 Burk, "Die Wächter des Sarkophags," 68.

roughly five years would have to pass before he explicitly thematized the Chernobyl catastrophe in conjunction with his "antitelevision" broadcasts.[118]

Forever obsessed with anniversaries because of their overdetermined status as preludes to change, the opportunities continually lost therein, and the customarily overlooked call for memory work they exhort, Kluge first commemorated the year 1986 in a twenty-five-minute broadcast that first aired in July 1991 by largely emulating television's usual conflation of news and *faits-divers* much like he did in *Miscellaneous News*. A calendar of that year's catastrophes, the show entitled "Wir sind noch einmal davongekommen / Jahresring 1986" [We Escaped Once Again / Growth Ring 1986] begins with a report about two hundred teenagers who perished in a burning youth center; touches upon the *Challenger* disaster; mentions briefly the death of the oldest man alive; climaxes with the Chernobyl meltdown; and then closes with the official launch of commercial television in West Germany.[119] In subsequent broadcasts, Kluge wrestled less diachronically with the general hopelessness of that year—he has regularly regarded 1986 as the "antipode to 1968," a year full of utopian aspirations—and instead proceeded synchronically by interviewing eyewitnesses who experienced the explosion of reactor four and the tragic consequences firsthand.[120] This shift in approach is significant, for it marks precisely how he moved away from merely registering the paralysis of everyday life and politics indexically (as is the case in *Miscellaneous News*) and replicating the undifferentiated dimensions of televisual information (as reflected in "Jahresring 1986").

What we usually call mass media—film and television, for example—count for Kluge as just "forms," that is, formal conditions under which the real medium in question—namely people and their experiences, wishes, and fantasies—take shape.[121] As for the particular attributes of television's form, Kluge insisted already in 1985 that television is essentially not unlike the usual agents of the classical bourgeois public sphere (e.g., newspapers, theater, literature, film); it, too, can traffic in the two primary categories—uniqueness and permanence—necessary

---

118 Kluge, "Medialization—Musealization," 294.

119 For a transcript of the broadcast, see: Kluge, "Jahresring 1986," 117–28.

120 Kluge, "Jahresring 1986," 117.

121 Alexander Kluge, "Rohstoff, Nachrichten," in *Die Patriotin: Texts/Bilder 1–6* (Frankfurt am Main, 1979) 294.

for conveying everyday experience.[122] Yet, under the yoke of commercial interests, the dominant forms of television are marked more often
than not by transitoriness and repeatability, qualities that apportion,
moderate, and impair the immediacy of experience.[123] Under the right
conditions, television is actually a "hybrid" medium, one intrinsically
capable of resembling the forms of cinema in contradistinction to those
frenetic and predictable ones characteristic of digital media.[124] When
considered in this light, what makes Kluge's Chernobyl programs from
the first half of the nineties so unique in his three-decade panoply of
broadcasting are their techniques for manufacturing dimensions in the
form of boundaries and barriers for the spectator—the actual medium—
in spite of the homologous, unbounded effects of both private television
and nuclear catastrophe. Looking back at Chernobyl, ten years later,
Kluge framed his aspirations for his broadcasts about the catastrophe not
in terms of any moral imperative. Rather, his broadcasts were conceived
"practically" as a means for holding on to the "actual feeling" of immediate experience when the mediated experience promised by new media
threatened to do away with any such feeling altogether.[125] Kluge and
Negt explain in *History and Obstinacy* that historical experience is unreal
when it is full of abstractions; without a concomitant dose of antirealist feelings—feelings of "protest against unbearable relations" brought
on by abstractions—experience will forever remain prone to favorable
conditions for catastrophe.[126] For West Germans at the periphery of the
Chernobyl catastrophe, bystanders for whom the experience of nuclear
catastrophe in April 1986 was thoroughly unrealistic, the task then was
to "read" the far-off, abstract event "like writing on the wall."[127] Referring
to Daniel from the Old Testament, who deciphers divine writing that
prophesies the imminent downfall of King Belshazzar, Kluge has suggested that such code, once addressed exclusively to self-righteous kings,
has morphed into ubiquitous "public signs" that largely go unread. "In
addition, the warnings contain lots of 'fine print,'" he continues, "often

122 Alexander Kluge, "On the Expressions 'Media' and 'New Media': A Selection of
Keywords," trans. Richard Lambert, in *Difference and Orientation*, 255; cf. Benjamin,
"The Work of Art in the Age of Its Technical Reproducibility," 105.
123 Kluge, "On the Expressions 'Media' and 'New Media,'" 255.
124 Kluge, "On the Expressions 'Media' and 'New Media,'" 255.
125 Kluge, introduction to *Die Wächter des Sarkophags*, 15.
126 Kluge and Negt 139.
127 Kluge, introduction to *Die Wächter des Sarkophags*, 9.

Figure 4.4. Still from Kluge's 1993 *Primetime/Spätausgabe* broadcast "The Death Zone as Sanctuary" with Svetlana Alexievich and Rosemarie Tietze. © Alexander Kluge.

composed of rather inconspicuous messages. It is difficult to read these signs that rarely manifest themselves in writing."[128] In order to read these foreboding signs and engender conditions for antirealist feeling, Kluge deploys, once again, a *mise en abyme*, a screen within the screen, one that requires not one but two translations.

Midway through Kluge's second television broadcast about the nuclear catastrophe, "Die Wächter des Sarkophags von Tschernobyl" [The Guardians of Chernobyl's Sarcophagus] from 1992, we see once again the now familiar intertitle "Summer 1986." Translator Rosemarie Tietze sits in front of a television and renders into German the raw, Russian-language footage from BBC Horizon's extraordinary 1991 documentary "Inside Chernobyl's Sarcophagus."[129] Pointing to a closed-circuit television screen showing Red Army volunteers disposing of radioactive debris into the breach of the deadly reactor, military scientist and general Nikolai

---

128 Alexander Kluge and Martin Weinmann, *Album*, in Kluge, *Seen sind für Fische Inseln: Fernseharbeiten, 1987–2008* (Frankfurt am Main: Zweitausendeins, 2007) 53.

129 Edward Briffa, dir., "Inside Chernobyl's Sarcophagus," *Horizon*, BBC in association with WGBH Boston, April 22, 1991.

Tarakanov highlights for new recruits the exemplary work and says, according to Tietze, the following: "You have one minute to fulfill the following task. Watch your colleagues!"[130] In a subsequent broadcast entitled "You Have 40 Seconds," Kluge sits across from Romanian photojournalist Igor Kostin. "Where are you standing now?" Kluge asks as he reaches across the table, on which sits a large format print of Kostin's iconic photograph of "liquidators" or "bio-robots" disposing of the rubble. "Possibly a half meter ... away," Kostin's translator replies, attesting to the fact that Kostin, too, was exposed to deadly radiation for up to forty seconds at a time. "I intentionally exposed that longer," Kostin goes on to say, "so you can see how strong the radioactivity was."[131] In yet another broadcast, Belarusian journalist Svetlana Alexievich and translator Tietze sit together in front of a television screen while footage plays silently from Alexievich's filmed interviews with Tajik refugees who found shelter in Chernobyl's "exclusion zone" immediately after the Soviet Union dissolved and many of its republics succumbed to civil war (see fig. 4.4):

TIETZE: Svetlana N. is sitting in the middle there at the edge of the frame. They are afraid to mention their last names. They have a certain fear of the Tajik mafia that can be found everywhere ...

KLUGE: Is she pregnant?

TIETZE: (*first inquires with Alexievich in Russian and then replies to Kluge in German*) Yes, she is pregnant ... I asked her, "How come you decided to give birth to your child here when you are pregnant?" ... And she said that the ultimate reason for leaving was seeing a newborn killed right before her eyes.[132]

In all three broadcasts, reading images taken by eyewitnesses from within ground zero is fundamental. Yet this translation of experience into images is neither what conveys stories nor engenders knowledge of the catastrophe. Rather, it is Kluge's translators who disrupt the pull of

130 Kluge, *Die Wächter des Sarkophags*, 91.

131 Kluge, *Die Wächter des Sarkophags*, 50; see also: Alexander Kluge, dir., "Abschied von der sicheren Seite des Lebens: Geschichten aus Tschernobyl"; Kluge, dir., *Seen sind für Fische Inseln*, Zweitausendeins/dctp, 2009, DVD 4, track 3.

132 This exchange is missing in: Kluge, *Die Wächter des Sarkophags*, 142–47. The dialogue is taken from: Alexander Kluge, dir., "Die Todeszone als Zufluchtsort," *Primetime/Spätausgabe*, RTL plus, December 19, 1993; see also Svetlana Alexievich, *Voices from Chernobyl*, trans. Keith Gessen (Normal, IL: Dalkey Archive Press, 2005) 54–64.

the immersive spectacle by mediating for the spectator linguistically the eyewitnesses' accounts of either their own or another's stories about the images on view. The central role played by Kluge's translators says, in a word, that TV images alone can never suffice when reading the writing on the wall. What goes missing from, or rather what gets buried beneath, the televisual field is the everyday lived experience—the *faits-divers*—of catastrophe. Without the translation of storytelling, the images themselves tell little if anything of the gravity of Chernobyl's threat to human life. Further complicating the task of catastrophic reading is the fact that Kluge's eyewitnesses—investigative journalists, scientists, and former government officials—do not convey experiences infused with any antirealist feelings that he and Negt say are necessary for steering clear of future catastrophe. The bio-robots willingly put their lives on the line to minimize the contamination. In spite of the dangers to his own health, the photojournalist exposed himself in order to preserve for all of posterity the history of the quickly forgotten liquidators. Compared with the bloodshed at home, a slow death in the exclusion zone was for refugees like Svetlana N. a far better fate. In every instance, the contradictions characteristic of antagonistic reality have vanished. In Kluge and Negt's language, "everything appears unreal" for these individuals.[133] And the same could be said of West Germans in the summer of 1986. Flipping Michel's slogan on its head—"everyday life cannot be narrated"—Kluge's interviews suggest that neither catastrophe, in general, nor any antirealist feelings of protests against it, in particular, can ever be narrated by the victims or their translators. What storytelling transmits is the unrealness of everyday reality in the catastrophe. The conditions for reviving a critical sensibility lie ultimately elsewhere, namely in the real locus of the interview, in that sense of amazement about everyday life in the catastrophe conveyed by Kluge and his questions.

In his eighth thesis on the concept of history, Benjamin argues that there is nothing philosophical about the amazement we feel when "the things we are experiencing are 'still' possible in the twentieth century." "This amazement," he adds, "is not the beginning of knowledge—unless it is the knowledge that the view of history which gives rise to it is untenable."[134] When, in yet another interview with nuclear engineer Oxana Pentak, Kluge asks not about the technical details of the

---

133 Kluge and Negt 239.
134 Walter Benjamin, "On the Concept of History," trans. Harry Zohn, in *Selected*

explosion on April 26, 1986, but rather the details of her everyday life in the immediate shadow of catastrophe, he effectively divulges his own astonishment:

KLUGE: ... How long did you then stay in the reactor's immediate sphere of influence?
...
KLUGE: And what did you do? You are a technician and scientist. Did you shower? What does one do in such an instance?
...
KLUGE: What rules are there? How should one behave after that kind of catastrophe? Wash one's clothes?[135]

In her deft reading of Benjamin's intricate thesis on amazement, Sigrid Weigel points out that, when carefully parsed, the proposition does not actually petition for moral outrage against the normalization of disaster and catastrophe in the forward march of human history. Instead, Benjamin's calculated language singles out amazement as a "condition of possibility for a different type of perception" of history, a non-philosophical response that "distinguishes amazement at what we have experienced in the twentieth century from the figure of what is 'still' possible."[136] Evident by his line of questioning, Kluge's amazement has not to do with the incorporation of catastrophe into historical progress, but rather with the dialectic of everydayness in a new era of global nuclear catastrophe. What remains of everyday life when nuclear catastrophe is everyday? If the grievances of publicness were first its disregard for and, then later, its predation of everydayness, everyday life as we once knew it—once thought of as those unexceptional experiences produced in everyday life and work—stands to vanish altogether. Like Benjamin, Kluge's amazement is one nevertheless imbued with utopian élan. Writing a decade and a half after Kluge entered into the morass of private television, American media theorists Jay Bolter and Richard

---

Writings, vol. 4: *1938–1940*, eds. Howard Eiland and Michael W. Jennings (Cambridge, MA: Belknap Press, 1974) 392.

135 Kluge, *Die Wächter des Sarkophags*, 33, 34, 36.

136 Sigrid Weigel, "Non-Philosophical Amazement—Writing in Amazement: Benjamin's Position in the Aftermath of the Holocaust," in *Body- and Image-Space: Re-reading Walter Benjamin*, trans. Georgina Paul et al. (London: Routledge, 1996) 147, 148.

Grusin rechristened the word "remediation" to describe the contemporary social desire to multiply media while erasing all traces of any
mediation.[137] A moderately clever *bon mot* intended to capture this contradictory logic, Bolter and Grusin's remediation stifles, however, the
word's primary meaning, namely to remedy, to cure, to reverse, or to
bring to a full stop. Remediation, in this other sense, is precisely what
Kluge achieves with his mediation of experience. Using a constellation
composed of appropriated images taken from historical catastrophe,
eyewitness accounts, and translators, as well as his own long-standing
investment in championing every human being's right to their own
everyday life, Kluge engenders in his Chernobyl broadcasts temporal
and spatial differences that information-driven television literally has no
time or space for. Unlike Bolter and Grusin's remediation that, arguably,
operates within the media conditions of clouds where near and far collapse into one, Kluge's cultural windows on television strive to restore the
condition of possibility for the human sensorium's perception of time
and space and, by extension, the distinctions between uniqueness and
duration versus transitoriness and repeatability that allow amazement—
in Kluge's own words, an intense antirealistic feeling—to transpire at all
in the face of imminent permanent catastrophe.

*

Referring to the influence of digital technologies on the organization of
social life at the millennium, Slavoj Žižek has argued that "the standard
opposition of public and private" is no more. "A new space [has been
created]," he goes on to say, "the paradoxical space of *shared, collective
privacy*."[138] Countless scholars have struggled to give this new space an
adequate name, a space that also has as much to do with the fall of the
Berlin Wall, the disintegration of Soviet communism, the widespread
legitimation of neoliberalism, and the acceleration of global capitalism
as it does with recent advances in digital technologies. In Baudrillard's
mind, this new space marks the "end of the social."[139] Writing over a

137 Jay David Bolter and Richard Grusin, *Remediation: Understanding New Media*
(Cambridge, MA: MIT Press, 1999) 5.

138 Slavoj Žižek, "The Future of Politics (I)," *Die Gazette* (August 8, 2001).

139 Jean Baudrillard, *In the Shadow of the Silent Majorities … or, the End of the Social
and other Essays*, trans. Paul Foss, Paul Patton, and John Johnston (New York: Semio-
text(e), 1983) 65–91.

decade later, Peter Sloterdijk proffered instead the idea of a republic of spaces best elucidated by the figure of foam, an aggregate of countless tiny, hermetically sealed, egotistical bubbles.[140] Perhaps the most significant upshot of this widely recognized transformation of social space is what Beck, writing in the year of the Chernobyl catastrophe, called the society of risk's "disempowerment of politics."[141] In a similar vein, Jacques Rancière, echoing Baudrillard before him, has gone so far as to write more recently of the "end of politics."[142] Less bombastic than these dire pronouncements yet no less earnest, Zygmunt Bauman has claimed that our liquid modernity has merely fostered an end to politics with a capital P—"the activity charged with the task of translating private problems into public issues"; in other words, big P politics disintegrated into the small p life-politics of the "gossip column."[143] As if heeding Benjamin's charge that "nothing that has ever happened should be regarded as lost to history," Kluge has developed a political pedagogy of the senses focused on countering that bourgeois catastrophe-prone tendency intent on curtailing the dimensions of experience by throwing into stark relief *faits-divers*—the life-politics of the gossip column—against the backdrop of looming permanent catastrophe.[144] The political challenge for Negt and Kluge is thus the fortification of our faculties of differentiation necessary for reflecting on and communicating the catastrophic fate of everyday life when the basic conditions for this differentiation—*"time, recognizable places, the autonomous abilities of subjects"*—have been destroyed by the "long-distance effects" of Chernobyl.[145] Using the very medium that has exacerbated more often than not what we might in a word call our critical sensibility of this postmodern implosion of time and space, Kluge's media praxis essentially remediated in tiny, twenty-five-minute televisual doses the necessary dimensions for the political judgment that catastrophe in all its many guises threatens to collapse.

140 Peter Sloterdijk, *Spheres*, vol. 3: *Foams*, trans. Wieland Hoban (Los Angeles, CA: Semiotext(e), 2011) pp. 23, 53–55.

141 Beck 191.

142 Jacques Rancière, *On the Shores of Politics*, trans. Liz Heron (London: Verso, 1995) 5.

143 Zygmunt Bauman, *Liquid Modernity* (Cambridge, UK: Polity Press 2000) 70, 71.

144 Benjamin, "On the Concept of History," 390.

145 Negt and Kluge, *Maßverhältnisse des Politischen*, 10.

Aesthetic Praxis: Video, Television, Film, Literature

Figure 5.1. "How does film think?" Sergei Eisenstein cutting *October* in 1928.

Figure 5.2. "Cells know everything from here to the stars …"

Two stills from *News from Ideological Antiquity: Marx-Eisenstein-Capital*.
© Alexander Kluge.

5

Outlines for a Digital Critique of Capital: Forms of Cinematic Thinking

Which Ideological Antiquity?

The verdict was out not long after the bright orange DVD box set hit German bookstores at the close of 2008, mere months after the sudden collapse of the investment bank Lehman Brothers in September that year and the ensuing global panic that culminated in the Great Recession. Journalists and film scholars alike quickly proclaimed the nine-hour video *News from Ideological Antiquity: Marx-Eisenstein-Capital* to be Alexander Kluge's "magnum opus," a crowning achievement in what one critic called his ongoing Wagnerian *Gesamtkunstwerk*-in-progress that seemed to embody one of Kluge's guiding principles, *kairos*.[1] Or did it? A derivation of the minor Greek god Caerus, *kairos* marks the time of both good fortune and opportunity and stands in opposition to *chronos*—linear, chronological time that consumes everything—named after the Titan king Cronus who ate his children. "*Kairos* is portrayed as a god with wings on his feet, a thick lock of hair on his forehead, and no hair in the back," Kluge once explained. "Whoever fails to grab him

---

1 Ekkehard Knörer, "Versteinertes verflüssigen. *Nachrichten aus der ideologischen Antike*, Powered by Sergei Eisenstein," *die tageszeitung* (November 12, 2008): 15; and Julia Vassilieva, "Capital and Co.: Kluge/Eisenstein/Marx," *Screening the Past* 31 (2011), www.screeningthepast.com/2011/08/capital-and-co-klugeeisensteinmarx/.

by his tuft of hair at the right time ends up sliding off the bare backside of his head."[2] Given the fact that Kluge's video arrived in the immediate wake of the worst global recession since the 1930s, the collective attention he suddenly directed at capitalism's greatest critic along with the Soviet filmmaker who once toyed with a film adaptation of *Capital* came arguably not in the nick of time but rather a moment too late. Disaster had already struck. Banks, markets, communities, and lives would continue to tumble for years to come. Nevertheless, critics found Kluge's video nothing less than prophetic. American Marxist literary critic Fredric Jameson suggested, for example, that Kluge's video reveals just how productive "the category of classical antiquity" can be for a global left intent on reinventing "an energizing past for itself."[3] In the words of a media studies scholar, *News from Ideological Antiquity* is a timely attempt at showing what the critique of political economy might mean in the twenty-first century.[4] In conjunction with a screening of the film in Beijing in the spring of 2012, Chinese sociologist Wang Hui proffered the idea that Kluge's video is an archaeological dig containing clues for solving the ongoing financial crisis.[5] For these and other commentators, there was no question that Kluge's news from antiquity could not have been timelier on account of its germane political and economic insights.[6] But what exactly are these insights?

To suggest, however, that Kluge was prescient of the Great Recession would certainly overlook the fact that the video's origins reach back to the early nineties, when Germany in particular found itself in very different economic strain due to reunification. Moreover, it would dismiss the fact that *News from Ideological Antiquity* was, for Kluge, initially a fuzzy idea at best. "In the beginning," he confessed later in an interview, "I could not even say whether it was going to be a book,

---

2 Alexander Kluge, "On the Expressions 'Media' and 'New Media': A Selection of Keywords," trans. Richard Lambert, in *Difference and Orientation: An Alexander Kluge Reader*, ed. Richard Langston (Ithaca, NY: Cornell University Press, 2019) 271.

3 Fredric Jameson, "Marx and Montage," *New Left Review* 58 (July–August 2009): 117.

4 Christophe Van Eecke, "Stock Footage and Shock Tactics: Eisenstein, Marx and Filming *Capital*," *ThRu* (2009): 2, kluge-alexander.de/uploads/media/KapitalChristophe VanEecke.pdf.

5 Alexander Kluge, "An Instance of Internet Telephony over the Himalayas," trans. Emma Woelk, in *Difference and Orientation*, 492.

6 Sven Lütticken, "Film Capital: On Cinemarxism in the Twenty-First Century," in *Aesthetic Marx*, eds. Samir Gandesha and Johan Hartle (London: Bloomsbury, 2017) 233.

a film, an online contribution, a DVD, an evening at the movies or a sort of counter-program on television."[7] Kluge's impetus was originally a treasure others found while digging underneath layers of what he calls "historical debris."[8] Shortly after the fall of the Iron Curtain, Kluge began dialoguing with New York film scholar Annette Michelson, who back in 1976 had introduced the English-language world to Eisenstein's recently unearthed notes on his plans for "cinematizing" Marx's *Capital*.[9] In light of the Soviet Bloc's swift demise, the disintegration of European hopes for a post-communist revolution, and the concomitant loss of "trust in history as a process directly shaped by human consciousness," Kluge saw little in the nineties that echoed the turbulent conditions orbiting around the publication of Marx's magnum opus or the calamity of the Stock Market Crash of 1929.[10] Eisenstein's ambition to film *Capital* seemed just as alien on the eve of the new millennium as *Capital* itself did.[11] What made Eisenstein and Marx seem so strange for Kluge haunted sundry interviews recorded for his television broadcasts well before he embarked on *News from Ideological Antiquity* in earnest. With literary scholar Joseph Vogl, he investigated, for example, the relationship between narration and stock markets.[12] With his longtime collaborator Oskar Negt, he queried how best to approach *Capital* cinematographically.[13] Additional recorded interviews with Russian Eisenstein scholar

---

7 Gertrud Koch, "Undercurrents of Capital: An Interview with Alexander Kluge," trans. Gerrit Jackson, *Germanic Review* 85 (2010): 361; see also: Stefan Grissemann, "Karl Marx ist der Dichter unserer Krise: Im Gespräch, Alexander Kluge," *Frankfurter Allgemeine Zeitung* (October 22, 2008): 33.

8 Alexander Kluge, booklet, *Nachrichten aus der ideologischen Antike: Marx – Eisenstein – Das Kapital* (Frankfurt am Main: Suhrkamp Verlag, 2008) 4.

9 Kluge, booklet, *Nachrichten aus der ideologischen Antike*, 5; Sergei Eisenstein, "Notes for a Film of *Capital*," trans. Maciej Sliwowski, Jay Leyda, and Annette Michelson, *October* 2 (Summer 1976): 3–26. Kluge reveals his indebtedness to Michelson in: Alexander Kluge, *Cinema Stories*, trans. Martin Brady and Helen Hughes (New York: New Directions, 2007) 101.

10 Kluge, booklet, *Nachrichten aus der ideologischen Antike*, 4.

11 Kluge, booklet, *Nachrichten aus der ideologischen Antike*, 4.

12 Alexander Kluge and Joseph Vogl, "Was für einen Roman erzählt die Börse?," in *Soll und Haben: Fernsehgespräche* (Berlin: diaphanes, 2009) 247–58. Originally broadcast on *10 till 11*, RTL, May 22, 2000.

13 Alexander Kluge, dir., "Der 'Mehrwert' & seine Bilder: Wie verfilmt man das *Kapital* von Marx?," in *Seen sind für Fische Inseln: Fernseharbeiten 1987–2008* (Frankfurt am Main: Zweitausendeins, 2009) DVD 13, chapter 4. Originally broadcast on *10 till 11*, RTL, December 12, 2005.

Oksana Bulgakowa solidified his grasp of the filmmaker's biography that later served as an anchor for the video's exposition on disc 1. As several commentators have aptly noted, and as Kluge himself confirms, the final result is neither a screen adaptation of Marx's critique of political economy nor a reconstruction of Eisenstein's unrealized notes. Eighty-five separate video tracks subdivided into six themes spread over three discs, the video circles back around to Eisenstein and Marx again and again, but what news Kluge bears exactly and why both Marx and Eisenstein represent the new millennium's antiquity is anything but obvious at first sight. If not of *kairos* and certainly not of *chronos*, then one might perhaps wager that Kluge's project is actually marked by and incommensurable with present time.

What is undoubtedly of its own present moment when it appeared in 2008 is the project's chosen medium. Commissioned by Suhrkamp Verlag's Ulla Unseld-Berkéwicz to inaugurate the press's new foray into video on DVD, *News from Ideological Antiquity* was designed to be a commercially available video packaged together with a sixty-page booklet containing essays and stories. Aside from a brief and limited distribution in Europe, Asia, and the Americas at art house theaters and cultural centers, where either the nine-hour original or an abbreviated ninety-minute version (with or without subtitles) was screened, the video was primarily intended for private consumption. Given the fact that all three discs contain additional text files, it is reasonable to assume that the project's imagined spectator would most likely sit at a computer rather than at a television.[14] For Kluge and Negt, the corporeal demands of the new medium made all the difference. "I lean back for TV," they note in *History and Obstinacy* with respect to the restructuring of intelligence in the digital age, "whereas I lean forward for the computer."[15] That Kluge settled on the DVD format for delivering his news from ideological antiquity was not entirely unprecedented. Just a year earlier, he released, with the assistance of Munich's Filmmuseum, the Goethe-Institut, and Zweitausendeins (the publisher of *Geschichte und Eigensinn*), a box set of

---

14 Cornell University Library's online archive *Alexander Kluge: Cultural History in Dialogue* is the only authorized online provider that streams all three parts of *News from Ideological Antiquity*. See: https://kluge.library.cornell.edu/films/ideological-antiquity. Portions of the video can be also be screened through Kluge's online Gardens of Information. See: http://www.dctp.tv/filme/nachrichten17/.

15 Alexander Kluge and Oskar Negt, *History and Obstinacy*, ed. Devin Fore, trans. Richard Langston et al. (New York: Zone Books, 2014) 197.

his entire filmography, thirty hours of shorts and features as well as a few select television programs including an interview with Jean-Luc Godard, essays, unrealized screenplays, and literary texts. After decades of reluctantly releasing only two of his twenty full-length films on VHS for commercial distribution, Kluge gave himself, as it were, the "Criterion treatment": high-quality digital transfers of all his films and unprecedented access to copious amounts of extra-textual materials. A similar box set of highlights from his television broadcasts since 1988 appeared less than two months after the release of *News from Ideological Antiquity*. Like these compendia, *News from Ideological Antiquity* includes navigable menus full of extras and additional reading material, not to mention detailed liner notes. While the Criterion Collection's principle of the home theater as "an important alternative space for film spectatorship" was hardly new to Kluge the television auteur, its lavish transformation of the DVD into "an archive of archives," however, was unprecedented.[16] Kluge acknowledged as much shortly after releasing his Marx-Eisenstein video. Asked what his "DVD-ification" of Eisenstein's plans to cinematize Marx's *Capital* along the lines of Joyce's literary adaption of Homer's *Odyssey*, he responded, "Technical possibilities have really been developed so far and are so ubiquitously available that [Walter Benjamin's] analysis [of technological reproducibility] is no longer [apt] in our time." DVDs, Kluge added, are both a storage medium and a raft: "You can tie a great number of logs together and then travel very safely. All of Polynesia was settled that way."[17]

According to media theoretician Boris Groys, the ground underneath Benjamin's seminal argument about the reproducible work of art has indeed shifted in the digital age. Whereas analog reproduction generated copies of an original that were removed from an authentic material flow, digital archiving is no longer concerned with originals or the technical denigration of their aura. "What remains is its metadata," Groys explains, "the information about the here and now of its original inscription into the material flow: photos, videos, textual testimonies."[18] Crucial for Groys, and arguably just as germane for Kluge, is the distinction between the irreversibility of analog material flows marked

---

16 James Kendrick, "What Is the Criterion? The Criterion Collection as an Archive of Film as Culture," *Journal of Film and Video* 53.2/3 (Summer/Fall 2001): 127, 134.

17 Koch 361.

18 Boris Groys, *In the Flow* (London: Verso, 2016) 4.

by the sign of *chronos* and the reversibility of the digital archive's data flows capable of generating aura devoid of any object. In other words, Kluge's deliberation on Eisenstein's unrealized plans for cinematizing Marx not only transpires entirely outside the analog environment in which it originally unfolded, but also explicitly makes use of the non-linear geometry of the digital archive in order to enact his own unique Marxian agenda. As will be argued over the course of this chapter, the antiquity that *News from Ideological Antiquity* reports actually belongs to neither Marx's nineteenth century nor to Eisenstein's early twentieth century, and the relationality it employs to that end also seems worlds apart from the constellations once championed by Benjamin. On the series format, Kluge's chosen organizational method for constructing his video "raft," Gilles Deleuze (in accordance with Gottfried Wilhelm Leibniz) contends that it is in fact what constitutes the world. "However, the series and sequences are apparent to us only in small sections, and in a disrupted or mixed-up order."[19] What remains to be seen is how Kluge deploys the series as dictated by the organizational logic of the DVD, and to what end the vertical depths of its archive and the horizontal breadth of its float serve in his twenty-first-century deliberation on Marxism. "We experience more about ourselves," Kluge says of digging through Eisenstein's plans for *Capital*, than the "shards and treasures [we find in this archaeological site]."[20] In order to arrive at the nature of this learning process, the ensuing chapter argues that *News from Ideological Antiquity* works strategically through various possibilities for cinema to think without ever attempting to enact the Marxian thought that Eisenstein aspired to with his outlines for an unrealized film he tentatively entitled "Capital."

Beyond the Movement-Image

In what is perhaps the clearest précis of *History and Obstinacy*, Negt explained his and Kluge's shared investment in Marxism in terms of two agendas, one complete and the other woefully incomplete. "*The agenda*

19 Gilles Deleuze, *Cinema 2: The Time-Image*, trans. Hugh Tomlinson and Robert Galeta (Minneapolis, MN: University of Minnesota Press, 1989) 14.

20 Alexander Kluge, "A Plan with the Force of a Battleship," trans. Martin Brady and Helen Hughes, in *Difference and Orientation*, 211.

of the analysis of capital has certainly been completed," he argued on the centennial commemoration of Marx's death.

> *Incomplete is the agenda concerning the constitution of the Subject.* Everything that Marx said is correct, but he did not say everything that we need in order to comprehend the modern world. *Capital* does not have to be written yet again ... If we distinguish complete from incomplete agendas, then we recognize simultaneously that Marx mainly undertook the scientific development of a field at the point at which an established science of it already existed. How could he speak scientifically about the constitution of the Subject when in his lifetime there was no psychology of internal development or of compulsive desires?[21]

What Marx refrained from undertaking because of his and Engel's overestimation of the working-class revolutionary will is what Negt calls a "cell analysis" of the vastly underestimated and compromised characteristics within proletarian subjects responsible for neutralizing and absorbing this very will.[22] That Frankfurt School elders had long given up on the proletariat as a class and substance was no reason, in Negt's estimation, to abandon the study of proletarian characteristics. Such characteristics, he adds, are "directed toward emancipation," engage in "permanent opposition," and presuppose a kind of organization capable of doing battle with the micro-physics of power that Michel Foucault attributes to the modern production of docile bodies.[23] In order to tackle this unfulfilled agenda, Negt calls for an exploration of the subject, one that departs from the realization that individuals are neither synthetic wholes nor inherently stable. And, finally, reinvigorating Marxism in the form of a micrological study of the subject must account for both the political economy of labor's valorization of some human characteristics and the opportunity seized by others for resistance. All of this, says Negt, must start with re-reading Marx anew, and this is precisely how Kluge begins *News from Ideological Antiquity.* After a thirty-minute

---

21 Oskar Negt, "What Is a Revival of Marxism and Why Do We Need One Today? Centennial Lecture Commemorating the Death of Karl Marx," trans. Michael Palencia-Roth, in *Marxism and the Interpretation of Culture*, eds. Cary Nelson and Lawrence Grossberg (Urbana: University of Illinois Press, 1988) 220.

22 Negt 222.

23 Negt 226; see also: Kluge and Negt 116.

exposition of Eisenstein's unrealized plans at the opening of disc 1, Kluge
turns to Marx in earnest and indexes Negt's (and by extension his own)
program through a series of recitations. In spite of its allusion to the late
Marx in its title—the Marx of freedom *from* labor—Kluge's video works
its way backward in time to the young Marx, the Marx of the subject's
freedom *through* labor.[24] A single passage from *Capital* (1867) on the
mature Marx's revised account of the labor process based on the science
of Hermann von Helmholtz segues to a brief excerpt from the introduction to *Grundrisse* (1857) before concluding with another bit from
the preface to Marx's 1843–44 "Contribution to the Critique of Hegel's
Philosophy of Law":

> A spider conducts operations that resemble those of a weaver, and a
> bee puts to shame many an architect in the construction of her cells.
> But what distinguishes the worst architect from the best of bees is this,
> that the architect raises his structure in imagination before he erects it
> in reality ...
>
> Man is a ζῷον πολιτιχόν [political animal] in the most literal sense:
> he is not only a social animal, but an animal that can isolate itself only
> within society ...
>
> But *man* is no abstract being encamped outside the world. Man is
> the *world of man* ...[25]

Described by Kluge himself as but a preamble designed to familiarize
viewers with Eisenstein's intentions, disc 1 of *News from Ideological
Antiquity* makes progressively clear that the video's theoretical concepts
come not from the mature Marx's critique of political economy at all.[26]
What these and subsequent citations produced on title cards all have in
common is their trajectory backward to the anthropological thrust of the
young Marx, the Marx in pursuit of a theory of the human being.[27]

---

24 Anson Rabinbach, *The Human Motor: Energy, Fatigue, and the Origins of Modernity* (New York: Basic Books, 1990) 80.

25 Karl Marx, *Capital: A Critique of Political Economy*, vol. 1, in *Collected Works*,
vol. 35 (London: Lawrence and Wishart, 1996) 188; Karl Marx, "Economic Manuscripts
of 1857–58," in *Collected Works*, vol. 28: *Karl Marx: 1857–61* (London: Lawrence and
Wishart, 1986) 18; Karl Marx, "Contribution to the Critique of Hegel's Philosophy of
Law: Introduction," in *Collected Works*, vol. 3: *Marx and Engels, 1843–1844* (London:
Lawrence and Wishart, 1975) 175.

26 Kluge, *Nachrichten aus der ideologischen Antike*, 31; see also: Koch 367.

27 Eberhard Knödler-Bunte, Hajo Funke, and Arno Widmann, "The History of

Whereas the spoken and printed word in this second section from disc 1 points to Negt and Kluge's own Marxian emphasis on the human factor, the thirteen minutes of interspersed montage sequences of factories, assembly plants, warehouses, grocery stores, and humanoid robots accompanied by music keep the mature Marx of *Capital* literally in view. In Kluge's exposition of Marx's thinking, these components and their theoretical indices are separated from one another entirely. The reverse motion of Kluge's Marx quotations, all of which deliberate on the question of the human being, actually point forward to their unresolved relationship to the mature Marx.[28] Does, in other words, the human factor have any bearing on the evolutionary trajectory of capitalism into a society of androids? Far from providing an answer, *News from Ideological Antiquity* pushes forward with a surprising jump. Addressed as denizens of the cosmos, spectators see a swirling sea of stars set to noise taken from an experimental album called *Leichenschrei* [The Scream of the Corpses].[29] The bay doors of an observatory then open and we behold a telescope pointing toward the heavens, a cinematic projection spinning ever so slightly. A time-lapse shot of a rotating Mars segues to yet another string of title cards taken from neither the young nor the mature Marx, but, rather, from the work where Negt's proposed revival of Marxism was first outlined, namely his and Kluge's very own *History and Obstinacy*: "The Milky Way is a flat stellar mass arranged in spiral shape. Here, a view of its center. The earth moves around the sun. The sun moves at 750,000 kilometers per hour around the center. For one orbit it needs 250 million years. Planet earth is roughly four billion years old."[30] A brief lesson on our place within the vastness of cosmic space and time, this cinematization of Kluge and Negt's original caption taken from *History and Obstinacy* is merely a counterpoint to a second quotation, one accompanied this time by screams and the sound of breaking glass: "Intercourse with four billion years of evolution, 2,000 years of historical time, the cumulative landscapes of industry, and the emotions of the entire body is both **objective** and **definite**. Cells know everything all the way to the stars but the mind has either never experienced any such

Living Labor Power: A Discussion with Oskar Negt and Alexander Kluge," trans. Fiona Elliot, *October* 149 (Summer 2014): 39

28 Deleuze 186.

29 Socialistisches Patienten Kollektiv, "Internal Bleeding," *Leichenschrei*, Thermidor Records, 1982.

30 Kluge and Negt 157.

a thing or simply forgot it if it did."[31] Following the final title card, a series
of faces from ancient sculptures are then superimposed onto the same
sea of swirling stars the telescope set its sights on earlier (see fig. 5.2).
Section two concludes with a final quotation from *Grundrisse*, namely
Marx's famous rumination on the difficulties moderns have with trying
to understand ancient art and poetry.[32] Far from shifting his categories
to matters of classical philology, Kluge's chosen quotes juxtaposed with
his series of images point to a glaring discrepancy: we study the heavens
but know very little about ourselves let alone where we came from. This
conundrum is compounded further in a subsequent scene from part 3,
in which two actors dressed as East German non-commissioned officers
(one of whom is Kluge's own daughter) prepare for an exam on Marx.
Holding copies of Negt and Kluge's *Geschichte und Eigensinn* in their
hands, Officers Müller and Pflüger first recite from Marx's "Economic
and Philosophic Manuscripts." What Negt and Kluge carefully gloss line
by line, namely Marx's deliberations on "real, corporeal *man*" and "his
real, objective, *essential powers*," eludes the East German officers entirely.[33] "How do you understand naturalism in this context?" Müller asks.
Unsatisfied with Pflüger's guess at an answer, he retorts, "But what does
being natural mean?" "Not thinking," she replies. "No, I don't believe
that," he responds in a flash. To embark on a Marxian study of subjective
characteristics departing from the young Marx's own writings proves as
difficult as understanding the Greeks.

At this point, less than an hour into the nine-hour video, those viewers
attentive to the origins of these granular details may very well have the
sneaking suspicion that the remainder of *News from Ideological Antiquity*
amounts to nothing more than a cinematization of Kluge and Negt's own
History and Obstinacy. Indeed, Kluge seems to intimate as much when,
in the accompanying booklet, he confesses, "I am not so much interested
in the ways Marx's texts describe the external economy and its 'laws' than
I am, above all, in the CAPITALISM IN US."[34] However, as the video
marches forward through its many interviews, fictional dialogues, Marx

---

31 Kluge and Negt 158. Translation slightly modified.

32 Marx, "Economic Manuscripts of 1857–58," 47–48.

33 Karl Marx, "Economic and Philosophic Manuscripts of 1844," in Karl Marx and
Friedrich Engels, *Collected Works*, vol. 3: *Marx and Engels, 1843–1844* (London: Lawrence and Wishart, 1975) 336.

34 Kluge, booklet, *Nachrichten aus der ideologischen Antike*, 6.

recitations and exegeses, musical performances, and title cards, recurring reference to the possibilities of two different mediums—first film
and then video—makes progressively clear that Kluge's project is anything but an illustration of his and Negt's magnum opus. Following a
dialogue about the peculiarities of translating the young Marx's thoughts
about the historical formation of the human sensorium into Russian, we
see a contrastive montage: a title card poses the question "How does film
think?" below a photograph of Eisenstein editing *October* in 1928 (see
fig. 5.1). And then the video cuts to a brief clip, not from any of Eisenstein's films, but rather from the very last sequence in Dziga Vertov's
Lullaby from 1937; a pouty infant, gently rocking in a hammock, turns its
head to look beyond the frame and then cracks a smile. An unmistakable
allusion to the language of Gilles Deleuze, the aforementioned intertitle
sets the tone for the many ensuing clues on all three discs. Concerned
with developing a taxonomy of cinema's different regimes of time and
thought, Deleuze affirms Kluge's question entirely when in his *Cinema
2* he writes that Eisenstein "made cinema the cerebral art *par excellence*"
and he did so by way of montage.[35] Yet Deleuze did not stop there. He
singles Eisenstein out, in particular, as an exemplar of what he calls the
"movement-image." "A cinematographic Hegel," he writes, Eisenstein's
films, renowned for their dialectical montage, embody "an ideal of
knowledge as harmonious totality."[36] This regime's attendant notion of
truth, both singular and steadfast, subordinates time such that it is only
indirectly represented, "because it flows from the montage which links
one movement-image to another."[37] Equally applicable to both Eisenstein
and Vertov, not to mention American silent and French impressionist
film as well, the movement-image traffics in chronological time within an
identitarian universe wholly deterministic in nature.[38] Bringing Deleuze
into conversation with Kluge at this early juncture will certainly raise
red flags from some, for Deleuze's association of the movement-image
with chronological time drags Eisenstein into the morass of mechanical
time, *chronos*, that Kluge has actively worked against his entire career.
What seemed at first like a video intent on valorizing Eisenstein's plans

---

35 Deleuze 211.
36 Deleuze 210.
37 Deleuze 35.
38 D.N. Rodowick, *Gilles Deleuze's Time Machine* (Durham, NC: Duke University
Press, 1997) 15.

for Marx's *Capital*, when parsed in conjunction with Deleuze's concepts, *News from Ideological Antiquity* suddenly raises doubts. Above all, why would Kluge make Eisenstein his subject when, in the words of Fredric Jameson, both he and Negt "explicitly repudiate conceptions of the dialectic that aim at restoring some primal unity?"[39]

It would be a gross oversight to conflate this one image of Eisenstein at the cutting table as a single point of orientation for understanding the entirety of *News from Ideological Antiquity*. Deleuze does indeed matter for a comprehensive understanding of Kluge's video, but his account of the thinking characteristic of the movement-image does not have the final say. In fact, the ensuing sequence of Vertov's rocking child confirms that the question of how film thinks, for both Eisenstein and Vertov, actually serves as a historical query for Kluge that should not be confused with the overall aspirations of his video. Why Kluge singles out Vertov's *Lullaby* has, in all probability, to do with a backwards movement to that preceding sequence in which Austrian actress Sophie Rois recites the aforementioned final paragraph from Marx's introduction to *Grundrisse*: "An adult cannot become a child again, or he becomes childish. But does not the naiveté of the child give him pleasure, and must he not himself endeavor to reproduce the child's veracity on a higher level?" "The Greeks," Marx goes on to write, "were normal children. The charm their art has for us ... is ... inseparably linked with the fact that the immature social conditions which gave rise ... to this art can never recur."[40] Rois's reading includes no substantial commentary other than a piano accompaniment, a transcription of "Oh, rimembranza" ("Oh, What Memories!") from Vincenzo Bellini's opera *Norma* (1831). When brought into dialogue with one another, Vertov's image and Marx's quotation make clear that, for Kluge, Soviet cinema is the charming yet naïve antiquity in question that not only eludes simple comprehension but that will also never happen again. A memory not to be repeated, Soviet cinema is, in other words, a historical reference point for Kluge's own contemporary interest in engaging, on the one hand, capitalism's colonization of the interior world of human life and, on the other, the subjective powers set on resisting this domination. Invoking Deleuze's

---

39 Fredric Jameson, "On Negt and Kluge," *October* 46 (Autumn 1988) 160.
40 Marx, "Economic Manuscripts of 1857–58," 47–48. Kluge reproduces this excerpt in: Kluge, booklet, *Nachrichten aus der ideologischen Antike*, 33.

language again and again, *News from Ideological Antiquity* acknowledges the need to move beyond the organicism of the movement-image. In the second lengthy interview on disc 1, one with Marxist writer Dietmar Dath, Kluge invokes Eisenstein's meeting with James Joyce in late 1929. "Eisenstein decides either to film Joyce's book—simultaneously with *Capital*—or to adapt *Capital*, using the literary method of *Ulysses*," Kluge explains.[41] "What all would they have talked about?" he asks Dath. Unsatisfied with Joyce's universal conceptualization of the human being, Dath retorts, "I think Eisenstein would have had quite a lot to discuss with Charles Dickens about a film adaptation of *Capital*." Referring to Eisenstein, Kluge concurs, "It would not be possible for him to express the Joycean way of associating things in film." In order to achieve his vision, Kluge then conjectured, Eisenstein "would actually have to have what is at the beginning of film time as equally present at the end." In a lengthy interview with Peter Sloterdijk, on disc 2, that ponders the belated human propensity to internalize capitalism's external transformation of industry, Sloterdijk ponders aloud, "I, too, believe that the best approach to ... the analysis of Marx's *Capital* should be carried out from the perspective of a theory of fairy tales." In this vein, the best antidote to what Kluge calls the "false objectivity" of positivist Marxism is, says Sloterdijk, "the *Metamorphoses* by Ovid." And, on disc 3, Kluge proposes that images—what he calls "crystalized moments"—could map out the images of life under capital, to which Negt retorts, "The trained analysts from the Frankfurt School have their difficulties developing image worlds that make concrete what their analyses of knowledge and truth present." On this lingering aporia between image and concept, Kluge then suggests, "One would have to learn how to deal with images arranged serially, meaning apposing an image to its variation and another variation and yet another variation, et cetera, so as to learn how to comment with images." Just three of many oblique allusions to essential features of Deleuze's second regime of cinema—the time-image—scattered in no particular order, these references to time, metamorphosis, and the crystalline image in series all suggest that a realization of Eisenstein's plans for *Capital* would, at the very least, have to move beyond the regime of the movement-image.

---

41 Kluge, "A Plan with the Force of a Battleship," 209.

The Unfilmed Criticizes the Filmed

The crucial turning point in Deleuze's account of cinema transpires at that moment when Eisenstein's organic image is superseded by a new image regime he calls "crystalline." Such images, no longer subject to the movement of sensory-motor perception, are purely optical and acoustic, and their organization, no longer beholden to chronological time, becomes irrational, discontinuous, and undecidable. Essential for the modern cinema of the time-image is the serial order of its independent images (along with their corresponding irrational cuts) marked by categories that freely pass into one another. Unlike the harmonious totality of truth characteristic of the classical regime of the movement-image, this new cinema produces images in series that exert what Deleuze, borrowing from Friedrich Nietzsche, calls the "power of the false." "Everywhere it is the metamorphoses of the false which replace the form of the true," he explains.[42] First exemplified in Italian neorealism and the ensuing new waves but raised to the level of something akin to the novel by none other than Kluge's paragon Jean-Luc Godard, the time-image brings time to the fore of thinking—it brings together, he writes, "the before and the after in a becoming"—that sets free otherwise subordinate powers of life capable of refuting the world of appearances and their grasp on truth.[43] Compared with Godard's films of the sixties featured in Deleuze's philosophical theory, Kluge's *News from Ideological Antiquity* hardly looks like any of Deleuze's exemplars of the time-image. For all its talk about the value of the metamorphosis (Sloterdijk) in the image series (Negt) that thinks from the beyond (Dath), Kluge's video is fairly poor in images. In fact, roughly two-thirds of the entire nine-hour video is composed of discourse-laden interviews with scholars or artists. As was the case with the aforementioned sequence on disc 1 that weaves thought-images of the mature Marx's economic critique into the young Marx's anthropological discourse, all three discs are populated with sundry images, but none are crystalline as Deleuze defines it, for in the final analysis *News from Ideological Antiquity* tells of no story for any crystal moments to lay bare direct-time from beyond, nor does it live up to Deleuze's ambiguous category of fabulation. So what then is *News from Ideological*

---

42 Deleuze 134.

43 Deleuze 155. Kluge writes in *Cinema Stories*: "I have only seen Godard, for me a paradigm in the world of cinema, three times in my life" (105).

Antiquity? In order to settle on an answer, the process of eliminiation must make two more strikes. While we may with reason choose not to take him by his word, Kluge has nevertheless insisted both in his notes and in interviews that his video aspires to be neither an imitation nor a realization of Eisenstein's designs. And, secondly, Kluge acknowledges Eisenstein's own awareness that "cinema does not possess [the] means of expression" necessary for bringing about his vision for *Capital*.[44] "Film," he emphatically explains to Negt on disc 3, "is actually not suitable." Kluge's reasoning once again harks back to the perils of *chronos*: "Above all, every new impression purges the preceding ones." Were Eisenstein to accept Joyce's challenge of framing *Capital* as a day-in-the-life *story* in the form of a "chain" that actually triggers a non-linear "play" of conceptual "associations," then cinema would have to move beyond the plane of chronological time.[45]

Of course, Deleuze's cinematic taxonomy is not the only model for cinematic thinking. If what Eisenstein sought was unrealizable in his own time and is also not reflected *in* Kluge's video that nevertheless reflects *on* conditions necessary for realizing Eisenstein's Marx project, then what *News from Ideological Antiquity* is is arguably best described with the help of another thinker, someone admittedly worlds apart from Deleuze, namely Theodor W. Adorno. In his seminal essay on the essay, Adorno insists on the form's reliance on play and luck, its aversion to methods and systems, as well as its open, fragmentary character. These are just some of the many features that made it for him "the critical form par excellence."[46] The essay's unique claim to truth—or more accurately its repudiation of culture's untruths by penetrating "what hides behind the façade under the name of objectivity"—is also a function of its ability to stand in relation to other spheres of experience and knowledge without ever replicating them. Neither a pure and tidy philosophy nor an "aconceptual intuitive" art, the essay nevertheless "has something like aesthetic autonomy," Adorno insists, and aspires to its own conceptual thought while behaving "cautiously toward theory."[47] It is furthermore not the essayist who thinks but rather the form itself—Adorno calls it

---

44 Eisenstein, 26.
45 Eisenstein, 15.
46 Theodor W. Adorno, "The Essay as Form," in *Notes on Literature*, vol. 1, trans. Shierry Weber Nicholsen (New York: Columbia University Press, 1991) 18.
47 Adorno, "The Essay as Form," 4, 7, 8, 5, 18.

"an arena for intellectual experience"—and it does so idiosyncratically and in opposition to dominant modes of thought predicated on scientific and philosophical notions of truth.[48] To this end, the essay negates the "compulsion of identity" and instead "allows for the consciousness of nonidentity."[49] On the actual form of the essay, he explains:

> All concepts are to be presented in such a way that they support one another, that each becomes articulated through its configuration with others. In the essay discrete elements set off against one another come together to form a readable context; the essay erects no scaffolding and no structure. But the elements crystallize as a configuration through their motion. The constellation is a force field, just as every intellectual structure is necessarily transformed into a force field under the essay's gaze.[50]

Much of what Adorno describes can be found in *News from Ideological Antiquity*—play, fragmentation, nonidentity, critique—but Kluge's most noticeable departure from these prescriptions takes leave of the essay's crystallized constellation. Without any explicit recourse to the ontological presuppositions operating in Deleuze's work, Kluge replaces the astronomical figure of the constellation with a hallmark of the time-image, namely the series. Presumably describing Eisenstein's ambitions, Kluge could not have been more accurate describing his own media praxis when in the booklet to his video he writes: "Eisenstein wanted to arrange a series of such 'monads' ... Different images—irreconcilable and autonomous—plus the gap that arises from their juxtaposition yield a new relationality."[51] Whereas Eisenstein dreamt of monadic images, Kluge's essay video has serialized concepts capable of entering into new relationalities by virtue of the DVD's post-filmic potential: its interactive interface and the multi-directionality of its expansive archive, as well as its play with and disruption of linear time. Yet these technological features are just an introductory lesson in what ideally transpires at the level of thinking itself. What this ultimately means is that the sequence of six thematic series burned into the three discs of *News from Ideological*

---

48 Adorno, "The Essay as Form," 13, 11.
49 Adorno, "The Essay as Form," 17, 9.
50 Adorno, "The Essay as Form," 13.
51 Kluge, "A Plan with the Force of a Battleship," 216.

Antiquity dissolves in the realm of thought such that any number of other series can take shape. For novices, Kluge actually provides one of many primers for how to start thinking gravitationally according to what he calls his Eisensteinian "spherical dramaturgies": "The story of steam and electricity (DVD II, extra track 4) corresponds, i.e., to REVOLUTIONS ARE THE LOCOMOTIVES OF HISTORY (DVD II, chapter 9.)"[52] In other words, thinking seeks correspondences, and to this end one must be prepared to move across all three discs out of order; one can move backwards in viewing time and forward in lived history; one may move from imagined pasts on screen to one's own present; and one may jump out of line altogether, leave the medium of video, and find oneself in the midst of a story or an essay only then to return to the fray of moving images where one left off.

As much as it might seem like Kluge smuggled essayistic thinking back into Deleuze's universe, there are actually significant differences. What separates Kluge's serial thinking above all from what Deleuzian scholars call the "digital fold" is the fact that it is inscribed. Though fragmentary and incomplete, Kluge's video does not promote nomadism in the endless labyrinth typical of the fold.[53] Rather, it harnesses thinking as a combinatory exercise within a perforated sphere. These boundaries and the focus they engender are what allows *News from Ideological Antiquity* to retain the contradiction and nonidentity and therefore the critical force central to the essay as Adorno defines it. The consciousness of nonidentity finds its definitive expression in the video's final dialogue with Negt on Marx. When Kluge declares film a weak medium for Eisenstein's purposes in the aforementioned conversation with Negt, Negt then conjectures that what Eisenstein had in mind with filming *Capital* "was certainly not to make a film about *Capital*. It's not the same thing," he asserts.

> KLUGE: In this case, he wanted to go further and say, "I want to leave behind the anecdotal, exemplary, and doctrinal that we find in *October* and *Battleship Potemkin*. Instead, I want to reach the subtext in people." ...

---

52 Kluge, "A Plan with the Force of a Battleship," 211; Kluge, booklet, *Nachrichten aus der ideologischen Antike*, 39.

53 Timothy Murray, *Digital Baroque: New Media and Cinematic Folds* (Minneapolis: University of Minnesota Press, 2008) 5ff. Kluge, *Nachrichten aus der ideologischen Antike*, 22.

NEGT: Nevertheless, the question in my mind is where does this lead? What's the additional explanatory value? Even if he didn't want to produce a didactic film like *Potemkin*, what did he want? ...

KLUGE: He says that the best-case scenario would be a critique of film such that the medium changes. But perhaps film can also support thinking, to wit not as a prosthesis or aid, but rather as a means of securing autonomous thinking in a different way. It doesn't take place in the study and is not limited to language. It is not restricted to the exclusive communication among scholars. Instead, it transpires among different segments of the population and for that I need situations, and I can secure situations better with images than with just words.

The most succinct statement about Eisenstein's ambitions in the entire video, Kluge's clarification only leads to uncertainty. In agreement that *Capital* does contain a precious few "poetic" situations suitable for transforming into images (i.e., the commodity fetish, primitive accumulation), Negt recognizes the potential for mapping the differences between disparate historical experiences, but then rightly wonders whether Marx's theory would be necessary in the first place for such an endeavor. Even more disconcerting, he adds, is the fact that the sensational nature of such images, very likely of oppressed peoples, could be employed in the name of empire building just as they could serve the purposes of Eisenstein's envisioned visual language. While a constellation of concepts may very well convey Adorno's negative force field, an arrangement of images, regardless of whether it is constellative or serial, proves resistant to theory and politics alike. Essentially caught between two positions Benjamin mapped out before and after German fascism's rise to power—an emancipatory apparatus theory (his account of the "optical unconscious") and his theory of the aestheticization of politics—Negt and Kluge close without really choosing either.[54] At best, one can stitch together very different images in the hopes of "cross-mapping" historical difference, but

---

54 See: Walter Benjamin, "Little History of Photography," trans. Edmund Jephcott and Kingsley Shorter, in *Selected Writings*, eds. Michael W. Jennings, Howard Eiland, and Gary Smith (Cambridge, MA: Belknap Press, 1999) 507–30; and Walter Benjamin, "The Work of Art in the Age of Its Technological Reproducibility: Second Version," in *Selected Writings*, eds. Howard Eiland and Michael W. Jennings (Cambridge, MA: Belknap Press, 2002) 101–33.

neither the "visual instruction in the dialectical method" as Eisenstein described it nor the development of a politicized art as Benjamin envisioned it present themselves as certain paths forward at the end of the video.[55] In fact, the final word is ceded to the culture industry. In an interview with Eisenstein's fictional film composer Fyodor Rostopchin, played by comedian Helge Schneider, Rostopchin explains, "People don't want to die in the movies. They want happy endings." Cathartic film music in keeping with Andrew Lloyd Webber's musical theater ensues: "And then everyone applauds. The movie's over. And they leave the cinema for their homes and suddenly everything is beautiful," Schneider declares before the screen goes black.

Kluge's video essay defines itself according to what it refuses to be. On the one hand, it is an homage to Eisenstein's utopian aspirations and, on the other, it is a critical recognition of not just his vision's limits but also the potential dangers of ocularizing Marxist theory. What remains is what so many have found perplexing about Kluge's video in the first place, for it indulges far more in the production of discourse about images than producing the images themselves. In fact, Kluge says as much when in an interview with film scholar Gertrud Koch he explained, "I do longer passages of text with very few images in between. I starve the images, as it were, which makes them stronger."[56] This is not to suggest, however, that Kluge the filmmaker has advanced in the age of video to "literarize" his film projects. On the contrary, discourse in *News from Ideological Antiquity* demarcates historically specific boundaries and points toward the utopian possibilities of the time-image regime without ever returning to that mode of filmic thought (to which Kluge's own *Yesterday Girl* arguably belongs). To do so would entail, however, running the risk that Negt identifies as occuring not in words but in gesture: in a non-narrative world of images, theory would lose its connection to material experience altogether. In lieu of a grand utopian vision, Kluge settles for a minor utopia: Trying to imagine a workaround, he proposes a solution that calls

---

55 Eisenstein, 16. On cross-mapping, Kluge explains: "When stories are laid on top of each other like maps *cross-mapping* occurs. A Dadaist line commands: 'Wander through the Harz region of Germany while blindly following the directions of a map of London.' This is productive when you become keenly aware of falling into an abyss. You can experience a lot with an incorrect map. We can never say exactly which maps are correct." See: Alexander Kluge, "The Peacemaker," trans. Emma Woelk, in *Difference and Orientation*, 72.

56 Koch 363.

on the audience's experience and imagination: "You could say, 'I'll only make fragments and hope that the spectators fill the gaps between the fragments themselves … That's not entirely utopian. That's possible … in another kind of cinema. That's heterotopia." According to Foucault, heterotopia is a mixed experience best exemplified by the visual experience of looking into a mirror. "The mirror is, after all, a utopia," he explains, "since it is a placeless place. In the mirror, I see myself there where I am not, in an unreal, virtual space that opens up behind the surface … But it is also a heterotopia in so far as the mirror does exist in reality, where it exerts a sort of counteraction on the position that I occupy. From the standpoint of the mirror I discover my absence from the place where I am since I see myself over there."[57] If cross-mapping is the name Kluge gives to the order of cinematic heterotopia that unfolds between the spectator and a fragmentary film, then another order also operates between *News from Ideological Antiquity* and Eisenstein's plans for Marx's *Capital*. From the standpoint of *News from Ideological Antiquity*, Eisenstein's film remains a filmless film, but from the standpoint of the Eisenstein mirror Kluge peers into, Kluge's video essay occupies an absence as well. Transposed into the realm of time, Kluge's video turns the linearity of *chronos* into an incomplete circuit that affords not so much the experience of *kairos* as opportunities for viewers to grasp hold of this auspicious time. In the end, Kluge's video fulfills one of Kluge's own directives extrapolated from Adorno's essay on the essay, namely to invoke that which has not been or can never be filmed in order to criticize what has been filmed.[58] The point of such critique is not limited to just the cinematic productivity Kluge recognizes in Adorno's iconoclasm. It also delivers this same negativity to the objectivity dominating (the reception of) Marx's *Capital*.[59] This is why of all the many avenues into Marx's *Capital*, Kluge opts for the one he and Negt chose in *History and Obstinacy*: "The economy of this labor capacity is capital's polar opposite. It constitutes COUNTERCAPITAL."[60]

---

57 Michel Foucault, "Of Other Spaces," trans. Jay Miskowiec, *Diacritics* 16.1 (Spring 1986): 24.

58 Alexander Kluge, "Das Nichtverfilmte kritisiert das Verfilmte," in *In Gefahr und grösster Not bringt der Mittelweg den Tod: Texte zu Kino, Film, Politik* (Berlin: Vorwerk 8, 1999) 60–61.

59 Alexander Kluge, "Bits of Conversation," trans. Emma Woelk, in *Difference and Orientation*, 148: KLUGE: "Adorno once said mockingly that what bothered him about film was really just the image."

60 Kluge and Negt 73.

Figure 6.1. ANITA G.: "It's impossible to learn not to learn." Still from *Yesterday Girl* (1966). © Alexander Kluge.

Figure 6.2. OSKAR NEGT: "Kant says …" Still from "Independent Thought / Immanuel Kant's Text: 'What Is Orientation in Thinking?'" *Ten to Eleven*, RTL, September 19, 2005. © Alexander Kluge.

6

Dialogue and Dialectics:
The Ethics of Fantasy

Different Discussions

After the anticipated completion of *Aesthetic Theory*, slated for the summer of 1970, Theodor Adorno planned a treatise on moral philosophy that was intended to round out his major philosophical trilogy initiated in 1966 with *Negative Dialectics*.[1] Due to his untimely death in August 1969, Adorno's plans failed to come to fruition; the place of moral philosophy within his vision of critical theory was, in the words of one scholar, a "testament" to be realized by later generations.[2] Prior to Adorno's demise, Jürgen Habermas was well underway with the constituents of his own vision of critical theory, one that would soon culminate into a full-fledged ethical system. For intellectual historians and philosophers alike, intent on assessing the vicissitudes of critical theory's passage from its first to second generations, Adorno's unrealized moral philosophy leaves us with only a few of his scattered critiques of morality —his "minor ethics" first laid out in *Minima Moralia*, for example, and then picked up again in *Negative Dialectics* as well as in his transcribed

1 Theodor W. Adorno, *Gesammelte Schriften*, vol. 7, eds. Rolf Tiedemann et al. (Frankfurt am Main: Suhrkamp, 1986) 537.

2 Robert Schurz, *Ethik nach Adorno* (Frankfurt am Main: Stroemfeld/Roter Stern, 1985) 11.

lectures on moral philosophy from 1963. Woven together, they bespeak, according to Christoph Menke, the first generation's overall skepticism toward morality.[3] Conversely, the centrality of morality as *the* category of inquiry for Habermas (along with Karl-Otto Apel) evinces a substantial generational rift, a charitable reevaluation of morality that Habermas's critics have picked apart due to his overestimation of normativity and his underestimation of Adorno's testament.[4]

As if to counter these critical historical accounts of critical theory's legacy gone awry, Habermas himself has insisted that the unity of critical theory before he reconstructed it was a historiographic invention; to accuse him of betrayal of an earlier generation is also to presume its coherency.[5] From Habermas's vantage point, the legacies of the Frankfurt School under Horkheimer and Adorno have been so heterogeneous and divergent after Adorno's passing that some strains now travel in "diametrically opposed directions."[6] Instead of laying down a linear narrative of critical theory's evolution like Rolf Wiggershaus's magisterial history of the School, Habermas has opted for a constellation of "related discussions," in which its original positions still retain relevance in the present.[7] And yet, as Albrecht Wellmer has countered, Habermas's singular achievement of delivering critical theory from the cul-de-sac of Max Horkheimer and Adorno's dialectical negativity and messianism has advanced him as the indubitable heir and custodian of what once was more or less inscribed by the Frankfurt School moniker. "It is not possible," Wellmer exclaimed, "to discuss 'the significance of the Frankfurt School today' without ... discussing the theories of Jürgen Habermas."[8]

---

3 Christoph Menke, "Critique and Self-Reflection: The Problematization of Morality," in *Critical Theory: Current States and Future Prospects*, eds. Peter-Uwe Hohendahl and Jaimey Fischer (New York: Berghahn, 2001) 119.

4 See: Jaimey Fischer, "Normativity and Its Limits: Toward a Residual Ethics in Critical Theory," in *Critical Theory: Current States and Future Prospects*, eds. Peter-Uwe Hohendahl and Jaimey Fischer (New York: Berghahn, 2001) 263–86. For a sustained example of charges against Habermas's linguistic turn and its betrayal of critical theory's legacy, see Gerhard Bolte, ed., *Unkritische Theorie: Gegen Habermas* (Lüneburg: Zu Klampen, 1989).

5 Jürgen Habermas, "Drei Thesen zur Wirkungsgeschichte der Frankfurter Schule," in *Die Frankfurter Schule und die Folgen*, eds. Axel Honneth and Albrecht Wellmer (Berlin: de Gruyter, 1986) 9–11.

6 Habermas 10.

7 Habermas 11.

8 Albrecht Wellmer, "The Significance of the Frankfurt School Today: Five Theses,"

In short, Habermas's metaphor of the constellation only obscures the unavoidable impact his own shifts and turns have had on the younger arbiters and affiliates of critical theory. Precisely because of the enormity of Habermas's creative new syntheses of old and new thinkers alike for the "*critical* continuation" of critical theory, Wellmer infers the critical value of fleshing out the latent productivity of Habermas's constellation metaphor.[9] By shifting our heuristic away from the evolution of Habermas's reevaluation of morality and toward "related discussions" with and against him, we can identify how other critical theorists of the so-called second generation have laid bare the aporias in his ethics.[10] Were we to transfer our critique from a diachronic to a synchronic axis, Wellmer suggests, we would productively query other synchronic accounts of morality, ones that Habermas's categories of communication, consensus, and discourse cannot comprehend. Where, then, in the constellation of critical theory's present-day "discussions" might we find another account of moral philosophy after Adorno?

In spite of his repeated confessions of faithfulness to the "chief rabbis" of critical theory (e.g., "Walter Benjamin, Adorno, Bloch, Marx"), Alexander Kluge's theoretical work penned with collaborator Oskar Negt certainly belongs to this constellation of younger theoretical "discussions."[11] Like Negt, who counts not only Horkheimer and Adorno but also Habermas among his closest "critical companions," Kluge is quick to acknowledge the indispensable value of Habermas's work.[12] "Habermas's thought belongs to the floor plan where I roam," Kluge explained. "If I have second thoughts, I'll glean Habermas's work and can orient myself."[13] Habermas, too, has lauded both authors for their influential "cult books" even though his assessments of their contents are lacking in both accuracy and precision.[14] For all their mutual respect, Habermas and Negt

---

in *Endgames: The Irreconcilable Nature of Modernity: Essays and Lectures*, trans. David Midgley (Cambridge, MA: MIT Press, 1998) 257.

9 Wellmer 256.

10 Wellmer 256.

11 Alexander Kluge, *Macht der Gefühle* (Frankfurt am Main: Zweitausendeins, 1984) 178.

12 Oskar Negt, *Kant und Marx: Ein Epochengespräch* (Göttingen: Steidl, 2003) 10.

13 Alexander Kluge, "Der Theoretiker als Navigator," in *Über Habermas: Gespräche mit Zeitgenossen*, ed. Michael Funken (Darmstadt: Wissenschaftliche Buchgesellschaft, 2008) 171.

14 Jürgen Habermas, "The Useful Mole Who Ruins the Beautiful Lawn: The Lessing Prize for Alexander Kluge," in *The Liberating Power of Symbols: Philosophical Essays*,

and Kluge have not been participating in the same discussion. While still Habermas's assistant at the Goethe-University Frankfurt, Negt co-edited in 1968 (along with Wolfgang Abendroth and others) an attack on Habermas's rebuke of the West German student movement; some twenty years later, Negt would apologize publicly for his involvement in the imprudent "Anti-Habermas" campaign.[15] The real substantive point of friction between Habermas and Negt and Kluge was, however, the latter's 1962 habilitation *The Structural Transformation of the Public Sphere*. In what was surely yet another provocative answer to Habermas's thought, Negt and Kluge's first collaboration from 1972, *Public Sphere and Experience*, took polite exception to Habermas's normative (and thus exclusionary) installation of a single liberal-bourgeois public sphere in his historical account of the denigration of democratic politics.[16] At once a sequel and prequel to their own obstinate theory of counterpublic spheres, their second collaboration, *Geschichte und Eigensinn* from 1981, obscured its fundamental differences with Habermas's linguistic turn in a smattering of footnotes. More discreet than ever before, they again obliquely part ways from Habermas's reaction to postmodernity's impenetrability in their 1992 tract "Measured Relations of the Political."

Thought of as a coherent body of philosophy, Negt and Kluge's trilogy spanning two decades leaves readers with enough evidence to suggest a deep-seated gulf between them and the doyen of critical theory. But, apart from their explicit systematic commentary on Habermas's work predating his linguistic turn in the early seventies, Negt and Kluge have seemingly refrained from tackling the constituents and the consequences of Habermas's communication theory, let alone the discourse ethics that soon emerged from it. With their emphases on proletarian counterpublic spheres, the obstinate will of unalienated labor, and interrelated politics

---

trans. Peter Dews (Cambridge, MA: MIT Press, 2001) 113; on Habermas's misguided view of Negt and Kluge's work, see also: Christian Schulte and Rainer Stollmann, "Moles Don't Use Systems: A Conversation with Oskar Negt," trans. Fiona Elliot, *October* 149 (Summer 2014): 71.

15 See Wolfgang Abendroth et al., eds., *Die Linke antwortet Jürgen Habermas* (Frankfurt am Main: Europäische Verlagsanstalt, 1968) 32; see also Oskar Negt's apology in: "Autonomie und Eingriff: Ein deutscher Intellektueller mit politischem Urteilsvermögen: Jürgen Habermas," *Frankfurter Rundschau* (June 16, 1989): 3 (supplement).

16 On the distinctions between Habermas's habilitation and Negt and Kluge's debut, see: Miriam Hansen, "Unstable Mixtures, Dilated Spheres: Negt and Kluge's *The Public Sphere and Experience*, Twenty Years Later." *Public Culture* 5.2 (Winter 1993): 191–92, 197–201.

of individual autonomy and community, Negt and Kluge appear, on the one hand, to have programmatically ignored the core of Habermas's system—a universal ethics underlying communicative rationality. On the other hand, if "*communicative action*" is a "symbolically mediated interaction ... recognized by at least two acting subjects," as Habermas propounded very early on, then Negt and Kluge have been very well acquainted with Habermas's terms of engagement all along.[17] In fact, the origins and the technique as well as the final outcome of their collaborations are dialogic through and through. Described in detail in Kluge's foreword to the 2001 edition of their two-volume compendium of philosophy, the "art and technique" of "critical dialogue" have subtended each of their three aforementioned works.[18] Kluge paraphrases the "principle of orality" underlying their collective work as such: "A conversation begins as follows: I don't know the answer. This is not acceptable. Perhaps you know the answer? There is always some answer."[19] As for the actual writing process, Negt and Kluge have recently recollected how the dialogic give-and-take of their own "theory marathons," when not smoothed over by their amanuensis later on, is actually discernible in the finished product:[20]

NEGT: Habermas came to me one day ... and he said: "What are you doing there? Are you two writing that sentence for sentence? That's just a metaphor [for your method—RL]. That can't really be so."

KLUGE: He was mistaken.

NEGT: And I showed him the tables at which we sat across from one another. Usually in this situation Kluge would start to spin out a text ...

KLUGE: That is, I would recite something and then I would notice from his facial expressions that something wasn't right.

...

17 Jürgen Habermas, "Objectivist and Subjectivist Approaches to the Theory Formation in the Social Sciences," in *On the Pragmatics of Social Interaction: Preliminary Studies in the Theory of Communicative Action*, trans. Barbara Fultner (Cambridge, MA: MIT Press, 2001) 12.

18 Alexander Kluge, "Momentaufnahmen aus unserer Zusammenarbeit," in Oskar Negt and Alexander Kluge, *Der unterschätzte Mensch: Gemeinsame Philosophie in zwei Bänden*, vol. 1 (Frankfurt am Main: Zweitausendeins, 2001) 6, 8.

19 Kluge, "Momentaufnahmen aus unserer Zusammenarbeit," 9.

20 Kluge, "Momentaufnahmen aus unserer Zusammenarbeit," 15.

NEGT: ... In principle, we never competed with one another. If we had
to discuss a sentence more than five minutes, then it remained as
it was originally proposed. He dictated for ten minutes and then I
took over such that in certain sentences the first half was from him
and the second half from me.[21]

In fact, the origins of Negt and Kluge's dialogic relationship reach back
further than Habermas's own turn to intersubjective understanding in
the early seventies and arose out of entirely different circumstances. The
founding moment of Negt and Kluge's working relationship, the West
German student movement's ethos of "patient and devoted debate,"
in which "every speaker is tolerated regardless of his concerns and his
opposing interests," was particularly characteristic of Negt's own political
pedagogy, be it in the classroom at universities in Frankfurt and Hanover
or in extracurricular roundtable discussions with other leftists.[22] The
origins of Kluge's professional interest in dialogue very likely emerged
during his training as a lawyer at the Philipps-University in Marburg
in the early fifties. But it was in the wake of his professional reinvention
as author, filmmaker, and film school instructor at the Ulm School of
Design in the early sixties when Kluge first began reflecting on the critical potential of dialogue. Arguing that dialogue in commercial film plays
an inconsequential second fiddle to narrative action, Kluge (along with
Edgar Reitz and Wilfried Reinke) contended early on that film dialogue
must lose its function *as* dialogue. "Because it no longer serves any narrative purpose, dialogue is now available as a medium of reflection," the
film instructors argued in 1965. Taking Jean-Luc Godard as their model,
Kluge, Reitz, and Reinke petitioned auteur filmmakers to "apply to dialogue the same principles of montage as to the image track."[23] Freed from
its diegetic burden, so went their logic, dialogue could become a powerful medium of thought in its own right.

Already, some of the contours of Negt and Kluge's interest in dialogue should begin to come into view. Yet these early constituents of

21 Alexander Kluge, "Öffentlichkeit und Erfahrung, Faust: Alexander Kluge und
Oskar Negt im Gespräch mit Claus Philipp," in *Magazin des Glücks*, eds., Sebastian
Huber and Claus Philipp (Vienna: Springer Verlag, 2007) 95–96.

22 Kluge, "Momentaufnahmen aus unserer Zusammenarbeit," 13, 15.

23 Edgar Reitz, Alexander Kluge, and Wilfried Reinke, "Word and Film," trans.
Miriam Hansen, in *Difference and Orientation: An Alexander Kluge Reader*, ed. Richard
Langston (Ithaca, NY: Cornell University Press, 2019) 133.

the foundation of their project—a nascent politics of recognition of the other and the fragmentary aesthetic of a Franco-German auteur cinema —tell us little of the philosophical rationale, the relation of dialogue to the larger body of their thinking, let alone the socio-political consequences—"philosophical systems," Negt has argued, are for "clarifying problems that besiege our lives"—of their long-standing yet largely unspoken reliance on dialogue.[24] Far more importantly, these preliminary findings reveal little of their points of contact and friction with, as well as lines of flight away from, Habermas's own system of ethics. Consistently dialogic yet suspiciously silent on matters of communication, Negt and Kluge have much to tell us about another strain of critical theory's legacy equally invested in moral philosophy, one in which "communicative rationality" does not play a key role. While Negt and Kluge do steer clear of Habermas's communicative theory built upon a universal pragmatics, linguistic competency, and moral consciousness, they do ultimately seek out through dialogue philosophical ends not unlike Habermas's own ethics. In order to unlock the logic of Negt and Kluge's dialogues and render their moral dimension legible, we must shift our focus away from their aforementioned works since, instead of addressing ethical matters outright, their trilogy takes on the public sphere, culture of work, and the political, respectively; we should consider, rather, how *through* their many televised dialogues recorded since 1988 they both perform and theorize the preconditions for what Wellmer has called in another context an "ethics of dialogue."[25] As should become clear over the course of the ensuing chapter, the ethical dimension of dialogue is, for Negt and Kluge, never inscribed by the linguistic exchange between two speakers. Neither a generic dialogic form (containing Habermasian features like an argument and consensus) nor a generator of technical or practical knowledge, dialogue for Negt and Kluge is, rather, always open and propaedeutic. Dialogue is a form through which others— third parties like listeners or spectators—are voluntarily enlisted into an

---

24 Negt 7.
25 Rainer Stollmann, "Vernunft ist ein Gefühl für Zusammenhang," in *Der Maulwurf kennt kein System: Beiträge zur gemeinsamen Philosophie von Oskar Negt und Alexander Kluge*, eds. Christian Schulte and Rainer Stollmann (Bielefeld: transcript Verlag, 2005) 233; the distinction here between "dialogic ethics" and "ethics of dialogue" is developed in: Albrecht Wellmer, "Ethics and Dialogue: Elements of Moral Judgment in Kant and Discourse Ethics," in *The Persistence of Modernity: Essays on Aesthetics, Ethics and Postmodernism*, trans. David Midgley (Cambridge, MA: MIT Press, 1991) 142.

ethical labor of the fantasy necessary for realizing moral relationships. Never the product of labor but rather the process of laboring itself, this morality is always in a state of emergence.

Terms of Engagement: *Sein* and *Sollen*

The era of Kluge's television format is officially over. Since launching his online "theme park" in 2009, Gardens of Information (along with its ancillary YouTube channel, Facebook page, and Twitter feed), and publishing long-format films with Suhrkamp Verlag's and *Neue Zürcher Zeitung*'s DVD imprints starting in 2008, Kluge the filmmaker poured his energies into producing either one-minute or ten-hour films.[26] Although his television programs *News & Stories* and *10 till 11* continued to air regularly until their licence finally expired in June 2019, Kluge's "cultural windows" were no longer at the forefront of his labor, especially given the fact that the leading media at the dawn of the twenty-first century had become increasingly personal, digital, and mobile. A significant side effect of this media shift has been the commercial release of digital prints of Kluge's entire filmography as well as a representative portion of his massive videography. Before the 2009 release of Kluge's second box set of subtitled DVDs, *Seen sind für Fische Inseln* [Lakes Are Islands for Fish], containing 137 of his roughly 1,500 hours of recorded airtime between 1988 and 2008, English-speaking viewers had extremely limited access to Kluge's television work; only those German-speaking scholars dedicated enough to record Kluge's weekly installments on RTL plus, SAT.1, and Vox (or personally ask Kluge for access) could collect enough source material for scholarly analysis. Prior to his digital shift, Kluge allowed for several exceptions to this media exclusivity. As was the case with the publication of many of his screenplays after their premiere, Kluge released several selections of transcripts of televised interviews conducted with regular and particularly dear conversation partners. The twenty-six transcripts of interviews with Oskar Negt entitled *Suchbegriffe*, which

---

26 Alexander Kluge, personal interview, 3 March 2010. See also: "Kluges wundersame Web-Welt," *Spiegel Online* (May 8, 2009), https://www.spiegel.de/kultur/gesellschaft/dctp-tv-kluges-wundersame-web-welt-a-623639.html. With his 2018 co-production *Happy Lamento* made with Filipino director Khavn De La Cruz, Kluge returned after a thirty-two-year hiatus to making ninety-minute films.

constitute the first third of their collected philosophical writings, are, by far, the most extensive to date. (Kluge's two volumes of transcribed televised interviews with author Heiner Müller come in second; the 2009 publication of dialogues with literary scholar Joseph Vogl takes third place.)[27] Counting the additional interviews with Negt included on the box set as well as other miscellaneous transcribed interviews printed elsewhere, the available interviews between Negt and Kluge represent roughly three-fifths of their dialogues recorded to date.

While Negt and Kluge's interviews have entertained a wide range of themes ranging, for example, from opera to modern German history and politics, a majority of their interviews, much like their theory trilogy, wrestles with philosophical questions. In keeping with Negt's own intellectual biography, the two thinkers who consume the greatest amount of their concentration are Immanuel Kant and Karl Marx, the "beginning and ending of the bourgeois world between an idealized conception of self and the self torn asunder." For Negt, the persistent polarities between Kant and Marx, two thinkers for whom critique was the "substance of judicious thought," have consumed an entire lifetime of thinking.[28] In summing up his career as a social philosopher, Negt outlines their fundamental antinomy as *the* term of engagement for a serviceable moral philosophy today:

As much as the subject-position of the modern world assumes a central role in both theories, they differ from one another axiomatically according to how they weigh the truth and reality content of knowledge … Marx's entire body of research and theoretical production focuses on grasping the reality conditions of societal life relations as well as on analyzing the societal becoming and decaying of social orders. *Quid facti?* is for him the key question. For Marx, definitions of truth are grounded in the reality content of knowledge … For [Kant], that which differentiates humans unmistakably from all other life forms rests clearly within the realm legislating reason, namely the question: *What should I do?* And at this juncture knowledge plays no

---

27 Alexander Kluge, *Ich schulde der Welt einen Toten: Gespräche* (Hamburg: Rotbuch Verlag, 1995); Alexander Kluge, *"Ich bin ein Landvermesser": Gespräche mit Heiner Müller, Neue Folge* (Hamburg: Rotbuch Verlag, 1996); and Alexander Kluge and Joseph Vogl, *Soll und Haben: Fernsehgespräche* (Zürich: diaphanes, 2009).

28 Negt 22.

role at all. A comprehensive knowledge of the causality of relations adds nothing to the moral quality of my actions. In this respect, the question *Quid iuris?*—timeless validity—constitutes for Kant the truth content of an action.[29]

While Negt is quick to remind his audience of the vastness of Kant's thought, it is the terrain of his moral philosophy where an imaginary dialogue between him and Marx still has yet to unfold satisfactorily. For Negt (as for many Hegelians before him), Kant's proof of pure practical reason contains a wrinkle; by containing moral law apart from the causality of empirical sensual experience, Kant fortifies the absolute character of human freedom, autonomy, and dignity. But, in doing so, he also rules out the possibility of knowledge and individual decision resulting from, let alone playing a role in, the intelligibility of moral law. Although Marx advances knowledge as the agent of human freedom, Negt contends that the various Marxist social experiments in social freedom that evolved in Marx's wake committed a grandiose ethical blunder; with the production of ever-more orthodox bodies of Marxian knowledge, the laws of human dignity and justice were shrouded in ideology, downgraded, relativized, and ultimately dissolved. Bridging the gulf between the *Sollen* (the ought) at work in Kant's timeless Categorical Imperative and the *Sein* (the is) of Marx's historical materialism—a project undertaken by philosophers like Karl Vorländer, Leonard Nelson, the early Georg Lukács, Adorno, and Hans Jonas—acquires renewed urgency in our current post-Marxist age, Negt insists. Not only increasingly larger bodies of scientific knowledge but also nature itself have become ethical problems in their own right. Nevertheless, Negt argues that for an ethics to take hold in the twenty-first century it must follow both Marx's call for a high degree of critical knowledge as well as Kant's prohibition of any and all forms of moral relativity.

Although Negt does clearly call for carrying on a dialogue about framing an ethics for the new century between the cornerstones laid down by Marx and Kant, his 2002 meditation refrains from prescribing a concrete path forward. Upon initial examination, Negt's televised dialogues with Kluge appear to preclude such a sophisticated level of philosophical discourse as well.[30] Anywhere from roughly fifteen to

29 Negt 15–16.
30 The only existing discussion—Markus Bauer, "On the Road: Zu den Gesprächen

thirty minutes in length, Negt and Kluge's conversations about Kant or Marx certainly strike the uninitiated as highfalutin philosophical conversations recorded in midstream. With either both speakers on camera sitting across from one another (see fig. 0.3 on page 3 of the introduction) or, as is more recently the case, with only Negt on screen (see fig. 6.2 that begins this chapter), Negt and Kluge's exchanges usually take off from simple questions: "What is a concept actually?" "What is real?" "Is unhappiness productive?"[31] But, as Vogl has eloquently pointed out, Kluge's deceptively elementary leading questions aim at multiplying a single fundamental problem of understanding into an impenetrable field composed of ancillary questions in which answers are far less important than the constellation of limitlessly interrelatable queries.[32]

The effects of Kluge's Socratic method do apparently little to illuminate their shared thoughts on morality; for some unforgiving critics, the result of Negt and Kluge's string of associative volleys is nothing less than confusion or condescension.[33] Such criticisms seem warranted in light of their interviews' often disparate nature; referring to Kant's 1784 eponymous essay, for example, Kluge's question "What is enlightenment?" posed to Negt on their April 1, 1990, broadcast leads to the equally straightforward follow-up "What does *sapere aude* mean?," which then moves onward to discussions of Friedrich Schiller's interpretation of Kant's idea, Kant's place within legal philosophy, the generational contract underlying Kant's Categorical Imperative, bio-engineering, and Marx's reflections on private property.[34] After fourteen minutes of back-and-forth, viewers are left wondering what exactly constituted the core of Negt and Kluge's exchange. Conversely, gambits from other dialogues

---

zwischen Alexander Kluge und Oskar Negt," in *Der Maulwurf kennt kein System: Beiträge zur gemeinsamen Philosophie von Oskar Negt und Alexander Kluge*, eds. Christian Schulte and Rainer Stollmann (Bielefeld: transcript Verlag, 2005) 93–102—refrains from grounding their interviews in their collaborative philosophy.

31 Oskar Negt and Alexander Kluge, *Suchbegriffe: TV-Gespräche*, in *Der unterschätzte Mensch: Gemeinsame Philosophie in zwei Bänden*, vol. 1 (Frankfurt am Main: Zweitausendeins, 2001) 44, 122, 281. Many of these dialogues as well as others not yet transcribed can also be found on Cornell University Library's online archive *Alexander Kluge: Cultural History in Dialogue*: https://kluge.library.cornell.edu/conversations/negt.

32 Joseph Vogl, "Kluges Fragen," *Maske und Kothurn: Internationale Beiträge zur Theater-, Film- und Medienwissenschaft* 53.1 (2007): 122–23.

33 See the overview of such criticisms in: Matthias Uecker, *Anti-Fernsehen? Alexander Kluges Fernsehproduktionen* (Marburg: Schüren, 2000.) 111–12, 148–65.

34 Negt and Kluge, *Suchbegriffe*, 64.

like "What is Kant's *Critique of the Power of Judgment* about?" "What is the Categorical Imperative?" "There exists a new kind of Categorical Imperative ... Describe [it] for me," "What do feelings mean for Immanuel Kant?," or "What does metaphysics mean?" may very likely convey the sense of a patronizing philosophy primer for those unfamiliar with an underlying critical thrust at work in their Kantian dialogues.[35] In spite of these early criticisms (as well as the ways in which the interviews provoke them), the transcription and digital distribution of Negt and Kluge's television dialogues must be considered a vital culmination of their dialogues' original protracted production and serial release over the course of two decades; out of the stockpile of footage broadcast only once on private television, Kluge, in particular, has created a topographical arrangement of dialogues that synchronously link up with one another across different storage media (book, DVD, Internet). From this spatial constellation, Negt and Kluge offer us neither evidence of their "assimilation of Enlightenment motifs," as Winfried Siebers has claimed, nor a simple realization of their motifs in the form of "processual knowledge" rendered comprehensible through "intuitive associations."[36] Instead, the entirety of Negt and Kluge's interviews undertake a dialogic recovery—as opposed to what Habermas calls a reconstruction—of Kant's ethics in the name of making viable a post-Marxian project of creating a sphere of thinking ethical subjects.

Reinstating the Subject after Intersubjectivity

Before the aforementioned April 1, 1990, broadcast of *Primetime* ever revealed its title, viewers were confronted by Anita G., the protagonist from Kluge's first feature film, *Yesterday Girl* (1966). Without any knowledge of Anita's life on the run, her string of low-paying jobs, or her flight from the law, we see Anita engaged in pillow talk with the first of her three lovers, a student (fig. 6.1).

---

35 Negt and Kluge, *Suchbegriffe*, 108, 125, 240, 274, 290.
36 Winfried Siebers, "Weltkasten mit Digressionen: Spuren der Aufklärung in Oskar Negts und Alexander Kluges gemeinsamer Philosophie," in *Der Maulwurf kennt kein System: Beiträge zur gemeinsamen Philosophie von Oskar Negt und Alexander Kluge*, eds. Christian Schulte and Rainer Stollmann (Bielefeld: transcript Verlag, 2005) 210.

ANITA: I really want to learn, but it's impossible to learn not to learn.

THE YOUNG MAN: But you simply can't not learn at all.

ANITA: But I can always still learn, you know? Nobody can learn not to learn. Are you still in high school?

THE YOUNG MAN: Yes.

ANITA: Did you learn that there?

THE YOUNG MAN: No.[37]

Anita's problem is, ultimately, a Kantian one. Entirely independent and sovereign in her thinking, she announces that the human capacity for learning can never be acquired from another person. Yet the imposed acquisition of this capacity is precisely Anita's conundrum throughout the film. She is examined by a prosecuting attorney for her thievery, proselytized by her devout parole officer, bossed around by her employer, lectured to by professors, and above all subjected to a protracted civilizing education by her third and final lover, Manfred Pichota, an employee in the Hessian Ministry of Culture. Without ever explicitly performing a reading of the film, Negt and Kluge together parse Anita's profound Kantian insight that goes unused throughout the film's circular narrative.

KLUGE: If you take the sentence "You cannot learn not to learn," what would you understand such a sentence to mean?

NEGT: When one learns or, more specifically, when one acquires the ability to learn—it is a very animated faculty in the brain and in the learning of my senses—then one unleashes learning. One cannot simultaneously lay down a blockade and then say to oneself or convey to others: I'm stopping here! A person who comprehends what, for example, enlightenment is cannot decide at a certain point: I'm done with the enlightenment ...

KLUGE: What is enlightenment?[38]

After sketching the principles of Kant's exposition on enlightenment, Kluge summarizes before Negt moves onward to legal matters. "Thus Kant would say," Kluge adds, "the core of this is autonomy, maturity,

37 Alexander Kluge, *Abschied von gestern: Protokoll* (Frankfurt am Main: Verlag Filmkritik, 1967) 43–44. Translation slightly modified. See also: Negt and Kluge, *Suchbegriffe*, 62.

38 Negt and Kluge, *Suchbegriffe*, 63–64.

and freedom from the tutelage of others, even from other knowledge-
able people."[39] Performing much more than a close reading of Anita's
persistent immaturity, Negt and Kluge assert with conviction that Kant's
1784 essay still carries the utmost relevance in the modern age. A foil
with which to lay down Kant's "thoroughly current train of thought,"
Anita's conundrum from the immediate postwar period serves as a point
of departure for Negt and Kluge to propound further Kant's relevancy
in the age of atomic warfare, human cloning, and environmental disasters of global proportions.[40] The dialogue's shift from Kant's original
attention to "man's emergence" to "the living conditions of our children,"
though true to Kant's own concern with "unalterable ... doctrines ... to
secure for all time a constant guardianship," leaves unanswered the question opening Kluge's original story "Anita G." on which *Yesterday Girl* is
based: "Don't you know a more cheerful story?"[41] Why does Anita fail to
use her own understanding?

In his own reading of *Yesterday Girl* from 1990, Habermas suggests
the problem has less to do with Anita than those around her. "The world
of the prosecuting attorney," Habermas conjectures, "is not rational
enough to permit an answer to such obvious questions" like the one
regarding the impulses driving Anita's life: "incomprehensible motives,
anxieties and desires."[42] What Habermas alludes to in his brief commentary is the diminished if not altogether absent role of ethical discourse
within the lifeworld of postwar West Germany. If, as Habermas argued at
the dawn of his linguistic turn, the "public process of formation of will"
and "consensus free from domination" are the most basic hallmarks of
practical discourse, then the prosecuting attorney, by virtue of the fact
that he refuses to field questions or provide answers, entirely forestalls
any such possibility for intersubjective agreement.[43] In contradistinction
to his subsequent more affirmative thinking on the institutionalization
of discourse ethics (e.g., *Between Facts and Norms* [1992]), Habermas

---

39 Negt and Kluge, *Suchbegriffe*, 65.

40 Negt and Kluge, *Suchbegriffe*, 66.

41 Immanuel Kant, "An Answer to the Question: 'What Is Enlightenment?'" in
Political Writings, 2nd ed., ed. Hans Reiss, trans. H.B. Nisbet (Cambridge: Cambridge
University Press, 1991) 54, 57; Kluge, *Case Histories*, trans. Leila Vennewitz (New York:
Holmes & Meier, 1962) 85.

42 Habermas, "The Useful Mole Who Ruins the Beautiful Lawn," 116.

43 Jürgen Habermas, *Philosophical-Political Profiles*, trans. Frederick G. Lawrence
(Cambridge, MA: MIT Press, 1981) 119.

attributes Anita's problem to the world of law; it is nothing less than a gigantic bureaucracy of "irrational rationality."[44] And yet Negt and Kluge would certainly add that the dilemma is not merely institutional in nature. Anita must be held accountable *not*, as Habermas might suggest, for failing to call into question the validity claims of legal norms, but rather for failing to think consistently by and for herself and others:

KLUGE: [Kant's Categorical Imperative] is actually not really normative
...
NEGT: No, it has to do with consistent thinking. Kant says this as well.
KLUGE: Consistent thinking ... when I say I respect others as I respect myself, when I acknowledge all other people with respect, then I cannot want something that is immoral. ...
NEGT: ... It is very closely related to a type of thinking for oneself ...
KLUGE: ... consistent thinking ...
NEGT: ... and thinking in the categories of others, which is related to thinking consistently. Very very closely. Kant would say, if I were to think everything through to the end, then I would reach the point where I cannot want, for example, robbery to become a universal law.
KLUGE: No, then I would be robbing myself.
NEGT: Yes, I am destroying myself.
KLUGE: Yes.[45]

Anita's deviant tendencies—she borrows cash from her boss without permission, fails to pay her rent and later her hotel bill, and steals a cardigan from another woman—all come back to haunt her. On the lam, after deceiving her lover Pichota once and for all, Anita turns herself in to the police and soon finds herself (and her child) a ward of the state. The discrepancy between the center of gravity of Negt and Kluge's Kantian dialogues, which repeatedly orbit around the question of morality, and Habermas's own inferred discourse-based approach to reading *Yesterday*

---

44 Habermas, "The Useful Mole Who Ruins the Beautiful Lawn," 116.

45 Alexander Kluge, dir., "Selbstdenken: Immanuel Kants Schrift: Was heißt: sich im Denken orientieren?," *Seen sind für Fische Inseln: Fernseharbeiten, 1987–2008* (Frankfurt am Main: Zweitausendeins, 2009) DVD 13, track 7. This was originally aired on: *10 till 11*, RTL, September 19, 2005, https://kluge.library.cornell.edu/conversations/negt/film/2114

Girl—the former emphasize an individual person's natural propensity to learn; the latter, discourse's unredeemed promise to justify norms and actions for a community—are indicative of just how divergent these thinkers' reliance on Kant is. As Habermas himself has made explicit all along, his discourse ethics is as indebted to Kant as it is critical of him.[46] The point of departure of Habermas's reconstruction of the Categorical Imperative is the primacy of Kant's moral subject; because Kant rejects the ontological mandate of "unalterable … doctrines" and because he insists on the derivation of norms from within the subject, the universal validity of norms between subjects becomes irreconcilable. Habermas's linguistic solution—the intersubjectivity of practical discourse—to the critique of Kant's moral philosophy leveled by Georg Wilhelm Friedrich Hegel entails a series of related shifts: (a) a shift from the transcendental realm of free will and duty to a post-metaphysical realm of everyday communicative praxis; (b) a shift from the abstract universalism of moral intuition (the imperative) to a set of presuppositions about universal pragmatism and communicative competency (the argument); and, above all, (c) a shift from the monologic subject to dialogic discourse between at least two cooperative subjects.[47]

Compared with Habermas's sophisticated downgrade and redeployment of Kant's Categorical Imperative, Negt and Kluge's faithful retention of the primacy of the Kantian subject would appear to set them up for the very same criticisms Hegel and now Habermas make of Kant (namely charges of formalism, abstract universalism, the unconciousness of oughtness, and pure intuition).[48] Nothing could, however, be further from the truth. For one, Negt (and by extension Kluge as well) has clearly acknowledged Kant's shortcomings; in his Kant-Marx dialogue from 2003, Negt, for example, reiterates Habermas's own critique of Kant's foreclosure of any causality between the realms of the intelligible and the sensible.[49] Moreover, Negt and Kluge have undertaken, like Habermas before them, their own unique shift in order to stave off the monologic aporia of Kant's moral philosophy. To this end,

46 On the critical reception of Habermas's Kantianism, see: Paul Saurette, *The Kantian Imperative: Humiliation, Common Sense, Politics* (Toronto: University of Toronto Press, 2005) 161–96.

47 Jürgen Habermas, *Moral Consciousness and Communicative Action*, trans. Christian Lenhardt and Shierry Weber Nicholsen (Cambridge, MA: MIT Press, 1990) 203–7.

48 Habermas, *Moral Consciousness and Communicative Action*, 195–96.

49 Negt 42; Habermas, *Philosophical-Political Profiles*, 118–19.

Kluge and Negt expound upon Kant's reply to the question "What is Enlightenment?" by asking "What is Enlightenment in the Relations of Relationships?"[50] Riffing on a recurrent theme in Habermas's own writings from the seventies—"If labor and interaction are equiprimordial," Habermas wrote in 1970, "then the life of the human race depends in equal measure on the material conditions of production and the ethical conditions of social organization"—Kluge and Negt take up the former category and graft it onto matters of morality, while Habermas went on to pursue the latter one.[51] Labor, for Kluge and Negt, is not merely that Marxian category of dead labor extracted from humans in the name of capital. A second considerable portion of labor power is expended in the name of upholding private relationships. And a third and final share of it goes into maintaining a balance between the demands of the first and second portions. Enlightenment, as Kant defined it, is primarily a solitary subjective labor—Kant writes how "each separate individual [must] work his way out of ... immaturity"—that, when introduced into the sphere of relationships, Kluge and Negt claim, is capable of either undoing or augmenting both the relationship as well as expended labor spent to nurture it.[52] In order for this labor of enlightenment to affect both a person and that person's relationship with another it must assume a specific form, a political stance, that brings forth not just one's own understanding and autonomy but also the understanding and autonomy of the other.

Exactly how this maieutic labor of relationships precipitates enlightenment receives only the most cursory of explanations. We read that it must "consist of assuming a stance, not just talking."[53] In assuming a political form or stance, this labor of enlightenment must, while working with the existing forces at work within a relationship, violate its usual inertia; each member of the relationship must be thrown into confusion by a "tender force," their individual motives dislodged, and their contradictions sublated and constructed anew.[54] This enlightenment arises, therefore, not from the "resolution or courage to use one's own characteristics without

50 Alexander Kluge and Oskar Negt, *History and Obstinacy*, ed. Devin Fore, trans. Richard Langston et al. (New York: Zone Book, 2014) 373.
51 Habermas, *Philosophical-Political Profiles*, 120; Kluge and Negt 157.
52 Kant 54; Kluge and Negt 376.
53 Kluge and Negt 376.
54 Kluge and Negt 383.

Figure 6.3. Kant as pool shark.

the guidance of another"; without the tender violence of the other, the forces within oneself will not break free from their gravitational field.[55] We are also to understand that enlightenment in relationships cannot follow a mechanical logic whereby the tools of rationality are applied to pliable willing materials. The relationship and its individual members require instead their own time and reason to incubate. And lastly, the authors explain that enlightenment is not "produced by two participants at any single moment, but emerges collectively and as a side effect of multiple instances of paying and receiving attention that come about one after the other."[56]

Power of Imagination, the Labor of Fantasy

At this juncture, the distinctions setting Negt and Kluge's dialogues apart from Habermas's discourse ethics should begin to come into view. Whereas Habermas thinks in terms of intersubjective dialogue, Negt

55 Kluge and Negt 382.
56 Kluge and Negt 384.

Figure 6.4. Kant candy: "Orientation corresponds to the objective world." Two stills from "Man Is Only Fully Human When He Plays." *Primetime/Spätausgabe*, RTL, November 13, 2005. © Alexander Kluge.

and Kluge retain the primacy of Kant's autonomous thinking subject. Whereas Habermas elevates the dialogue as a communal form for morality, Negt and Kluge adopt the "equiprimordial" category of labor as the basis for forming moral relationships. The conditions for this labor to engender enlightenment in relationships—its extra-linguistic character, the nature of its "tender force," its unique temporality, and its collective "side effects"—are unsurprisingly not as straightforward as they might seem. If there is a tender force at work in Negt and Kluge's own intercourse, then it surely manifests itself in Kluge's intermittent questions from left field (e.g., "[Kant's] system is like Metternich's, can one say that?" "If Kant came back to … Königsberg as a visionary, how would he encounter himself?" "[Did Kant have] big eyes?").[57] In each instance, Negt does pause for a moment to think and respond. However long or often Kluge derails Negt, this tender force still transpires within the realm of talking and within the temporal frame of private television's

---

57 Negt and Kluge, *Suchbegriffe*, 275, 295; Alexander Kluge, dir., "Der Mensch ist nur dort ganz Mensch, wo er spielt," *Primetime*, RTL, November 13, 2005.

fifteen- to thirty-minute programming. After decades and decades of collaborations between Negt and Kluge, it is, however, not possible to argue that they still repeatedly deconstruct their working relationship in the name of deriving a higher sublated form of cooperation; unlike the love relationships fraught with strife described in *History and Obstinacy*, theirs, for all their individual differences, is conspicuously harmonious and non-argumentative.[58] If we are to locate the real force of Negt and Kluge's Kantian dialogue, then we must look not within the dialogic frame of speaking but rather outside the frame of print and broadcast media (be they books, cable television, or DVDs), and query how the mediated form of their dialogues assumes a political stance that exercises a tender violence on the viewer.

"Third parties," Kluge and Negt explain in the context of the enlightenment of relationships, "can look on to see how [it] functions and even take away an experience from it."[59] In this respect, the tender violence of Negt and Kluge's dialogues is a side effect both cognitive and phenomenological in nature. On the one hand, viewers are challenged to think along with Negt and Kluge about the moral consequences that Kant spells out regarding humankind's natural ability to reason. The intensity of their dialogues, the sophistication of Kant's own thinking, and its consequences for everyday life are neither easily accessible nor self-evident and thus require a mental labor on the part of the viewer. On the other hand, Kluge's production of the dialogues adds a second register of complexity, insofar as their ticker-tape titles containing provocative questions that often go unanswered, colored intertitles, and interposed stills regularly tease, distract, confuse, and even mislead. Take, for example, Negt and Kluge's dialogue on Kant's *Critique of the Power of Judgment* from November 2005. Introduced as a dialogue about Kant's position on "good entertainment," the frame of Negt and Kluge's dialogue regularly cuts away to stills of Königsberg, partial quotes from the *Critique*, portraits of Kant, but also to altered images illustrating Kant's passion for billiards (fig. 6.3) as well as an advertisement for a chocolate bar called Kant (fig. 6.4). Negt and Kluge actually explicate together

---

58 In his discussion of the labor subtending Kluge's interviews, Christian Schulte sites Kluge's interviewee as the primary laborer. Such a unilateral relationship would actually violate the "inscribed third party" vital for Negt and Kluge's ethics. See: "Die Rennstrecke der Hoffnung: Alexander Kluges Kulturmagazine." *Medienwissenschaft* 1 (1999): 16.

59 Kluge and Negt 384.

Kluge's method and, by extension, the task of the viewer as residing, in part, within the realm of fantasy:

> KLUGE: An ability resides in human beings to introduce an idea into the world playfully and then to watch what would happen. A person performs a test. Incidentally, a person can also perform a test using errors.
>
> NEGT: Yes.
>
> KLUGE: A person can then notice how the world reacts to … repudiates the error. And this bat-like ability to throw echoes and then to learn from that which bounces back, that is something Kant would certainly not consider completely absurd.
>
> NEGT: No, not at all. Quite the contrary … This echo method—that is, constantly trying out places in the objective world where I implement my fantasy and reason—must be sensual. He also says here, the world is actually the epitome of the objects of possible experience. That means, orientation corresponds to the objective world [*fig. 6.4 appears on screen here* – RL]. For Kant, discharging the power of the imagination and fantasy is one of the most basic of human needs. Incidentally, it is also not only in the realm of fancy, but also in the need for specific things we cannot illustrate: the need for God, immortality. Those are …
>
> KLUGE: … thoughts, tests.[60]

If, as Negt explains, Kantian orientation in the world arises "not only [from] the starry sky, but also [from] moral law and sensory experience," then Negt and Kluge's interviews—like a bar of chocolate—must be thought of as a means for testing sensory experience in the material world.[61] It is not the dialogue per se or even the authority of knowledge conveyed therein that bestows this orientation. In keeping with Kant, Negt and Kluge contend it is instead the feelings—quite possibly ranging from hostility to indifference—about the television program inspired by the tender force of its disparate words and images and generated by the viewer's fantasy that ultimately trigger a person to appeal to their own faculties of reason.[62] The subject of this imaginative labor—its

---

60 Kluge, "Der Mensch ist nur dort ganz Mensch, wo er spielt."
61 Kluge, "Selbstdenken."
62 Negt and Kluge address the role of feeling in Kant's philosophy, and repeatedly

telos being a relationship with other thinkers like Negt and Kluge—is not at all arbitrary, but rather is focused specifically on rendering that imaginable which cannot be illustrated, namely one's own capacity for reason. In this respect, the slight changes in Kluge's simple *mise-en-scène* and cinematography have always been an open political form in which a third party outside the frame is always inscribed into the process of thinking. By virtue of our identification as spectators with the apparatus, the framed dyad in *Yesterday Girl* (fig. 6.1) becomes a triad. The pair we enter into when we watch the static medium shots of Negt (fig. 6.2) are always accompanied by the third party of Kluge's voice-over outside the frame. And any passive voyeuristic tendency to watch Negt and Kluge dialogue across a table (fig. 0.3 on page 3 of the introduction) is always rendered active by the program's disruptions in the form of words and images directed at the voyeur. In effect a script to a play, Negt and Kluge's transcribed dialogues only unfold when we play them out in our heads. This triangulation, which has as much if not more to do with looking into the faces of others as it does with "listening and speaking," brings into view the cognitive moral dimension of Negt and Kluge's Kantian dialogues (and, for that matter, the entirety of Kluge's interviews with and without Negt).[63] For them, morality is contingent upon one's own emergence from immaturity *and* the labor of thinking with others. Kluge once asked, "How does moral law enter into a person?" Negt then answered, "It is very closely related to a type of thinking for oneself and a thinking … in categories of the other."[64] In effect, the open forms of Negt and Kluge's recorded dialogues adhere to the maxim they derive from Kant's Categorical Imperative: "Treat other people in such a way that you give them more of yourself than they would have had were you not to exist."[65]

Negt clarifies that for Kant feeling (and by extension knowledge) cannot gain purchase on reason. See: Negt and Kluge, *Suchbegriffe*, 274; see also: Immanuel Kant, "Groundwork for the Metaphysics of Morals," in *Practical Philosophy*, trans. and eds. Mary J. Gregor (Cambridge: Cambridge University Press, 1996) 56; and Kluge, *Macht der Gefühle*, 180–86.

63 Kluge and Negt 384. One influential forerunner for Negt and Kluge's face-to-face dialogues is Heinrich von Kleist, addressed in the introduction to *Dark Matter*. See: Heinrich von Kleist, "On the Gradual Production of Thoughts Whilst Speaking," in *Selected Writings*, ed. and trans. David Constantine (Indianapolis, IN: Hackett Publishing Company, 1997) 405–9. On Kleist's role in what Kluge calls the "oral tradition," see also: Alexander Kluge, "On the Expressions 'Media' and 'New Media': A Selection of Keywords," trans. Richard Lambert, in *Difference and Orientation*, 255–57.

64 Kluge, "Selbstdenken."

65 Kluge, "Selbstdenken."

For Negt and Kluge, this treatment is nothing more than an invitation to have the courage to indulge one's imagination.

According to Kant, the concept of the imagination (*Einbildungskraft*) designates that natural human faculty "for representing an object even without its presence in intuition."[66] A condition of possibility for all experience, Kant's imagination is a transcendental figurative synthesis that belongs a priori to our capacity for cognition. It would be wholly inaccurate, however, to conclude that Negt and Kluge's appeal to the labor power of their spectators' imagination has Kant's concept in mind. To be sure, Negt and Kluge neither call for the cultivation of this capacity of the soul for the realization of enlightenment in relationships, nor do they champion, for that matter, the coherent totality of Kant's autonomous subject. A crucial point of departure from Kant, Negt and Kluge uproot the imagination from the timeless ontology subtending Kant's *Sollen* and transplant it in the historically critical province of a Freudo-Marxian *Sein*. In order to account for capital's historical imprint, Negt and Kluge exchange the imagination for the category of fantasy (*Phantasie, Vorstellungsvermögen, Traum-arbeit*). As is the case with every human being's labor power, fantasy has always been subject to the exploitative forces of capital. Of an individual's modicum of living labor left unconsumed by capital there exists, Negt and Kluge maintain, just enough to compensate for the unbearableness of alienated reality under capital. Yet the unconscious practical critique of capital inscribed in this fantasy gets lost the more escapist it becomes. Complicating matters further, fantasy's capacity for the autonomous organization of one's own experiences is encumbered by "structures of consciousness, attention spans, and stereotypes molded by the culture industry."[67] Above, all, the transformation of fantasy into "collective practical emancipation" is hard pressed to control and organize fantasy's idiosyncratic and tenacious wishes, ideas, and movements in each and every individual.[68] For precisely these reasons, the dimension of fantasy to which Negt and Kluge attach the greatest importance is not the product of any one individual's mental labor. Nor is it synonymous with that private film, which "assembles itself

66 Immanuel Kant, *Critique of Pure Reason*, trans. and eds. Paul Guyer and Allen W. Wood. (Cambridge: Cambridge University Press, 1998) B151.

67 Oskar Negt and Alexander Kluge, *Public Sphere and Experience: Toward an Analysis of the Bourgeois and Proletarian Public Sphere*, trans. Peter Labanyi, Jamie Owen Daniel, and Assenka Oksiloff (Minneapolis: University of Minnesota Press, 1993) 34.

68 Negt and Kluge, *Public Sphere and Experience*, 33.

in the mind of the spectator" (as Kluge has long insisted about his own auteur cinema), presumably accessible only through a reader-response approach.[69] Negt and Kluge instead identify fantasy's promise in terms of its grounding in sensory experience, its resistance to the valorization interests of capital and, most importantly, its potential for reorganizing and rearticulating "the relations of human beings to one another and to nature."[70] Far from wanting to reassemble a single paradise lost, Negt and Kluge see in the relational labor of fantasy the promise of making an infinite number of possible connections—both reasoned and erroneous ones—within and between fractured subjects, the multiple worlds they inhabit, and the present impressions, past wishes, and future will fulfillments these subjects have experienced. It is not then what is fantasized but rather that subjects think among one another within a mediated space at all that is the point.

To conclude, Negt and Kluge's dialogues are not dialogues per se. If thinking, for Negt and Kluge, is the epitome of a collective process, then their intercourse actually strives to open up for others conditions of possibility of thinking autonomously in the company of other thinking subjects. The central importance of the fantasy in this process is the decisive factor separating them from Habermas's discourse ethics. Building upon Wellmer's and Cornelius Castoriadis's critiques of Habermas, Kenneth MacKendrick has recently argued that, in order to dispel the specter of the subject, Habermas's post-metaphysical, post-conventional ethics must repress the moral-imaginary dimension in Kant's thought.[71] While the particulars of MacKendrick's detailed arguments regarding the transcendental contradictions underlying Habermas's thought cannot concern us at the close of this chapter, it is nevertheless significant to consider, in short, how the absence of the extra-linguistic (and even pre-linguistic) dimensions of moral consciousness in Habermas's theory, as pointed out by MacKendrick, is precisely what Negt and Kluge preserve in their own thought. (In this respect, it is therefore not feasible to speak of a Habermasian turn in Negt and Kluge's thinking![72]) But

69 Alexander Kluge, "Bits of Conversation," trans. Emma Woelk, in *Difference and Orientation*, 148.

70 Negt and Kluge, *Public Sphere and Experience*, 37.

71 Kenneth MacKendrick, "The Moral Imaginary of Discourse Ethics," in *Critical Theory after Habermas*, eds. Dieter Freundlieb et al. (Leiden: Brill, 2004) 280–306.

72 The most explicit claim for a Habermasian turn in Kluge's work, for example, can be found in Hansen, "Unstable Mixtures, Dilated Spheres," 206n48.

perhaps the most decisive distinction between their bodies of thought resides in their relationship to practice. Referring to the practical deployment of discourse ethics at the dawn of the twenty-first century, Negt has contended that something has gone awry. "So-called discourse ethics," says Negt, has not only been rendered ineffectual within the quarantined confines of academia, but has also been redeemed by governments intent on benefiting not social but rather economic interests.[73] Out of Habermas's reconstruction of Kant's Categorical Imperative—one early formulation of Habermas's precept reads: "I must submit my maxim to all others for purposes of discursively testing its claim to universality"—a new discursive imperative has emerged: "Act in such a way," Negt summarizes, "that dominant economic interests suffer no damages, even when human interests, which the general formulation of law ought take into consideration, are supposed to be involved."[74] While certainly no immediate fault of Habermas's own, this pseudo-ethical instrumentalization stands no chance of making any economic use of Negt and Kluge's dialogues, let alone their underlying imperative derived from Heraclitus: "engaging-the-self-with-others."[75] Moral law can be neither exclusively communicative nor procedural, they argue, for morality itself is always contingent upon those subjects in dialogue who bring other subjects outside dialogue into a shared sphere of autonomous thinking with one another. The viability of this moral community of thinkers has little to do with the direction or telos of those thoughts engendered by the "tender force" of dialogue; the bottom line is that thinking transpires in concert with others. If we wish then to locate an "ethics of dialogue" at work in Negt and Kluge's intercourse, then this ethical dimension—an unrealized potential of fantasy work that can "advocate motivational forces for reason and understanding"—is to be found outside the immediate frame of dialogic exchange.[76] It might thus be said that theirs is a morality of eavesdroppers, furtive spectators, and even dreamers.

---

73 Negt 66.
74 Habermas, *Moral Consciousness and Communicative Action*, 67; Negt 66.
75 Kluge, "Momentaufnahmen aus unserer Zusammenarbeit," 6.
76 Negt and Kluge, *Suchbegriffe*, 274.

Figure 7.1. Corporate enemy Roswitha Bronski selling sausages. *Part-Time Work of a Domestic Slave* (1973). © Alexander Kluge.

Figure 7.2. A fair exchange: fifty marks for a child. *The Assault of the Present on the Rest of Time*. © Alexander Kluge.

7

The Antigone Complex: Obstinacy and the Dramaturgy of Emotions

"Interest in the Womens' Films"

First there was Jewish refugee Anita. And then came circus reformer Leni. After backroom abortionist Roswitha came brief appearances by the sex thief Inge and the GDR spy Rita. And then history teacher Gabi made her debut. Several years later, an entire cast emerged all at once: defendant G., charged with murdering her rapist husband, the nameless forlorn lover, whose suicide attempt is thwarted by a lecherous salesman on his way home from work, the matchmaker Frau Bärlamm, the prostitute Knautsch-Betty, the unemployed Frau Dr. Eilers, foster mother Gertrud Meinecke, the West African asylum seeker Frau Fasassi, and, finally, the terminally ill Frau Kügelgen. These leading ladies driving Kluge's feature films are, without question, keystones in his theory and praxis of filmic narration. That they once got him into hot water is a fact that appears—from a twenty-first-century standpoint—no longer to be the breaking point it once was for feminists in the early seventies. Called a "cynic" and a "trivializing" "anti-feminist," Kluge was originally taken to task because his interest in female protagonists was allegedly only disingenuously "progressive," for in actuality its "tasteless" and uninformed "sexism" appeared to uphold the "patriarchy" and was therefore deemed both "wrong and dangerous."[1] Writing from an American perspective in

---

1 This collage of criticisms is taken from: Marlies Kallweit, Helke Sander, and Mädi Kemper, "Zu Kluges 'Gelegenheitsarbeit einer Sklavin,'" *Frauen und Film* 3 (November

1983, B. Ruby Rich encapsulated the crux of West German feminist criticisms originally leveled at Kluge in 1974 in terms of foreclosed female
agency: "In a film … in which the filmmaker and narrator are male and
the protagonist is a woman, the sexual politics are sharply etched within
the film's form. The narrator, in league with the author (Kluge), whose
point of view he comes to represent and whose words become inflected
through the intertitles, consistently undermines the film's female protagonist by a process in which the audience is actively complicitous."[2]
There are arguably many reasons for the diminished presence of these
feminist charges in scholarship on Kluge today. One obvious explanation
would be that feminism spared itself the additional effort since it already
dismissed Kluge's films as bad objects. Secondly, the political landscape
in which feminism's offensive against Kluge—his 1973 film *Part-Time
Work of a Domestic Slave* about a female abortionist—shifted drastically
beginning in 1974, when one of the main organizing principles of the
women's movement—West Germany's restrictive abortion laws—started
to unravel. Thirdly, the severity of feminism's original charges may have
also lost their edge when the essentialist concerns for womanhood in
the seventies eventually gave way to poststructuralist interrogations
into the discursive constructions of gender beginning in the eighties
and nineties. And lastly, the primary grounds for feminism's critique—
Kluge's female leads—underwent a contemporaneous metamorphosis.
After a twenty-year run that resulted in fourteen feature films, Kluge
left behind both the medium of film and his screenplays driven by their
heroines.

Of course, all the many actual and fictional women populating Kluge's
television broadcasts since the mid-eighties, along with the many thousand stories since his literary comeback in the year 2000, are testimony
that his "enthusiasm for women," as he once called it in 1974, remains
indefatigable, even though he seems to tread more lightly than ever in
the long shadow of feminism's criticisms.[3] "I take this criticism seriously,"

1974): 12, 13, 17, 20; and B. Ruby Rich, "She Says, He Says: The Power of the Narrator in
Modernist Film Politics," *Discourse* 6 (Fall 1983): 43.

2 Rich 32.

3 For Kluge's statement, see the reproduction of Henner Bechtle's article "Frauen
begeistern mich" from Berlin's tabloid *BZ* (8 Feb. 1974) in: Marlies Kallweit, Helke
Sander, and Mädi Kemper, "Zu Kluges 'Gelegenheitsarbeit einer Sklavin,'" *Frauen und
Film* 3 (November 1974): 25.

he insisted in a 1976 interview, "and have grappled with it thorough-ly."[4] Whether and, if so, how exactly Kluge's later work compensates for second-wave feminism's attacks on his portrayal of women is, in hind-sight, a question of perhaps limited utility, especially as feminism has, in the words of one feminist scholar, "splintered" into "ever-proliferating positions" to the point of its "unrecognizability."[5] Even more importantly, feminists already in the 1980s began finding productive ways to rehabili-tate the larger field of Kluge's thought with not just feminist but also queer and subaltern concerns. As Leslie A. Adelson has pointed out, Teresa de Lauretis productively engaged Kluge and Oskar Negt's *Public Sphere and Experience*, written immediately before the release of Kluge's *Part-Time Work of a Domestic Slave*, in her landmark 1984 study on cinema, representation, and female subjectivity.[6] Acutely aware of the problems with not just Kluge's but also Negt and Kluge's "idealization of female subjectivity," Miriam Hansen imagined roughly a decade later how their work on counterpublic spheres "could contribute to the current debate, in particular questions raised from feminist, gay/lesbian, diasporic, and subaltern perspectives."[7] Writing at the same time, Adelson identified in Kluge and Negt's *History and Obstinacy* a model for "history as a bodily sense," capable of moving feminism beyond traditional notions of sub-jective identity and agency that fueled Rich et al.'s criticism.[8] Another decade later, Caryl Flinn identified overlooked affinities between Kluge's de-auraticization of opera and queer studies' attention to the cultural pol-itics of its physicality.[9] Since the original altercation, feminists have made considerable room at the table for both Kluge and Negt by bracketing

4 Alexander Kluge, interview by Ulrich Gregor, *Herzog/Kluge/Straub*, eds. Peter W. Jansen and Wolfram Schütte (Munich: Carl Hanser Verlag, 1976) 160.

5 On this diversification of feminism, see Misha Kavka's introduction to *Feminist Consequences*, eds. Elisabeth Bronfen and Misha Kavka (New York: Columbia University Press, 2001) ix. See also the essays therein.

6 Leslie A. Adelson, *Making Bodies, Making History: Feminism and German Iden-tity* (Lincoln: University of Nebraska Press, 1993) 17. Adelson is referring to Teresa de Lauretis's *Alice Doesn't: Feminism, Semiotics, Cinema* (Bloomington: Indiana University Press, 1984).

7 Miriam Hansen, foreword to Oskar Negt and Alexander Kluge, *Public Sphere and Experience: Toward an Analysis of the Bourgeois and Proletarian Public Sphere*, trans. Peter Labanyi, Jamie Owen Daniel, and Assenka Oksiloff (Minneapolis: University of Minnesota Press, 1993) xxviii.

8 Adelson 12.

9 Caryl Flinn, *The New German Cinema: Music, History, and the Matter of Style* (Berkeley, CA: University of California Press, 2004) 165–66.

out Kluge's original offense and moving other components of his and
Negt's thought into productive feminist frameworks. Nevertheless, the
jolt that comes when reconsidering Kluge's most troubling heroines like
the abortionist Roswitha, the prostitute Betty, or the asylum seeker Frau
Fasassi invariably returns spectators to the raw debates from the early
seventies.

To reopen the unfinished business of assessing Kluge's women on the
silver screen is certainly to stir up a hornet's nest that, in all likelihood,
might merely end up confirming the original grounds for reproaching
Kluge as well as the need to emphasize Negt and Kluge's theory over
Kluge's films. Yet it is in Kluge's heroine-driven films where we find both
an anticipation and the continuation of his and Negt's seminal theory
of protest and resistance articulated in their *History and Obstinacy*.
Conversely, it is Kluge and Negt's *History and Obstinacy* that points
to a theoretical and socio-historical problem manifest in that greatest
of obstinate women, Antigone, that populates practically every one of
Kluge's films in one guise or another. Kluge and Negt pique our interest
with what they call at the close of an excursus on German fairy tales
the "Antigone complex," but ultimately say very little about what this
complex is. We are told that to understand the human characteristic
of obstinacy, we must look not only to the Grimm brothers' tale "The
Obstinate Child" but also to Sophocles's *Antigone*.[10] Whereas the former
illustrates how discipline invariably fails to expropriate a person's autonomous senses entirely (even after death), the latter illustrates something
even more astonishing, namely the fact that compliant submission to discipline can and does regularly eclipse obstinacy altogether. Why, Kluge
and Negt ask, would a person—a wife or mother, for example—allow
themselves, like Antigone, to be walled into a marriage or motherhood
without ever articulating that rebellious sense of protest that imperiled
Antigone in the first place? In order to figure out how to bring down "the
Antigone complex," a study of self-subjection in patriarchal relations
would need to uncover how social forces ensure the reproduction of
society by neutralizing obstinacy.[11] Kluge and Negt are certainly neither
the first nor the only ones to ponder why Sigmund Freud never followed
Sophocles's Theban plays to their conclusion in order to develop a theory

---

10 Alexander Kluge and Oskar Negt, *History and Obstinacy*, ed. Devin Fore, trans.
Richard Langston et al. (New York: Zone Books, 2014) 292–95.

11 Kluge and Negt 294.

of feminine psychodynamics on par with the Oedipus complex. In contemporary feminist and queer theory alone, important interventions have sought to remedy this. Cecilia Sjöholm has petitioned, for example, for an Antigone complex she defines in terms of an ethics of feminine desire.[12] Judith Butler has not so much pinned a psychoanalytic complex to Antigone as identified her as a disruption to kinship laws and a sign of future non-normative relationships to come.[13] Taking Butler to task for neutralizing Antigone's radical potential by projecting her into the future, Lee Edelman has found in Antigone's entombment a queer model for refusing heteronormative intelligibility.[14] To suggest that Negt and Kluge anticipated this recent flurry of deliberations on Antigone would be, however, just as much an overstep as to assert that they presaged a second development in gender and queer studies that also emerged around the end of the millennium, namely affect theory.[15]

English-language readers are regularly reminded that the German concept of *Eigensinn* as Kluge and Negt deploy it in *History and Obstinacy* —literally "one's own sense" but usually rendered as "obstinacy"—eludes simple translation.[16] What gets lost in this and other unsuccessful proposals are the layers of bodily sensuousness conveyed therein. "We are interested," they underscore in chapter 2 of their magnum opus, "in the nature of cells, the skin, bodies, the brain, the five senses."[17] A paradigm shift in the North American academy that began to materialize in 1995 and, since then, has come into its own, affect theory might have found this first half of Kluge and Negt's proclamation potentially promising, for pioneering thinkers like Eve Kosofsky Sedgwick and Brian Massumi recognized in the lived materialities of bodies, albeit in very different ways, a new opening for theorizing autonomy and freedom.[18] Also interested in

---

12 Cecilia Sjöholm, *The Antigone Complex: Ethics and the Intervention of Feminine Desire* (Stanford, CA: Stanford University Press, 2004).

13 Judith Butler, *Antigone's Claim: Kinship between Life and Death* (New York: Columbia University Press, 2000).

14 Lee Edelman, *No Future: Queer Theory and the Death Drive* (Durham, NC: Duke University Press, 2004).

15 I am following here the overview of recent work on Antigone in: Bonnie Honig, *Antigone, Interrupted* (Cambridge: Cambridge University Press, 2013).

16 On the search for a suitable translation, see: Fredric Jameson, "On Negt and Kluge," *October* 46 (Autumn 1988) 158.

17 Kluge and Negt 98.

18 Clare Hemmings, "Invoking Affect: Cultural Theory and the Ontological Turn," *Cultural Studies* 19.5 (September 2005) 548–67.

"social organs" like "love, knowledge, mourning, memory" that are built on top of the corporeal ones mentioned above, Negt and Kluge actually steer clear from the ontological straightjacket that so much affect theory entails—ontology, they note, is singular for its separation of philosophy from experience—and they also refrain from limiting their interest in Antigone to an exclusively feminist or queer agenda, as is the case with the thinkers noted above.[19] Obstinacy, they underscore, "has long had an influence on the sensuousness of social processes and is in no way confined to women."[20] But, if this is indeed the case, then we cannot help but ask why Kluge's feature-length films consistently present heroines as the bearers of this feeling. Rather than venturing down the path as to whether Kluge's intention in his films can be reconciled, the following chapter instead queries what consequences the debates revolving around these films had for both his very late work on celluloid as well as the theory of feeling he developed as a counterpart to his work on obstinacy with Negt. Kluge's theory of emotion presupposes an aesthetic politics, a pedagogy to be precise, that wrestles with the representability of feeling in both narrative and cinematic form. Kluge's films explore again and again the question as to how cinema can promote the consequences of obstinacy. In other words, how can cinema bring down the problem of confused, blocked, misled, unfocused, and oppressed feelings called the Antigone complex? Rather than "exercising emotional influence" on its imagined spectators, as Sergei Eisenstein once prescribed, Kluge's cinema evolves to create aesthetic spaces where feelings both strong and weak can assemble side by side—a parliament of feelings as it were—and, to this end, he adapts models from the Weimar Republic that Bertolt Brecht extoled for his own political pedagogy of feeling.[21]

Obstinacy and Narrative

The reason why *Eigensinn* is best conveyed in English as obstinacy in the context of Kluge and Negt's work (compared with alternatives

19 Oskar Negt and Alexander Kluge, *Geschichte und Eigensinn, Der unterschätzte Mensch: Gemeinsame Philosophie in zwei Bänden*, vol. 2 (Frankfurt am Main: Zweitausendeins, 2001) 1145.

20 Kluge and Negt 295.

21 S.M. Eisenstein, "The Montage of Film Attractions," in *Selected Works*, vol. 1: *Writings, 1922–34*, ed. and trans. Richard Taylor (London: BFI Books, 1988) 39.

like "self-will" or "willful meaning") has everything to do with how G.W.F. Hegel locates *Eigensinn* in his *Phenomenology of Spirit* (1807).[22] At the close of his seminal excursus on the dialectical nature of self-consciousness illustrated by the countervailing recognition of the lord and bondsman, Hegel qualifies the bondsman's being-for-self. Through this object that labor engenders, the bondsman "becomes aware that being-for-self belongs to him, that he himself exists essentially and actually in his own right."[23] As long as this awareness is not endangered by what Hegel calls "absolute fear"—the fear of death—determinate being acquires "a 'mind of its own,'" a "self-will, freedom which is still enmeshed in servitude."[24] On this unhappy consciousness characteristic among bondsmen, Hegel writes, "Self-will [*Eigensinn*] is the freedom which entrenches itself in some particularity and is still in bondage."[25] In her reading of Hegel's account of this stubbornness, Judith Butler draws attention to the bondsman's fundamental body-mind schism and therewith helps us throw into relief just how different Kluge and Negt's deliberations on *Eigensinn* are. In the state of unhappy consciousness described by Hegel, "the recognition of the body's death is averted," she explains. "The bondsman takes the place of the lord by recognizing his own formative capacity, but once the lord is displaced, the bondsman becomes lord over himself, more specifically, lord over his own body."[26] Freedom in servitude involves, in other words, a mental operation that jettisons the body from consciousness. In keeping with Marx's own reversal of Hegel, Kluge and Negt define *Eigensinn* in the reverse by standing Hegel's (and Butler's) account on its head. In extreme cases, obstinacy disavows the psyche. Taking Marx at his word when he wrote "the five senses is a labour of the entire history of the world down to the present," Kluge and Negt see the body's senses as a complicated, self-regulating admixture of matter (i.e., natural characteristics of first nature) overlaid and extended by culture (i.e., second nature).[27] Yet the material construction of the body sets limits to its suggestibility. Expropriated or pushed

---

22 Jameson, "On Negt and Kluge," 158.

23 G.W.F. Hegel, *Phenomenology of Spirit*, trans. A.V. Miller (Oxford: Oxford University Press, 1977) 118.

24 Hegel 119.

25 Hegel 121.

26 Judith Butler, *The Psychic Life of Power: Theories in Subjection* (Stanford, CA: Stanford University Press, 1997) 42.

27 Marx, "Economic and Philosophic Manuscripts of 1844," 302.

to extremes that endanger their homeostasis, the senses can reach a breaking point such that they shirk heteronomy (e.g., sensory demands of second nature). Obstinacy may express itself as a feature for the maintenance of the body's concomitant household, but it may also culminate in conditions favorable for revolution, namely "when those below are no longer willing and those above no longer can."[28] On the level of first nature, the unnatural sense called obstinacy arises out of a provocation in order to ensure the continued health of a cell or organ. On the level of second nature, obstinacy can acquire a political motive capable of exploding the relations of production. In the end, whether obstinacy accumulates such revolutionary potential is a matter of the admixture and its thresholds, a tolerance for disruption, and the influence of compensatory interferences.

In a certain sense, obstinacy is Kluge and Negt's answer to Max Horkheimer and Theodor W. Adorno's account of cunning in *Dialectic of Enlightenment*. If cunning is that higher cognitive faculty Odysseus exploits to preserve his self "by throwing [it] away" in the face of nature, then obstinacy is the characteristic that bodies have recourse to in order to preserve their (first and/or second) nature under attack.[29] At its core, obstinacy is a feeling that makes a claim to primitive property, one's right to one or more particularities that suddenly balk at any and all forms of exchange. "It is the protest," they explain, "against ... the expropriation of one's own senses that interface with the external world."[30] Obstinacy brings with it an attitude toward the world, the attendant feelings of which Kluge and Negt call both irrational and antirealistic (see figure 1.4). Intolerance to and protest against the reality principle is, however, not obstinacy's telos. Only when a way out of the intolerable conditions is found does the agitation come to rest that brought obstinacy into being in the first place. First outlined in his acceptance speech of the Fontane Prize in 1979 and then woven into *Geschichte und Eigensinn* two years later, the emancipatory trajectory to Kluge's concept of antirealism of feeling only receives sustained study another two years later in conjunction with his 1983 film *The Power of Emotion*.[31] "When I started

---

28 Kluge and Negt 102.

29 Max Horkheimer and Theodor W. Adorno, *The Dialectic of Enlightenment: Philosophical Fragments*, ed. Gunzelin Schmid Noerr, trans. Edmund Jephcott (Stanford, CA: Stanford University Press, 2002) 39.

30 Kluge and Negt 290.

31 For Kluge's speech, see: Alexander Kluge, "The Political Intensity of Everyday

the film," Kluge confessed, "I was in no rational state of mind ... I have yet to come to terms with my motivation, the fact that my mother died, that I really learned from her 'how emotions move,' and *how* she died."[32] Far from debilitating Kluge, the overwhelming feelings unleashed by the death of his mother brought forth a sense of obstinacy and purpose: "I feel deep down," he explained about the making of the film, "a disbelief in the tragic; I am, so to speak, against the melancholy that our culture is in love with."[33] A cinematic protest against personal feelings of loss, *The Power of Emotion* sharpens Kluge's optic to ask, "Why do emotions that move the world lead to so much unhappiness in the end, especially when each and every one of them are theologians of happiness"?[34] For Kluge, it is no mystery why emotions fail to fulfill their inherent desire for happiness. They are often too few in number or there are too many of them in play at once; they speak a language entirely different than that of instrumental reason or they are disproportionate to grand feelings like greed or jealousy. In other words, the feeling of obstinacy and the motive that may guide it lose their way on account of other feelings that get in the way. If feelings are suggestible to a certain degree, then they can be taught to shield themselves from the lure of tragic melancholy.[35]

One of Kluge's first programmatic statements on film and pedagogy came in the shadow of debates over his *Part-Time Work of a Domestic Slave*. "It must be possible," he insisted, "to present reality as the historical fiction that it is."[36] With Walter Benjamin's essay "Author as Producer" on his mind, Kluge makes clear that the cinematic apparatus is always implicated in the dominant means of production. In order to proceed, the film must express for its audience a perceptible difference between its product and external reality in the form of "disharmony."[37] That disharmony in *Part-Time Work of a Domestic Slave* is an exaggerated metaphor for a

---

Feelings," trans. Andrew Bowie, in *Alexander Kluge: Raw Materials for the Imagination*, ed. Tara Forrest (Amsterdam: Amsterdam University Press, 2012) 283–90.

32 Alexander Kluge, *Die Macht der Gefühle* (Frankfurt am Main: Zweitausendeins, 1984) 45.

33 Kluge, *Die Macht der Gefühle*, 176.

34 Kluge, *Die Macht der Gefühle*, 166.

35 For a detailed account of this dialectics of feeling, see: Philipp Ekardt, *Toward Fewer Images: The Work of Alexander Kluge* (Cambridge, MA: MIT Press, 2018) 147–65.

36 Alexander Kluge, "The Sharpest Ideology: That Reality Appeals to Its Realistic Character," trans. David Roberts, in *Alexander Kluge: Raw Materials for the Imagination*, 191.

37 Kluge, "The Sharpest Ideology," 194.

contradiction that, says Kluge, exists in every family.[38] This contradiction at work in the unlikely story of Roswitha Bronski—wife, mother, and backroom abortionist—revolves around the fact that she, like Antigone, knowingly breaks the law. She also disobeys her husband in order to earn money outside the private sphere so she can afford to raise more children at home. In order to expand the capacity of living labor within the realm of her maternal production, she resorts to what is at once both a dead labor and a labor of death. Her ability to satisfy needs within the family stands in stark opposition to the needs outside her family that go unmet or come undone. Essential for the realization of Kluge's metaphor is his and Negt's conceptualization of the splintered subject first articulated in *Public Sphere and Experience*. "Real historical developments do not move on the side of the 'complete person' and 'whole proletarian,'" they write, "but on the side of their individual characteristics."[39] Unlike those masculine characteristics validated under capital (her husband's professional diligence and his academic ambitions), Roswitha's proletarian characteristics (her tenacious commitment to family and her care for her patients) go unappreciated. "I forbid you," her husband decrees early in the film, "to have anything to do with that abortion practice!" Of course, obstinacy ensues, but no happy ending results. Roswitha's practice is shut down by the authorities. Her husband takes the blame, goes to jail, and loses his job. Left to support her family by herself, she maintains her proletarian characteristics by selling sausages not far from her husband's former employer. Unbeknownst to the corporate spies who track her activities from afar, Roswitha wraps her wares in anti-corporate broadsides (see fig. 7.1). In her scathing 1974 critique of *Part-Time Work of a Domestic Slave*, Marlies Kallweit charged that, on account of its exclusive interest in Roswitha's characteristics, Kluge's film renders its heroine a

---

38 Jan Dawson, ed., "But Why Are the Questions So Abstract? An Interview with Alexander Kluge," in *Alexander Kluge and the Occasional Work of a Female Slave* (Perth, AU: Perth Film Festival, 1974) 28.

39 Negt and Kluge, *Public Sphere and Experience*, 296–97. When Marx writes of the "*emancipation* of all human senses and characteristics" in his "Economic and Philosophic Manuscripts," his language for characteristics is identical to Negt and Kluge's, even though this parallel gets lost in translation. The translation of the German *Eigenschaften* in both originals is modified here from "qualities" to "characteristics" in order to retain the etymological sense of a characteristic's malleability. For a more detailed explanation, see: Kluge and Negt 477n1. See also: Karl Marx, "Economic and Philosophic Manuscripts of 1844," in Karl Marx and Friedrich Engels, *Collected Works*, vol. 3: *Marx and Engels, 1843–1844* (London: Lawrence and Wishart, 1975) 300.

heteronormative breeding machine; as a consequence, her "sensuousness ... toward her children, her husband, her girlfriend, and her clients are repudiated all at once."[40] Similarly, Helke Sander contended that the only reasonable explanation for Roswitha's intolerable powerlessness, naiveté, and stupidity is the fact that "Kluge is enthusiastic about those female characteristics that are the sign of their oppression."[41] Sander's strikes a blow against Kluge's dialectics. Excluded from the reality principle, these characteristics appear weak, when in fact, he says, their very exclusion ensures their un-co-opted strength, thus making them an ideal "raw material for political production."[42] Under what conditions within the smallest social unit, he asks, is cooperation possible? How might other repressed social classes—white- and blue-collar workers, small business owners, and farmers—learn from one another's characteristics so as to leverage a way out of their shared alienation?

It is precisely this point that feminist film scholar Heide Schlüpmann pursues in her own takedown of Kluge's gender politics, namely that of representation: "The ability to represent [specifically female characteristics] in Kluge's films seems to be blocked ...," she argued over a decade after the initial debates.[43] Isolated for careful study, female characteristics operative within the "experience of oppression" are supposed, Kluge argues, to be rendered "comprehensible" in film so that they can serve as learning processes for all other oppressed classes.[44] Not only is feminism right to criticize how Kluge employs his heroine "for the emancipation of other 'classes,'" but Kluge's film never renders perceptible, says Schlüpmann, any learning process or, for that matter, any relationship between oppressed classes or their shared characteristics: "He separates the theme of femininity as a productive force from that of the relationship with the sexes, and that of sexuality within society, and never reunites them."[45] This trouble ultimately resides in whether the subject of oppression can

40 Marlies Kallweit, "Zu Kluges 'Gelegenheitsarbeit einer Sklavin,'" *Frauen und Film* 3 (November 1974): 15.

41 Helke Sander, "Zu Kluges 'Gelegenheitsarbeit einer Sklavin,'" *Frauen und Film* 3 (November 1974): 18, 22n2.

42 Alexander Kluge, "Das Interesse an Frauenfilm: Zusammenhang der gesellschaftlichen Produktionsweisen," in *Gelegenheitsarbeit einer Sklavin: Zur realistischen Methode* (Frankfurt am Main: Suhrkamp Verlag, 1975) 237.

43 Heide Schlüpmann, "Femininity as Productive Force: Kluge and Critical Theory," *New German Critique* 49 (Winter 1990): 75, 77.

44 Kluge, "Das Interesse an Frauenfilm," 224, 239.

45 Schlüpmann 77.

be represented. What we see on screen is a character study of woman as mother, not her splintered characteristics per se.[46] This fact certainly does not pass Kluge by. He admits himself that any re-education of the senses invariably runs the risk of succumbing to the deficient capacities of perception on the part of spectators, on the one hand, and an unavoidable "aporia of representation," on the other hand.[47] Any attempt at making oppressed characteristics clear on screen is a deception, he concedes, for oppression's complexities invariably look like gibberish or they get too simplified.[48] It is for this reason that he needs to qualify his antirealism in conjunction with his interest in the woman's film; unlike "ideological realism," which is complicit with the "official apparatus of consciousness," his antagonistic realism built on montage is one that strives to articulate the "resistance" of the physical "senses" against dominant reality by producing in the perception of the spectator a capacity for differentiating reality from unreality.[49] Quoting once again from the young Marx on estranged physical senses, he sees this solution as one that ideally negates this estrangement by producing cinematically a "sensuousness of relationality" made out of "disharmony."[50] But, for feminists like Kallweit, Sander, Rich, and Schlüpmann, this capacity fails to materialize not only because of their very different notions of subjecthood, but also because of the harmony between Roswitha's dominant reality and that of her spectators. Were it possible, as Kluge insists, to represent reality as the fiction that it really is, then this possibility of cinematic representation would eventually have to look beyond Marx's language of "senses" and "characteristics" in order to effectively render the difference of protest palatable.[51] And, in lieu of the senses and characteristics, Kluge eventually shifts his attention to the concept of feeling, in general,

46 Alexander Kluge, "The Realistic Method and the 'Filmic,'" trans. Rory Bradley, in *Difference and Orientation: An Alexander Kluge Reader*, ed. Richard Langston (Ithaca, NY: Cornell University Press, 2019) 160.

47 Alexander Kluge, "Roswithas Program," in *Gelegenheitsarbeit einer Sklavin: Zur realistischen Methode* (Frankfurt am Main: Suhrkamp Verlag, 1975) 186; Kluge, "Das Interesse an Frauenfilm," 237.

48 Kluge, "Das Interesse an Frauenfilm," 237.

49 Kluge, "The Realistic Method and the 'Filmic,'" 163, 161; Alexander Kluge, "Die fünf Sinne: Sinnlichkeit des Zusammenhangs,'" in *Gelegenheitsarbeit einer Sklavin: Zur realistischen Methode* (Frankfurt am Main: Suhrkamp Verlag 1975) 217.

50 Kluge, "Das Interesse an Frauenfilm," 241; Kluge, "The Sharpest Ideology," 194.

51 Kluge, "Die fünf Sinne: Sinnlichkeit des Zusammenhangs,'" 212. Marx, "Economic and Philosophic Manuscripts of 1844," 300.

and the narrative conditions for happiness, in particular. Feeling was an operative category for Kluge from the start of his film career, but it only came into its own after he himself was overwhelmed by feeling.

The General Assembly of Feelings

Harking back to the assaults on Kluge launched by the journal *Frauen und Film* in 1974 on account of the liberties taken in *Part-Time Work of a Domestic Slave*, feminist Jutta Brückner was hardly impressed by (let alone aware of) the conceptual shift in Kluge new 1983 film *The Power of Emotion*: "Kluge's plea for emancipated feelings is close to his conception of woman's mode of production as mother," she wrote, adding that, contrary to Kluge, the world of feeling is undeniably "two-gendered."[52] Still wedded to cultural feminism's emphasis on the visible, Brückner failed, however, to see that with his turn to feeling Kluge shifted his sights once again to the affective structures of film itself. Reinventing film dramaturgy had already been a central concern for Kluge and his comrades at the Ulm School of Design at the dawn of new German cinema. Initially categorized under the heading "diversification of dramaturgy," Kluge's call for the cinematic miniature, variations on a single theme, and the mixing of documentary and fiction, as well as the "antirealism of feeling" versus the "realism of worldly facts" was originally concocted as a challenge to the standard form of the ninety-minute feature film and its suppression of fantasy.[53] But with his deliberate conceptual turn to feeling in the eighties, the rationale for and the targets of his idiosyncratic dramaturgy shifted as well. No longer bound by the representational quandary that resulted from his earlier cinematic investigations of splintered subjects and their oppressed characteristics, Kluge's new cinema of feeling focused instead on rewiring what he came to see as a direct correlation between the forms of popular entertainment and the structures of social feeling. Kluge's logic runs something like this: if cinema can just manage to disrupt both nineteenth-century tragic opera's intensification of feeling that usually breaks down in the fifth act, as well as Hollywood dramaturgy's conciliatory happy endings, then it may very

---

52 Kluge, "Die Macht der Gefühle," 231.
53 Klaus Eder and Alexander Kluge, in *Ulmer Dramaturgien: Reibungsverluste* (Munich: Carl Hanser Verlag, 1980) 5–7.

well be possible for feelings to organize themselves such that they find real happiness.

Writing the same year *The Power of Emotion* debuted, Kluge argued that the success of the variety format, the "number dramaturgy," as developed in the pre-cinematic circus, was measured according to its stark opposition to the largely undramatic relations of social reality.[54] Marked by a high degree of contrast and a maximum amount of contact area, circus dramaturgy reemerged after the ascendency of opera in the nineteenth century to become what Miriam Hansen called the "primitive diversity" of early twentieth-century cinema.[55] As Hansen has observed as well, the logic of the nickelodeon has long been a keystone for Kluge's oppositional public sphere work. While *The Power of Emotion* does "[abound] with primitive devices," it is arguable that with his turn to feeling in the eighties, his admiration for and incorporation of the variety principle was less a matter of invoking distraction à la Benjamin's optical unconscious (with its involuntary memory and associational processes) than serving the pedagogy necessary for bringing down the Antigone complex. It is also conceivable that Kluge is channeling Eisenstein's admiration for circus programming and his practice of numbering of scenes.[56] What tilts, however, the scales in favor of Brecht, who repeatedly wrote of the "number character" of his epic theater, and his theory of that dramatic form, is Brecht's emphasis on theater's resolve to jettison empathy in favor of "new, manifold, socially productive emotions."[57] Even though Brecht's importance for Kluge cannot be overstated, scholarly attention has been largely cursory. In English-language scholarship, David Roberts was one of the first who underscored the Brechtian influence on Kluge's concept of realism.[58] Anton Kaes argued for Kluge's indebtedness to Brecht's montage manifest in his call for making film literary through the

---

54 Alexander Kluge, "Nummern-Dramaturgie," in *Bestandsaufnahme: Utopie Film* (Frankfurt am Main: Zweitausendeins, 1983) 105.

55 Miriam Hansen, "Reinventing the Nickelodeon: Notes on Kluge and Early Cinema," *October* 46 (Autumn 1988) 190ff. See also: Miriam Hansen, *Babel and Babylon: Spectatorship in American Silent Film* (Cambridge, MA: Harvard University Press, 1991) 30.

56 Eisenstein 35.

57 Bertolt Brecht, "A Little Private Tuition for My Friend Max Gorelik," in *Brecht on Theatre: The Development of an Aesthetic*, ed. and trans. John Willett (London: Eyre Methuen, 1974) 161.

58 David Roberts, "Alexander Kluge and German History: 'The Air Raid on Halberstadt on 8.4.1945,'" in *Alexander Kluge: Raw Materials for the Imagination*, 128. This article was originally published in German in 1983. See also Kluge and Negt 236; and

incorporation of verbal elements.[59] And Jameson drew attention to similarities and differences between Brecht's and Negt and Kluge's pedagogy.[60] Without question Brechtian, but never systematically studied, Kluge has also reportedly parted ways with Brecht, too. One scholar has cautioned, for example, against applying Brechtian distantiation to Kluge's films.[61] Another has rightfully called attention to his distance to Brecht's affiliation with class struggle as well as his prescriptions for political change.[62] Formally beholden to Brecht but politically circumspect when compared with him, Kluge is, without question, a disciple, but where and why he parts ways with the master of epic theater remains an open question. While Adorno's disdain and Jean-Luc Godard's admiration for Brecht could explain away this tension in terms of influence, a closer look into Brecht's theory of emotion reveals that Kluge's alterations follow careful study of Brecht's own theory of feeling.

For Brecht, emotion and feeling are essential dramaturgical concerns because they serve as the primary conduit between stage and audience. Spectators in classical theater are pulled into the action on stage and its emotional highs and lows. As a result, they indulge in an illusory identification that not only fails to get audiences inside a character's skin but also precludes a critical analysis of the ideology responsible for the dominant emotional economy in the first place. Unlike Aristotelian dramaturgy that traffics in the passivity of empathy (*Einfühlung*), Brecht's objective, far from obviating feelings altogether, rests on activating an individual spectator's faculties of perception and judgment *through* emotion. Predicated on proscribing just one feeling, namely empathy, the dramaturgy of epic theater can avail itself of any number of means to achieve this goal; its actors can, for example, aim at triggering Brecht's renowned alienation effect through an asymmetry between performed emotions and emotional effect. Jarred on account of the contradiction that emerges out of this emotional displacement, audiences are to arrive

Peter C. Lutze, *Alexander Kluge: The Last Modernist* (Detroit, MI: Wayne State University Press, 1998) 130.

59 Anton Kaes, *From Hitler to Heimat: The Return of History as Film* (Cambridge, MA: Harvard University Press, 1989) 114. This book was originally published in German in 1987.

60 Jameson 166. See also: Fredric Jameson, *Brecht and Method* (London: Verso, 1998) 120–21.

61 Hansen 190.

62 Jan Bruck, "Brecht's and Kluge's Aesthetics of Realism," *Poetics* 17 (1988): 65–66.

at feeling and recognizing a situation's "double aspect": manifest emotions as well as their latent, resolutely unemotional causes.[63] The telos of
Brecht's dramaturgical theory and praxis of emotion strives to establish a
link between collective feeling and the cognitive recognition of universal
needs and interests. On the nature of this learning process, he writes:
"We need a type of theatre which not only releases the feelings, insights
and impulses possible within the particular historical field of human
relations in which the action takes place, but employs and encour-
ages those thoughts and feelings which help transform the field itself."[64]
Kluge's own theory of emotions shares with Brecht's above all the conviction that emotions engage in intercourse. Whereas Brecht's dramaturgy
is ultimately aimed at derailing one-to-one emotional communication
between stage and audience in search of another, better emotional
economy, Kluge identifies the problem outside the work of art entirely
in terms of the exchange itself. When grasped from an anthropological
vantage point, individual human emotions appear to have always suf-
fered from the sacrifices demanded by exchange societies. "With every
sacrifice," he explains, "there arises on the side a feeling for how it can be
avoided, for how cunning can be exercised, for which exit strategies and
subterfuges could be devised, and for how valuable whatever I was sacri-
ficed for must be."[65] As Kluge tells it, for a cinematic politics of emotion to
emerge, the tyrannical singularity of the dominant feeling accompanying any one given form of exchange—greed, lust, jealousy, etc.—would
have to cede to other weaker emotions. To that end, the work of art's
task is to create as many points of contact between individual emotions,
both weak ones otherwise suppressed and strong ones, such that the singularity of the one gives way to what Kluge calls "a general assembly of
feelings."[66] This proves to be the way out that allows obstinacy's motive
to prevail in spite of the odds. That Kluge's late films conceived in the

---

63 Bertolt Brecht, "Conversation about Being Forced into Empathy," in *Brecht on
Theatre: The Development of an Aesthetic*, ed. and trans. John Willett (London: Eyre
Methuen, 1974) 271.

64 Bertolt Brecht, "A Short Organum for the Theater," in *Brecht on Theatre: The Development of an Aesthetic*, ed. and trans. John Willett (London: Eyre Methuen, 1974) 190.

65 Florian Hopf, "'Feelings Can Move Mountains ... ': An Interview with Alexander
Kluge on the Film *The Power of Feelings*," trans. Robert Savage, in *Alexander Kluge: Raw
Materials for the Imagination*, 242.

66 Kluge, "Kluge on Opera, Film, and Feelings," trans. Miriam Hansen and Sara S.
Poor, *New German Critique* 49 (Winter 1990): 106.

shadow of *Geschichte und Eigensinn* turn to the variety format en force should therefore come as no surprise, for its high capacity for contrast and maximum surface area allow for as many emotions as possible to come into contact with one another within the span of one hundred and some minutes.

As much as Kluge's penultimate film *The Assault of the Present on the Rest of Time* (1985) can be read as a eulogy for film, it is also very much a continuation of the same themes that shaped its immediate forerunner, *The Power of Emotion*.[67] In fact, both the gloom from the medium of film's pending death due to the onslaught of new media and the human sacrifices in each of the former film's stories must be regarded as countervailing narratives. Whether a way out of this melancholy is possible ultimately boils down, as we shall see, to whether there exist cinematic alternatives to the principle of exchange subtending all the many sacrifices both human and non-human throughout the film's many scenes, sequences, and stories. The film begins with a dramatization of act 2 from *Tosca*, when the heroine is strong-armed into sacrificing her relationship with Cavaradossi; after securing his safety, she kills Baron Scarpia, the chief of the secret police. The Wronskis, caretakers of an abandoned film studio in wartime Poland, marry away their daughter to a predatory German soldier; their hope is that the enemy will help save the studio's treasures. Family physician Anna Eilers is replaced by a young hotshot; unwilling to play second fiddle, she quits her job without notice. In between each of these opening stories, the film inserts any number of city sequences, stills, early film footage, and interviews. In the first thirty minutes of the film, the range of emotions runs the gamut from ressentiment to confusion, hope to humor, and grief to gruff. Before the Antigone complex ever makes an appearance in the second half of the film, three overlapping stories are told. The first introduces a nameless wealthy woman whose businessman husband has little if any time for her. Later we are told, "Her husband is three years younger than her. In four years he'll dump her." The second story tells of Lisa, who survives a car crash that kills her parents. The third story, which operates as a point of contact for the two equally powerful emotions from the preceding stories, the unhappiness from the first and tragedy from the second, is the story entitled "Handing over the Child." Originally

---

67 See Lutze 143–77.

conceived in conjunction with *The Power of Emotion*, the story begins with a medium shot of Gertrud Meinecke counting money at home. Calculating and anything but indifferent, she has quit her job as a civil servant because of the state's indifference. After Lisa passes in and out of children's homes for two years, Gertrud decides to take her in. Lisa and Gertrud's is an awkward yet functional relationship, one presumably motivated by Gertrud's compensation as a foster parent. However, when the courts identify Lisa's aunt, the wealthy woman from the first story solely interested in setting up her villa, as her next of kin, Gertrud complies with the directive to hand over the child.[68] "That was very nice of you," says the nameless woman dressed in furs before she hands Gertrud fifty marks for her troubles (fig. 7.2). Treated with disdain by Lisa's new guardian, Gertrud first grows wary and then distrustful and angered by the aunt's cold, "technocratic" demeanor.[69] Nonetheless, she remains dutiful and waits hours on end with the hope that the busy aunt finds a moment to have a reasonable word about the traumatized child's needs. That moment never arrives. Unable to hand the child over in good conscience, Gertrud returns the fifty marks and absconds with Lisa.

Nothing less than an Antigone story about breaking the law for a higher purpose, "Handing over the Child" is remarkable precisely because of its happy ending entirely devoid of sacrifice. The Antigone complex, that inability to parlay feelings of obstinacy and the motives they carry into good fortune, never gets the upper hand here. Gertrud succeeds where Antigone failed. What Kluge calls a "small feeling" not usually validated in cinema (in this case Gertrud's intolerance for indifference, her earnestness) sets off an obstinate chain reaction that leads to her antirealistic decision to go on the lam with Lisa in order protect the child's interests.[70] Neither Gertrud's sudden rage nor the wealthy aunt's proposed monetary exchange derails the telos of Gertrud's feelings because of the

---

68 This is the point where the screenplay begins. See: Kluge, *Die Macht der Gefühle*, 218. The story is also reproduced in: Alexander Kluge, *Der Angriff der Gegenwart auf die übrige Zeit: Das Drehbuch zum Film* (Frankfurt am Main: Syndikat, 1985) 91–104; and Alexander Kluge, "Übergabe des Kindes," in *Chronik der Gefühle*, vol. 1: *Basisgeschichten* (Frankfurt am Main: Suhrkamp, 2000) 321–26. See also the analysis of Kluge's story in: Christian Schulte, "Alexander Kluge: Übergabe des Kindes," in *Deutsche Kurzprosa der Gegenwart*, eds. Werner Bellmann and Christine Hummel (Stuttgart: Reclam, 2006) 169–74.

69 Kluge, "Übergabe des Kindes," 323.

70 Kluge, *Die Macht der Gefühle*, 200.

compartmentalization of their narratives. Separated into three narrative sequences that overlap by dint of the child, the three stories evolve such that the only one charged by obstinacy comes out on top. What makes happy endings in life so difficult, says Kluge, is the fact that "the dramaturgy of experience is gravitational, hardly ever linear."[71] What makes the provisional happy ending in *The Assault of the Present on the Rest of Time* possible is, however, the linearity of the film's imbricated miniatures. On account of its embrace of earlier dramaturgical forms dating back to the folk play, the circus, and epic theater, Kluge's "number dramaturgy" strives to unfurl emotions and their attendant stories without the interference typical of the gravitational dramaturgy of experience. While it is indeed imaginable that beyond the narrative frame the law will eventually catch up to Gertrud such that some sacrifice might ensue, Kluge's dramaturgy of emotion nevertheless makes use of the times and spaces unique to cinema in order to accommodate the temporal and spatial needs for feelings to stake their claim. "Feelings have their own time," he insists in his screenplay to *The Power of Emotion*.[72] To recognize the development of Kluge's cinematic praxis from the single fragmented narrative in *Part-Time Work of a Domestic Slave* to the multiple narrative fragments in *The Assault of the Present on the Rest of Time* is certainly not enough to allay feminism's deep misgivings reaching back to the seventies. (As Schlüpmann sees it, the real problem is a theoretical one; Kluge unfortunately relies on Horkheimer's bourgeois conflation of a feminine productive force with motherliness.) Still a set of characteristics and a corresponding "superior mode of production," Kluge's notion of femininity in his late homages to the variety format make no grand gesture to redress the glaring absence of female experience (e.g., feminine sexuality and erotics) found in his early work.[73] Grasped in terms of their chiastic relationship, Kluge's early and late films do evince, however, an essential shift. Whereas Roswitha sought to profit from the outside exchange economy in order to support her motherly production within the private sphere, Gertrud enters into a non-biological maternal-like role in exchange for money from the state, only then to rebuff a private exchange in order to save someone else's child from indifference and

---

71 Alexander Kluge, "An Answer to Two Opera Quotations," trans. Miriam Hansen and Sara S. Poor, in *Difference and Orientation*, 243.

72 Kluge, *Die Macht der Gefühle*, 211.

73 Negt and Kluge, *Public Sphere and Experience*, 22n36.

neglect. Whereas Roswitha's obstinacy succumbs to the law and the force of the exchange economy, Gertrud's refuses both and in so doing she comes into what appears like the beginning of humane sensuousness, the very thing lacking in Roswitha. While Kluge may very well never get off the hook for his concept of femininity, the formal and narrative trajectory of his films nevertheless makes clear that bringing down the Antigone complex must entail nothing less than a wholesale rejection of capital's logic of exchange and its juridical enforcement. That cinema manages to imagine the utopian conditions for this paradise is the reason why Kluge sees it as one of obstinacy's most important allies.

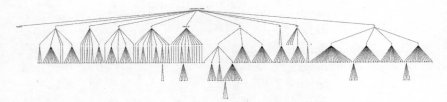

Figure 8.1. Tree diagram of Alexander Kluge's *Case Histories* (1962; trans. 1988). Note parent node five, the eighteen-page account of Anita G., which became Kluge's first feature film, *Yesterday Girl* (1966). © Richard Langston

Figure 8.2. Tree diagram of Alexander Kluge's *Tür an Tür mit einem anderen Leben: 350 neue Geschichten* [Next Door to Another Life: 350 New Stories] (2006). © Richard Langston

8

Beyond the Kernel and the Shell: Poetic Ambiguity and the Aesthetics of Life

Writing the Self, Writing the Novel

Of all their many mentors, it is arguably Walter Benjamin who did more than any other Frankfurt School affiliate to lay down a precedent for Oskar Negt's and Alexander Kluge's many forays into autobiography. To write a history of the autobiographical subject is fraught with peril for Benjamin, for it assumes unfettered access to a coherent, stable, and autonomous self that presumably unfolds logically in the course of forward-marching time. According to scholar Gerhard Richter, Benjamin repudiated the ideological fictions that alleged sovereign subjects concocted with their autobiographical writing. Nevertheless, Benjamin did recognize in auto-biography a genre capable of "problematiz[ing] the interrelations of the self (*autos*), life (*bios*), and the act of writing (*graphe*)."[1] As exemplified by works like *Moscow Diary* (1926–27), *A Berlin Chronicle* (1932), and *Berlin Childhood around 1900* (1932–38), Benjamin dared to enter this fray by advancing a mode of autobiography Richter calls "archaeolog-ical montage" that ruptures and displaces the self's identity as well as its place in historical time. Benjamin's lessons certainly did not escape Negt or Kluge. Even though he regularly inserted brief autobiographical

---

1 Gerhard Richter, *Walter Benjamin and the Corpus of Autobiography* (Detroit, MI: Wayne State University Press, 2000) 48.

accounts in many of his theoretical works, Negt only began channeling key features of Benjamin's prescriptions in his two-volume autobiographical "voyage in thinking" entitled *Überlebensglück* [The Luck of Survival] (2016) and *Erfahrungsspuren* [Traces of Experience] (2019). "This autobiography," Negt explains at the outset of volume 1, "shall not be a collection of events told in chronological succession and condensed into stories." As if referring to Benjamin's own autobiographical mode, Negt continues by insisting that his own autobiographical fragment "has something akin to a collage in which old links are broken and re-established albeit without any conscious action in play."[2] Going beyond these formal and substantive limits, volume 2 goes even further by declaring outright that self-writing must entail stepping outside of oneself in order to behold oneself as a foreigner might.[3] Autobiography must entail, in a word, an act of self-alienation.

Whereas Negt regards autobiography as an unavoidable unmaking of the self, Kluge has increasingly found in the concept of *Lebenslauf* writerly techniques for producing the self. In everyday German parlance, *Lebenslauf* usually refers to a résumé outlining a person's educational and professional achievements. Literally, *Lebenslauf* means the course or span of a life. Fiendishly difficult to translate, the title of Kluge's first storybook, *Lebensläufe* (1962), has proven resistant both times it was translated into English; neither *Attendance List for a Funeral* nor *Case Histories* comes anywhere close to capturing the sundry meanings in book's German title, let alone its content. What eludes even a literal translation is how courses or spans of life in Kluge's hands is neither whole nor singular and as a result rends asunder Enlightenment fictions of coherent personhood. Astonished by Kluge's debut, Siegfried Kracauer, for whom biography was a longstanding concern due to how the genre strives to sustain the bourgeois myth of the sovereign individual while crystalizing the otherwise elusive work of history, commended the author personally for his book's unparalleled, meticulous, and shocking account of modern experience torn from the playbook of conventional biography and "pieced together crookedly from scraps."[4] Kluge's preoc-

---

2 Oskar Negt, *Überlebensglück: Eine autobiographische Spurensuche* (Göttingen: Steidl Verlag, 2016) 12–13, 16–17

3 Oskar Negt, *Erfahrungsspuren: Eine autobiographische Denkreise* (Göttingen: Steidl Verlag, 2019) 25: "Only when I wagered the step of standing outside of myself, in other words alienating myself, was I able to formulate a kind of running text."

4 Siegfried Kracauer, "The Biography as an Art Form of the New Bourgeoisie," *The*

cupation since the early sixties, the challenge of how to write the courses of a life, has continued to concern him well into the new millennium, as a recent exchange with writer Hans Magnus Enzensberger illustrates:

> KLUGE: The course of a person's life, their life span is something quite strange. Measured according to what happened objectively, it is actually often too short or too long. There are life spans from under which history has pulled out the rug.
>
> ENZENSBERGER: Yes, but on the other hand every life span is much richer than any old vessel that could contain it. As a result, narration must be discontinuous. You as a filmmaker have always worked with montage, and I myself can hardly imagine a life span as an uninterrupted, progressive, continuous story. Rather, it also depends on the variety of sources. A life span is always polyphonic and the cut is as extremely important as leaving material out is. I cannot narrate everything ...[5]

Writing a self's many selves by jumping, cutting, and omitting counts as just some of the many techniques Kluge has deployed in his many biographical portraits. Although he has long incorporated traces of his family history into his prose and films, only since the new millennium has he turned his attention to the courses of his own life in what he has provocatively called his novels.

Scholars have recently made important arguments for the literary miniature as a productive heuristic for grappling with the idiosyncratic forms characteristic of Kluge's prose written in the new millennium.[6]

Mass Ornament: Weimar Essays, ed. and trans. Thomas Y. Levin (Cambridge: Harvard University Press, 1995) 102–3. Siegfried Kracauer to Alexander Kluge, December 24, 1962, in Jörg Später, *Siegfried Kracauer: Eine Biografie* (Berlin: Suhrkamp 2016) 554. In a telling reference back to Benjamin, Kracauer adds: "I wrote Adorno that Benjamin would have perhaps said of your book what he once said of my novel *Ginster*, namely that only in Germany could such a book have been written." I thank Steffen Andrae for bringing this letter to my attention.

5 Alexander Kluge, dir., "Ohne Rücksicht auf Verluste! Hanz Magnuz Enzensberger: Wie erzählt man Lebensläufe?," *News & Stories*, SAT.1, September 27, 2009. Broadcast included on DVD 2 of: Hans Magnus Enzensberger, *Ich bin keiner von uns: Filme, Porträts, Interviews* (Frankfurt am Main: Suhrkamp Verlag, 2009). This dctp broadcast is also available via Cornell University Library's online archive *Alexander Kluge: Cultural History in Dialogue*: https://kluge.library.cornell.edu/conversations/enzensberger/film/1970.

6 Leslie A. Adelson, *Cosmic Miniatures and the Future Sense: Alexander Kluge's 21st-Century Literary Experiments in German Culture and Narrative Form* (Berlin: De

While the miniature has indeed been a staple for Kluge ever since his work as a film instructor at the Ulm School of Design (1963–68), he has also made an unmistakable case for the novel not long after his literary comeback in 2000.[7] On the novel's necessary historical transformation at the dawn of the new millennium, he explained in an interview from 2001: "Basically, the form of the novel at the end of this century would have to take on a different form than it had at the beginning of the century."[8] This transformation—he goes on to note in another interview from around the same time—initially entails two countervailing operations: compression and multiplication: "I think that you would need about 400 authors, a Balzacian collective, to describe the footprint of our experience. All of my stories are really novels in disguise. Under the growing pressure of our intensified reality, a novel like *Buddenbrooks* gets compressed into fourteen pages."[9] Accordingly, compressing the novel, be it realist or modernist, also calls for the accumulation and concatenation of many such condensed forms that together give rise to an entirely unique morphology whose innumerable ruptures produce a radical heterogeneity. A third, unspoken, yet essential operation is that of elastic constructivism: Kluge's short forms are carefully arranged into an array of both unmistakable and abstruse relationships that lend the entire volume to which they belong an underlying cohesion that, while never an index of any totality, does verge on epic proportions. But unlike the "universalizing dream" characteristic of the maximalist novel growing in popularity among contemporary German-language novelists, especially since the new millennium—e.g., Peter Handke, Navid Kermani, Clemens J. Setz, Uwe Tellkamp, Frank Witzel, etc.—Kluge has remained true to both his suspicion of totality and, conversely, his long-standing penchant for the productive force in the cut.[10] Packaged in oftentimes hefty books that, by

Gruyter, 2017); see also Andreas Huyssen, *Miniature Metropolis: Literature in an Age of Photography and Film* (Cambridge, MA: Harvard University Press, 2015) 13.

7 Daniela Sannwald, *Von der Filmkrise zum Neuen Deutschen Film: Filmausbildung an der Hochschule für Gestaltung Ulm 1959–1968* (Berlin: Wissenschaftsverlag Spiess, 1997) 100–102.

8 Alexander Kluge, *Verdeckte Ermittlung: Ein Gespräch mit Christian Schulte und Rainer Stollmann* (Berlin: Merve Verlag, 2001) 51.

9 Alexander Kluge, "Storytelling Is the Representation of Differences," trans. Steffen Kaupp, in *Difference and Orientation: An Alexander Kluge Reader*, ed. Richard Langston (Ithaca, NY: Cornell University Press, 2019) 67.

10 Stefano Ercolino, *The Maximalist Novel: From Thomas Pynchon's* Gravity's Rainbow *to Roberto Bolaño's* 2066, trans. Albert Sbragia (New York: Bloomsbury Academic, 2014).

their weight alone, could pass for novels at first sight—his *Chronik der Gefühle* [Chronicle of Feeling] from 2000 clocks in at over two thousand pages!—Kluge's disguised novels are far more apt to exacerbate than to resolve the contradictions that arise from their formal organization.[11]

With knowledge of his reconstructive intentions for the long form of the contemporary novel, Kluge's readers find themselves in an exegetical dilemma. What does it mean to read any one of Kluge's books as a refashioned "novel" appropriate for the pressures of the new millennium? Is any single one of his books, composed of anywhere from 48 to 500 stories, the "novel"? Or is the "novel" located rather in each and every story that in turn is concatenated into thematic clusters and chapters? Or is Kluge's new "novel" an intermediary phenomenon somewhere in between these micrological and macrological levels? In a word, on which strata is meaning in Kluge's books generated? On the nominal problem of naming Kluge's storybooks, it was Enzensberger who tackled this elusive question of genre in a 1977 review of Kluge's fourth collection of stories by comparing Kluge's "writing style" with a field of ruins full of "splinters and fragments," an approximation of the catastrophes of modernity that, when transposed into literary form, inevitably produce confusion in the reader.[12] Conversely, Helmut Heißenbüttel petitioned that Kluge's "fragmentary narrative style full of gaps" transcends the medium of literature altogether and thereby activates the reader's imagination.[13] Beyond these older appeals to either a catastrophic object or the contingencies of the ideal subject's imagination, more recent efforts intent on tackling this nagging question—why are Kluge's books so difficult?—have explored other paths focused on Kluge's personae that, for example, pin the elusive nature of the "genre Kluge" to his inserting his own powerful subjectivity into both text and an extra-literary world inhabited by his readers and spectators.[14] Another vein is the inference derived from isolating Kluge's "preface politics"—nearly all of his storybooks begin with a foreword that recycles "catchwords" from his long-established materialist

---

11 Cf. Franco Moretti, "The End of the Beginning," *New Left Review* 41 (September–October 2006): 73. In late 2019, Kluge began preparing a revised, twelve-volume English translation of *Chronik der Gefühle* to be published by Seagull Press.

12 Hans Magnus Enzensberger, "Ein herzloser Schriftsteller," *Der Spiegel* 1 (1978): 81.

13 Helmut Heißenbüttel, "Der Text ist die Wahrheit," *Text + Kritik* 85/86 (1985): 4.

14 Jan Philipp Reemtsma, "Unvertrautheit und Urvertrauen: Die 'Gattung Kluge' – Laudatio auf Alexander Kluge," in *Deutsche Akademie für Sprache und Dichtung Jahrbuch* (Göttingen: Wallstein, 2003) 173.

aesthetics—that his prose battles against the ever more heightened forms of alienated experience endemic to what sociologist Zygmunt Bauman calls "liquid modernity."[15]

What is particularly intriguing about these more recent arguments about genre is the implication that Kluge's prose masterfully deploys a largely invisible authorial self in its bulwark against one of liquid modernity's unavoidable waste products, namely unprecedented levels of ambivalence. For Bauman, the structuration of an otherwise "contingent world of randomness"—both its nominalization and classification—has long been a hallmark of modernity intent on preventing the proliferation of ambivalence; ordering the world invariably entails, however, making distinctions and with every resulting exclusion greater levels of "polysemy, cognitive dissonance, polyvalent definitions, [and] contingency" emerge inadvertently.[16] According to this logic, Kluge's "antagonistic realism," as he himself calls it, would belong to a previous order of modernity characterized by both its solidity and heft guaranteed by linguistic strategies intent on reducing and containing ambivalence.[17] What has allegedly changed in the new millennium, one marked by a lighter and more deliquescent iteration of modernity—once called postmodernity, second modernity, and surmodernity, it is now more closely associated with globalization and neoliberalism—is ambivalence's own waning antagonistic status. Previously an intolerable byproduct of linguistic structuration, ambivalence is arguably now a core structural feature of our predominantly audio-visual, very late modernity. Put differently, liquid modernity is swimming in its own sea of ambivalent waste. So, while Kluge's literary project ostensibly remains committed to doing battle against ambivalence, social life at large—so Bauman's argument goes—has been lulled into an alliance with it. Complicating these newer attempts to categorize Kluge's prose is the implication that the meticulous structuration so intrinsic to his writing increases the production of

---

15 Harro Müller, "Die authentische Methode: Alexander Kluges antirealistisches Realismusprojekt," in *Realitätskonstruktionen in der zeitgenössischen Kultur: Beiträge zu Literatur, Kunst, Fotografie, Film und zum Alltagsleben*, ed. Susanne Knaller (Vienna: Böhlau Verlag, 2008) 130, 135–36; see also: Zygmunt Bauman, *Liquid Modernity* (Cambridge, UK: Polity Press, 2000) 1–15.

16 Zygmunt Bauman, *Modernity and Ambivalence* (Ithaca, NY: Cornell University Press, 1991) 1, 9.

17 Bauman, *Liquid Modernity*, 25: "Kluge's antirealist realism project is a project of incomplete modernity." See: Müller 131.

the very ambivalence it seeks to counter. In contradistinction to such a contradictory reading that effectively overlooks Kluge's investment in writing *Lebensläufe*, this chapter sites the secret of ambivalence as an originary impetus not just for Kluge's recent call to reconstruct the novel but also for all his poetics and aesthetics. What, however, cannot be said of Kluge's prose, both new and old, is that ambivalence is its unintended result. Rather, Kluge's poetics evince signs of the premodern science of alchemy intent on revealing secret knowledge about the self by way of the "admixture of opposites."[18]

Alchemical Solutions: Reading for Multidimensional Ambiguity

In her book *Alchemical Mercury*, scholar Karen Pinkus writes, "Ambivalence is intolerable."[19] In the chemical sciences, the co-existence of two similar charges or valences around an atom simply does not exist, whereas in psychology the ambivalence that arises when subjects fail to master a lost object prolongs the mourning process. Ambivalence, she underscores, "is binary, and stubbornly so. It refuses to open itself up to multiplicities just as resolutely as it refuses to reduce itself to one."[20] The only option left is any number of alchemical techniques that seek out "a state of suspension in which various elements (often two, perhaps more) exist together."[21] A carryover from his writings on cinematic realism first published in 1975, Kluge's excursus on the "antirealistic attitude," co-authored with Negt and reproduced in *History and Obstinacy*, is remarkable for just how much it resonates with Pinkus's observations on the intolerable nature of ambivalence.[22] On how to comport oneself antagonistically vis-à-vis the intolerable conditions sustained by political economy, Kluge and Negt contend that ambivalence in the lives of people counts as one of the greatest challenges to translating the antirealism rooted in bodily feelings—think, for example, of the proverbial "gut feeling"—into the requisite attitude for protest. An encounter between

---

18 Karen Pinkus, *Alchemical Mercury: A Theory of Ambivalence* (Stanford, CA: Stanford University Press, 2010) 4–6.

19 Pinkus 64.

20 Pinkus 65.

21 Pinkus 65.

22 Alexander Kluge and Oskar Negt, *History and Obstinacy*, ed. Devin Fore, trans. Richard Langston et al. (New York: Zone Books, 2014) 139–40.

strangers devoid of predictability and credibility automatically gives rise
to an ambivalence that can be obviated in at least one of two ways. For
Negt, *ambi*-valence is primarily a matter of twos that can, in theory, be
surmounted dialectically: "Ambivalence is today essentially a conceptual substitute for dialectics," he explained in an interview from 2012.
"Whoever thinks relationally thinks dialectically. In other words, relationalities are not just fragments, but rather fragments in their dynamic
logic. Regardless what kind of fragment goes missing, the libinal energy
of its absence leads to further development. That would, in a sense, put
the dialectical process back on track and set it in motion."[23] Whereas
Negt sees in the dialectic a potential for a third path forward beyond the
suspension of binary difference, Kluge travels in the reverse direction:
"Multidimensionality," he counters, "is also a category of relationality and
can be dialectical, but it does not have to be so. Now take, for example,
the co-existence of different times, meaning all our ancestors we carry
in us as it were … In this respect, we are polyphonic creatures that live
in multiverses interlaced with one another."[24] Multidimensionality not
only compensates for the deficiencies in the insufferable state of affairs
in reality, Kluge insists, but it also dodges the hierarchies of the universal and the particular that so often produce both small- and large-scale
tragedies. Furthermore, it arrests the intolerability of *ambivalence*—the
persistence of the binary—with the *ambiguity* of multiple alternatives
and indecisiveness.[25]

Long committed to translating this antirealism of feeling into aesthetic
form, Kluge's alchemical poetics has long relied on three principal techniques. Asked in 2008 what holds his many stories together, he pointed
out these otherwise elusive features and their attendant morphology
subtending both his recent storybooks and feature films as well as his
streaming video portal—www.dctp.tv:

A reader can do very little with finished buildings. He is better off
when he builds his own house, but not arbitrarily. All 350 stories in
my book *Tür an Tür mit einem anderen Leben* [Next Door to Another
Life] have a single core, just as there is a core at the center of the Earth

---

23 Richard Langston, "'Das ist die umgekehrte Flaschenpost': Ein montiertes Interview mit Oskar Negt und Alexander Kluge," *Alexander Kluge-Jahrbuch* 2 (2015): 61.
24 Langston 64.
25 Pinkus 61, 173.

from which gravitational relations emerge. This gravitational thinking holds things on the sphere's surface together, but also the sphere itself, and this corresponds with other spheres that zip around in space like planets.[26]

Firstly, there is the core. Reminiscent of Kluge's long-ago homage to Gottfried Benn's "orange style," the core operates as a central organizing principle in each of his storybooks.[27] Referring specifically to the afore-mentioned *Chronik der Gefühle*, Kluge once insisted "my stories all stand in a single relationality with one another. I could also write these 2,000 pages in seven sentences, but they would not be completely decipherable."[28] Decrypting the core can thus proceed only indirectly according to the second feature, namely the gravitational forces fanning outward from the core. "I narrate," he once explained, "from the center of my own interest outwardly toward every horizon."[29] And thirdly, the individual stories commune with one another not only by virtue of their shared tether to a core, but also because of the coincidental intercourse among one another. "They are autonomously formulated stories," he remarked, "that come into contact with others also formulated autonomously. They are like Leibniz's monads and communicate quite well even though they are blind."[30] Alas, Kluge's readers are limited on account of their quo-tidian powers of comprehension and description when trying to access all the many subcutaneous relationalities lurking beneath these blind monads. Kluge merely offers here a deeply ambiguous metaphor; his books, he insists, are geocentric worlds coasting through some sort of intergalactic space (of thought) along with other celestial bodies pre-sumably of both Kluge's own making and his aforementioned "Balzacian collective."

26 Alexander Kluge, "Storytelling Means Dissolving Relations," trans. Emma Woelk, in *Difference and Orientation*, 95. Regarding the English translation of Kluge's title *Tür an Tür mit einem anderen Leben*, Adelson has proposed a more literal approach with "Door to Door with an Other Life." I have opted here for a more condensed though more liberal rendition that emphasizes the parallelism conveyed in the German. A partial English translation of *Tür an Tüt mit einem anderen Leben* is to be included in Kluge's forthcom-ing expanded, twelve-volume English-language edition of *Chronik der Gefühle*.
27 Richard Langston, *Visions of Violence: German Avant-Gardes after Fascism* (Evan-ston, IL: Northwestern University Press, 2008) 212.
28 Kluge, *Verdeckte Ermittlung*, 52.
29 Kluge, *Verdeckte Ermittlung*, 51.
30 Kluge, "Storytelling Means Dissolving Relations," 95.

Far less prone to the wild vagaries typical of a rich metaphor like the cosmos, the figure of the tree—long deployed by both modern philosophers and scientists alike—reduces the focal length in question considerably and thereby allows for visualization and comparison of the complex relationships at work in Kluge's prose. Although the language of taxonomy's phylogenetic tree (root, branch, node) does appear to map effortlessly onto Kluge's own poetic concepts (core, gravitation, sphere), the point of plotting the architecture by which a Kluge book arranges its many stories can only serve as a point of departure and is not without risk. It cannot, for example, effortlessly deduce the meaning of the core/root that guides the entire book. The gravitational lines from core to sphere do not trace any evolutionary development, as is the case with a phylogenetic tree's branches. A tree cannot account for the blind communication transpiring between stories located on disparate lines. And, above all, taxonomy's quest for mastery projects order onto Kluge's chaotic prose that invariably gives rise to a vicious circle. Let us not forget, Bauman reminds us, that "ambivalence is a side-product of the labor of classification; and it calls for yet more classifying effort."[31] What trees can elucidate, however, is the historical continuity of the breadth and depth endemic to Kluge's morphology, and this leads to a very different explanation for the origins and motives of Kluge's ambiguous multidimensionality. Consider, for example, the first edition of Kluge's first book of prose, *Case Histories* [*Lebensläufe*] (1962; trans. 1988) and the aforementioned "Next Door to Another Life" (2006). Following taxonomic terminology, the root in "Next Door to Another Life" (fig. 8.2) fissions just as it does in *Case Histories* (fig. 8.1) into nine branches leading to nine parent nodes (chapters), which in turn contain either end-nodes (single stories) or polytomic nodes leading to multiple descendants (story clusters). Like *Case Histories*, the majority of populations (stories) in "Next Door to Another Life" are found in the third and fourth strata descending downward from the root (core). Skeptics may be reasonably dubious of what looks here like distant reading's notorious disdain for the interpretation of particulars, which both Kluge and Negt hold in high regard. (The duo writes, for example, "As a category of primitive property, the particular is finally something powerful and universal [*Allgemeines*]; it also produces a community that emerges out of multiple particularities, my own

31 Bauman, *Modernity and Ambivalence*, 3

community.")[32] The skeptics will nevertheless agree that, morphologically, "Next Door to Another Life" looks a lot like *Case Histories*. All this is to make clear that Kluge's call at the new millennium for the reconstruction of the novel's form rooted in compression, multiplication, and constructivism is actually nothing new at all. The ambiguity arising from the multidimensional sphere of stories and its underlying morphology is just as much a function of the "debatable unity" of "form and content" in Kluge's early reckoning with the legacies of German history in *Case Histories* as it is in his motley assortment of stories in "Next Door to Another Life."[33] What separates these two volumes beyond their identifiable subject matter and the forty-four intervening years are their formal aspirations and the intensity of their focalization. Whereas *Case Histories* aspired in its own time to count as merely a volume about a "sad chronicle" centered on recent German "tradition" dating from 1933 to 1962, Kluge casts "Next Door to Another Life" against the backdrop of the long form—a new novel for a new millennium—and casts his storytelling net backwards in time some 630 million years.[34]

Ambiguity from Separation: The Problem of the Crypt

"Next Door to Another Life" actively eludes comprehension. The title's ambivalent allusion to two concurrent lives separated by a door quickly devolves into full-fledged ambiguity. The book's preface provides few if any additional clues. Plowing ahead and reading in sequential order from left to right, cover to cover—a practice Kluge has discounted together with Negt in favor of the "autonomous activity of the reader"—only exacerbates confusion.[35] It is not unclear at first sight how the thirty-

---

32 Kluge and Negt 141.

33 See Helmut Heißenbüttel's review, in which he praises Kluge's debut as a rare meeting of form and content: "Von der Kunst des Erzählens im Jahre 1962," *Deutsche Zeitung* (October 20–21, 1962): 20.

34 Kluge begins *Case Histories* with the following caveat: "The stories in this volume question tradition from a number of very different aspects." See: Alexander Kluge, *Case Histories*, trans. Leila Vennewitz (New York: Holmes & Meier, 1962) viii; *Tür an Tür mit einem anderen Leben* begins with the declaration, "630 million years ago the earth was a ball encrusted in ice." See: Alexander Kluge, *Tür an Tür mit einem anderen Leben: 350 neue Geschichten* (Frankfurt am Main: Suhrkamp Verlag, 2006) 7.

35 Oskar Negt and Alexander Kluge, *Geschichte und Eigensinn, Der unterschätzte*

one stories about globalization in chapter 1 link up with those contained in the subsequent eight chapters. What—the reader is left to ponder—does globalization have to do with World War I, the subject of chapter 2's stories? And what about chapter 3's focus on philosopher Friedrich Nietzsche's idea of the Overman; or chapter 4's attention to the Final Solution; or chapter 5's detailed analysis of our deficient perception of time; or chapter 6's account of the history of the locomotive; or the circus stories in chapter 7; or the love stories in chapter 8? And then there is the usual potpourri of largely autobiographical stories in chapter 9. Echoing Enzenberger's assessment some three decades earlier, one literary critic admitted, "The stories resist being reduced to a common denominator."[36] Ancillary evidence in the form of illustrations peppered throughout the book, and the back matter's critical apparatus containing annotated citations and cross-references, as well as the concluding eleven-page table of contents (a customary practice for German-language books) do little in and of themselves to alleviate this bewilderment. In spite of the continuity of Kluge's morphology and the heightened explosion of ambiguity in "Next Door to Another Life," there is indeed something new afoot in "Next Door to Another Life" that both critics quickly called out and Kluge has addressed unabashedly in person. In one of the book's very first reviews, another critic noted: "Kluge's interest in knowledge always aims at social contexts, ... and thus it comes as no small surprise that Kluge makes a private confession at the end of his new book of 350 stories."[37] The confession in question, which comes to light in an account of Kluge's actual confrontation with another renowned German writer, divulges the real autobiographical impetus that compelled him to write prose in the first place in spite of his mentor Theodor W. Adorno's long-ago admonition that "you cannot be better than Proust."[38] In light of the unprecedented autobiographical content of the stories contained in

Mensch: Gemeinsame Philosophie in zwei Bänden, vol. 2 (Frankfurt am Main: Zweitausendeins, 2001) 1283.

36 Thomas Rothschild, "Sokrates und die Frau vom Zirkus: Alexander Kluge beglückt mit 350 neuen Geschichten," *Stuttgarter Zeitung* (October 13, 2006): 40.

37 Martin Krumbholz, "Wölfe sind gutmütig, wenn sie satt sind: Alexander Kluges neue Geschichten *Tür an Tür mit einem anderen Leben*," *Neue Zürcher Zeitung* (October 2, 2006): 50.

38 Alexander Kluge, "The Peacemaker," trans. Emma Woelk, in *Difference and Orientation: An Alexander Kluge Reader*, ed. Richard Langston (Ithaca, NY: Cornell University Press, 2019) 78.

chapter 9, Kluge's revelation is nothing less than the author recognizing the intolerability of a persistent ambivalence in his own (auto)biography. What shall also come to light shortly is how Kluge's multidimensional poetics seeks to counter this ambivalence.

Lodged between two clusters of stories, one about Kluge's father Ernst and the other about his mother Alice, Kluge's confession appears in a seemingly unsuspecting story entitled "My True Motive" that begins with the aforementioned chance encounter on New Year's Eve 2001 with preeminent postwar German novelist Martin Walser at Zurich's Schauspielhaus.[39] Sensing a potential conflict due to his own longstanding political reputation as a leftist and debates from around 2000 that charged Walser, himself once a committed communist, with the sins of historical revisionism, the first-person narrator Kluge tells how he initially made small talk with Walser. "After an hour of talking back and forth without making any real contact," Kluge then explains, "he asked me why I write stories." "Such a direct question," he continues,

> implies that I could also refrain from writing stories altogether. Such brashness leads one to search for a direct response. It was clear to me that basically everything I do serves to establish peace between my parents, a revocation of their divorce ... All my research into parallel worlds or the concession to a second life circles around the possibility of rehabilitating this "union" that confusingly enough was no union but that should have been one.[40]

On what it would take for his parent's union to work, Kluge muses that had he possessed as a child the negotiation skills that he later deployed throughout his adult career, then the nine-year-old Kluge would have surely been able to bring his parents back together. Unwilling to let bygones be bygones, he adds that souls like those of his parents who did indeed divorce acrimoniously in 1943 can still cross paths again in the

39 The story "My True Motive" stands out in many reviews, interviews, and analyses as a key access point for making sense of *Tür an Tür mit einem anderen Leben*. (For example, see: Thomas Combrink, "'Ein Arzt aus Halberstadt': Über Alexander Kluges Vater," *Text + Kritik* 85/86, rev. ed. [2011]: 84; Alexander Kluge, "Die Geduld der Bücher: Alexander Kluge im Gespräch mit Claus Philipp," *Volltext: Magazin für Literatur* 6 [December–January 2006]: 30; Krumbholz 50; and Müller 132.) Adelson's reading (198–205) is the first important analysis to move beyond (auto)biographical reconstructions.
40 Kluge, *Tür an Tür mit einem anderen Leben*, 594–5.

future. Rematerializing this union would be, however, nothing less than a literary feat. In response to Kluge's confession, Walser's doubts were dispelled; Kluge's identity as a fellow author suddenly became unassailable. Then the story abruptly cuts to an excerpt from Kluge and Walser's actual dialogue:[41]

> – Then the whole élan for ENLIGHTENMENT, FOR WHICH YOU ARE KNOWN, is based on a private motive?
> – And a hopeless one at that.[42]

Asked about the nature of his mother's misgivings, Kluge responds: "A 'school for lovers' should have been created. Both needed to be schooled on the path of adult education. It would not have been ruled out that their feelings, so far removed from one another, could have grown back together."[43] Readers unfamiliar with either Kluge's return to prose since 2000 or his previous books, films, and videos may very well see nothing peculiar in this confidential revelation. Conversely, an awareness that Kluge had long been "reticent about revealing his own biography," that until the publication of "Next Door to Another Life" in 2006 only a rudimentary biography could be gleaned from "traces" strewn throughout out his work makes clear above all the sea change in Kluge's authorial relationship to a secret that ostensibly touched off his literary career in the first place.[44] "What flabbergasted me," Kluge professed in a dialogue from late 2006 with Vienna art house director Claus Philipp, "is that my parents appear for the first time by name and that it works."[45] Specifically, what works here is the revelation of an autobiographical secret in Kluge's long-standing pursuit of an ambiguous, multidimensional long form that he calls, for the lack of a better word, a novel. What this divulgence affords this novel in particular is, however, not so much an exorcism of the secret or even a reunification of the parents so much as a poetic response to the foundational place separation plays not only

---

41 Thomas Combrink, "'Ein Arzt aus Halberstadt': Über Alexander Kluges Vater," *Text + Kritik* 85/86, rev. ed. (2011): 84.

42 Kluge, *Tür an Tür mit einem anderen Leben*, 595.

43 Kluge, *Tür an Tür mit einem anderen Leben*, 596.

44 Peter C. Lutze, *Alexander Kluge: The Last Modernist* (Detroit, MI: Wayne State University Press, 1998) 37; and Rainer Stollmann, "Biographische Spuren im Werk," in *Alexander Kluge zur Einführung* (Hamburg: Junius Verlag 1998) 138.

45 Kluge, "Die Geduld der Bücher," 29–30.

in his biography but also in the historical formation of all human subjectivity. For the Hungarian-French psychoanalysts Nicolas Abraham
and Maria Torok, secrets are what patients in therapy avoid at all costs.
Secrets burrow down into that space within the psychic apparatus they
call "the kernel," that inaccessible, sheltered place where the ego resides.[46]
Revising Sigmund Freud's thoughts on the symptom as trace material
of latent repressed sexual desires, Abraham and Torok's concept of the
"crypt"—the psychic place within the ego where we bury our secrets—
arises not from the effects of catastrophes or disasters per se.[47] Within
the mental life of individuals burdened with one or more secrets, crypts
must always be kept under lock and key. The disavowal of this reality is
not only a continual activity, but this labor of entombment must also
resist language. The secret, they underscore, "is precisely a matter of
... unspeakable words buried alive" and "stripped of their customary
communicative function."[48] Essential in the maintenance of this status
quo is the work of fantasy. Fantasy arises from the secret contents of the
kernel's crypt, and yet fantasy invariably conceals, obfuscates, and lies
such that in the end it produces a vast array of misleading words and
images that envelop like a shell the secret from within.[49] This fantastic
labor is characterized, they add, by a "back-and-forth motion" between
kernel and shell, an "ambivalence" between speaking of the secret and
shrouding it.[50] Taking Kluge by his word regarding the central place
this family secret plays in his life's work would mean then grasping his
alchemical poetics as a series of highly productive failures at trying to
overcome a secret about the never-ending, psychic coexistence of a two
halves that, for both the eleven-year-old and the seventy-four-year-old

---

46 Nicolas Abraham and Maria Torok, "The Topography of Reality: Sketching a
Metapsychology of Secrets," in *The Shell and the Kernel: Renewals of Psychoanalysis*, ed.
and trans. Nicholas T. Rand (Chicago: University of Chicago Press, 1994) 157.

47 Nicolas T. Rand, "Psychoanalysis with Literature: An Abstract of Nicolas Abraham
and Maria Torok's *The Shell and the Kernel*," *Oxford Literary Review* 12 (1990): 59; Nicolas
T. Rand, "Introduction: Renewals of Psychoanalysis," in *The Shell and the Kernel: Renewals of Psychoanalysis*, ed. and trans. Nicholas T. Rand (Chicago: University of Chicago
Press, 1994) 4–11.

48 Abraham and Torok 159–60.

49 Nicolas Abraham, "The Shell and the Kernel: The Scope and Originality of Freudian Psychoanalysis," in *The Shell and the Kernel: Renewals of Psychoanalysis*, ed. and trans.
Nicholas T. Rand (Chicago: University of Chicago Press, 1994) 88–90.

50 Nicolas Abraham and Maria Torok, *The Wolf Man's Magic Word: A Cryptonymy*,
trans. Nicolas Rand (Minneapolis: University of Minnesota Press, 1986) 82.

Kluge alike, should have remained a single bond. A book whose very title could evoke either a sense of parallel worlds or two parallel iterations of a single life, "Next Door to Another Life" concedes that the very idea of another reality afforded by a poetics of multidimensionality could conceivably reconcile the intolerability of twos characteristic of ambivalence. As Kluge's rapid-fire literary output since 2000 attests, the poetic ambiguity that emerges from his morphology not only ends up having to reproduce itself again and again on account of the psychic interminability of the broken couple, but also always necessarily stands in opposition to this originary ambivalence. As a result, a higher-order ambivalence emerges vis-à-vis experience and perception on account of the aesthetically mediated possibility of another form of being—a being-next-door-to-another—radically different than the one found in the quotidian reality that otherwise destroys people and, what is more, their relationships.[51]

There are then at least two possible readings of the secret revealed in "My True Motive" along with the blind communication it presumably engages in with the rest of Kluge's many other stories, books, films, and videos. On the one hand, it could be parsed as a self-effacing autobiographical confession that deflates both Kluge's authorial personae and his aesthetic productions as mere compensatory strategies for a central primal scene in the author's psychosexual development; accordingly, this path would frame Kluge's alleged reinvention of the novel for the twenty-first century as the aesthetic expression of the author's fantasy life organized by a childhood trauma into a series of crypts. In contradistinction to such a symptomological reading played out strictly on the ontogenetic plane, casting this one story as the ontogenetic recapitulation of a crucial phase in phylogenetic development—something actually hinted at at the close of the story—would move away from an exclusively autobiographical reading of Kluge's familial stories and instead underscore their essential place in not just his multidimensional prose's response to the problem of a particular historical separation (his parent's divorce) but also the foundational role it and, by extension, ambivalence play throughout all of human history.[52] In the final paragraph to "My True Motive," Kluge the narrator begins with a confession about his

51 Kluge, *Tür an Tür mit einem anderen Leben*, 7.

52 Stephen Jay Gould, *Ontogeny and Phylogeny* (Cambridge, MA: Belknap Press, 1977) 164–65.

confession to Walser. "But what I could not say to my 'literary father confessor,' whom I trusted on account of the trust he placed in my direct feelings, was this: the same longing existed beneath both my parents' remarkably different temperaments and bodies, to 'be able to devote oneself without being deceived.' Both were cautious."[53] A shared desire to surrender oneself to the other that could have led to the formation of a single bond was something neither of his parents was willing to risk, Kluge professes. Both were so deeply cautious that any such union was foreclosed. What makes two lovers so cautious toward one another that they end up thwarting the consummation of their common, deep-seated desires? What is it about the ego that inevitably results in the cleaving of one into two?

The final chapter of "Next Door to Another Life," just like the entire book itself, makes clear that answers to these fundamental questions are not to be limited to the biographies of the author's mother and father or their relatives for that matter. Rather, the closing chapter of "Next Door to Another Life" tells stories about, on the one hand, the supercontinent Pangea and the Great Extinction from 250 million years ago, and, more recently, the birth of the human ego in ancient Mesopotamia and Kluge's present-day daydreams of his previous self residing in ancient Syria, on the other, in order to concatenate a grand evolutionary account of terrestrial fusion and separation with intimate human stories.[54] This is, in part, the crux of Negt and Kluge's focus as stated in *Geschichte und Eigensinn*: "We are interested," they explain in the book's preface, "in what exactly labor achieves when it alters matter in a world in which catastrophes obviously occur. What carries out this labor are historical labor capacities formed from processes of separation and armed with obstinacy that defends them against this separation."[55] If processes of separation are the organizational moments of human history that elicit antagonistic responses (like obstinacy and caution) that, in turn, generate more separations (and ambivalence), they are but only more recent, smaller-scale episodes preceded and precipitated by larger-scale, planetary events. But the "double perspective" that arises from yoking Kluge's own life span (*Lebenslauf*) to "world history" underscores, above all, that the ambivalent consequences of subject formation arising out of separation are

53 Kluge, *Tür an Tür mit einem anderen Leben*, 596.
54 Kluge, *Tür an Tür mit einem anderen Leben*, 539, 543, 581, 606.
55 Negt and Kluge, *Geschichte und Eigensinn*, 5.

neither predetermined nor inevitable.[56] This explains why towards the middle of his story "My True Motive" Kluge the narrator exclaims, "The political is personal."[57] The evolutionary perspective reveals just how much a "barricade ... and longing" were also essential for the development of biological difference and human evolution.[58] In other words, Ernst and Alice's sad story did not have to end the way it did.

Alchemical Writing

If ambivalence is indeed intolerable, then, when Kluge calls upon Freud in his aforementioned interview with Philipp, it would seem that, for him, his alchemical solution of multidimensionality is nothing less than the philosopher's stone: "Happiness is the fulfillment of a childhood wish according to Freud. I always wanted a watch and I get a watch, but I no longer have the wish: that is the problem with childhood wishes. In this book, I fulfilled a series of childhood wishes."[59] Unlike a childhood wish that wanes with age, Kluge's childhood desire to prevent his parents' divorce and similarly his adult desire to forge a posthumous peace between them and therewith rescind their separation after death obviously persist, but exactly how "Next Door to Another Life" fulfills these wishes let alone brokers happiness is not entirely obvious from the book's generic form or its individual stories. The narrator Kluge's conviction in a "groundswell" shared by both his father and mother never culminates in a fictional story from some parallel world where his parent's marriage finds its happy ending.[60] On the contrary, "Next Door to Another Life" leaves its readers with a penultimate parting shot of Ernst and Alice on their way to their Parisian honeymoon, that moment four years before Kluge's birth when their bond was still intact and the scales had not yet tipped; it was not yet clear whether Ernst and Alice would become "saviors and angels" or "belligerents."[61] Far from simply arresting his parents' personal history at that moment of its apex and basking

56 Kluge, "Die Geduld der Bücher," 30.
57 Kluge, *Tür an Tür mit einem anderen Leben*, 596
58 Kluge, *Tür an Tür mit einem anderen Leben*, 540.
59 Kluge, "Die Geduld der Bücher," 28.
60 Kluge, *Tür an Tür mit einem anderen Leben*, 596, 571.
61 Kluge, *Tür an Tür mit einem anderen Leben*, 605.

in its glow, the happiness afforded by "Next Door to Another Life" is to be found entirely elsewhere. Addressing the early modern alchemical process called *opus alchymicum*, whereby common elements were to be transmuted into precious metals, philosopher Giorgio Agamben writes, "The search for and production of the philosopher's stone coincides with the spiritual creation or recreation of the subject that carries it out."[62] This alchemical transformation of the subject did not go entirely unnoticed among moderns. In fact, there exists a small canon of writers who have deployed their literary work "as the protocol for the carrying out of an operation on oneself."[63] In pursuit of this extra-textual practice, alchemical literature, says Agamben, is generally marked by a volatility between concocting fiction and conveying real experience, between keeping secrets and revealing knowledge, and between shaping an opus and giving form to one's life. The purpose of such undecidability was arguably best theorized by philosopher Michel Foucault who, in arguing that the subject can only emerge out of a relationship to the self, implied that the "relationship with oneself and the work on oneself" can assume the guise of creative activity and this, in turn, affords the potential for happiness.[64] "By writing ... you give to your existence," Foucault insisted in an interview from 1968, "a form of absolution ... It's not the writing that's happy, it's the joy of existing that's attached to writing."[65]

That writing and life are so intimately intertwined with one another was precisely why Walser seemed so very unexpectedly to go for the jugular after an hour of small talk with Kluge in Zurich on New Year's Eve. In a follow-up conversation from 2006, Kluge questioned his "literary father confessor" on the dearth of extra-literary content in his recently published diaries *Leben und Schreiben* [Living and Writing] spanning the first full decade of the Federal Republic of Germany.[66] Neither the Korean War nor the Spiegel Affair of 1962 or any other intervening

---

62 Giorgio Agamben, *The Fire and the Tale*, trans. Lorenzo Chiesa (Stanford, CA: Stanford University Press, 2017) 122.

63 Agamben, *The Fire and the Tale*, 114.

64 Agamben, *The Fire and the Tale*, 134. See also: Michel Foucault, *The Hermeneutics of the Subject: Lectures at the Collège de France, 1981–82*, trans. Graham Burchell (New York: Palgrave Macmillan, 2005) 533.

65 Michel Foucault, *Speech Begins after Death: In Conversation with Claude Bonnefoy*, ed. Philippe Artières, trans. Robert Bononno (Minneapolis, MN: University of Minnesota Press, 2013) 64.

66 Kluge, *Tür an Tür mit einem anderen Leben*, 596.

historical event commonly associated with Chancellor Adenauer's term in office is mentioned. "I noticed precisely this," Kluge remarked. "Nothing about it appears."[67] As if to say recounting political events and creative practices carried out in the name of working on the self transpire on two entirely different strata, Walser retorted, "Indeed, it is life and writing. What inspired me to write? … Here in the freedom of a journal I only wrote heedlessly about what drove me to write."[68] In this respect, that earlier confrontational moment in Zurich when Kluge hastily presumed Walser to be a hostile critic on account of his old reputation in the sixties as a leftist was, in fact, Walser merely probing whether Kluge, too, was an alchemist committed to the "aesthetics of existence."[69] If his subsequent conversation with Walser were not enough irrefutable proof of their kindred relationship toward writing, Kluge concludes "Next Door to Another Life," published a mere eight months later, with a story that leaves little doubt that writing the self is indeed both his and the work's objective. The title of this final story—a play on the beginning of Kant's conclusion to *Critique of Practical Reason*—is "Der Sechsjährige in mir und der gestirnte Himmel über mir" [The Six-Year-Old within Me and the Starry Sky above Me], and ostensibly transpires in the extra-literary present.[70] But, suddenly, the authorial narrator transports himself to other times and places. Kluge, trapped in a boring business meeting held in an underground, windowless boardroom, declares to himself in writing: "I hear the six-year-old in me who I once was AND WHO IN PRINCIPLE I AM AT EVERY MOMENT OF MY LIFE … If I shut my eyes for a moment, it can be the case that I return to this hall from an earlier time. I have the impression I lived on an estate in ancient Syria."[71] A polyphonic chorus composed of the septuagenarian's many younger selves as well as the human species' selves that date back to the cradle of human civilization

---

67 Alexander Kluge and Martin Walser, "Wenn Du einen Roman schreibst, ist die ganze Welt eine einzige Zulieferung," *Text + Kritik* 85/86, rev. ed. (2011) 60. This was originally broadcast as: Alexander Kluge, dir., "Schreiben als Lebensart: Martin Walser aus Anlass seiner Tagebücher 1951–62," *10 till 11*, RTL, 27. Feb. 2006.

68 Kluge and Walser, "Wenn Du einen Roman schreibst," 60

69 Agamben, *The Fire and the Tale*, 130.

70 Kant concludes his second Critique as follows: "Two things fill the mind with ever new and increasing admiration and reverence, the more often and more steadily one reflects on them: *the starry heavens above me and the moral law within me*." See: Immanuel Kant, "Critique of Practice Reason," in *Practical Philosophy*, ed. and trans. Mary J. Gregor (Cambridge University Press, 1996) 269.

71 Kluge, *Tür an Tür mit einem anderen Leben*, 607.

in Upper Mesopotamia, Kluge's acoustic fantasy is both an ontogenetic and phylogenetic foil for his alchemy. It points back to the photograph displayed in the beginning of "Next Door to Another Life," of Kluge the six-year-old child playing under a table while his parents—their marriage was already on the rocks—take pleasure in listening to friends and strangers gossip: "I wanted to hear them, even without understanding them, because my parents loved these conversations."[72] This ontogenetic recollection of fleeting happiness that ends regardless in divorce stands alongside a phylogenetic one recorded in *The Epic of Gilgamesh*, in which human hubris leads not only to a bloody battle against the gods but also the loss of friends, happiness, and the "unbridled delight in battle, play, and pleasure."[73] A corollary to that formative moment when Kluge's life-long childhood wish began to materialize, this ancient "hour when the EGO develops" is no time or place for identification with ideal selves.[74] Rather, both it and the childhood wish count as events intimately bound up with the emergence of the very ambivalence—one historical, the other structural—against which Kluge has written for a half a century. "The real alchemist," Agamben contends, "is ... the one who—in the opus and through the opus—contemplates only the potentiality that produced it."[75] In other words, alchemical writing actualizes the self's potentiality; the work is merely a facilitator. In Kluge's case, this potentiality is propelled forward not only in the opus's strategic recollection of these ambivalent moments but also the ambiguity that arises from its interwoven multidimensionality and the being-next-door-to-another it engenders. Yet the poetic form these actions and reactions assume ultimately affords an exclusive relationship to the writing self, one we readers can only glean as an impersonal record, a cipher of a life that only Kluge has lived, yet one that we as egos, too, also know a thing or two about.

Kluge once implied that what he does in his writing is really no different than what Ovid does in *Metamorphoses*. Ovid crafts his individual stories just as Kluge narrates outwardly in a spiral toward every possible horizon: "By narrating from a center point, the novel would orient itself to the oral tradition and not merely to the written one. In this respect, Ovid's short stories are all novels, each one of them, and together they

---

72 Kluge, *Tür an Tür mit einem anderen Leben*, 6, 149.
73 Kluge, *Tür an Tür mit einem anderen Leben*, 582.
74 Kluge, *Tür an Tür mit einem anderen Leben*, 582.
75 Agamben, *The Fire and the Tale*, 137.

are the *Metamorphoses*."[76] To the question as to whether Kluge writes miniatures or whether he invented a new idiosyncratic novel, perhaps the best, most accurate response is both and neither. To take Kluge by his word would mean that each of the 350 stories in "Next Door to Another Life" is a miniature novel. Yet this leaves largely unanswered the overarching questions regarding their relationships to one another and the formal nature of their vessel, as well as this container's recurrence over time. Sidestepping this binary conundrum, Kluge would very likely advance a third term for his preferred long form, namely that of "metamorphoses." On the necessity of both facts and fakes for storytelling, he once noted: "In his *Metamorphoses*, Ovid writes that suffering creatures would rather transform themselves than to go on suffering. This is the entire story of his *Metamorphoses*."[77] If it is possible to speak of a single story coursing through "Next Door to Another Life"—one that radiates outward from its core—then it is no different than the one contained in Kluge's favorite book by Ovid, for it is suffering precipitated by the ambivalence of separation that both works seek to alleviate using ambiguity. But unlike Ovid's intention to "tell of bodies changed / to different forms," Kluge's metamorphoses—"loosely Ovidian [in] structure and tone"—are the means by which he changes his own self from one mired in a hopelessly unrealizable wish into many selves no longer confronted by the interminability of ambivalence.[78] In so doing, Kluge arrives at Benjamin's injunction against autobiographical writing in the reverse direction; rather than rationing the self, he renders it wholly arbitrary and contingent by throwing into relief all its many other selves populating sundry times past, present, and future and places both near and far.

76 Kluge, *Verdeckte Ermittlung*, 51–52.

77 Alexander Kluge, "The Art of Drawing Distinctions," trans. Emma Woelk, in *Difference and Orientation*, 418.

78 Ovid, *Metamorphoses*, trans. Rolfe Humphries (Bloomington, IN: Indiana University Press, 1983) 3; Theodore Ziolkowski, *Ovid and the Moderns* (Ithaca, NY: Cornell University Press, 200) 251n34.

Figure 9.1. The unborn. KIEFER: "Indeed, mature sunflowers always reminded me of the firmament." Alexander Kluge, dir., "The Unborn: A Meeting with Anselm Kiefer in His Studio in Croissy-Beauregard," *News & Stories*, SAT.1, September 1, 2013. © Alexander Kluge.

Epilogue
Orientation and Critique

How Critical Is It?

Thinking gravitationally presupposes a steadfast difference between at least two people invested in trying to think together. That difference may express itself in terms of life experience or training, vocation or allegiances, language or culture. Gravitational thinking involves making considerable effort on each party's part to meet one another almost halfway, a point where near gravitationlessness allows for points of contact to emerge. Where gravitational thinkers meet is a place no single thinker could reach alone. Where this thinking starts is just as unpredictable as where it leads to. Gravitational thinking is not about the art of persuasion or the founding of communities based on communicative reason. Its primary aim is to achieve a togetherness in thinking through thinking together. It therefore requires both generosity toward the other and a ferocious adherence to one's center of gravity. Because of this tension, it may momentarily falter or come unhinged. It may require clarification or correction. It might even entail talking or writing past the other person. It is full of pauses, jumps, twists, and surprises. Gravitational thinking is thus an experiment. Whether it is successful or a failure is immaterial. Essential is the thinking itself. As argued in the preceding chapters, gravitational thinking is a hallmark of social philosopher Oskar Negt and multimedia polymath Alexander

Kluge's four decades of collaborations. Their need to expand the breadth of their gravitational thinking eventually brought them to engage other thinkers. As demonstrated in the first four chapters of *Dark Matter*, markedly different thinkers far less sympathetic to their Frankfurt roots found astonishingly productive roles in their thinking process. Their objective was often to work through seminal problems regarding thinking itself, labor, community, and the political. The second half of *Dark Matter* underscored how gravitational thinking also forms the bedrock of Kluge's aesthetic praxis in all his chosen mediums.

If what separates Negt and Kluge is not their loyalty to the Frankfurt School but rather their vocations—theory and the aesthetic—then what remains to be addressed in sustained fashion is whether or not gravitational thinking adheres to the core principles of critical theory. For gravitational thinking to remain true to the tenets of both thinkers' intellectual roots, would not both need to hail from the same school or tradition? Can an author be trusted with carrying the torch alone without theoretical oversight on hand? When thinking together, Kluge and Negt are unequivocal in their allegiance to critique. "*Critique behaves inequitably toward misery*," they write in *History and Obstinacy*.[1] But without Negt's counterbalance, Kluge has sometimes seemed to come untethered from his professed roots. Fellow Frankfurt School scion and essayist Michael Rutschky exclaimed in 2000, for example, that when let loose and unchecked by the likes of Negt, Kluge was uncharacteristically uncritical. In spite of his long professed allegiance to the chief rabbis of critical theory—"Walter Benjamin, Adorno, Bloch, Marx"—nothing seems "more alien to [Kluge] than *Ideologiekritik*, the dismantling of false consciousness."[2] Adorno's crucial lesson in differentiating negation from affirmation often seems to elude Kluge entirely. Given the chance, Kluge would surely talk to Adorno's arch nemesis Martin Heidegger. Nevertheless, Kluge has regularly insisted that critique does play a role in his work. A cursory glance at just some of his claims to critique confirms

---

1 Alexander Kluge and Oskar Negt, *History and Obstinacy*, ed. Devin Fore, trans. Richard Langston et al. (New York: Zone Books, 2014) 200.

2 Alexander Kluge, *Die Macht der Gefühle* (Frankfurt am Main: Zweitausendeins, 1984) 178; Michael Rutschky, "Quasseln und Lakonik," *die tageszeitung* (December 16, 2000): 13; I am following here: Christian Schulte, "Kritik und Kairos: Essayismus zwischen den Medien bei Alexander Kluge," in *Inszenierung und Gedächtnis: Soziokulturelle und ästhetische Praxis*, eds. Hermann Blume et al. (Bielefeld: transcript Verlag, 2014) 250–54.

that he has long taken to heart his and Negt's claim from *Geschichte und Eigensinn* that "there is not just one form of critique but many."[3] Critique, he proffered in his Frankfurt poetics lectures held in 2012, is the continuation of poetics by other means. In an interview from 2000, he claimed that critique is a heightened faculty to differentiate.[4] "Critique," he reiterated in 2007, "is the positive capacity to differentiate between something new and an old falsehood."[5] Critique is what every film never made does toward every movie brought to life.[6] And critique is what narration does when it pits subjective experience against the reigning power of intelligence fueled by algorithms and information capital. In closing, *Dark Matter* motions for adding orientation to this list. Critique for Negt and Kluge can also manifest itself in the search for orientation that leads to ways out of the reality principle's hallmarks: immaturity (in the Kantian sense), alienation, and oppression. Yet there is no guarantee that orientation is intrinsically critical. Not only can techniques for orientation serve nefarious aims, but modernity's catastrophes can uproot our frames of reference entirely making the search for ways out virtually impossible.[7] If "migratory birds orient themselves … amidst the storm," how, Kluge asks, can we humans do the same?[8] A far greater challenge than storms raging outside are the challenges to achieving orientation from within. Our powers of perception can often pit, for example, one constituent of orientation against another. In order for it to retain its critical power, orientation must retain practical tools capable of "measuring the relations of relationships" and to this end Negt and Kluge's gravitational thinking has persisted since the millennium as a pillar of Kluge's

---

3 Oskar Negt and Alexander Kluge, *Geschichte und Eigensinn*, in *Der unterschätzte Mensch: Gemeinsame Philosophie in zwei Bänden*, vol. 2 (Frankfurt am Main: Zweitausendeins, 2001) 475.

4 Alexander Kluge, *Verdeckte Ermittlung: Ein Gespräch mit Christian Schulte und Rainer Stollmann* (Berlin: Merve Verlag, 2001) 49.

5 Alexander Kluge, "Critique, Up Close and Personal," trans. Emma Woelk, in *Difference and Orientation: An Alexander Kluge Reader*, ed. Richard Langston (Ithaca, NY: Cornell University Press, 2019) 440.

6 Alexander Kluge, "Das Nichtverfilmte kritisierte das Verfilmte," in *In Gefahr und größter Not bringt der Mittelweg den Tod: Texte zu Kino, Film, Politik* (Berlin: Vorwerk 8, 1999) 60.

7 Alexander Kluge, "Theory of Storytelling: Lecture One," trans. Nathan Wagner, in *Difference and Orientation*, 101.

8 Alexander Kluge, "Die Poetische Kraft der Theorie," *Alexander Kluge-Jahrbuch* 6 (2019): 31, 43.

encounters with others often radically different than both Negt and himself.[9] Certainly not the first but arguably one of the most productive of his many recent collaborations in the art museum, Kluge's dialogues with painter Anselm Kiefer not only revolve around some of the many challenges to orientation but they also reveal how Kluge has succeeded in retaining orientation's critical potential with the help of his longstanding relational poetics.

*

In one of many televised interviews with Oskar Negt about Immanuel Kant, Alexander Kluge's September 2005 broadcast entitled "Thinking for Oneself" takes a sharp turn backward in time to the subject matter that concluded *Geschichte und Eigensinn* from 1981. "What," Kluge asks his longtime collaborator, "is the philosopher Immanuel Kant's relationship to the stars?"[10] After reciting from the conclusion to Kant's *Critique of Practical Reason*—"*the starry heavens above me and the moral law within me*"—Negt underscores how for Kant "the metaphor [of] the stars plays a big role," only then to have Kluge finish his sentence with the words "for orientation."[11] In contradistinction to what Max Horkheimer and Theodor W. Adorno call "the basic text of European civilization," namely Homer's tale of the Phoenician sailor Odysseus who navigated according to celestial bodies, Negt and Kluge maintain at the close of *Geschichte und Eigensinn* that the history of continental Europe knows no such orientational prospects.[12] Instead of Odysseus's and Kant's starry heavens, central Europe of both high and late modernity is more like the fantastic stuff of a sailor's yarn with its tales of "fog banks," "whirlpools," and fabled "magnetic mountains" capable of tearing ships asunder.[13] To the question of what to do when our sense of trust can rely on neither external constants nor bodily organs capable of sensing, such as, for

---

9 Negt and Kluge 1002.

10 Alexander Kluge, dir., "Selbstdenken: Immanuel Kants Schrift: Was heißt: sich im Denken orientieren?," *10 Till 11*, September 19, 2005, https://kluge.library.cornell.edu/conversations/negt/film/2114.

11 Kluge, "Selbstdenken." See also: Immanuel Kant, "Critique of Practical Reason," in *Practical Philosophy*, ed. and trans. Mary J. Gregor (Cambridge: Cambridge University Press, 1996) 269.

12 Max Horkheimer and Theodor W. Adorno, *Dialectic of Enlightenment: Philosophical Fragments*, trans. Edmund Jephcott (Stanford: Stanford University Press, 2002) 37.

13 Negt and Kluge 1004.

example, a bat's echolocation or a bird's magnetoreception, Negt and Kluge propose the juxtaposition and collaboration of three orientational practices—the commentary, the dialogue, and experimentation—modeled after the ascetic scribe St. Jerome, Heinrich von Kleist's spoken discourse with his sister, and the restless experimenter Galileo Galilei who leaves the cave and ventures out "into the prairie."[14] Yet, when sized up against the "monsters of experience" like wars between enemies or even lovers, these techniques for orientation reveal their Achilles' heel. Since they require both calm and concentration, they cannot compete with the haste typical of more instinctive defense mechanisms like the psychology of introjection, projection, substitution, and displacement. Orientation requires extra time, they say, something invariably in short supply, especially in catastrophic times.

What appears puzzling if not downright troubling is the intensity with which Kluge has reappraised elsewhere the starry heavens, especially since the new millennium. Of the three aforementioned orders of orientation it is the third modeled after Galileo—the exploration of great distances and the expansion of our horizons—that appears at face value to have consumed him the most. If we imagine momentarily Negt and Kluge's guidelines for promoting practical orientation as a rebuttal to Georg Lukács's grim assertion some sixty-five years earlier that "Kant's starry firmament ... no longer lights any ... path," then Kluge's seemingly new, amplified interest in the heavens, in general, and the scientific disciplines relevant to physical cosmology, in particular, just might seem to suggest that the fog has finally lifted and the stars are twinkling brighter than ever before.[15] There are, to be sure, ample correspondences that suggest the upswing, beginning around the year 2000, in the number of Kluge's conversations with astrophysicists as well as his many stories about the cosmos consciously follows on the heels of cosmological breakthroughs made since the nineties. (Indeed, Kluge has drawn considerable attention to the quantity of dramatic breakthroughs in scientific knowledge including, but certainly not limited to, the field of astrophysics.)[16] Yet the science of the Big Bang, supernovas, and black

14 Negt and Kluge 1006, 1009.
15 Georg Lukács, *The Theory of the Novel: A Historico-Philosophical Essay on the Forms of Great Epic Literature*, trans. Anna Bostock (Cambridge, MA: MIT Press, 1971) 36.
16 Alexander Kluge, "'Ich liebe das Lakonische,'" *Der Spiegel*, 45 (November 6, 2000): 336.

holes—all matters of great interest to Kluge—is hardly serviceable for orientation in the "literal sense" that so concerned him and Negt well over twenty years earlier.[17] One need not know the intricacies of the science to realize that mariners and wanderers could never find their way through this world using cosmic phenomena like dark matter neither visible nor directly accessible to the unaided human eye. So, while Negt and Kluge may have indeed rehashed decades later the Kantian core of their prescription for orientation, one is left to wonder whether Kluge's own contemporary interests in the heavens have retreated away from what he and Negt identified as the antipode to practical orientation, namely "mere knowledge."[18] When grasped solely in terms of that third Galilean form of orientation (i.e., "the exploration of long-term effects by way of experimentation") Kluge's interviews with expert astrophysicists can seem like "bizarre tidbits" of "specialized knowledge," as Miriam Hansen once argued.[19] But Kluge's interest in the cosmos also taps into that first, more introverted order of orientation modeled after St. Jerome who wrote his scriptural commentaries in a cave—"a second skin," Negt and Kluge explain—far removed from the outside world. The most basic form of orientation, they contend, begins with feelings rooted in the "body's internal processes" and this orientation finds its emblematic expression in St. Jerome's penchant for pouring his living labor into writing commentaries about "the dead thought" captured in books.[20]

Negt and Kluge have given this other order of orientation different names over time—among them "antirealism," "obstinacy," and "the political"—but the common denominator has always been its source, a reservoir full of other kinds of feelings that "protest against unbearable relations."[21] In *History and Obstinacy*, Kluge and Negt initially lead us to believe that these feelings of protest are wholly terrestrial in nature; the innate characteristics of human cells and organs—unchanged for

---

17 Negt and Kluge 1002.

18 Negt and Kluge 1002.

19 Negt and Kluge 1010; Miriam Hansen, "Fictional Experts: Role-Play and Authority in Kluge's Work," *Maske und Kothurn: Internationale Beiträge zur Theater-, Film-, und Medienwissenschaft* 53.1 (2007): 69, 71.

20 Negt and Kluge 1007.

21 Alexander Kluge, "The Sharpest Ideology: That Reality Appeals to Its Realistic Character," trans. David Roberts, in *Alexander Kluge: Raw Materials for the Imagination*, ed. Tara Forrest (Amsterdam: Amsterdam University Press, 2012) 193; see also: Kluge and Negt 139.

thousands and thousands of years—are resolute in their resistance to the demands of historical progress propelled forward by capital. Individual cells, they go on to say, take orders from neither reason nor its masters.[22] But, then, it is presumably Kluge, the volume's co-illustrator, who catches readers by surprise by casting these feelings into outer space in a short, untranslated section of *Geschichte und Eigensinn* entitled "Unfulfilled Program" that begins with an image of an infant's developing neurons and closes with another of an electroencephalogram captioned "No human brain has ever seen stars."[23] Sandwiched in between are still more images including ones of the Milky Way, Jupiter, Saturn, and their moons, and the equally perplexing assertion "Cells know everything from here to the stars, but the mind [*der Kopf*] has never experienced any such thing and thus has never forgotten it either."[24] Cast in the language of Kant's first *Critique*, the second half of this proposition is largely unremarkable for it echoes Kant's own characterization of the second of his three regulative principles, which nature, the world, and the cosmos undergird, as a transcendental idea of pure reason beyond both experience and intuition.[25] As such, the cosmos in its infiniteness can be neither remembered nor forgotten. Turning to the first half of Negt and Kluge's axiom, however, readers attuned to Kant are left to wonder what on earth the authors exactly mean. How is it possible that our own cells possess transcendent knowledge of the universe unfettered by Kant's seminal distinctions between the world of phenomenal appearances and the world of unknowable *noumena*? In other words, how can the cellular labor of St. Jerome the commentator be at the same time like Galileo's measurements of the moon, the planets, and the stars? Instead of charging Negt and Kluge with the fatal flaw of transcendental realism, as Kant himself might do, we must look for answers to this conundrum elsewhere, for Negt and Kluge's fleeting reference to cellular knowledge about the cosmos seems to suggest that a messy entanglement of orientation's different orders has emerged in late modernity's disruptive times. If, as Negt and Kluge have argued, "no single form of orientational labor can achieve anything cohesive on its own," then how can any

22 Kluge and Negt 105.

23 Negt and Kluge 153.

24 Negt and Kluge 151.

25 Immanuel Kant, *Critique of Pure Reason*, trans. Paul Guyer and Allen W. Wood (Cambridge: Cambridge University Press, 1998) 606–13.

cooperation among all three orders of orientation successfully transpire when one assumes the guise (not to mention the effects) of another?[26] How is the critical power of orientation still at all possible when the difference between its orders collapse?

Alchemical Correspondences

If there is one interest that binds all five of Kluge's remarkable interviews with the artist Anselm Kiefer—Kiefer later described them as the rarest form of "spiritual communication"—then it is without question the protoscience of alchemy.[27] Filmed in galleries on the occasion of solo exhibitions, in Kiefer's Parisian home, and at his studio in the south of France, the interviews take place among the artist's distinctive large-format, mixed-media paintings; his glass vitrines filled with sundry objects; and his massive, site-specific installations. Enraptured by the images around him as well as the artist's muses and methods, Kluge repeatedly pitches his interlocutor questions regarding his approach to orientation. Asked in their first interview from late 2010 about the significance of tunnels in Kiefer's two-hundred-acre studio, for example, the artist points to seventeenth-century English Paracelsian Robert Fludd's Kabbalistic cosmology: "The original idea was the seven heavenly palaces from merkabah mysticism ... I built terrestrial palaces out of glass and through the tunnels you can descend into the earth ... The idea from merkabah mysticism is the same as Robert Fludd's that when someone ascends, they simultaneously descend."[28] A year later at Kiefer's exhibition in Salzburg, Kluge asks of the show's principal painting, "What does the word *alkahest* mean that I see up there?" "That refers," Kiefer replies, "to a substance in alchemy capable of dissolving everything."[29] After a third interview in the

---

26 Negt and Kluge 868.

27 Anselm Kiefer, "'Alexander, You Are a Particle Accelerator,'" trans. Martin Brady and Helen Hughes, *Alexander Kluge-Jahrbuch* 2 (2015): 181.

28 Alexander Kluge, dir., "Gärten zweier Welten: Anselm Kiefer über das geheime Leben der Kunst," *News & Stories*, SAT.1, January 16, 2011. This and all subsequent television dialogues with Kiefer can be found on the box set of DVDs: Anseln Kiefer and Alexander Kluge, *Dancing with Pictures: Films and Dialogues* (Berlin: Suhrkamp Verlag, 2017).

29 Alexander Kluge, dir. "Alkahest: Anselm Kiefers neuer Werkzyklus in der Galarie Thaddaeus Ropac in Salzburg," *News & Stories*, SAT.1, October 9, 2011.

south of France also peppered with alchemical references, Kluge finally gets Kiefer to come clean while at home in Paris: "Everyone knows that you have a love for alchemy, but would you say that you are an alchemist in the truest sense of the word?" Without hesitation, Kiefer answers in the affirmative and, when asked whether alchemy is akin to gardening—a recurring metaphor for Kluge's own aesthetic practice intent on "building connections between places, people, and situations"—Kiefer demurs: "There's a difference," he insists.[30] "Unlike the alchemist, the gardener respects the laws of nature. The alchemist wants springtime twice in row without any of the other seasons in between. That's why it's so dangerous."[31] In their fifth interview from June 2016, Kluge's inquiry into Kiefer's preferred mode of orientation hits yet another telling snag. As to whether Kiefer has one role model above all, Kluge offers up options and thereby attributes to Kiefer's art, on account of its extensive allusions to modern literature, that first order from his and Negt's program for orientation, namely St. Jerome's penchant for commentary:

KLUGE: You essentially still comment on writers like Hölderlin, Ingeborg Bachmann, Paul Celan, and Rimbaud.
KIEFER: No, I don't comment, I make correspondences.[32]

In spite of the exceptional synergy between the two, it would appear that Kluge initially misrecognized Kiefer's art and the orientation sought therein. Whereas Kluge saw in Kiefer the kind of cellular work typical of St. Jerome the commentator, Kiefer actually aligned his interests according to the very same experimental orientation that consumed Kluge in the new millennium. However, there is much more to Kluge and Kiefer's dialogues than just a case of crossed wires.

At the heart of all alchemy, Karen Pinkus has explained, is "the admixture of opposites, dominated by the couple *inside* and *outside*."[33] While

30 Kluge and Negt 389; see also Alexander Kluge, "Der Autor als Dompteur oder Gärtner," in *Personen und Reden: Lessing, Böll, Huch, Schiller, Adorno, Habermas, Müller, Augstein, Gaus, Schlingensief, Ad me ipsum* (Berlin: Verlag Klaus Wagenbach, 2012) 26.

31 Alexander Kluge, dir., "Ein Vormittag mit Anselm Kiefer: Gespräch im Atlier des Künstlers bei Paris," *News & Stories*, SAT.1, August 3, 2014.

32 Alexander Kluge, dir., "Der mit den Bildern tanzt," *News & Stories*, SAT.1, June 29, 2016.

33 Karen Pinkus, *Alchemical Mercury: A Theory of Ambivalence* (Stanford: Stanford University Press, 2010) 5.

Kiefer does explicitly address with Kluge familiar alchemical themes in his paintings like the philosopher's stone as well as attendant esoteric subject matter like Hermeticism, Neoplatonism, and Gnosticism, it is the figure of the sunflower that Kiefer associates most closely in his interviews with his predisposition to forge correspondences. Dating back to the mid-nineties when Kiefer pivoted away from his long-standing pre-occupation with German history, "mature sunflowers," he expounds in his third interview with Kluge, "always reminded me of the firmament ... I've often laid down in fields of sunflowers where the mature ones point their heads downward. If you look up, you see nothing but galaxies" (see fig. 9.1).[34] In his second interview with Kluge, Kiefer further explains the link between sunflowers and stars displayed in a brief sequence from their first encounter, in which a gallerist flips through Kiefer's large-format 1996 book entitled *For Robert Fludd*. A contemporary of Galileo, Fludd, says Kiefer,

> was a Rosicrucian, possibly a freemason, both an alchemist and chemist, and a philosopher who united everything together ... Initially, I only knew a single sentence by him: *every flower on earth has its correspondence in heaven in the form of a star*. This ... fascinated me so much because [Fludd] devised a relation between the macrocosmos and microcosmos that Einstein failed ... to achieve.[35]

There are certainly many correspondences subtending Fludd's mystical alchemy—e.g., the sun's status as heavenly heart; its metabolic connection to the human heart; divine, life-giving light and the unknowable darkness where god's oneness resides—that resonate in Kiefer's many reworkings of this union of sunflower and cosmos.[36] Far from imputing Fludd's medico-theosophical aims to Kiefer's design, some have convincingly attributed to the artist's work an infatuation with what Michel

34 Daniel Arasse, *Anselm Kiefer*, trans. Mary Whitthall (London: Thames & Hudson Ltd., 2001) 187–88; Alexander Kluge, dir., "Die Ungeborenen: Begegnung mit Anselm Kiefer in seinem Atelier in Croissy-Beauregard," *News & Stories*, SAT.1, September 1, 2013.

35 Kluge, "Alkahest."

36 Allen G. Debus, *The English Paracelsians* (London: Oldbourne, 1965) 113–15; see also Wilhelm Schmidt-Biggemann, "Robert Fludd's Kabbalistic Cosmos," trans. Geoff Dumbreck and Douglas Hedley, in *Platonism at the Origins of Modernity: Studies on Platonism and Early Modern Philosophy*, eds. Douglas Hedley and Sarah Hutton (Dordrecht: Springer, 2008) 83.

Foucault labeled—citing another contemporary alchemist who wrote "the stars are the matrix of all the plants"—the Renaissance's episteme rooted in the logic of resemblance.[37] At stake in Kiefer's employ of the logic of resemblance is nothing less than an alchemical admixture of two orders of orientation as outlined by Negt and Kluge: the commentary of St. Jerome and the experimentation of Galileo. Kluge begins to recognize the alchemical nature of Kiefer's thinking when in another interview he asks him what he thinks about the glacial pace of tectonic shifts. "There's, of course, the relativity of time," Kiefer replies, "I've always felt extremely at ease there because I feel transported into another time."

> KLUGE: Another reality?
>
> KIEFER: Another, real reality where I feel at home. There exist three temporalities: cosmological time, geological time, and our time. If I harness myself to cosmic time, then right away I'm naturally much more at peace because I then have more time ahead of me.
>
> KLUGE: And this time is relevant for us because our cells know all about it.
>
> KIEFER: Certainly. Not just the mind but cells, too, contain our memories. Cells are memory to begin with.
>
> KLUGE: Three stars must cease to exist in order for that matter to develop, of which our cells are made ... This is what you're dealing with when you say something like "Every flower has its star."
>
> KIEFER: Yes, yes. And then I tether the earthly to the cosmic ...
>
> KLUGE: It's sometimes been said that the [cosmos] is also a creature that just reacts differently than we do.
>
> ...
>
> KIEFER: I think there's life that we can't even see. Perhaps there's life here next to us that we don't see but is nevertheless there.
>
> KLUGE: A parallel world.
>
> KIEFER: Right here on this very spot ... And we don't yet have the equipment [to see it]. I see perhaps only one-tenth of what exists.

---

37 Cf. Arasse 262–67; Foucault is quoting from German alchemist Oswald Croll's 1609 *De signaturis internis rerum*. See: *The Order of Things: An Archaeology of the Human Sciences* (New York: Vintage Books, 1973) 20. Compare this also with Walter Benjamin's observation from "One Way Street" that "the ancients' intercourse with the cosmos had been different: the ecstatic trance." See: "One Way Street," trans. Edmund Jephcott, in *Selected Writings*, vol. 1: *1913–1926*, eds. Marcus Bulloch and Michael W. Jennings (Cambridge, MA: Belknap Press, 1996) 486.

KLUGE: But that's something art can do with its capacity for intuition.
KIEFER: Yes.[38]

Whereas Kluge initially anticipated having to meet Kiefer half way by imputing to his work that introverted form of orientation personified by St. Jerome, Kiefer responds with nothing less than an alchemical variation of Negt and Kluge's own enigmatic allusion in *Geschichte und Eigensinn* to the body's cellular knowledge of the cosmos. Quite suddenly, Negt and Kluge appear more like alchemists than ever before, or so it would seem. Whereas orientation, as Negt and Kluge define it in *Geschichte und Eigensinn*, queries the hardness of existing conditions in order to find ways out, feelings are defensive, insofar as they "vehemently obstruct this hardness" of reality due to their conviction in reality's changeability.[39] But, as Kiefer himself suggests above, and as Kluge concurs, this change is far more fundamental than just searching for the next available exit out of the "unbearable relations" endemic to terrestrial reality. Instead, it presumes the existence of other realities or worlds characterized, above all, by temporalities different than our own, slower realities to which we can tether ourselves and thereby acquire more time than what is otherwise at our disposal, realities that quite possibly shelter life forms about which we know nothing, life forms that the work of art is purportedly well suited to intuit. For such otherworldly realities to come into view, orientation must transcend its concrete telluric foundations. St. Jerome and Galileo must join forces. Cells and stars must find their common thread. If "cells know everything from here to the stars," then that "everything" pertains to states of radical alterity—other possible times and spaces where other beings dwell—all because we're literally made of stars. From the vantage point of unbearable suffering, radical alterity represents a model way out; however, from the vantage point of critique, it threatens to turn orientation into escapism.

On the Limits of Metaphysical Being

Speaking on the occasion of Kluge's acceptance of the 2014 Heinrich Heine Prize, Kiefer extolled Kluge's prose in his laudation, not for its

---

38 Kluge, "Gärten zweier Welten."
39 Negt and Kluge 868.

correspondences but rather for its voids: "The real essence of your books," he explained, "is in what is left out." "We both love this empty space."[40] It is certainly no mystery to those familiar with Kluge's theory of cinematic montage that the "concrete relations between two images," so paradigmatic for his feature films, seeks to flag as a cipher that which no human eye can see and what no camera can show.[41] Montage, Kluge adds, is no different than what the seafaring Odysseus does when he takes measurements in order to orient himself according to the stars.[42] An indirect solution to the problem that arises when social relations slip into what Bertolt Brecht called the functional dimension and then become abstract, this principle of relationality applies equally, Kluge insists, to his literature (see figure 1.4). In his 2012 lectures on poetics held in Frankfurt, he explained, for example, that "storytelling require[s] that contrasts are left open such that there's a story here and another there and a third somewhere else in space. In so doing, a narrative space emerges that's not identical to any one single story but rather lays bare so much in-between space such that the remainders—what is untold—can be sensed."[43] For all the implied similarities between the formal worlds of Kluge's film and literature, there is arguably at least one, if not several, crucial differences. Whereas Kluge's theory of cinematic montage once advocated montage's abilities to index the functional by using contrasting images, literary montage has advanced—at least in some of Kluge's most recent prose—as a tool for detecting indirectly what cells already "know." Yet a closer look at Kluge's literary collaborations with Kiefer reveals few if any traces of the alchemical admixtures and conceptual entanglements found in their aforementioned exchanges. Unlike the many other worlds so central in Kluge's storybook *Tür an Tür mit einem anderen Leben* [Next Door to Another Life] (2006), for example, his stories written in direct dialogue with Kiefer's paintings are decidedly anti-alchemical.

In conjunction with Kiefer's exhibition entitled "The Unborn" held at Thaddaeus Ropac's Parisian gallery in 2012, Kluge dedicated to Kiefer seventeen stories, "the center of which"—he explains in his introductory

---

40 Kiefer 181.

41 Alexander Kluge, "On Film and the Public Sphere," trans. Thomas Y. Levin and Miriam B. Hansen, in *Alexander Kluge: Raw Materials for the Imagination*, 46.

42 Kluge, "On Film and the Public Sphere," 47–48.

43 Alexander Kluge, "Erzählraum des Nichterzählten," in *Theorie der Erzählung: Frankfurter Poetikvorlesung* (Berlin: Suhrkamp Verlag, 2013) disc 2, track 2.

remarks—"lies in [Kiefer's] paintings."[44] This conceit proves to be, however, a ruse already in the first story, entitled "Between the Cosmos and the Thames," for there exists no such painting in Kiefer's catalogue that corresponds to Kluge's story. Inspired by a segment from their first dialogue about Kiefer's iconoclasm as exemplified by a pair of roller skates he once found in the Thames River, Kluge's story begins as Odysseus would—by measuring the stars.[45] With the help of optical equipment—readers are told—stargazers can use the principle of stellar parallax to measure three deep-space objects including the star cluster Pleiades, once vital for ancient mariners on the Mediterranean Sea, in order to triangulate our solar system precisely with respect to the center of the Milky Way. "Thirty thousand light years separate the starfield we call home from the core of our galaxy."[46] This pithy preamble abruptly shifts away from matters of Galilean orientation occurring at some undisclosed location on earth and transports us readers to the University of Leiden, where astrophysicist Simon Portegies Zwart crunches data at the oldest university observatory in the world. Rather than looking up directly into the heavens, Zwart (whose fitting surname is derived from the proto-Germanic for "black") relies on computers that compile data— strings of numbers and symbols—into a map that only computers could ever conceive:

> At night the data dreams, he says. Were they let loose, they would unite to form a MIGHTY STAR CHART that reveals a PATH orbiting majestically around the center of the galaxy. No admiral could ever helm such a convoy. Gravitational storms as well as curvatures in time and space, caused when massive bodies and collisions of stars and galaxies emit gravitational waves, nudge them from their trajectory.[47]

---

44 Alexander Kluge, introduction to Anselm Kiefer, *Die Ungeborenen* (Paris: Galerie Thaddaeus Ropac, 2012) 129.

45 See, Kluge, "Gärten zweier Welten":
KIEFER: I once found in the Thames at low tide a roller skate completely rusted and covered in mud. That would be an emblem that could possible serve that purpose.
KLUGE: You still have it?
KIEFER: Oh yes, it's waiting. […] I have shelves full of found objects, all of which are waiting for their context.

46 Alexander Kluge, "Zwischen Kosmos und Themse," in Anselm Kiefer, *Die Ungeborenen* (Paris: Galerie Thaddaeus Ropac, 2012) 130.

47 Kluge, "Zwischen Kosmos und Themse," 130.

Without ever saying so explicity, this second station indexes just how far removed contemporary astrophysics is from the older concerns of experimental orientation; rather than venturing out into the world, Zwart retreats like St. Jerome into cave full of dreaming computers. The story's final station concludes with Kiefer and his rescued roller skates, which he later adds to his Parisian collection of disused objects waiting to become part of a future work of art. Regardless of what the future holds for the skates, the narrative voice maintains that the found object is much like Kiefer's sunflowers. It not only corresponds to the speeds and distances our galaxy has traveled, but it also records earth's geological time. "In this respect," the narrator asserts, "not only plants but also things are connected to the cosmos."[48] Referring to an imaginary painting that Kiefer never made, the narrator finally proclaims, "Images of this sort, neither abstract nor representational, are alchemical devices of the spirit."[49]

As much as Kluge's narrator appears in the end to champion the alchemy subtending Kiefer's aesthetic of mystical correspondences, there are significant differences between the former's prose and the latter's painting, differences that underscore just how far apart Negt and Kluge's cellular knowledge really is from Kiefer's alchemy. In spite of its title's interest in measuring geographic distances, Kluge's story actually belongs to that first order of orientation. "My actual literary form," Kluge explained in an interview from 2008, "is that of the commentary. Commentaries tend to create constellations." This is why Kluge also cautions us from "grasp[ing] stories in isolation but rather always in relationship to others."[50] Instead of providing readers with a robust narrative replete with fleshed-out characters in crisis, the first station in his story-cum-commentary elucidates the viability of Galileo's approach to measuring the stars for cosmic orientation. The second one explicates how data science threatens to render experimental orientation wholly unintelligible to the human mind.[51] At first glance, the third station reads like marginalia on the process and meaning of Kiefer's painterly alchemy.

---

48 Kluge, "Zwischen Kosmos und Themse," 130.

49 Kluge, "Zwischen Kosmos und Themse," 130.

50 Alexander Kluge, "Storytelling Means Dissolving Relations," trans. Emma Woelk, in *Difference and Orientation*, 92.

51 On data science's constitution of a new order of second nature, Kluge writes: "It remains to be seen whether or not we are able to apprehend the new signs of the algorithms, data networks, and Artificial Intelligence in their true dimensions." Alexander Kluge, "Reading and Writing: How Can I Live? How Can I Know? What Does the Future

However, by virtue of the sequential differences that Kluge's juxtaposed stations throw into relief, all three operate together as a commentary on three historical iterations of experimental orientation. The third station is especially significant insofar as it initially seems to provide a protoscientific commentary on the scientific extravagences in the previous station. Yet a significant substitution transpires in this third station that not only parts ways with the primacy of the natural world in Kiefer's alchemy but also clarifies an essential difference between Negt and Kluge's materialist understanding of cellular knowledge and Kiefer's far more mystical grasp of the astral body. In lieu of Kiefer's sunflowers and the otherwise hidden cosmic fabric to which it is pinned, Kluge imagines a future painting by Kiefer that incorporates a disused commodity. By reclaiming the roller skates from their watery grave, this painting would salvage the dead labor that succumbed to the logic of obsolescence long ago. In so doing, it would also recast this labor into temporal relationships much longer in scope than the already long-range time frames according to which capital organizes itself. Instead of pinning the skates to the "time of machines" and their owners, Kluge's imagined Kiefer painting would yoke the dead labor of the skates to the times, speeds, and spaces of the cosmos. Still ticking long after the cells that brought it into being perished—the narrator decrees that "the roller skates are a CLOCK"—the dead labor petrified within the commodity is transformed under the aegis of the work of art into a chronograph capable of keeping both earthly and cosmic time.[52] While this imagined afterlife of the commodity would entail for Kluge a certain reanimation of subjective-objective relations, it would be neither mystical nor metaphysical as is the case with Kiefer's sunflowers. That Kluge's story must imagine a painting that Kiefer himself would never conceivably make is significant, for the dimension of human labor—at the heart of which lies cells either willing or unwilling to comply to the relations of production—is entirely foreign to his interests in mysticism and myth.[53] At that moment when Kluge and Kiefer seem to speak like kindred spirits, it turns out that their understanding of human cells and their relation to human life, earth, and the universe is really worlds apart. What initially appeared like identical instances of entangled orders of

---

Hold?," in *The New Alphabet: Opening Days*, eds. Bernd Scherer and Olga von Schubert (Berlin: HKW, 2019) 34.

52 Kluge and Negt 129; Kluge, "Zwischen Kosmos und Themse," 130.

53 Kluge and Negt, 102–3.

orientation—a potentially uncritical conflation of the internal workings of the body with experiments on the natural world—is in fact Kluge's poetic mobilization of the *longue durée* in order to reinsert the human factor back into our present-day posthuman world in which computers dream up maps that no human could ever put to practical use in order to find ways out of the reality principle. Compared to the historical transformations of experimental orientation, that other dimension of orientation—commentary—proves resolutely critical when fragmented and arranged into a constellation insofar as its montage casts light on not just what has gone missing but how poetics can imagine alternatives that harness our capacity to differentiate.

"Tied to the realm of aesthetics," Pinkus argues, "alchemy is not the normal business of ... philosophers."[54] And yet so much of what binds Kiefer and Kluge together is their mutual love for thinking together, what Negt and Kluge call the second Kleistian order of orientation, namely discourse in the "company of another person."[55] "I'm not really a painter at heart," Kiefer confessed in his second interview with Kluge, "rather I think through painting."[56] Given the well-known importance of Theodor W. Adorno for Kluge's own thinking through stories and images, it is remarkable to consider in hindsight just how much common ground Kluge's and Kiefer's gravitational thinking finds in spite of Kiefer's long-recognized indebtedness to Adorno's nemesis, Martin Heidegger.[57] It all boils down perhaps to Kiefer's and Kluge's shared investment in a single, albeit contentious word. There is a short passage in *Negative Dialectics* where Adorno revels in picking apart what he sees as Heidegger's deeply problematic case for the "metaphysical dignity of being."[58] In Heidegger's "Letter on 'Humanism,'" he contends that "the essence of the human being consists in his being more than merely human."[59] Heidegger is quick to qualify the "more" as what is "more originally and therefore

54 Karen Pinkus, *Alchemical Mercury: A Theory of Ambivalence* (Stanford, CA: Stanford University Press, 2010) 5.

55 Negt and Kluge 1009.

56 Kluge, "Alkahest."

57 Matthew Biro, *Anselm Kiefer and the Philosophy of Martin Heidegger* (Cambridge: Cambridge University Press, 1998).

58 Theodor W. Adorno, *Negative Dialectics*, trans. E.B. Ashton (New York: Continuum, 1995) 105.

59 Martin Heidegger, "Letter on 'Humanism,'" trans. Frank A Capuzzi, in *Pathmarks*, ed. William McNeill (Cambridge: Cambridge University Press, 1998) 260.

more essentially in terms of [man's] essence." What troubled Adorno
so deeply about "the more" is not the importance Heidegger places on
it so much as where it resides; jettisoned beyond both the subject and
the object, Heidegger's "more" forecloses thinking altogether, something
Adorno flat out rejects. "No concept would be thinkable," he counters,
"indeed none would even be possible without the 'more.'"[60] So, instead of
discarding the more like that roller skate abandoned in the Thames, he
retrieves it and weaves into being: "What echoes in the word 'Being' ... :
that everything is more than it is."[61] According to Gerhard Schweppenhäuser, "metaphysical experience for Adorno is actually the anticipation
of happiness." It comports itself, however, negatively, especially in the
work of art where it asks over and over again, "Can this be everything?"[62]
Left entirely to his own devices, Kiefer may have just chosen to channel
Heidegger's infatuation with Friedrich Hölderlin as a model for art's aspiration to unify heaven and earth as a "more tender infinite relation."[63]
But instead of opting for what Adorno disparaged as Heidegger's call for
absolute appearance, he momentarily goes along with Kluge. Regardless
of who follows whom, it is in that abaric point where the two meet and
where their gravitational thinking about the conditions of possibility
for the more transpires. That Kluge the storyteller later returns to his
center of gravity to reimagine a more materialist Kiefer should, however,
not eclipse the fact that both agree that the more is anchored not only
into our cells but also in the voids of space—dark matter—that science
and the aesthetic can detect indirectly and that bring the promise of this
more—happiness—to resonate forth.

60 Adorno 106.
61 Adorno 106.
62 Gerhard Schweppenhäuser, *Die Antinomie des Universalismus: Zum moralphi-
losophischen Diskurs der Moderne* (Würzburg: Königshausen & Neumann, 2005) 290;
Adorno 375.
63 Martin Heidegger, "Hölderlin's Earth and Heaven," in *Elucidations of Hölderlin's
Poetry*, trans. Keith Hoeller (New York: Humanity Books, 2000) 187.

Index

on "temporal core" *(Zeitkern)*, 123
on tension between internal feeling
    and external action, 74–5
Theoriearbeit (theory labor), 24
on theory labor, 78, 150–1, 157
theory of intelligence, 93
theory of knowledge, 89–90
theory of learning processes, 63, 98
on "third parties," 262
Überlebensglück (The Luck of
    Survival), 143–4, 292
on unfulfilled program, 39
"The Wolf and the Seven Young
    Kids" (Der Wolf und die sieben
    Gießlein), 121–2, 136
on working brain, 74–5, 76f
Nelson, Leonard, 252
Netzwerke (networks), 163–9, 167n92
Neumann, Franz, 181
neural pathways, 87f
neutral point, 25–6
New Left, 82
new order of second nature, 329–30n51
*News from Ideological Antiquity: Marx-
    Eisenstein-Capital*, 220f, 221–4,
    227–37, 239–40
News & Stories (TV program), 14, 250,
    314f
Niagara, Horseshoe Falls (film), 159
Nietzsche, Friedrich
    about, 89, 234, 302
    "On the Uses and Disadvantages of
        History for Life," 60
Nolte, Helmut, 111–2
no-man's-land of the normative, 93–4
Norma (opera), 232
noumenal knowledge, 26
number dramaturgy, 282

Oberhausen Manifesto, 13–4
obstinacy, 13, 269–88
"The Obstinate Child," 123, 272
Odysseus, 318
Öffentlichkeit und Erfahrung, 167n92
"On the Uses and Disadvantages of
    History for Life" (Nietzsche), 60
Oort, Jan, 5–6n2
opus alchymicum, 309
"orange style," 299
organization, 77–89, 167
orientation, critique and, 315–32

The Origin of the German Tragic Drama
    (Benjamin), 57
Overman, 302
Ovid
    About, 44
    Metamorphoses, 311–2

paradigm shift
    Beck's, 188
    from digital capitalism, 145
Parisian Manuscripts (Marx), 16
Parmenides, 23
partial publics, 147, 147n18
Part-Time work of a Domestic Slave
    (film), 102f, 104, 268f, 270–1, 277–9,
    281, 287
The Patriot (film), 37–8, 102f, 104,
    123–4, 124f
Payback (Schirrmacher), 95–6
Peirce, Charles Sanders, 68
Pentak, Oxana, 214–5
phenomenal realm, 26
Phenomenology of Spirit (Hegel),
    274–5
Philipp, Claus, 304
philosophical anthropology, 109–10
philosophical method (Adorno),
    113–4
philosophical thinking, 107
philosophy, 5, 60–1
Piaget, Jean, 69
Pinkus, Karen
    about, 323–4, 331
    Alchemical Mercury, 297
Place de l'Opéra, 159
pleasure principle, 23
poetic ambiguity, 291–312
political, theorizing the, 190–6
political action, 192–4
political economy, 224
politics
    aestheticization of, 84
    Weber on, 23
Popper, Karl, 112
postmodernity, Beck's pursuit of, 187–8
power
    of the false, 234
    of imagination, 260–7
The Power of Emotion (film), 131, 132f–
    4f, 139, 276–7, 281, 282, 285, 287
preface politics, 295–6